Rika Benveniste

THOSE WHO SURVIVED
The Resistance, Deportation, and Return
of the Jews from Salonika in the 1940s

Rika Benveniste

THOSE WHO SURVIVED

The Resistance, Deportation, and Return
of the Jews from Salonika in the 1940s

Translated from the German by Susan Kennedy

YAD VASHEM
THE WORLD HOLOCAUST
REMEMBRANCE CENTER

THE INTERNATIONAL INSTITUTE
FOR HOLOCAUST RESEARCH

Rika Benveniste

Αυτοί που επέζησαν.

Αντίσταση, Εκτόπιση, Επιστροφή. Θεσσαλονικείς Εβραίοι στη δεκαετία του 1940

Die Überlebenden. Widerstand, Deportation, Rückkehr. Juden aus Thessaloniki in den 1940er Jahren

Language and Production Editor: Rebecca Wolpe

© 2022 All rights reserved to Yad Vashem
P.O.B. 3477, Jerusalem 9103401, Israel
publications.marketing@yadvashem.org.il
First published in Greek by Polis Editions, 2014
And in German by Edition Romiosini, 2016

ISBN 978-965-308-658-6

Typesetting: Hava Salzman

Printed in Israel by Offset Natan Shlomo Press, Jerusalem

For Kostas Chatzikyriakou

Table of Contents

Introduction

lthough Greek historiography arrived relatively late on the Holocaust research scene, and the Jewish history scene in general, a number of significant historical accounts, as well as innovative studies, were published in the last two decades of the twentieth century.[1] The

1 Hagen Fleischer, *Im Kreuzschatten der Mächte: Griechenland 1941–44: Okkupation, Resistance, Kollaboration* (Frankfurt am Main: Peter Lang, 1986); Mark Mazower, *Inside Hitler's Greece: The Experience of Occupation, 1941–44* (New Haven: Yale University Press, 2001); see the papers given at the first conference concerning the history of Greek Jews under occupation: Rika Benveniste, ed., *The Jews of Greece during the Occupation* (Greek) (Thessaloniki: Vanias, 1998). In parallel to international interest in this field, Fragiski Abatzopoulou studied Greek testimonies concerning the Holocaust. See, for example, the contribution to the volume Erika Kounio-Amarilio and Albertos Nar, eds., *Oral Testimonies of Jews of Salonika on the Holocaust* (Greek) (Thessaloniki: Paratiritis, 1998) and her book *The Holocaust in the Greek Jews' Testimonies* (Greek) (Thessaloniki: Paratiritis, 1993). Since then, the research literature has broadened in scope, see Gabriella Etkmektsoglou, "The Holocaust of Greek Jews," in Christos Chatziiosif and Prokopis Papastratis, eds., *History of Greece in the Twentieth Century: World War II, 1940–1945. Occupation-Resistance* (Greek) (Athens: Vivliorama, 2010), pp. 175–196; Steven B. Bowman, *The Agony of Greek Jews, 1940–1945* (Stanford: Stanford University Press, 2009). The latter also dedicated a book to the participation of Jews in the resistance: Steven B. Bowman, *Jewish Resistance in Wartime Greece* (London: Vallentine Mitchell, 2006). On the same theme see Michael Matsas, *The Illusion of Safety: The Story of the Greek Jews during the Second World War* (New York: Pella, 1997). Interesting contributions can also be found in: Giorgos Antoniou, Stratos Dordanas, Nikos Zaikos, and Nikos Marantzidis, eds., *The Holocaust in the Balkans* (Greek) (Thessaloniki: Epikendro, 2001); Vasiliki Georgiadou and Alkis Rigos, eds., *Auschwitz: The Event and Its Memory: Historical, Social, Psychoanalytical and Political Aspects of the Genocide* (Greek) (Athens: Kastaniotis, 2007). Important lectures were delivered at the conference organized by the "Group for the Study

of the History of the Jews of Greece" in cooperation with the Department of Political Science at the Aristotle University of Thessaloniki (AUTh) in the framework of a session on "The Economy of the Occupation Era and the Fate of Jewish Money" (Thessaloniki, May 2, 2009), and at a conference held on April 5–6, 2013, by the same university to commemorate the seventieth anniversary of the deportation of the Jews from Salonika, see Maria Kavala, ed., *Modern Greek Jewry: Dynamic Presence, Painful Absence* (Greek) (Thessaloniki: University Studio Press, 2020). For new research see also Andrew Apostolou, "The Exception of Salonika: Greek Christian Reactions to the Holocaust" (PhD diss., St. Anthony's College, Oxford, 2007); Maria Kavala, "Salonika during the German Occupation (1941–1944): Society, Economy, Persecution of Jews" (Greek) (PhD diss., University of Crete, Rethymnon, 2009); Stratos Dordanas, *Greeks Against Greeks: The World of the Security Battalions in Occupied Salonika, 1941–44* (Greek) (Thessaloniki: Epikentro, 2006); Stratos Dordanas, "Extermination and Plunder: Agency for the Custody of Jewish Properties," in Antoniou, Dordanas, Zaikos, and Marantzidis, *The Holocaust in the Balkans*, pp. 331–352; Vasilis Ritzaleos, "The Jewish Community of Kavala under Bulgarian Occupation: Organization, Exploitation, Dissolution (1942–1944)," in V. Dalkavoukis, E. Pashaloudi, I. Skoulidas, and K. Tskekou, eds., *Narratives on the 1940s: From the Occupied State's Discourse to Postmodern Historiography* (Greek) (Thessaloniki: Epikendro, 2012), pp. 69–90; and Vasilis Ritzaleos, "The Greek Orthodox Church in Salonika and the Holocaust," in Antoniou, Dordanas, Zaikos, and Marantzidis, *The Holocaust in the Balkans*, pp. 295–330; Nikos Tzafleris, "Survival and Resistance in Volos under the Occupation (1941–1944)" (Greek) (PhD diss., University of Thessaly, 2007); Nikos Tzafleris, "Persecution and Rescue of the Jews of Volos during the Holocaust in Greece (1943–1944)," in Dan Michman, ed., *Hiding, Sheltering, and Borrowing Identities: Avenues of Rescue during the Holocaust* (Jerusalem: Yad Vashem, 2017), pp. 125–144; Pothiti Hantzaroula, "The Social Dimension of Memory in Holocaust Survivors' Testimonies," in R. B. Bouschoten et al., eds., *Bridging Generations: Interdisciplinarity and Life-Histories in the Twenty-First Century* (Greek) (Volos: Oral History Association, 2013), pp. 217–234. Concerning a proposal for questioning historiographical myths, see Rena Molho, "Myths and Reality on the Extermination of the Jews of Salonika," *Athens Review of Books* (Greek), 27 (2013), pp. 38–42, as well as Karina Lampsa and Yakov Schiby, *Rescue: World's Silence, Resistance in the Ghettos and the Camps. Greek Jews during the German Occupation* (Greek) (Athens: Capon, 2012). Since the first edition of my book, published in Greek in 2014, more books on the Holocaust in Greece have been published, see Rena Molho, *The Holocaust of Greek Jews: Studies on History and Memory* (Greek) (Athens: Patakis, 2014); Maria Kavala, *The Destruction of the Jews of Greece, 1941–1944* (Greek) (Athens: Hellenic Academic Libraries, 2015); Giorgos Antoniou and Dirk Moses, eds., *The Holocaust in Greece* (Cambridge: Cambridge University Press, 2019); Leon Saltiel, *The Holocaust in Thessaloniki: Reactions to the Anti-Jewish Persecution, 1942–1943* (London: Routledge, 2020); Andreas K. Bouroutis, *The Holocaust*

extraordinarily high proportion of Shoah victims in Greece,[2] and especially in Salonika, has often masked the fact that the history of Greek Jewry in the years of the occupation represents a mosaic of individual cases in a multitude of regions and a plethora of personal and collective destinies: deportation and almost complete annihilation (in Salonika, Ioannina, and elsewhere); the salvation of entire communities (on the island of Zakynthos); a very high survival rate (Volos); escape to Mandatory Palestine; passage to the mountains and armed struggle as partisans fighting the Germans and their collaborators; denunciations; and hiding in towns and villages, aided by Christian citizens. Even if one claims that it is far from exceptional, the Greek case is of special interest because—apart from the constraints pertaining to all the occupied countries—the sociocultural human geography of the Jewish communities (Sephardic or Romaniote; large and cosmopolitan or small and disconnected from the outside world) and the division of the country into different occupation zones, as well as the staggered process of deportations, all make this country a unique case. When the Germans invaded Greece in April 1941, massive extermination by deportation had not yet begun. Anti-Jewish measures were gradually introduced, yet the deportations of the

---

in Salonika: The Italian Stance and the Jewish Pupils of Umberto Primo (Greek) (Athens: Alexandria, 2020); Pothiti Hantzaroula, *Child Survivors of the Holocaust in Greece: Memory, Testimony and Subjectivity* (London: Routledge, 2020); Anna-Maria Droumbouki, *An Endless Negotiation: The Reconstruction of the Jewish Communities and German Reparations, 1945–1961* (Greek) (Athens: Potamos, 2019); Iasonas Handrinos, *Fellow Fighter: EAM and the Jews of Greece* (Greek) (Athens: Psifides, 2020); Eleni Beze, "Greek Jews: Memories and Identities after World War II" (Greek) (PhD diss., University of Thessaly, Volos, 2021); Eleni Beze, "Being Leftist and Jewish in Greece during the Civil War and Its Aftermath: Constraints and Choices," *Historein*, 18:2 (2019), https://doi.org/10.12681/historein.14601 (accessed October 1, 2021); Andreas K. Bouroutis, ed., *After the War: Salonika and the Fate of the Jewish Assets* (Greek) (Athens: Alexandria, 2021).

2 Before the war, 75,307 Jews lived in Greece and prewar Salonika had a population of around 56,000 Jews. According to the information given by the Jewish Central Board, published by *Israilitikon Vima* (Jewish Tribune) (August 3, 1946), between 1943 and 1944 around 65,000 Jews were deported. After the war, the Jewish population of Greece amounted to around 10,026, of which 1,950 survivors were to be found in Salonika.

Jews of Salonika only began in March 1943, twenty-three months after the Germans entered the city. What information did the Jews possess at that time and, perhaps most importantly, how was it received and interpreted in an atmosphere permeated by fear, uncertainty, but also hope? What scope was there for action and for the expression of solidarity? What was the significance of the deportation of the last Greek Jews in the summer of 1944, as the German Reich was already collapsing? A new history of the Greek Jews under occupation must consider the diverse histories of the Jewish communities in Greece, locating them in the context of the war in Europe. Indeed, the implementation of these measures was accompanied at every step by the subjugation and cooperation of politicians and local authorities, by the passivity of neighbors, or their assistance, and by the victims' desire to gain time, especially in view of their limited room for maneuver. Local institutions and relationships, existing networks, rivalries, and solidarity also played an important role in this context, and a thorough exploration is still pending. For good reasons, the current picture of the Shoah in Greece has been shaped by the case of Salonika, which boasted a significant community and suffered an extremely high proportion of losses. The history of the Jews of Rhodes or Corfu, for example—or of the relatively small Jewish community in Athens—has not yet been written. Furthermore, some chapters of the history of Salonika remain unexplored.

Indeed, we lack an "integrated history" of the Jewish communities in Greece during the occupation. When I speak of "communities," I mean a totality of people who were united by traditional institutions but at the same time differentiated or layered, if not entirely heterogeneous. In the words of Holocaust historian Saul Friedländer, history can only be considered "integrated" if we do not assign a key role to its perpetrators and the machinery of persecution set in motion and perpetuated by them.[3] Instead, "integrated history" focuses on the persecuted;

---

3   Saul Friedländer, *Nazi Germany and the Jews: The Years of Persecution, 1933–1939* (New York: Harper Collins, 1997); Saul Friedländer, *The Years of Extermination: Nazi Germany and the Jews, 1939–1945* (New York: Harper Collins, 2007).

their thoughts, feelings, and options for action, assigning an active role to the onlookers and neighbors who betrayed them, were indifferent to their fate, or supported them. Of course, such an approach considers both the personal and collective Jewish sources as well as the testimonies of contemporary Jewish witnesses and relates them to documents from diplomatic, military, and police archives in addition to government, judicial, and community archives.

Over time, the history of the Shoah has come to include a vast number of studies and a significant body of knowledge. We have attained a profound understanding of and sensitivity to the past. For many of its major historians, the Holocaust was "contemporary history," a traumatic experience that they themselves survived. They were thus required to extrapolate from the present to the past and to the future, to reproduce history from "their double identity as acting subjects and interpreters."[4] With younger historians entering the field of research in recent decades, the situation has changed; in the future, we will be able to appreciate the results of this change.

* * *

The present book also makes a methodological proposal for a **new history** of the annihilation of Greek Jewry, which I will try to apply here to the case of Salonika. The particular questions that I ask in my investigation are largely guided by "locality" and "altering the scale of observation," to which I shall return later. Adopting a microhistorical approach to the Shoah, following the paths of various **groups** of people from Salonika who shared experiences of the occupation and deportation, I try to grasp the relationships between individuals and groups, to fathom experiences that were bound up with a concrete geographical place, to discover what these people could have known at a particular time, what options for

---

4   François Bédarida, "Le temps présent et l'historiographie contemporaine," *Vingtième Siècle: Revue d'histoire*, 69 (2001), pp. 153–160; Dominick La Capra, *Writing History, Writing Trauma* (Baltimore: Johns Hopkins University Press, 2001).

action were available to them, and what resources they possessed to pursue them. This includes the results of their decisions, which of course they themselves could not have known in advance. The narration of these experiences requires a comparison and combination of the subjective testimonies provided by these people with archival sources of various kinds. My account seeks to clarify the tension between the particular and the general. And if "the particular" in this case is the story of a family or a group, "the general" is war, Judeo-Christian relations, social and economic circumstances, etc. Such an inquiry requires a thorough examination of oral and written testimonies, the comparison of personal and collective memories, as well as an understanding of cultural traditions and Jewish identity as dynamic processes. The results of my research led me to analyze the historical context and to focus on moments at which choosing one path or the other became a question of life or death. Thus, when exploring archival documents, specifically those that contain subjective and collective memories of what happened, and when reflecting upon the kind of language appropriate for an analysis and description of these events, we find answers to questions concerning deportation, resistance, and the return of the Jews. As such, I endeavor to produce a historiography based on empirical studies but which at the same time recognizes the theoretical claims and the ideological stakes that are a necessary part of any modern account of the Holocaust.

More precisely, my approach revolves around three axes:

1. Locality and microhistory. The fact that the Holocaust towered over almost the whole of Europe should not obscure the fact that it concerned real life stories in concrete places. A careful exploration of devastated Jewish communities often calls into question generalizations and abstractions.[5] The topography, in our case the particular social context of German-occupied Salonika, should not be understood *a priori* either as a mere reflection of the

---

5   It is sufficient to mention Isaiah Trunk, *Jüdenrat: The Jewish Councils in Eastern Europe under Nazi Occupation* (New York: Macmillan, 1972) or the more recent study by Jan T. Gross regarding the relations between Jews and Christians in Poland: *Neighbors: The Destruction of the Jewish Community in Jedwabne, Poland* (Princeton: Princeton University Press, 2001).

prevailing schema or as an exception, but rather as a challenge that enables us to gain valuable new knowledge. At the same time, apart from altering the scale of observation, microhistory provides us with the epistemological coordinates of historiographical practice over a long period. In the history of the Holocaust,[6] in particular, microhistorical approaches have made significant contributions: focusing on a small town,[7] a ghetto,[8] a camp,[9] a person,[10] and so on have proven to be extremely useful in understanding the relationships between people, social networks, the knowledge available to people at a given time, the means available to the persecuted, and the paths they then chose to take.

2. Extending the time period from the first years of the occupation to the entire 1940s. Certainly the genocide was the result of military occupation and Nazi ideology. However, if we want to understand **how** the deportations took place or, **how**, in rare cases, some people were rescued, we must return to the eve of the war. Furthermore, if we want to grasp the consequences of the genocide, we must enquire about the circumstances under which the survivors returned and the years after the war: the Greek Civil

6   See, for example, Claire Zalc, Tal Bruttmann, and Ivan Ermakoff, *Pour une Microhistoire de la Shoah* (Paris: Seuil, 2012).

7   Nicolas Mariot and Claire Zalc, *Face à la persécution: 991 juifs dans la guerre* (Paris: Seuil, 2010), relates the story of 991 Jews from the city of Lens between 1940 and 1945. The authors record the divergent paths of the residents, the dilemmas and options for action in different phases, from the moment they were "identified" as Jews until their deportation. Dilemmas and biographies are discussed in relation to the demographic and social context, occupational characteristics, and legal status.

8   Tim Cole, *Traces of the Holocaust: Journeying in and out of the Ghettos* (London and New York: Continuum, 2011).

9   See Christopher R. Browning, *Collected Memories: Holocaust History and Post-War Testimony* (Madison: University of Wisconsin Press, 2003), see the chapter entitled "Survivor Testimonies from Starachowice: Writing the History of a Factory Slave Labor Camp," pp. 27–59.

10   Götz Aly, *Into the Tunnel: The Brief Life of Marion Samuel, 1931–1943* (New York: Metropolitan Books, 2007). The book is about an eleven-year-old girl who was murdered in Auschwitz. The author collected everything that can be learned about her life and death from various sources: the declarations concerning the value of her family's estate, civil documents, photo albums, school records, and deportation lists, etc.

War, the reconstruction of Greece and the Jewish communities, the economic situation, and the survivors' departure for Israel[11] or elsewhere.

3. Examining the "traditional" questions of Holocaust historiography alongside other issues that have occupied researchers in the last two decades. More specifically, I revisit two classical problems of historiography—the victims' resistance and the role played by the Jewish Councils (Judenräte). In addition, I explore a topic neglected by Greek historiography: the options open to the survivors in the first years after the liberation of the concentration camps.

Obviously, my study is a social and cultural history of the Jews in the Holocaust era, which, without underestimating the classical problems, lends its results a temporal and cultural depth.[12] The subject under study is the significance that historical subjects attribute to the experience of occupation and deportation. In this regard, we must reexamine ideologies, considering not only their consciously and logically structured components but also their delusions[13] and sensibilities. In addition, we must not reduce power relations to mere economics but also include the range of meanings attributed to them in the context of a crisis of traditional structures under conditions of extreme violence. From this point

---

11 Karina Lampsa and Yakov Schiby, *Life from the Start: The Migration of Greek Jews to Palestine* (1945–1948) (Greek) (Athens: Alexandria, 2010); Katherine Fleming, *Greece: A Jewish History* (Princeton: Princeton University Press, 2009).

12 Fifteen years ago, I formulated an agenda of "classic" open questions concerning the study of the Shoah in Greece: "The Historiography of the Holocaust in Greece: A Survey," *Sychrona Themata* (Greek), 76/77 (2001), pp. 104–109; see also my text "On the Historiography of the Shoah: The International Scene and the Greek Perspectives," in the Festschrift in honor of Hagen Fleischer; K. Gardika, A. M. Droumbouki, V. Karamanolakis, and K. Raptis, eds., *The Long Shadow of the 1940s. Heritages and Memories: War, Occupation, Resistance, Civil War* (Greek) (Athens: Alexandria, 2015), pp. 153–170; Minna Rozen's contribution is an example of the approach to tackling an old problem: "Jews and Greeks Remember Their Past: The Political Career of Rabbi Tzvi Koretz (1933–1943)," *Jewish Social Studies*, 12:1 (2005), pp. 111–166.

13 See Dan Stone, "Holocaust Historiography and Cultural History," *Dapim: Studies on the Holocaust*, 23 (2009), pp. 52–55; Alon Confino, "Fantasies about the Jews, Cultural Reflections on the Holocaust," *History and Memory*, 17:1/2 (2005), pp. 296–322.

of view, the time-honored and weighty problems (collaboration with the conqueror, Jewish resistance, the role of the church or diplomacy, etc.) are by no means suppressed but rather analyzed from a perspective that rejects monocausal interpretations, perhaps paving the way for a new political history. I set out to tell the story of the catastrophe as it was experienced by different people who were subject to the same persecution, people who walked different paths, paths that occasionally crossed and then diverged again. Focusing on a series of testimonies written at different times and under various external conditions by people who underwent similar experiences, it is possible to capture both the idiosyncrasies of each narrative and those features common to all, without prematurely imposing a single voice on all the stories.

The first part of the book examines Jewish partisans from Salonika. Among the 30,000 resistance fighters (*andartes* in Greek) in the ELAS (the Greek People's Liberation Army), there were about 1,000 Jews.[14] They are invisible if you read the illegal press of the time, hidden behind Christian pseudonyms. The civil war and the concomitant persecution of the Left resulted in the silencing and self-censorship of the former Jewish partisans. Their experiences left virtually no written evidence. However, we possess at least a dozen oral testimonies of former Jewish partisans. This is a typical case in which the voices of contemporaneous witnesses help us to construct an edifice of facts, providing a starting point to reconsider the common perception of Jewish resistance. They invite us to take a critical look at the frequently assumed passivity of the Jews and to recognize the limited opportunities available, as well as the dangers that any personal or collective action entailed. In so doing, the initial lethargy that shaped the experience of the persecuted, as well as the extraordinary pressure exerted by the impending deportation, becomes tangible. Here I encountered the following problem: how to narrate the history of Jewish participation in the resistance in Salonika given that it encompassed people with very different socioeconomic profiles who took very divergent paths in life, paths that crossed only because of the persecution?

14 Bowman, *Jewish Resistance in Wartime Greece*, p. xxii.

The microhistory of a group of about twenty Jewish partisans from Salonika sheds light on three particular themes that are important in delineating the common path: (a) the conditions under which the decision to "go to the mountains" was made and the conjunctural nature of the decision-making: the social profile of the young men; risks and dilemmas associated with escape; the family, neighborhood, and political or resistance networks to which they had access; timing, planning, and the realization of flight; b) the geography and nature of partisan war, daily life, and struggles against the Germans and their collaborators; c) Jewish identity, liberation, and the difficult return to a "normal life" as well as the political reintegration of the former partisans during the civil war that followed the war years.

The second part of the book focuses on about 100 Jews from Salonika who were defined as "displaced persons" according to the bureaucratic terminology of the postwar period. Having been liberated from the concentration camps, they remained in Germany for a few months or a few years, in the Feldafing DP (Displaced Persons) camp near Munich in the American zone. Their story is complicated and includes events that place them between the Germans and the Allies, between the past of their war experiences and the future of their new lives, between Greece, America, and *Eretz Israel*. Behind the stage of postwar international relations and political history, one encounters stories that contradict the image of Jews as "passive subjects." We discover that these Jews from Salonika formed a group that shared the experience of deportation and a common path of torment: from Auschwitz-Birkenau to Warsaw, where they cleared the ghetto ruins, and from there to Dachau and its subcamps, where they remained until their liberation by the American army and their transport to Feldafing on May 1, 1945. These people are further connected by their decision not to return to Greece. In tracing their paths and decisions, I try to understand who they were and why they stayed in Germany awaiting immigration permits. I seek to observe their daily living conditions, the black market, their love stories, weddings, and marriages, their commitment to the Zionist vision, their desperate efforts to reach America, their similarities with other survivors from Central and Eastern Europe, but also their differences, and, finally, to recount the founding of a "Sephardi Federation" (see Part 2).

The third part of my study focuses on the story of a single family. This family, the head of which was a member of the Jewish Council (Judenrat), was deported from Salonika to Bergen-Belsen on August 2, 1943. As we know, all previous transports had arrived at Auschwitz-Birkenau. The transport that took place on August 2 included 367 Jews from Salonika in possession of Spanish passports and a mixed group of seventy-four people: certain notables, including two of the fourteen members of the Judenrat and the committee that worked with it, Chief Rabbi Zvi Koretz, Jewish community employees, Jacques Albala, who had replaced Koretz as the head of the community in April 1943 after the chief rabbi fell out of favor with the Germans, as well as certain Nazi employees, all of them accompanied by their families.

The head of the family I studied did not survive the deportation. Only his widow, together with her three children, returned to Salonika. As is often stated in the study of the Holocaust, family testimonies allow us to reconstruct the relationships between concrete events and our general knowledge. The benefit of a biographical study lies in finding a balance between the particularity of the testimonies of a single family and the analysis of the social context that allows us to decide what is "unique" and "paradigmatic" in a story. The letters exchanged between the spouses in the first months of the occupation, when the mother had taken her children to Athens, archival documents, as well as the widow's correspondence in the first months after the liberation, led me to reconsider a number of issues: the "new normality"[15] under occupation; the circumstances of life, such as hunger and the confiscation of houses; but also the views shared by members of the wealthy elite. In other words, they enabled me to explore the real options for action and the illusions that reigned among the Jews in 1941 and 1942, before the intensification of anti-

---

15 According to the apt formulation by Kavala, "Salonika during the German Occupation," pp. 27, 152, 204.

Jewish measures and the beginning of the deportations. Again, I raise the question of the Judenrat, no longer focusing on Chief Rabbi Zvi Koretz, who after the war incurred the entire burden of responsibility and blame, but on the members of the many-headed elite who conducted the community affairs. At the center I place the council and the committee that "managed" the situation, in accordance or sometimes in opposition to Koretz but always in continuity with its prewar charitable activities: aid for the weak, ransoming community members from forced labor, certainties, and self-delusions. I examine the events in their chronological order and under conditions of a choice without alternatives, "choiceless choices," as Lawrence Langer put it: conditions that were inextricably linked to the extreme nature of events and the limited knowledge available to the victims.[16]

I follow the family members as they were deported to Bergen-Belsen, and through diaries and chronicles I try to enter the Star Camp, also called the Albala Camp, and the gradual transformation of this camp for the "privileged" into a universe of hunger, epidemic, and death. I then follow the family on the "Lost Train" that left the camp on April 10, 1945, headed for Theresienstadt, before it was liberated by the British. As a result of Allied bombings, the train, after wandering for some time, stopped near the small German town of Tröbitz, where the prisoners were eventually freed by the Red Army. After a four-month stay in Tröbitz, those who survived typhus returned to Salonika in September 1945, including the widow and her three children.

* * *

For the overwhelming majority of Jews from Salonika, the Shoah meant death in the concentration camp of Auschwitz-Birkenau. In that sense, the stories I tell here are marginal. Yet, when

---

16 Lawrence Langer, "The Dilemma of Choice in the Death Camps," *Centerpoint*, 4 (1980), pp. 222–231; see also Dan Diner, *Beyond the Conceivable: Studies on Germany, Nazism and the Holocaust* (Berkeley: University of California Press, 2000), in particular the chapter entitled "Beyond the Conceivable: The Judenrat as Borderline Experience," pp. 117–129.

studying the history of the Shoah, we must endeavor to find an answer to a crucial question: How can we transform something with which we are familiar as an experience or a testimony into an understanding of what happened? In other words: How can the information that I obtain about the experiences of particular groups of people be translated into an understanding of the epoch? My inquiry was guided by this question, as I tried to distinguish all the details and place them in context, and that question is the common thread running through my narrative. Ultimately, men and women make history. Their own perception of existing options for action and their actions may not always correspond to the impersonal structures that define the analytical categories within which the historian works. On many occasions, the results of studies into the circumstances of the occupation and the deportations appear surprising because they highlight individual actions and subjective experiences that contradict social and political structures. Mostly, such actions did not change the course of history, but they made a crucial difference for a group of people, a circle of people, or a community, the crucial difference between salvation and demise.

I wanted to write a book that reexamines the archives and testimonies, comparing them with collective memory, and which also reconsiders the dynamics of "Greco-Jewish identity." I mulled over the question of the appropriate language to use in describing what happened. Like every historian dealing with the extermination of European Jewry, I was confronted with the familiarity and also the sense of alienation that the Shoah still causes us to feel.

Acknowledgements

While preparing this book, dear friends and colleagues gave me the opportunity to share my research. Their comments and feedback contributed enormously to my work: Alexandra Bakalaki and Nora Skouteri (AUTH), Henriette Asséo, Maurice Kriegel, Sabina Loriga, and Annette Wieviorka in Paris (EHESS), Samar Farage, Joan Landes, the late Ted Norton, Sajay Samuel, and Nina Safran at State College (Penn State University), Joanna Bourke in London (Birkbeck College), and Patrizia Pizzorno Grimaldi in Florence (NY University La Pietra). I thank all those who participated in the informal seminar of the Working Group on the Study of the Jews of Greece that I organized between 2005 and 2011 together with Giorgos Antoniou, Tony Molho, and Paris Papamichos Chronakis in Salonika. Several friends and colleagues graciously assisted me for years (while others came on board more recently), listening to what I have to say and sharing their knowledge with me. I thank Efi Avdela, Odette Varon-Vassard, Edy and Izo Abraham, Fragiski Abatzopoulou, Polymeris Voglis, Stratos Dordanas, Maria Kavala, Tonia Kiousopoulou, the late Doron Lam, Giorgos Margaritis, Mark Mazower, Rena Molho, Eleni Beze, Kelly and Jacky Benmayor, Popi Polemi, Vasilis Ritzaleos, Minna Rozen, Yakov Schiby, Samy Taboch, Nikos Tzafleris, Hagen Fleischer, Maria Fragou, and Pothiti Hantzaroula. My colleagues at the Department of History, Archeology, and Social Anthropology in Volos gave me many opportunities for fruitful discussions. Polymeris Voglis, Maria Kavala, Giorgos Margaritis, and Pothiti Hantzaroula read an early version of the manuscript, pointed out my mistakes, and offered me useful advice. I did not always listen to them, and the responsibility for the final shape of this book lies solely with me. I am grateful to Aliki Aruch of the Historical Archive of the Jewish Community of Thessaloniki, who kindly allowed me access to the archives and generously assisted me with advice and support.

I would like to thank the publications team at Yad Vashem, in particular Dr. Ella Florsheim and Yasmine Garval, for making this English edition possible. I am grateful for their support, for their belief in this project, and for their help in finding the appropriate solutions to overcome various obstacles and facilitate its completion. Likewise, this English edition would not have been possible without the hard work of the translator, Susan Kennedy, and Rebecca Wolpe, the language and production editor, who attentively took care of all aspects of the book.

I could not have written this book without the love and constant support of Kostas Chatzikyriakou. To him I owe so much. His critical eye, his attention to detail, but also his patience have all helped me immensely. When, at the dinner table, he would ask me, "What news?" I would merely answer: "Today I read…" or "Today in the archives I discovered…" To this he would respond, "correcting" me, "But that's not news." However, he never fails to listen to me. That is why this book is dedicated to him.

Timeline[*]

October 28, 1940: The Italian ambassador in Athens presents the Greek prime minister with an ultimatum. He demands that the Greeks allow the Italian army to cross the border between Greece and Albania unhindered in order to occupy "strategically important points" in Greek territory. The prime minister's refusal signals the invasion of Greece and the beginning of the war.

April 6, 1941: The Germans invade Greece from Yugoslavia and Bulgaria.

April 9, 1941: The Germans invade Salonika.

April 11–18, 1941, Salonika: Jewish newspapers and press are banned. Confiscation of the Baron Hirsch hospital, Jewish homes, and schools. Arrest of members of the Community Council, community employees, and other prominent Jews. Looting of the community offices and confiscation of its archive.

April 21, 1941: In the restaurants of Salonika, antisemitic circles hang announcements in Greek and German declaring that Jews are not wanted in these establishments.

April 24, 1941: The Rosenberg Commando relocates to Salonika. On May 3, it begins overseeing the looting of synagogues and Jewish libraries, which continues until November.

---

[*] This timeline is neither a chronicle of the Shoah nor the history of World War II or the postwar years. It includes only events directly related to the topics discussed in this book.

April 27, 1941: The Germans march into Athens.

April 28, 1941: The Jews of Salonika are forced to give up their radios and pianos.

May 15, 1941: Foundation of the first resistance organization in Salonika, Eleftheria (Freedom).

May 17, 1941: Chief Rabbi of Salonika, Zvi Koretz, is arrested in Athens and deported to Vienna.

June 1941: The Germans appoint the former director of the community, Saby Saltiel, as community chairman. The members of the Community Council are released from custody.

June 29, 1941: Further confiscations of Jewish homes in Salonika.

July 12, 1941: In Salonika, there are mass arrests of Jews denounced as Communists.

September 1941: Soviet prisoners of war and Polish prisoners fall victim to the first extermination experiments using Zyklon B gas.

September 27, 1941: Establishment of the National Liberation Front, EAM, with the participation of the Communist Party of Greece, the Socialist Party of Greece, the Union of People's Democracy, and the Peasants' Party.

December 1941: The Germans execute three Jews from Salonika.

Winter 1941–Summer 1942: The population of Salonika is plagued by hunger and malaria, with the Jewish community suffering a higher-than-average mortality rate. In January 1942, leading members of the Jewish community form a central committee that assumes the task of providing social welfare, above all arranging for basic supplies, food, and care for children and the economically disadvantaged.

From December 8, 1941: In Chelmno, Poland, the Germans murder more than 150,000 Jews, gypsies, and Poles in special trucks, channeling exhaust fumes into them.

January 1942: Chief Rabbi Koretz is released and returns to Salonika to resume his post.

January 20, 1942: A meeting of the Nazi leadership in Wannsee, Berlin, chaired by the head of the Reich Main Security Office (RSHA), Reinhard Heydrich, decides on the Final Solution, initiating the annihilation of European Jewry. This was preceded in the summer of 1941 by the invasion of the Soviet Union and the arrest and murder of hundreds of thousands of Jews by the *Einsatzgruppen* (mobile killing squads). The minutes of the meeting include a list of Jews to be exterminated throughout Europe, among them the 69,600 Jews of Greece.

January/February 1942: The EAM Central Committee resolves to establish armed partisan groups under the name the Greek People's Liberation Army (ELAS). The first groups are active in central Greece.

February 7, 1942: After the arrest of employees of the American consulate (following the U.S. declaration of war on the Axis), the Jew David Tiano, one of the consulate employees, is executed.

March 25, 1942: On the occasion of Greek Independence Day, the first student protest against the German occupation takes place in Athens.

March 27, 1942: The German authorities begin the systematic deportation of French Jews.

April 1942: Prime Minister Georgios Tsolakoglou visits Salonika. Chief Rabbi Koretz and Saby Saltiel meet with him and thank him for his earlier statements, in which, among other things, he said, "There is no Jewish question in Greece." He also previously vouched that Jews who had proven their patriotism in the time of the Greco-Italian War would be treated no differently than any other Greek citizens.

April 22, 1942: The first general strike by civil servants takes place.

May 4, 1942: SS officers carry out the first selection in Auschwitz-Birkenau: the weak, the sick, and people deemed unsuited to forced labor are taken to the gas chambers. From May 1940 to January 1945, more than a million prisoners, 90% of them Jews, were murdered in the Auschwitz camp complex. About 865,000 of them were taken to the gas chambers immediately upon arrival at the camp.

May 18, 1942: *The New York Times* reports that more than 400,000 Jews were murdered by the Germans in the Soviet Union, eastern Poland, and Ukraine.

July 11, 1942: All Jewish men between the ages of eighteen and forty-five are ordered to report to the Platia Eleftherias in Salonika. Nine thousand men gather, suffering agony and humiliation under the scorching sun. They are registered to serve as forced laborers for the Todt company and for the German Müller firm (working in road construction, in mines, on railroad tracks, etc.). It takes three days, from July 13 to 15, to assign them all placements. These "workers" are sent to workplaces where the abysmal working conditions result in extremely high mortality rates.

July 22, 1942: Between July 22 and September 12, around 300,000 Jews are deported from the Warsaw ghetto. Most of them are murdered in the Treblinka death camp.

October 17, 1942: The Jewish community signs a protocol to ransom Jews from forced labor. They undertake to pay a ransom totaling 2 billion drachmas, which is collected by the community in the form of a compulsory levy. Maximilian (Max) Merten, *Kriegsverwaltungsrat* (military administration counselor) of the Nazi occupying forces in Salonika, had previously proposed the expropriation of the old Jewish cemetery, which he estimated to be worth 1.5 billion drachmas.

October 29, 1942: The first installment of the ransom is paid.

November 5, 1942: Arrest of Greek Jews in Paris. They are deported to Auschwitz-Birkenau on November 9 and 11.

November 1942, Salonika: Confiscation of goods from Jewish-owned printing and stationery shops. Even cinemas owned by Jews are confiscated by the German propaganda offices and given to their associates. At the request of the Germans, the city council decides to rename streets with Jewish names. The second installment of the ransom is paid.

December 5, 1942: The third installment of the ransom is paid, and the Jews begin to return from forced labor.

December 1942: Destruction of the Jewish cemetery in Salonika, which includes more than 500,000 graves. The community coordinates the exhumation of the dead, which is taken over by family members. Three months later, after a demand to this effect, tombstones and marble ornamentations from the Jewish cemetery are divided up by the city administration, to be used for the construction of public buildings, churches, and roads.

December 11, 1942: The representative of the Security Service (SD), Dr. Heinrich Calmes, assigns Chief Rabbi Koretz "the office of Chairman of the Jewish Congregation of Salonika from today and until further notice" and appoints a six-member board to advise him. Saby Saltiel is relieved of his duties as chairman.

January 15, 1943: The fourth and final installment of the ransom is paid.

February 2, 1943: A special unit of the security service, "Eichmann's men," including *SS-Hauptsturmführer* Dieter Wisliceny and Alois Brunner, arrives in Salonika to implement the plan for the deportation of the city's Jews.

February 1943: Implementation of the Nazi race laws in Salonika. On February 6, the German military commander of northern Greece and the Aegean orders all Jews with Greek citizenship to wear the yellow star. On February 7 and 10, all stocks of white paper are forcibly sold to a German-

Greek company, and Jewish-owned businesses dealing in machinery and hardware are confiscated. On February 11, the Jews are asked to draw up inventory lists. The next day, the demarcation of Jewish shops and houses is ordered. On February 13, the Jewish population is banned from moving to different neighborhoods and from using public transport and telephones. Jews are not permitted to leave their homes after sunset. The deadline for forcing the Jewish population into ghetto-like neighborhoods is February 25. On the same day, by order of the German military commander, it is requested that professional organizations exclude all Jewish members from their ranks. All Jewish employees in public service or in companies under public law are dismissed. At the end of February, all Jews are asked to submit a detailed declaration of their movable and immovable assets.

February 24 and March 5, 1943: The EAM conducts massive strikes and large-scale demonstrations in Athens against the threat of forcibly sending Greek civilians to Germany as workers. This leads to the failure of the German plan.

March 4, 1943: The Baron Hirsch neighborhood near the train station, in which the poorest Jewish families live, is cordoned off with boards and barbed wire; residents are not allowed to leave the neighborhood. On the same day, the Jews in the Bulgarian occupation zone (in Komotini, Alexandroupoli, Xanthi, Kavala, Serres, and Drama) are arrested and deported to Treblinka.

March 5, 1943: Mass rallies against the mobilization of citizens are held in Athens.

March 6, 1943: The ghetto-like Jewish neighborhoods of Salonika are demarcated with yellow tape.

March 7, 1943: The German occupying authorities instruct the Greek administration to set up offices in all Jewish companies for the purposes of implementing sequestration. A total of 104 Jewish dignitaries (regardless of their citizenship) are summoned and declared hostages to ensure the implementation of the anti-Jewish measures. They are not detained because Chief Rabbi Koretz vouches for them.

March 10, 1943: Prohibition against buying and selling any asset that belongs to a Jew. Wisliceny announces to a group of senior state officials that all Jewish assets are to be confiscated and transferred to the Greek state.

March 14, 1943: Chief Rabbi Koretz informs the residents of the Baron Hirsch ghetto of their imminent departure for Poland. He speaks of beginning a new life. They are all obliged to hand in money and valuables in return for bills of exchange in Polish currency (zloty).

March and April 1943: Around 400 weddings are held among members of the community to enable the couples to start their "new life" in an organized fashion.

Winter–Spring 1943: Armed resistance in rural areas increases. The partisans win several battles. From mid-1943, a relatively large liberated zone emerges in the heart of central Greece, "Free Greece."

March 15, 1943: A total of 2,800 residents of the Baron Hirsch ghetto are taken to the train station. Departure of the first train bound for Auschwitz-Birkenau. On the same day, an announcement is issued declaring that anyone who is involved in the looting of abandoned houses subsequent to "the emigration of the Jews" will incur severe penalties. From then on, the Baron Hirsch ghetto serves as a transit camp to which the Jews scheduled for deportation are brought and in which they remain until they are taken to the train station. The first transport from Salonika arrives in Auschwitz on March 20, 1943. Of the 2,800 deportees, 2,191 are taken directly to the gas chambers.

March 17, 1943: Departure of the second train, now with residents of the Stacion Tchico (Small Station) neighborhood, for Auschwitz-Birkenau, where the transport arrives on March

24. Of the roughly 2,800 deportees, 1,986 are taken directly to the gas chambers. On the day that this second transport departs, during a meeting held at the Monastiriot Synagogue, Chief Rabbi Koretz advises patience and perseverance.

March 18 and 22, 1943: Prime Minister Konstantinos Logothetopoulos, who collaborated with the Germans, submits a memorandum regarding the cessation of the deportations of Greek Jews to the plenipotentiary of the Reich in Athens, Günther Altenburg.

March 19, 1943: Departure of the third transport to Auschwitz-Birkenau, now with the residents of the Régie-Vardar neighborhood, who had previously been brought to the Baron Hirsch ghetto. They arrive in Auschwitz on March 25. Of the 1,901 deportees, 1,206 are taken directly to the gas chambers.

March 23, 1943: Departure of the fourth transport, which arrives in Auschwitz-Birkenau on March 30. Of the 2,501 deportees, 2,048 are taken directly to the gas chambers.

March 23 and 24, 1943: Archbishop Damaskinos of Athens and All Greece submits to Prime Minister Logothetopoulos and Günther Altenburg, the plenipotentiary of the Third Reich, a letter calling for the suspension of the deportations. The letter is cosigned by important figures in Greek society.

March 24, 1943: The remaining Jewish neighborhoods are cordoned off. A total of 151 men are arrested and transported to various workplaces for forced labor.

March 25, 1943: A large student demonstration against the German occupation takes place in Salonika.

March 27, 1943: Departure of the fifth transport, which arrives in Auschwitz-Birkenau on April 3. Of the 2,800 deportees, 2,208 are taken directly to the gas chambers.

March 29, 1943: After the evacuation of the western parts of the city and the ghetto in the city center, the Germans now turn to the eastern parts of the city. First, Jewish neighborhood 151 is evacuated and 7,500 Jews are brought to the Baron Hirsch ghetto.

End of March 1943: Rescue of the 30 Jews from the city of Katerini in northern Greece with the help of the population and the local authorities.

April 3, 1943: Departure of the sixth transport, which arrives in Auschwitz-Birkenau on April 9. Of the 2,500 deportees, 2,021 are taken directly to the gas chambers.

April 5, 1943: Departure of the seventh transport, which arrives in Auschwitz-Birkenau on April 10. Of the 2,750 deportees, 1,967 are taken directly to the gas chambers.

April 6, 1943: Evacuation of Jewish neighborhood 6, a property owned by the municipality of Salonika. The Jews go on foot to the Baron Hirsch ghetto.

April 7, 1943: The German occupying authorities set up the Rallis government. The eighth transport leaves on the same day. It arrives in Auschwitz-Birkenau on April 13. Of the 2,800 deportees, 1,936 are taken directly to the gas chambers. The Jewish quarter of Agia Triada is evacuated and residents walk to the Baron Hirsch ghetto.

April 9–11, 1943: The new prime minister, Ioannis Rallis, who collaborated with the Germans, visits Salonika to meet the German commander in chief. Chief Rabbi Koretz also succeeds in meeting Rallis (on April 10) and asks him to work to end the deportations. Rallis responds negatively; as a result of his initiative, Koretz is arrested the next day, dismissed from his position, and taken to the Baron Hirsch ghetto with his family. The German military commander of Northern Greece and the Aegean appoints Jacques Albala as chairman of the community.

April 10, 1943: Departure of the ninth transport, which arrives in Auschwitz-Birkenau on April 17. Of the 3,000 deportees, 2,271 are taken directly to the gas chambers.

April 13, 1943: Departure of the tenth transport, which arrives in Auschwitz-Birkenau on April 18. Of the 2,501 deportees, 1,897 are taken directly to the gas chambers.

April 16, 1943: Departure of the eleventh transport, which arrives in Auschwitz-Birkenau on April 22. Of the 2,800 deportees, 2,132 are taken directly to the gas chambers.

April 17, 1943: The municipality of Salonika decides to demolish neighborhood 6 for aesthetic reasons, selling the building materials obtained in the course of the demolition at an auction.

April 19–May 16, 1943: Uprising in the Warsaw ghetto—the first mass uprising in occupied Europe. The Jews of Warsaw oppose the evacuation of the ghetto by force; the Germans bomb the ghetto and eventually raze it to the ground. The survivors are deported and only very few manage to flee and join the partisans.

April 20, 1943: Departure of the twelfth transport, which arrives in Auschwitz-Birkenau on April 26. Of the 2,700 deportees, 2,062 are taken directly to the gas chambers.

April 22, 1943: Departure of the thirteenth transport, which arrives in Auschwitz-Birkenau on April 28. Of the 3,070 deportees, 2,529 are taken directly to the gas chambers.

April 28, 1943: Departure of the fourteenth transport, which arrives in Auschwitz-Birkenau on May 4. Of the 2,930 deportees, 2,392 are taken directly to the gas chambers.

May 3, 1943: Departure of the fifteenth transport, which arrives in Auschwitz-Birkenau on May 7. Of the 1,000 deportees, 932 are taken directly to the gas chambers.

Beginning of May 1943: Departure of the sixteenth transport, which arrives in Auschwitz-Birkenau on May 10. Of the 2,500 deportees, 1,685 are taken directly to the gas chambers.

May 9, 1943: Departure of the seventeenth transport, which arrives in Auschwitz-Birkenau on May 16. The 4,500 Jews on the transport include Jews from Salonika as well as Jews from the Evros region (Didymoticho, Nea Orestiada, Soufli) who were arrested on May 5. Of this number, 3,823 are taken directly to the gas chambers.

May 29, 1943: Founding of the YDIP (Jewish Properties Management Service or Service for the Disposal of Jewish Assets) in Salonika. Law 205, issued on June 1, regulates the "handling of assets confiscated by the occupying authorities or, rather, of Jewish assets left behind." The YDIP is the body through which the assets of the deportees are "lawfully" transferred to collaborators and supporters of the Germans.

June 1, 1943: Departure of the eighteenth transport, which arrives in Auschwitz-Birkenau on June 8. It includes members of the Community Council and committees as well as teachers and community employees, whom the Germans had promised to transport to Theresienstadt. Of the 880 deportees, 572 are taken directly to the gas chambers.

June 4, 1943: The areas of Macedonia under German occupation, the Aegean Islands, and the neutral Evros zone come under German administration. Max Merten is deployed as a civil commander, assisted by the governor general of Macedonia, Vasilios Simonidis, who collaborates with the Germans.

June 15, 1943: After mediation by the Italian consulate, 350 Jews from Salonika with Italian citizenship are brought to the Italian consulate in Athens.

July 1943: On July 10, there are rallies in Salonika and other cities in northern Greece against the alleged expansion of the Bulgarian zone of occupation. At the same time, a major strike takes place in Athens on July 22, 1943. Max Merten is meanwhile busy in Salonika settling disputes between candidates interested in taking over Jewish businesses.

August 2, 1943: The transport from Salonika to Bergen-Belsen departs. The transport includes seventy-four Jews from Salonika, among them Chief Rabbi Koretz, two members of the Community Council, community employees, militiamen, and others, as well as 367 Spanish citizens.

August 10, 1943: Departure of the nineteenth and last transport from Salonika to Auschwitz-Birkenau, arriving there on August 18. On board the train are 1,800 men who were arrested in the city in March and sent to forced labor. Of them, 1,529 are taken directly to the gas chambers. The day after the train departs, Brunner and Wisliceny, who have completed their work, leave Salonika by plane. Brunner goes on to organize the deportation of French Jews as commandant of the Drancy camp.

August 31–November 27, 1943: Around 1,000 Greek Jews and other prisoners are transported from Auschwitz-Birkenau to Warsaw in four transports. They are forced to clear the ruins of the ghetto.

September 8, 1943: Italy announces its surrender. The Germans close the Italian consulate in Salonika and begin persecuting and deporting the Jews in the former Italian zone. The rabbi of Athens, Elias Barzilai, escapes with the help of the resistance movement. Many Jews from Athens, Volos, and other cities manage to hide or join the partisans in the mountains.

Fall and Winter 1943: After Italy's surrender, the Italian Pinerolo Division surrenders to the ELAS. The latter's strength is significantly enhanced by securing the Italian weapons. From the end of 1943, the partisan groups increase their resistance activities against the Germans. Simultaneously, armed groups collaborating with the Germans expand their activities.

January 20, 1944: Passing of Law 1180 concerning "Confiscated Jewish Assets." The law extends the validity of Law 205/1943 to the entire area under German occupation. The YDIP is renamed KYDIP (Central Service for the Administration of Jewish Assets).

March 23–25, 1944: The Jews of Athens, Chalkida, Kastoria, Ioannina, Arta, Preveza, Larissa, Trikala, and Volos are rounded up. On April 2, their transport leaves for Auschwitz-Birkenau.

March–May 1944: After the occupation of Hungary (March 19), the Germans begin the extermination of one of the largest Jewish communities in Europe. Negotiations concerning the exchange and rescue of the Jews fail. About 570,000 Hungarian Jews are murdered in Auschwitz and other camps.

May–June 1944: On June 7, the Jews of Chania, on the island of Crete, are arrested. They are to be brought to the Piraeus harbor on board the steamer *Tanais*; the ship sinks and all its passengers drown. On June 9, the Jews of Corfu are arrested and deported to Auschwitz-Birkenau. On the island of Zakynthos, thanks to the initiative of Mayor Lukas Karrer and Archbishop of Athens Chrysostomos, all Jews are saved. On July 23 and 25, the 1,700 Jews on the islands of Rhodes and Kos are rounded up and brought to the concentration camp of Chaidari, from where they are deported to Auschwitz-Birkenau at the end of August.

October 7, 1944: Uprising of the *Sonderkommando* in the Auschwitz camp. About 250 inmates, those responsible for removing the dead from the gas chambers and taking the corpses to the crematoria, rebel, blowing up a crematorium and killing the guards. The uprising, in which 135 Greek Jews participated, is suppressed, and 200 prisoners are executed.

October 1944: Liberation of Greece. Athens is liberated on October 12, and Salonika on October 30. There are skirmishes with the retreating Germans and their collaborators. Celebrations and demonstrations in the liberated cities.

November 25, 1944: The SS begins to demolish the gas chambers and crematoria in Auschwitz-Birkenau.

December 1944: On December 3, armed clashes break out in Athens between government forces and the British army on the one hand and left-wing forces allied with the EAM, the ELAS, and the KKE on the other. The fighting, known as the *Dekemvriana*, lasts thirty-three days.

December 5, 1944: Jewish survivors who went into hiding or joined the resistance and then returned to Salonika meet in the Monastiriot Synagogue to discuss the reorganization of their community.

January 17, 1945: While the Soviet troops are advancing, SS units clear the Auschwitz-Birkenau camp complex and march the prisoners into the Reich. During these death marches, prisoners are killed or weakened to the point of collapse.

January 27, 1945: The Red Army liberates Auschwitz-Birkenau and the approximately 8,000 survivors remaining there.

February 12, 1945: Signing of the Varkiza Treaty by the Plastiras government and representatives of the EAM. Among other things, the treaty provides for the disarmament and demobilization of the ELAS.

March 15, 1945: The first survivor returns from Auschwitz to Salonika: Leon Bati. More survivors, individually or in groups, return to Salonika by the end of 1945.

April 1945: Liberation of the Bergen-Belsen camp on April 15 by the British. Most of the Jews from Greece interned there had already been "evacuated" from the camp on April 9. On April 23, near the town of Tröbitz, the Red Army liberates one of the trains on which they had been evacuated. In September 1945, the liberated return to Salonika. Spanish citizens from Greece had already been liberated in February 1944 and brought to the Spanish border.

May 2, 1945: The Red Army takes Berlin.

May 8, 1945: The unconditional surrender of Germany. The Soviet and Allied forces declare May 8 Victory in Europe Day (VE Day). The war in Europe is officially over.

June 1945: Foundation of the Central Council of Jewish Communities in Greece (KIS) as a legal entity under public law. Its main task is to rebuild the communities destroyed during the war. For many months or even years, Jewish survivors continue to demand the return of the houses and businesses taken from them.

1945–1952: More than 250,000 Jewish refugees—Displaced Persons (DPs)—including a core of former prisoners of the concentration and death camps, live in DP camps and urban centers in Germany, Austria, and Italy. They are under the administration of the Allied authorities and UNRRA.

August 1945: After the inspection of the refugee camps (DP camps) and on behalf of President Truman, Earl G. Harrison, the American representative to the Intergovernmental Committee on Refugees (ICG), presents his report. It sharply criticizes the attitude of the authorities regarding the DPs' living conditions.

August 1945: President Truman calls on the British to allow 110,000 Jewish refugees to enter Mandatory Palestine.

September 1945: The British set an upper limit for immigration to Mandatory Palestine: 1,500 refugees per month.

November 20, 1945–October 1, 1946: The Nuremberg Trials. Twenty-two Nazi political, military, and economic leaders are indicted before an international court made up of judges from the U.S., the U.K., the Soviet Union, and France. The court rules that obedience to orders from above does not justify the commission of "crimes against peace, war crimes, and crimes against humanity."

December 22, 1945: President Truman issues a directive regarding the preferential treatment of DPs who have applied for a visa to immigrate to the U.S.

January 1, 1946: The first postwar elections for the Jewish community of Salonika are held. The party of the former camp prisoners, the so-called "hostages," wins a majority over the Rebirth party, which was formed by Jews who hid during the war or who fought alongside the partisans.

1946: Foundation of a children's center in the Jewish community of Salonika. The JDC renovates an abandoned building on Spartis Street, converting it into a community and training center.

March 1946–August 1949: The Greek Civil War. Armed clashes between the National Army and the forces of the Democratic Army of Greece, DSE. Former Jewish partisans, as well as survivors from the camps, are drafted into military service and soon find themselves fighting on both sides.

July 1946: The Jewish community appears as a civil plaintiff in the trial of Nazi collaborators in Salonika; Jewish collaborators are also among the defendants. Survivors from the camps testify in court. Similar trials take place in Athens in 1947.

July 1946: As a result of the spread of defamatory rumors, Jewish survivors in Kielce, Poland, are attacked by an angry crowd. Forty Jews are killed and dozens more injured. This attack and similar pogroms lead to a wave of mass Jewish emigration from Poland and Eastern Europe to the refugee camps in Germany, Austria, and Italy.

February 1947: Great Britain raises the issue of Palestine at the United Nations.

July 11–September 8, 1947: The ship *Exodus 1947*, with Jewish refugees on board, sets sail from southern France for Mandatory Palestine. The British stop the ship and take it to the French port of Port-de-Bouc, where it is anchored for a month. The passengers are taken to Hamburg and then to camps in Cyprus. The incident provokes public outcry and Britain comes under pressure to allow Jews to enter Mandatory Palestine freely.

November 29, 1947: The General Assembly of the United Nations votes to divide Palestine into two states, one Jewish and one Arab. Jerusalem is to be placed under international control. The decision, which is supported by both the U.S. and the Soviet Union, is accepted by the Jewish side, but rejected by the Arab leadership.

May 14, 1948: David Ben-Gurion announces the founding of the State of Israel in Tel Aviv. He declares that the immigration of Jews to the new state should not be subject to any restrictions. Between 1948 and 1951, around 700,000 Jews immigrate to Israel, around two thirds of them DPs.

June 1948: The American Congress passes the Displaced Persons Act, which allows 200,000 DPs (Jews and non-Jews) to immigrate to the U.S. between 1949 and 1950. Originally, no preferential treatment was envisaged for the Jews, but the draft law is later changed. It is estimated that 80,000 Jewish DPs immigrated to the U.S. between 1945 and 1952.

March 1, 1949: Creation of the Organization for the Assistance and Rehabilitation of the Jews of Greece (OPAIE) to manage the assets appropriated by the YDIP. After the government issued Law 846 in January 1946, waiving its claims to Jewish assets without heirs in favor of a future organization to support and rehabilitate Jews, the founding of OPAIE was delayed by three years.

1949: Michael Molho and Joseph Nehama publish their book, *In Memoriam: Homage aux victimes juives des Nazis en Grèce*. This is the first detailed account of the persecution of Greek Jewry during the years of occupation.

PART ONE

"Be Well. Until Freedom Comes!"

In memory of David (Dick) Benveniste

CHAPTER ONE

Jews in Salonika, Partisans in the Mountains

In mid-February 1943, David (Dick) Benveniste (son of Yakov), who was born in 1921 and by this time was living at 13 Trapezountos Street, located in one of the ghettos in which the Germans had concentrated the Jews of Salonika, filled out two copies of a "declaration of assets" form:[1] a standardized version in German and one in Greek. The clear instructions given by the German occupying authorities read: "This statement is for statistical purposes. It must be completed on special paper, and the community council appointed by the Germans [Judenrat] recommends that people follow the instructions carefully and precisely, so as not to expose themselves to severe punishment by the German rulers." Rumors were circulating that the declarations served tax purposes, and the heads of Jewish families followed the instructions. Twenty-two-year-old Dick lived alone. His parents were already deceased, his older sister had been married for years, and she had a child of her own. As requested, he detailed cash and bank deposits, linens, outerwear, and underwear, as well as his share in a business holding. Prewar total value: 2,000 drachmas. On March 1, 1943,

---

1 Declaration of assets form, the Historical Archive of the Jewish Community of Thessaloniki (HAJCTh), Folder 0014: 0054–0057; see also Michael Molho and Joseph Nehama, *In Memoriam: Homage aux victimes juives des Nazis en Grèce*, 2nd ed. (Greek) (Thessaloniki: Jewish Community of Thessaloniki, 1973), pp. 84–86. For more details on these documents and their use in historical research, see Kavala, "Salonika during the German Occupation," pp. 267–287.

because of the massive wartime inflation, the total value of his assets was calculated at 818,000 drachmas.

Dick Benveniste, the son of a banker, came from an affluent family. However, the economic situation of the Benvenistes, like that of many other wealthy families, suffered a heavy blow during the global economic crisis, and in 1930 the family company, United Banks & Industries Benveniste, went bankrupt. In 1936, Dick graduated from the Altscheh business school, and he changed his job at least twice during the occupation. Nostalgically, he noted in his diary on December 23, 1944: "Two years ago, I opened my patisserie."[2] According to his discharge certificate from the tenth Division of ELAS (the Greek People's Liberation Army), Dick had been serving in the resistance since February 20, 1943. A far-sighted person who was known for making well-informed and balanced decisions, he had almost certainly already decided to go to the mountains when he completed his declaration of assets. An intermediary would have put him in contact with the resistance; then he would have packed a small backpack with thick leggings, a notebook, and a few essentials, waiting for the sign that would herald his departure.

Almost two years before, on April 9, 1941, the German occupying forces had marched into Salonika.[3] The Germans immediately shut down the Jewish newspapers, arrested the members of the community council, plundered the community offices, and set in motion the antisemitic propaganda machinery that was subsequently meticulously maintained by the *Nea Evropi* (New Europe) and *Apogevmatini* (Afternoon) newspapers. Racist ideology and the war had paved the way for the murder of the Jews, but the decision concerning the Final Solution to the Jewish Question had already been made. The implementation of this

---

2   The handwritten diary (numbering seventy-seven pages in total) in which he made daily entries from August 24, 1944, to February 19, 1945, the day on which he was discharged from his post, is found in my personal archive.

3   The best study of persecution is Molho and Nehama, *In Memoriam*. See also the recent study by Bowman, *The Agony*, as well as Yomtov Yakoel's testimony, *Memoirs 1941–1943* (Greek), edited and introduced by Fragiski Abatzopoulou (Thessaloniki: Paratiritis, 1993).

decision was in fact a process of increasingly radicalized anti-Jewish politics and the result of a series of individual decisions that were implemented and constantly expanded in the course of about a year—from the summer of 1941 and the mass murder of Jews in the framework of Operation Barbarossa against the Soviet Union until the summer of 1942 and the deadly attempt to assassinate Reinhard Heydrich in Prague.[4]

At the end of April 1941, the Rosenberg Commando, which was tasked with seizing libraries and religious artwork, arrived in Salonika.[5] Thanks to agents active in the area since the 1930s, the Nazi leadership possessed detailed information about the Jewish community, and the destruction of the Jewish community of Salonika was part of their plans as early as the fall of 1941.[6] The economic crisis and hunger hit the weakest strata, which accounted for most of the population. They were spared the worst until July 1942, when all adult men were ordered to report to Platia Eleftherias (Liberty Square) to register as forced laborers for German companies working with the Wehrmacht. The Judenrat, composed of new members, negotiated with the Germans to alleviate the burden on the weakest. It also organized the collection of ransom monies to redeem people from forced labor. At the same time, the expropriations and seizures of Jewish businesses continued, and, in December 1942, the city's ancient Jewish cemetery was destroyed in an act of great symbolic importance.[7] The Germans appointed Chief Rabbi Zvi Koretz

---

4   The discussion is well summarized in Ian Kershaw, *Hitler, the Germans and the Final Solution* (New Haven and London: Yale University Press, 2008), pp. 237–340.

5   Stratos Dordanas, "German Occupation Authorities and Greek Administration," in V. Gounaris and P. Papapolyviou, eds., *The "Blood Tax" in Occupied Thessaloniki: Foreign Domination, Resistance and Survival* (Greek) (Thessaloniki: Paratiritis, 2001), pp. 91–92.

6   Steven B. Bowman, "The Shoah in Salonika," in Randolph L. Braham, ed., *The Holocaust: Essays and Documents* (New York: East European Monographs, 2009), pp. 12ff.

7   Stella Salem, "The Old Jewish Cemetery of Salonika," *Chronika* (Greek), 181 (2005), pp. 6–17; Leon Saltiel, "Dehumanizing the Dead: The Destruction of Thessaloniki's Jewish Cemetery in the Light of New Sources," *Yad Vashem Studies*, 42:1 (2014), pp. 11–46.

as community leader. The decisive turning point occurred on February 2 and 3, 1943, when "Eichmann's men," a six-member commission responsible for carrying out the anti-Jewish measures, arrived in Salonika. The members of this commission included Dieter Wisliceny and Alois Brunner who worked with Max Merten. In his capacity as government councilor in the military administration, Merten often acted as the supreme commander for Macedonia and the Aegean. On February 6, 1943, Merten signed the ordinance ordering the Jews to wear the yellow star and to move into ghettos. On February 13, restrictions on freedom of movement and on the use of public transport and telephones were announced. The next day, a further restriction was publicized: Jewish shops were also required to display a special sign. On February 25, Max Merten dissolved all Jewish organizations. Sunny February 25 was the first day that the anti-Jewish measures were implemented in Salonika.

From February 1943, the Jews of Salonika marched to the rhythm of discriminatory regulations, decrees, restrictions, and prohibitions. Filling out their asset declaration forms, many still believed that there was room for negotiation and that it would perhaps even be possible to save the community. As the noose tightened, emotions changed: fear and resignation, thoughts of escape, hesitation, and the patient biding of time. In addition to the fear, uncertainty also fed a degree of confidence. Periods of relative calm discouraged radical decision-making and awakened hopes. Indeed, these hopes were deliberately nurtured by a language belying the fact that death awaited the Jews at the end of the train journey to Cracow. The Nazis systematically denied the Final Solution, declared the deportations "resettlement to the East," and tricked and appeased their victims by promising a new, albeit more difficult, life in labor camps. Using ambiguous terminology ("deportation, evacuation, relocation, transport"), the bureaucracy was able to ensure that matters remained vague, even though, as early as 1942, for the majority of Jews in the occupied countries, deportation meant transport to an extermination camp. With some probability, we can assume that the Jews of Salonika did not know of their impending fate at this stage.

For example, Dick did not know that the Greek Jews living in Paris, including his relatives, had been arrested in their homes by the French police at dawn on November 5, 1942, and taken to the Drancy transit camp.[8] From Drancy, they were then deported in two transports to Auschwitz, where most of them were immediately murdered in the gas chambers. Less than a month before March 15, 1943, the day on which the first train left for Auschwitz carrying the residents of the Baron Hirsch district, Dick left Salonika. He was not politically active, and he was not a leftist. Yet he was young, without family responsibilities,[9] and, based on the information available to him, he weighed his options and made the bold decision to flee to the mountains and join the partisan fighters.

How many Jews went to the mountains? Who did so and under what conditions? The problem that concerns me in the following pages can be formulated as follows: How can the common history of the Jews of Salonika who participated in the armed resistance be narrated, given that it involved very different people with divergent ways of life, whose paths crossed just briefly and then parted again? This question led me to reexamine age-old historiographic problems (such as resistance or collaboration with the enemy), assigning them different dimensions. It led me to relate the experience of the occupation to prewar and postwar history, and it calls once again for a comparison of the testimonies given by people and groups who shared common experiences in the war years yet came from very different social and geographical origins, held a range of political views, and so on. Focusing on a concrete case and its political and military context sheds light on

8   The mass arrests of the Jews in France were carried out in successive waves. However, overall responsibility lay with the French police. At the best-known mass arrest—which took place on July 16 and 17, 1942—more than 13,000 Jews were taken to the Paris "Wintervelodrom" (*Vel' d'Hiv*) and subsequently to various transit camps, before being transported to the Nazi concentration camps. Most of the Greek Jews living in Paris were arrested a few months later, on November 5, 1942.

9   His older sister, Ninette, lived with her husband, Joe Saporta, and their daughter, Andrée (Andy), in Athens. They had Spanish passports. They were deported to Bergen-Belsen and were liberated with the other Spaniards.

the particular experience of the partisans from Salonika. Their situation—and thus the conditions under which they made their decisions—differed from that of the Jews in Athens or Volos, for whom, in most cases, the adventure in the mountains did not begin until the Jews of Salonika had already been deported and eradicated. The stories of the resistance of Jews from other parts of Greece, sketched in detail in the books by Steven Bowman[10] and Karina Lampsa and Yakov Schiby,[11] belong to a slightly different context, and when reading them one should be careful not to draw hasty generalizations. Moreover, as we shall see below, in March 1943 resistance in general in Greece was in a very different phase than it would be a few months later, toward the end of the year.

Jewish Resistance

Any attempt to take a fresh look at Jewish participation in the resistance must be situated in the context of the historiographic developments that have accompanied public debate since the end of the war.[12] In other words, since the 1940s and 1950s, the political context has determined our understanding of the term "resistance" and its components—in Israel and in Europe. Perceptions have oscillated between the widespread view of the Jews as idealized

---

10 Bowman, *Jewish Resistance in Wartime Greece.*
11 Lampsa and Schiby, *Rescue*, pp. 307–384.
12 Israel Gutman, "Jewish Resistance: Questions and Assessments," in Israel Gutman and Gideon Greif, eds., *The Historiography of the Holocaust Period* (Jerusalem: Yad Vashem, 1988), pp. 641–677; Yehuda Bauer, "Forms of Jewish Resistance during the Holocaust," in John K. Roth and Michael Berenbaum, eds., *Holocaust: Religious and Philosophical Implications* (New York: Paragon House, 1989), pp. 136–155. Michael R. Marrus, "Jewish Resistance to the Holocaust," *Journal of Contemporary History*, 30:1 (1995), pp. 83–110; Nechama Tec, *Jewish Resistance: Facts, Omissions, and Distortions* (Washington, D.C.: United States Holocaust Memorial Museum and Miles Lerman Center for the Study of Jewish Resistance, 1997); Dan Michman, *Pour une historiographie de la Shoah* (Paris: Press Editions, 2001), especially the chapter "La résistance juive à la Shoah et sa signification: Orientations théoriques," pp. 237–284; Robert Rozett, "Jewish Resistance," in Dan Stone, ed., *The Historiography of the Holocaust* (New York: Palgrave Macmillan, 2004), pp. 344–363.

heroes who (like the fighters of the Warsaw ghetto) fell as rebels in an asymmetrical battle and the image of helpless, passive victims. "Sheep to the slaughter," "soap" in the extermination camps—these were disparaging terms used to describe the survivors.[13] In the search for those who could have led an uprising, survivors and historians alike looked to the leaders of the communities.

In the 1960s, Hannah Arendt, pinpointing the essence of a philosophical problem, yet at the same time misjudging its historical coordinates, or at least underestimating them, wrote that without exception the leaders of the Jewish communities in one way or another contributed to the Nazis' work. Indeed, she argued, while the catastrophe would of course have been enormous had the Jews confronted the Nazis in a completely disorganized fashion and without any guidance, the total number of casualties would nonetheless have been much smaller.[14]

At the same time, the eminent historian of the annihilation of European Jewry, Raul Hilberg, writing from the perspective of a political scientist, set a critical tone in his claims about the Judenräte: by accepting this role, Hilberg wrote, the leaders of the communities, even if they were morally impeccable and regardless of whether they desired the position or not, became cogs in the Nazi extermination machine.[15] In a later work, published in 1985, Hilberg reiterated his view, arguing that the main characteristic of European Jewish communities was their gradual adaptation to the escalating catastrophe. Yet, as he notes, certain Jews refused to adapt and deviated from the rule by choosing different ways out: suicide, hiding, escape, or resistance.[16]

13 Tal Bruttmann, "Qu'est-ce qu'un déporté?" in Tal Bruttmann, Annette Wieviorka, and Laurent Joly, eds., *Qu'est-ce qu'un déporté? Histoire et mémoires des déportations de la Seconde Guerre Mondiale* (Paris: CNRS, 2009), p. 19.

14 Hannah Arendt, *Eichmann in Jerusalem: A Report on the Banality of Evil* (New York: Viking Press, 1963). Giorgos Margaritis pointed out to me that, unlike other cases, for example the Armenian genocide, the perpetrators actually sought to ensure that their victims were organized, while the victims could do nothing but oppose the threat through their organization.

15 Raul Hilberg, *The Destruction of the European Jews*, vol. 3, 2nd ed. (New Haven: Yale University Press, 2003), pp. 217–218.

16 Raul Hilberg, *Perpetrators, Victims, Bystanders: The Jewish Catastrophe, 1933–1945* (New York: Harper Perennial, 1992).

These texts provoked, on the one hand, a series of "apologetic" responses. On the other hand, they led others to broaden the meaning of the term "resistance," no longer referring only to concrete, armed or unarmed, resistance but rather—in the sense of the Hebrew term *Amida*—also to intellectual resistance and all forms of response that can be implemented under conditions of extreme persecution, such as self-sacrifice, educational measures, food procurement, and more.

In this regard, Yehuda Bauer defined Jewish resistance as "any group action consciously taken in opposition to known or surmised laws, actions, or intentions directed against the Jews by the Germans and their supporters."[17] It should be remembered that the term "resistance," as noted by Angelos Elefantis, was not used in Greece in the years 1941–1944. The term originally came from France and was introduced shortly after the liberation. Until then, the (armed or political) struggle against the occupiers had always been referred to as *andartiko*, meaning the movement of partisans or rebels, the "struggle" (*agonas*), or the "struggle for national liberation" (*ethnikoapelevtherotikos agonas*). The armed struggle was the culmination of the spirit of resistance; it called for and created solidarity and mutual commitment among the combatants and the civilian population. The ideologically coherent network, Elefantis concludes, emerged from a resistance to Fascism, a national liberation struggle conducted from a leftist perspective, and it demonstrated, especially from the moment the Communists entered the stage, popular characteristics.[18]

Recent studies have managed to overcome the desire to ask why "the Jews did not resist," a question that is anything but harmless, often blaming the victims for their fate without taking into consideration the possibilities for resistance or the negligible probability that it was possible to alter the fate of those sentenced

17 Yehuda Bauer first articulated this in *The Jewish Emergence from Powerlessness* (Toronto: University of Toronto Press, 1979), p. 27, and later reiterated it in Yehuda Bauer, *Rethinking the Holocaust* (New Haven: Yale University Press, 2001), p. 119.

18 Angelos Elefantis, *They Took Athens from Us...Rereading History, 1941–1950* (Greek) (Athens: Vivliorama, 2002), p. 14.

to death in any way. In addition, the prejudices obscured a fact supported by all the historical sources: a Jewish resistance did indeed exist.[19] At the first international conference on resistance held in 1968 at Yad Vashem, young historians presented their research. Among them, Henri Michel came to the following, seemingly paradoxical, conclusion: it was in fact the other groups (such as prisoners in the concentration camps, Soviet prisoners of war, or workers in forced labor camps) who tended not to rise up and fight for their lives. This conclusion isolated the problem of resistance under conditions of extreme oppression from its correlation with factors such as national traditions or internalized behavioral patterns, turning researchers' attention to the catalytic influence exerted by severe violence and the paralyzing effect of totalitarian methods of oppression.[20]

Accordingly, shifting the emphasis from an ordinarily inevitable **result** (deportation to camps and subsequent mass extermination) to the **intentions** of the members of the Judenräte sheds light on a wide spectrum of behaviors and new problems.[21] What attitude did members of the Judenrat adopt, beyond the "red line" of betrayal and surrender of the Jews to the Germans; beyond active collaboration with the aggressor, which usually furthered personal enrichment? Did they try to protect the community? Were they corrupt or did they take risks and endanger their own families? These are questions that guard us against making premature generalizations. Most councils failed to protect their community or to save them, but their members often became aware that their actions were futile only when it was already too

---

19 See also Tec, *Jewish Resistance*.

20 Henri Michel, "Jewish Resistance and the European Resistance Movement," *Yad Vashem Studies*, 7 (1968), pp. 7–16.

21 Trunk, *Judenrat*; Aharon Weiss, "Jewish Leadership in Occupied Poland: Postures and Attitudes," *Yad Vashem Studies*, 12 (1977), pp. 335–365; Yehuda Bauer, "The Judenräte: Some Conclusions," in Israel Gutman and Cynthia J. Haft, eds., *Patterns of Jewish Leadership in Nazi Europe 1933–1945: Proceedings of the Third Yad Vashem International Conference, April 4–7, 1977* (Jerusalem: Yad Vashem, 1979), pp. 393–405. See also Barbara Spengler-Axiopoulou, "Methodological Thoughts for a Historical Approach to the Holocaust: The Case of Salonika," *Sychrona Themata* (Greek), 52–53 (1994), pp. 85–88.

late. Indeed, they frequently sought to save what could still be saved, even if there was no longer any hope (I will return to this problem in the third part of the book).

Vigorous resistance in all European countries was marked by the involvement of the masses as active agents, as Elefantis highlights.[22] Pieter Lagrou, who surveyed the resistance in the occupied countries of Western Europe, does not hide the fact that resistance, as opposed to collaboration with the aggressor, was a clear sign of a nation's moral health, a symbol of its rebirth. Thus, the fighters who revolted against the enemy became models for their nations. However, as Lagrou adds, the number of those actively involved in the resistance was extremely low, and the majority of citizens preferred to live their lives, avoiding conflict with the authorities and instead adapting to the new situation.[23] Although acts of resistance were by no means typical in countries such as Holland, France, or Belgium, they were appropriated by governments after the war in order to construct a collective "patriotic memory," serving as a unifying force that underscores an "eternal national value" and political tradition. The same trend was also manifest in discussions within French Jewish communities after the war.[24] In the survivors' newspapers, their leaders and intellectuals praised Jewish heroism, not just the armed struggle.[25]

Yet Jewish armed resistance was not and could never have been massive. The Jewish reaction to Nazi politics was strongly influenced by the extreme, "unbelievable" nature of the latter and by the fact that the extermination plans were shrouded in secrecy. When resistance cells finally mobilized in Eastern Europe, the catastrophe, that is, the deportation of the Jews to concentration

---

22 Elefantis, *They Took Athens from Us*, p. 16.
23 Pieter Lagrou, *The Legacy of Nazi Occupation: Patriotic Memory and National Recovery in Western Europe, 1945-1965* (Cambridge: Cambridge University Press, 2000).
24 Renée Poznanski, "Reflections on Jewish Resistance and Jewish Resistance in France," *Jewish Social Studies*, 2:1 (1995), pp. 124-158.
25 Boaz Cohen, *Israeli Holocaust Research: Birth and Evolution* (London: Routledge, 2013), pp. 212-214. Historians who, like N. Eck, were themselves among the survivors, use the Hebrew word *Amida* or the Yiddish *viderstand* in their texts.

camps and their subsequent extermination, was well underway.[26] Any attempt to assess the extent of the armed resistance or to compare the proportion of Jews in the resistance in relation to non-Jews must take into account special conditions and many parameters, such as the availability of weapons or the support given by resistance groups.

Piecing together these scattered elements creates an impressive picture.[27] A discrete or unified resistance certainly did not exist, certainly not in areas with a "mixed" population. For example, unlike the Communist resistance organizations, the nationalist Polish resistance did not accept Jews into its ranks. Yet about 25,000 Jews escaped from the ghettos of central and western Poland to join the partisans in the forests, while another 15,000 Jews fought in the western parts of Belarus. Very few of them survived. In Slovakia, 2,500 Jewish fighters took part in the uprising, and 10,000 men and women fought in Lithuania, while at least 20,000 Jews fought on the side of the Soviet partisans. Of course, the Jews' best-known resistance campaign was the Warsaw Ghetto Uprising in the spring of 1943. The Jews there knew that deportation to Treblinka spelt death, and the resistance groups subsequently succeeded in gaining control of ghetto life. There were also uprisings in other ghettos in Poland and Lithuania, such as those in Bialystok, Cracow, Czestochowa, Vilna, Kovno, and other places. In countries such as Belgium, France, Yugoslavia, Greece, and Italy, the Jews were accepted into resistance groups and

---

26 Yehuda Bauer, "Jewish Resistance and Passivity in the Face of the Holocaust," in François Furet, ed., *Unanswered Questions: Nazi Germany and the Genocide of the Jews* (New York: Schocken Books, 1989), p. 239.

27 Among the surveys offering an overview, see M. R. Marrus, *Jewish Resistance to the Holocaust* (London: Mecklermedia, 1989), as well as Yehuda Bauer, *History of the Holocaust* (New York: Franklin Watts, 2001). See also the following individual studies: Dov Levin, *Fighting Back: Lithuanian Jewry's Armed Resistance to the Nazis, 1941–1945* (New York: Holmes and Meier Publishers, 1985); Reuben Ainsztein, *Jewish Resistance in Nazi Dominated Eastern Europe* (New York: Elek, 1974); Renée Poznanski, "Résistance juive, résistants juifs: Retour à l'histoire," in Jean-Marie Guillon and Pierre Laborie, eds., *Mémoire et Histoire: La Résistance* (Toulouse: Privat, 1995), pp. 227–245; Israel Gutman, *The Jews of Warsaw: 1939–1943. Ghetto, Underground, Revolt* (Bloomington: Indiana University Press, 1989).

the national resistance. Nevertheless, there were also special Jewish groups elsewhere. In April 1943, in a unique act, Jewish resistance fighters in Belgium blew up a train bound for Auschwitz. In France, large numbers of Jews were involved in the resistance. Groups of Jewish resistance fighters helped other Jews escape and find shelter for children whose parents had already been deported. Most active were Communists and migrants from Eastern Europe.[28]

Although not a mass movement, the Jewish resistance was of great importance and manifested itself in a series of events that have become deeply rooted in the collective memory. In his farewell letter, Mordechai Anielewicz, the leader of the Warsaw Ghetto Uprising, wrote, "Self-defense in the ghetto will have been a reality. Jewish armed resistance and revenge are facts. I have been a witness to the magnificent, heroic fighting of Jewish men in battle."[29] An interesting question remains unanswered: to what extent did Jews participate in the resistance due to their particular situation as a persecuted people, or was it associated with other specificities of their identity—as Communists, workers, intellectuals, etc.? Likewise, was their Jewish identity during the war years (and also afterwards) influenced by their involvement in the resistance?

Since the 1970s, a scholarly consensus has distinguished between different forms of resistance without making any moral value judgments about them or placing them in a hierarchy. Such an attitude should not be misunderstood either as elevating a "gray zone" or as giving prominence to the "human" over the "political." It has more to do with a deep understanding of the schism and the tension between compulsory adaptation and rebellion. In addition, it relates to the understanding of a broader spectrum of responses and the complexity of behaviors. This means neither equating these behaviors nor leveling the differences that exist between them

---

28 Annette Wieviorka, *Ils étaient juifs, résistants, communistes* (Paris: Denoël, 1986).

29 The last letter from Mordechai Anielewicz, commander of the Warsaw Ghetto Uprising, April 23, 1943, in Yitzhak Arad, Israel Gutman, Abraham Margaliot, eds., *Documents on the Holocaust, Selected Sources on the Destruction of the Jews of Germany and Austria, Poland, and the Soviet Union* (Jerusalem and Lincoln: Yad Vashem and University of Nebraska, 1981), pp. 315–316.

but, on the contrary, underscoring the "red line" that separates compulsory adaptation from opportunism and conformism. In reality, it is not always easy to reach an opinion about such matters. As Enzo Traverso emphasizes,[30] it is by no means the case that there existed some kind of Weberian ideal type, subjects embodying dispositional ethics as opposed to those who embody the ethics of responsibility; those who follow an ethics of sacrifice, be it as fanatics, or simply those capable of killing for the good cause, while the latter consider the consequences of their actions for others. Such dilemmas tormented both sides, with contextual factors, or even just coincidence, causing the scales of decision to tilt toward one side or the other.

Historical research cannot circumvent epistemological investigations and inevitably contends with questions of a philosophical nature regarding the concept of "resistance." Ultimately, however, historical research presents its interpretations in the form of certain statements that often ignore political considerations. I would like to summarize them as follows: First, we cannot talk about **one** Jewish resistance, because the Jewish communities in Europe—and even within Greece—differed in terms of their composition and were in no way homogeneous. In addition, the Jews had **no** unified leadership and the relationship with their Christian fellow citizens varied from place to place.[31] Secondly, the decisions of the persecuted were largely determined by the course of the war, racial discrimination, the Final Solution, and the rhythm, timing, and conscious experience of its implementation on the ground (and less by information about what was happening in the camps in Poland and Germany). Third, the conditions of the occupation and the national resistance in all countries played a key role. In short, the local situation and the factors dictated by circumstances do not permit us to make either a depreciatory or a laudatory assessment of the Jews' participation

---

30 Enzo Traverso, *Fire and Blood: The European Civil War, 1914–1945* (New York: Verso, 2016), pp. 6–8.

31 On Greece, see Barbara Spengler-Axiopoulou, "Solidarity and Offering Help to the Greek Jews during the German Occupation, 1941–1945," in Benveniste, *Jews of Greece During the Occupation*, pp. 13–28.

in the armed resistance, nor can we fetishize the number of Jewish partisans involved. The relatively manageable scale of the Jews of Salonika allows us to rethink the questions posed above within their temporal framework as well as their political and social contexts.

Looking for Salonika's Jewish Partisans

As early as 1948, Rabbi Michael Molho addressed the difficult issue of resistance. Indeed, in a chapter entitled "Passivity of the Victims," he explains why, in his view, the Jews of Salonika could not avoid deportation. He provides a number of reasons for this:[32] the soothing and ultimately misleading speeches given by Chief Rabbi Koretz; the lack of financial resources necessary to buy salvation; the difficulty involved in concealing one's Jewish identity (due to the distinctive Judeo-Spanish accent among Salonika's Jews); the high denunciation rate; the panic that befell the terrorized population; the great distance from the resistance centers; family solidarity, which prevented the younger generation from leaving frail older relatives; the suddenness of the measures that preceded the deportations, such as forcing the Jewish population to append the yellow star to their clothing and to move to special neighborhoods, ghettos.

Chief Rabbi Zvi Koretz, who was appointed by the Germans as leader of the community in December 1942, incurred the wrath of nearly all the survivors. He was accused of failing to recognize the coming danger; of misleading the people and allaying their fears; and of demonstrating an exaggerated willingness to implement German orders immediately. Some witnesses explicitly describe his attitude as betrayal, suggesting that he worked with the Nazis for his own advantage, although this is difficult to prove.

As far as the assessment of the resistance is concerned, it was often determined by emotional and political considerations. In this light we should read what Asher Moisis, a scholar, Zionist,

---

32 Molho and Nechama, *In Memoriam*, pp. 114–116.

and prominent figure in the leadership of postwar Greek Jewry, who spent the years of the occupation in Athens, wrote to Joseph Nehama. His letter, dated December 6, 1962, states: "Unfortunately, we have no reason to be proud of our initiatives and resistance to the Germans during the persecution....In Salonika, passive resistance was rendered easy by the flight of one-tenth of the population, either to the Italian-occupied south of Greece or to the mountains (Vermio, Chasia, Pelion), where those young Jews who escaped with the help of the EAM [the National Liberation Front] joined the Resistance Army of the ELAS."[33] Asher Moisis saw Koretz's role absolutely negatively, noting at one point that when, in January 1943, emissaries of the EAM contacted him, he did not pay their proposals any heed.[34]

By contrast, the comprehensive catalog of an exhibition hosted by the Greek Jewish Museum in April 2013, which was entitled "Fellow Fighters: Greek Jews in the National Resistance," articulated the desire to restore "the lost page of history," to honor those who "fought and disproved the notion that the Jews in the Holocaust 'went like lambs to the slaughter,'" to acknowledge an "eternal lesson in collective dignity" and "militant solidarity."[35] To this end, the exhibition focused on the life stories of twenty-five men and women who took up arms. Of course, this exhibition and its catalog cannot replace historical analysis and interpretation. The phenomenon of Jewish participation in the resistance should be understood in the sense of two concentric circles: an "inner" circle of the Jewish community (community leadership, social differentiation, effects of anti-Jewish measures, etc.) and an "outer" circle of national resistance and the course of the war.

Giorgos Margaritis was one of the first to vividly describe the path from defeat to uprising, from hunger, occupation, and the feeling of betrayal to an unprecedented radical and mass

---

33 Asher Moisis, *Legacy*. Introduction and commentary by Rafail Moisis (Greek) (Athens: Asher Moisis, 2011), pp. 90ff.

34 Ibid., pp. 97–108.

35 Exhibition catalogue, *Fellow Fighters: Greek Jews in the National Resistance* (Greek) (Athens: Jewish Museum of Greece, 2014).

resistance of Greek citizens.[36] The lives of the Jews differed from city to city, depending on whether they were under German or Italian occupation, according to the time at which the anti-Jewish measures were implemented, the beginning of the deportations, the geographical situation, and the development of the resistance movement that the young Jews joined. Taking these preconditions into account, we reexamine the involvement of the Jews in Salonika in the armed resistance.

Under conditions we still need to understand, the Jewish inhabitants of Salonika, men and women alike, freely chose to "go to the mountains," a legendary and often inaccessible place of rebellion and refuge for persecuted persons who responded in different ways, taking up arms to ward off the enemy forces, to repel and defeat them. Certainly, there were other forms of resistance, from leafleting or the production of forged ID cards to the development of escape plans and hiding places in cities, in the countryside, or in Turkey, and later in Mandatory Palestine, usually with the help of the partisans.[37]

Steven Bowman estimates that there were around 1,000 Jewish partisans out of a total of about 30,000.[38] As we have already said, to interpret this figure we must consider factors such as access to the mountains, availability of weapons, on-site support, etc. The catalog of the abovementioned exhibition contains a number of revealing lists of names:[39] indeed, 106 of the Greek Jewish resistance fighters named were from Salonika. Twenty-four "fell while resisting," as well as twenty who were executed in the framework of retaliatory measures after they were arrested while fleeing or during military operations. In reality, it is difficult to distinguish between combatants, liaison personnel, and individuals arrested for a host of different reasons. In addition, the Jewish partisans, like many others, often used pseudonyms, sometimes even Christian

---

36 Giorgos Margaritis, *From Defeat to Revolt. Greece: Spring 1941–Fall 1942* (Greek) (Athens: Politis, 1993).

37 Lampsa and Schiby, *Rescue*, pp. 155ff; Matsas, *The Illusion of Safety*, pp. 102–110.

38 Bowman, *Jewish Resistance*, p. xxii.

39 Exhibition catalogue, *Fellow Fighters*, pp. 21–27.

ones, making it difficult to identify them. However, according to the testimonies of surviving partisans, their Jewish identity never presented a problem in the mountains and they never encountered antisemitic prejudice. Maurice Florentin took on the name Nikos; Beza, says Maurice, was called Takis: "That was enough. If you wanted, you said more," he said in an interview.

Bowman's most recent book concentrates on personal histories—one might say portraits—of Jewish resistance fighters. These are not woven into a common narrative thread but rather separate from the general framework of national resistance. In other words, this interesting prosopographic study does not attempt to explore the Jews as a group (albeit heterogeneous) within the resistance, essentially bypassing the need to reflect on Jewish resistance in general. It cannot be denied that a wealth of parameters often creates insurmountable difficulties: understanding the networks of evacuation routes to the mountains and joining the bands of fighters; the geography of their actions, which required that they remain constantly on the move; the geography of their missions and battles; and, of course, the importance of Jewish identity in these events. Furthermore, we must examine the shaping and transformation of subjects in terms of their political positions following the end of the war and during the civil war; their path to a "normal life" or to exile or prison; and their eventual emigration, leaving Greece for Israel or elsewhere. At the same time, we have few sources of information about the lives of the Jewish partisans in the mountains and their armed struggle.

In contrast to most other liberated countries, in Greece Nazi collaborators very soon joined the state mechanism and contributed to the delegitimization of the partisans. Undoubtedly, the civil war and the persecution of those on the political Left, which included many resistance fighters, contributed to the veil of silence that descended over this aspect of history. Nevertheless, and despite the self-censorship of many militants, today we have a number of autobiographical accounts[40] as well as a significant

---

40 Refer to the excellent autobiography by Moisis Bourlas, *Greek, Jew and Leftist* (Greek) (Skopelos: Nisides, 2009); see also the anonymous article, "Partisans

corpus of oral testimonies in various archives, upon which the following discussion draws.[41] One quickly realizes that the stories of the former partisans are very different from the memoirs of the partisan leaders, the *capetanioi*, who adopt an accusatory or apologetic tone when describing relations with other groups of partisans or with the British, and insist on the purely military or political decisions that pertained at the different levels of the resistance hierarchy. The *capetanioi* provide detailed accounts of the military achievements and deployment tactics, of armaments and casualties. As with all testimonies, those of the Jewish partisans are affected both by the time at which they were written and by the expectations of the intended audience and various institutions involved in collecting them.

Saving Jews: From the Diary of a Jewish Partisan," *Israilitikon Vima* (Greek), May 5, 1946; Joseph Matsas, "The Participation of the Greek Jews in the National Resistance, 1940–1944," *Journal of the Hellenic Diaspora,* 17 (1991), p. 55–68. Concerning the memoirs of a female partisan, see Renee Levine Melamed, "The Memoirs of a Partisan from Salonika," *Nashim* 7 (2004), pp. 151–173.

41 The oral, i.e., video and acoustically recorded, testimonies that I drew upon come from several archives: Yad Vashem Archives (YVA), Fortunoff Video Archive for Holocaust testimonies (HVT), the Visual History Archive of the USC Shoah Foundation (VHA), United States Holocaust Memorial Museum (USHMM), as well as Centropa Jewish Witness to a European Century. The interviews in VHA were recorded from 1996 onward, those in the Fortunoff Video Archive some years earlier. The testimonies of the following partisans are mentioned: Vital Aelion, VHA, 48010; David Aharon, YVA, O.3/3556218, O.3/3563156; Dario (David) and Yitzhak Amir, YVA, O.3/6733466; Emanuel Arouh, HVT, 3007; Markos Botton, VHA, 43906; Moisis Bourlas, VHA, 9368; David Broudo, VHA, 4466 and YVA, O.3/3740695; Solomon (Tsitso) Cohen, USHMM, RG-50.426*0008; Yakov Koumeris, VHA, 47768; Moise Eskaloni, VHA, 28007 and HVT, 2777; Maurice Florentin, Centropa, VHA, 42943, and HVT, 3013; Pepo Matalon, VHA, 49030; Yitzhak Moshe (Kapetan Kitsos), YVA, O.3/3558586; Moysis Esdra, VHA, 43906; Simantov Razon, USHMM, RG-50.120*0124; Jaques Serror, VHA, 1441. As part of a research program funded by the non-profit Latsis Foundation, a database has been created that greatly facilitates the study of visual and audio testimonies of Greek survivors. In addition to myself, as a coordinator of the program, the research group included Giorgos Antoniou, Pothiti Hantzaroula, Tony Molho, Paris Papamichos-Chronakis as well as Themis Dallas who was responsible for the database. The database is hosted on the homepage of the Department of History, Archaeology, and Social Anthropology at the University of Thessaly: http://gjst.ha.uth.gr/en/index.php (accessed April 5, 2016).

I followed the intersecting paths of a group of young people "at an age when you fear nothing and no one," as one of them, David Broudo, put it many years later. These paths took them from Salonika to the mountains of central and western Macedonia, where they served in the ELAS as fighters, interpreters, sentries guarding weapons and food, and in a range of other roles. Most of the Greek partisans were aged between fifteen and twenty, and more than half of them had fought on the Albanian front against the Italians (October 28, 1940–April 23, 1941), where they gained their first combat experiences. Among the soldiers who fought in the Greco-Italian War were also 12,898 Greek Jews. If we follow a group of individuals through the war and beyond, we are forced to take into account the diversity of their stories, to consider not only their common destiny but also their different ways of life, as dictated by the persecution.[42]

Thus, I try to trace the problems of a common history of persecution that manifested in a multitude of different ways, to bring to light options for action and decisions, and to understand the weight of the conditions that determined behavior. The story I tell unfolds in three chapters. First, there is affiliation with the partisan associations: the social and economic profile of those Jews who decided to go "to the mountains" and what they knew. When did they make their decisions? Did they wear the yellow star? Did they report to Platia Eleftherias in July 1942 to be registered as Jews? How did they bid goodbye to their relatives? When and how did they escape? Subsequently, we will learn about living conditions in the mountains, the geography of the resistance, and the battles. Finally, I will discuss the liberation, the Greek Civil War, and the dilemmas associated with, and the possibilities of, returning to the city of their birth.

Most of the Jews joined ELAS, the main resistance organization, which was closely linked to the EAM and the political Left, even though this step was not always determined by a conscious political decision.[43] To understand the mobilization of

42 Mariot and Zalc, *Face à la persécution.*
43 See Matsas, *The Illusion of Safety*, p. 343.

the Jewish partisans, we need to pause for a moment and recall the situation in Salonika and in the resistance movement when the hour arrived for the young Jews to make their all-important decision.

EAM/ELAS and the Resistance in Salonika

The National Liberation Front (EAM) was founded on September 27, 1941, at the initiative of four small left-wing parties: KKE, the Greek Communist Party; the Socialist Party; the Peasant Party; and the Union for People's Democracy. It brought together a wide range of social groups and started preparing people for armed action as early as October of that same year. In January 1942, the EAM and the KKE decided to set up the Greek People's Resistance Army (ELAS). Although an ELAS central committee was founded in February, the partisan movement remained uncoordinated for some time. Indeed, a certain period passed before the resistance movement became organized and coordinated (this applied to the rest of Europe as well, with the exception of the Balkans).[44] In the spring of 1942, Aris Velouchiotis took over the organization of the groups in central Greece.[45] The strengthening of the partisan movement was certainly also connected with the deterioration of the living conditions under the German occupation.

Networks were formed in Salonika at an early stage to provide hiding places for British parachutists and liaison agents and help them to flee. Following the German invasion of Salonika in April 1941, the Communists distributed leaflets calling for the people not to give up their weapons and to oppose the confiscation of

44 It is sufficient to recall that the Soviet partisan movement, although active from the start of the war (the summer of 1941) took two years to become organized; that Yugoslav resistance only strengthened after the capitulation of Italy (in September 1943); and that the French and Dutch resistance movements were not organized until the spring of 1943. However, resistance activity in Bosnia, Serbia, and Montenegro started already in the summer of 1941.

45 According to Mark Mazower, a year passed until the first local groupings and their leaders (*capetanioi*) formed a central armed forces staff. See Mazower, *Inside Hitler's Greece*, p. 298.

food. Toward the end of the same month, a resistance organization for national liberation, Eleftheria (Freedom), was founded. A year later, it was renamed EAM Macedonia. The flare-up of resistance in Macedonia was accelerated by the German attack on the Soviet Union. From September 1941, acts of sabotage, the disarming of gendarmes, and the bombing of railway lines were recorded. The armed actions led to retaliatory measures by the Germans (in Nigrita, Kilkis, and Almyros), and in November 1941 two students were executed in Salonika for the possession of illegal writings.[46]

At the same time, the Macedonian office of the KKE sought to coordinate the struggle and solve the problems of daily life. As part of the attacks on German collaborators, the Salonika home of Colonel Georgios Poulos, who collaborated with the occupiers, was blown up in December 1941. As the acts of sabotage increased, the Germans carried out mass retaliatory executions in prisons, and, consequently, the resistance abandoned the tactic of sabotage. This "retreat" had consequences for the Jews of Salonika. Yitzhak Nehama, in his testimony at the Eichmann trial in Jerusalem, described the Jews' return from the labor camps after the community had managed to ransom its members. At that time, he said,

> The partisans appeared on the scene and they wanted to take their revenge on the Germans. And who were the victims? — the Jews. The Germans decided to put Jewish guards in places where the railway had to pass. Every 20 kilometers there had to be a guard manned by young Jews, who were replaced every 24 hours. And they let it be known that if, Heaven forbid, something were to happen along the railway line, they would kill the entire Jewish guard. Imagine under what conditions the Jews lived then! The partisans knew about this and they refrained from doing anything.[47]

46 Giorgos Kaftantzis, *The University of Salonika during the Occupation* (Greek) (Salonika: Paratiritis, 1983), p. 17.
47 *The Trial of Adolf Eichmann: Record of Proceedings in the District Court of Jerusalem*, vol. 2 (Jerusalem: Ministry of Justice, 1992), p. 854.

In early 1942, Markos Vafiadis, a fugitive from the island of Gavdos, to which he had been exiled, arrived in Salonika. He assumed a post in the Macedonian office and in the Communist Party organization of Salonika. At that point, efforts were directed at attracting the lower classes of the population and tackling the problems of daily life: hunger and the sharp decline in wages. At the same time the party began to organize the printing of underground newspapers and political flyers.[48] Some voices in the party demanded an organic connection between the partisan movement and the population, which provided the necessary material goods and also formed an important source of combat reserves: the villages constituted a reservoir of food, shelter, information, and labor, without which the EAM/ELAS could not have survived.

In his memoirs, Stratis Anastasiadis mentions that in the winter of 1942 people asked the party for permission to go to the mountains to fight against the oppressors. The party responded that they were needed in Salonika, which greatly displeased them.[49] In fact, the EAM organized the urban population in Athens and Salonika quite successfully, with mass mobilizations and militant demonstrations for "Freedom and Bread." After the fall of 1942, the ELAS intensified its activities, and its initiatives became increasingly important from November, after the British, the EDES (Greek Democratic National Army, a nationalist guerilla force), and the ELAS together blew up the Gorgopotamos Bridge. In August 1942, the offices of the EEE Fascist organization in Salonika were attacked.[50] In late December and early January 1943, ELAS units became active in (Italian-occupied) western Macedonia, in the territories of Voio and Grevena; many Jewish partisans from Salonika were also involved in these actions. Members of the ELAS disarmed the gendarmerie, distributed grain, and moved into Siatista.

---

48 Petros Papapolyviou, "Resistance intra muros," in Gounaris and Papapolyviou, *The "Blood Tax,"* pp. 41–90.

49 Stratis Anastasiadis, *From Resistance to Disillusionment: Salonika, Bulkes, Vitsi* (Greek) (Thessaloniki: Epikendro, 2013), p. 43.

50 Andreas Kedros, *The Greek Resistance, 1940–1944* (Greek) (Athens: Themelio, 1976), p. 231.

On March 25, 1943, the youth organization of the EAM organized a mass rally in Salonika. After the students had crowned a bust of Rear Admiral Nikolaos Votsis (a symbol of liberation from Ottoman rule), they paraded past the home of Professor Theodoridis, who stepped onto his balcony and threw a Greek flag over them.[51] Other fighters also spoke at the same demonstration. Conspicuously, they did not mention any glimmer of solidarity with their Jewish fellow citizens, even though the deportations had begun ten days earlier. From the beginning of 1943, and in an atmosphere of relative optimism resulting from the victory in Stalingrad, the guerrillas' numbers increased, and, in the spring of 1943, they already numbered 12,000 combatants. A year later, in the spring of 1944, they amounted to around 26,000. In July 1943, the Supreme Military Council of the ELAS decided that the organization should be structured along the lines of a regular army system. The Macedonian headquarters and its local command posts was renamed the ninth division, "Division of Western Macedonia," and the establishment of the tenth division, "Division of Central Macedonia," was set in motion. Lieutenant Kikitsas and Capetan Markos Vafiadis were appointed as their respective commanders.

In 1942, political organization preceded the armed struggle. In February 1943, the EAM succeeded in transforming a series of what began as "economic" strikes into political actions against the German occupation.[52] In the spring of 1943, the movement protested against political mobilization in the service of the occupiers, and on April 16 a huge central rally was held in Salonika. Prior to this, there had been other rallies: a student mobilization on the second anniversary of the German invasion of the city and on the anniversary of the well-attended rally of March 25. The deportations had already begun at that time, but there was no voice of protest against the fate of the Jews, except, of course, Archbishop Damaskinos' formal objection of March 23, which bore twenty-

51 Eleftheria Drosaki, *In Salonika: From War to Occupation and Resistance* (Greek) (Thessaloniki: Odyseas, 2000), pp. 88–91.

52 Ioannis L. Hondros, "The Greek Resistance 1941–1944: A Reconsideration," in G. Iatridis, ed., *Greece in the Decade 1940–1950: A Nation in Crisis* (Greek) (Athens: Themelio, 1984), pp. 72–73.

seven additional signatures. The massive mobilizations reached their peak in July 1943, when most of the Jews had already been deported, and by the end of the year, with the creation of the Salonika ELAS Reserve, armed struggle had become a feature of city life.

Odette Varon-Vassard, who found two reports in the PEAN (Panhellenic Union of Young Combatants) newspaper, *Doxa*, which were published in Athens in September 1942 and October 1943, ultimately concludes that the persecution of Greek Jews had not entered the general consciousness as a "Greek problem."[53] Yet in an Athenian call-up issued by the EAM in January 1943, that is, before the deportations began, there is talk of "pogroms," and it is perfectly clear what was happening:

> To the whole Greek people, to the people of Athens. Brothers, the oppressor is preparing a new crime against our people. We are facing a new manifestation of Fascist brutality and bestiality, this time directed against the Jewish population among the Greek people. In Salonika, the bloodthirsty occupier is preparing a terrible and evil pogrom against the Greek Jews, like those it organized in Germany and Poland. Thousands of innocent people are being threatened by the evil Gestapo with execution, mass murder, and concentration camps. The wretched looters and murderers of the "new order" in Europe thirst for blood and for new hecatombs of victims…The pogrom against the Jews aims to weaken the powerful fighting spirit of our entire people, which has become a terrible nightmare now that it is shattered by the blows of our allies on the Eastern Front and in Italy. Therefore, the National Liberation Front calls on the people of Athens and all Greeks and Christians to help save the Jews. Let us thwart the horrendous anticipated

53 Odette Varon-Vassard, *The Emergence of a Difficult Memory* (Greek) (Athens: Estia, 2013), especially the chapter entitled "The Underground Press during the Occupation and the Deportation of the Jews: The Silence of Written Sources," pp. 19–30.

"pogrom" with mass protests, large committees, and general mobilization. We want to offer protection and refuge to every persecuted Jew. To crush every denunciator of the Jews.[54]

In April 1943, when the deportations were already underway in Salonika, the language became even more intense. In Athens, a call for "national solidarity" circulated:

A tragedy is taking place in Salonika. The monster craves sacrifice. And the mass of Jews gives him blood, blood, which has not sated Hitler and his followers even after their countless terrible crimes...They are beaten everywhere. They are made the scapegoat of German failure, the targets of the latter's schizophrenic worldview. Hundreds were transported in freight cars to Poland. Yet the wagons did not reach their destination. They stopped somewhere for ten days and there unimaginable events took place. A steady mass of people lived through the martyrdom of hunger, thirst, and slow asphyxiation, witnessing the terrible deaths of their neighbors, who remained in the sealed wagons. Those who did not meet their deaths lost their minds in Hitler's hell. Later they were thrown into pits. Others had to take their place...We feel the pain of the persecuted race as our own pain. Every Greek must protest against the sufferings of the Jews because they are part of the suffering that the oppressor brings on all the people who inhabit Greek soil.[55]

While the words of the flyer clearly indicate that the final destination of the Jews of Salonika was not known at the time—

---

54 The call-up, documented in the Jewish Museum of Greece, was discovered on an electricity meter during renovations to a shop. See "Pages of the National Resistance: A Flyer by EAM to save the Jews," *Chronika* (Greek), November–December 1989, p. 12ff.

55 From the archives of the Communist Party (KKE), published in the catalogue of an exhibition in the Jewish Museum of Greece. See *Fellow Fighters*, p. 9.

we shall return to this problem below—the motif of solidarity is highly explicit.

As part of the party's restructuring, the KKE organization of the Jews of Salonika, which now had around 150 members, was also reorganized. According to former partisan Markos Vafiadis,[56] the party members in general, and the Jewish members in particular, did not approve of mobilizations and protests opposing the racist discrimination measures. A general refusal to wear the yellow star also failed to rally support. He continues: "The Jews themselves were unrecognizable. Nothing was left of their former selves. Instead of pioneers and dedicated fighters, they were discouraged and inert." Vafiadis offers an explanation for this change, attributing responsibility to the "reactionary leadership" of the Jews. The KKE organization, he stressed, suggested that the Jews not sell their possessions but entrust them to "organized Greeks" and spread them over various locations. It was also advised that their children be placed with families outside Salonika.[57] Lastly, the Jewish party organization was asked to name those members who wanted to go to the mountains: about seventy-five or eighty came forward. Vafiadis continues:

> We divided them into three groups. The first group set off one night for the mountains. They had already gone quite far when they somehow learned that all Jews were

56 Vafiadis' interesting testimony articulates his skepticism about solidarity among the Jews, regardless of their social background, praises their militant participation in the workers' struggles in the years before the war, and confirms that the political influence of the party on the Jews was above average. See Markos Vafiadis, *Memoirs (1940–1944)* vol. 2 (Greek) (Athens: Papazisis, 1985).

57 In April 1945, a letter arrived, addressed to the community in Salonika. The undersigned explained that when the persecution of the Jews began, a father gave his children, aged ten and twelve, into his care. The father then set out "for the mountains to join the partisans, leaving the children with me. For eighteen months I hid them at home, and you can imagine the hardships and danger to which my wife and I were exposed." Jews who returned informed him that the father had been killed. The man admitted he had already received some help from the community but had since discovered that "the community gives loans to many citizens," and he implored it to help him with the orphans (HAJCTh, folder 00159: 00329).

gathered in an area surrounded by barbed-wire fencing near the train station [the Baron Hirsch ghetto]. Without thinking it over for very long, they too went there. They decided to return to their relatives, declaring: 'We know that we are going to our destruction, but it is our duty to be with our families.'"

Many years later, Panos Dimitriou, a fighter from Salonika and a left-wing leader, tried to sort through his memories, assessing them critically and attempting to determine who was responsible for the fact that the Jews did not flee en masse to the mountains:[58]

> When I arrived in Salonika on New Year's Day 1944, the crime of exterminating our Jewish fellow citizens had long been accomplished...Born and raised in Salonika, I could not help trying to clarify the circumstances and causes that led to their total annihilation, and above all in ascertaining why it had not been possible for at least part of the Jewish community to survive...I do not believe that the explanation lies in the indifference or insensitivity of the organizations mentioned. Because it is generally known that the KKE was the only Greek party that had a clear political position on the issue of minority rights, including Jewish rights, in the prewar period and consistently fought against discrimination and racism. It is also well known that a considerable number of Jews were integrated into the organizations of the KKE and OKNE [the federation of the Communist youth organizations of Greece], either as active members or even as cadres, and that the party also had a large number of affiliates.

Dimitriou's response to the questions asked above turns the spotlight on the attitude of the Jewish community and Koretz, as

---

58 Panos Dimitriou, *From the Depths of My Heart: Chronicle of a Life, of an Era* (Greek) (Athens: Themelio, 1997), pp. 111–114.

well as the illusion that the Jews would be able to save their lives with ransom money. As he continues:

> Because of the aforementioned circumstances, it is easy to understand why the KKE and the EAM organizations were reluctant to publicly denounce the genocide that was about to befall the Jews: indeed, they had no clear idea of the oppressor's intentions. As it was, they were reluctant to take responsibility for actions that were not expressly desired by the Jews themselves, and which could have been used as an excuse for even harsher measures to be taken against them. So, the only possible way out was to suggest that they flee to the mountains.

As with Vafiadis, Dimitriou's scale tends to tip toward placing responsibility on Koretz as well as the Jews' misguided self-deception. Perhaps he willfully disregards that other deception, the one that the Germans practiced. He does not hesitate to say: "There is another rather serious side to this subject, which concerns the attitude of some Greeks from Salonika toward the tragedy of their Jewish fellow citizens; they—luckily there were only a few—tried in every conceivable way to profit from the situation, and unfortunately were not outed in the Salonika resistance press."

The question of the relative silence in the resistance press, but also in the memories of the protests against the persecution of the Jews,[59] provokes a degree of embarrassment, even if this was not a singular Greek phenomenon.[60] It is not sufficient to cite a lack of knowledge, weakness, or antisemitism. The anti-Jewish measures and even the deportations were neither central to the resistance nor to public opinion, albeit for different reasons. Public opinion became accustomed to the "abnormal normality" of the occupation and accepted with a degree of equilibrium the

---

59 Kaftantzis, *The University of Salonika*.
60 See also Renée Poznanski, *Propagandes et Persécutions: La Resistance et le problème juif 1940–1944* (Paris: Fayard, 2008), pp. 2, 10–11.

misfortune that knocked on neighboring doors. The resistance viewed the persecution as part of the occupation policy rather than as a matter of particular priority that required specific action beyond self-evident denunciation. Good or bad, the solution for the persecuted Jews was the same as that for other Greeks: the mountains. Those Jews who went to the mountains believed— and rightly so—that their salvation would come only with the defeat of Fascism and that their struggle could only be fought in an alliance with the EAM. Whether for "national" or "class" reasons, or even a mixture of both, the character of the resistance movement did not allow the racial dimension to be perceived as a main axis of the Nazi occupation. The fate of the Jews was not considered a matter of high political stakes. Solidarity was a question of "humanity"—even after the first deportations in March 1943. Ignorance does not explain much, priorities explain a little more, and perhaps the leadership of the resistance, at least during the period of the deportations of the Jews, was not much more farsighted on this issue than the Jewish leadership was.

* * *

In any case, during the end of winter and in the spring of 1943, the ELAS stepped up its presence. The now palpable threat of deportation and the project of resistance to the Germans made the ELAS attractive to many young Jews from Salonika, especially but not exclusively leftist Jews. In addition, during the period of its great growth in 1944, the EAM turned to a wide range of social forces and to traditional bourgeois parties, and at the time of liberation the ELAS was able to muster 25,000 militants in Macedonia alone.

An interesting aspect of this theme is the cooperation of the Jewish Agency in Mandatory Palestine with the Greek government-in-exile in Cairo and the Greek resistance, albeit only from the summer of 1943. This involved supplying the partisans with clothing, blankets, military equipment, armaments, and medicines, as well as providing financial means to enable the partisans to hide and protect Jews or help them flee to Mandatory Palestine. Yakov Schiby mentions a meeting between representatives of the

Jewish Agency and the EAM, held in April 1944 in Cairo, with the goal of organizing an escape route via Euboea. He also mentions the correspondence of Alexandros Svolos (professor of law and left-leaning politician; in March 1944 he was appointed president of the Political Committee for National Liberation [PEEA], which was established by the EAM/ELAS) with the representative of the World Jewish Council in Cairo.[61] However, by the time all this happened, the struggle for the salvation of the Jews of Salonika was already lost.

61 Lampsa and Schiby, *Rescue*, pp. 312ff.

CHAPTER 2

Escape

Some Jews from Salonika had already fled to Athens and subsequently remained there, while others chose to follow suit. They joined the resistance, subsequently fighting in southern Greece.[1] Baruch Schiby,[2] for example, a leftist intellectual, journalist, and Zionist, had been in touch with the resistance and the EAM from an early stage. Following the German invasion, he understood that he would be arrested and fled to Athens, hoping to make his way to the Middle East. Wanted by the Gestapo, he hid in Athens, was involved in the resistance activities conducted by the EAM, and in the spring of 1944 helped Rabbi Barzilai to flee to the mountains. Manolis Aruch,[3] a medical student in Athens and a member of the Communist youth organization, joined the resistance early on. He later recalled how, together with twelve or fifteen other Jews, he formed a group that helped Athenian

---

1   For example, when Alberto Meir returned to Salonika in 1942, having been sent away for forced labor, he informed his father that he had decided to flee to Athens. Thanks to his political connections, he soon managed to contact the resistance, joined the ELAS, and fought in southern Greece. I thank his son Itzhak (Sakis) for this information.

2   Miriam Novitch, *Le Passage des Barbares: Contribution à l'histoire de la déportation et de la résistance des Juifs Grecs* (Paris: Presses du Temps Présent, 1967), pp. 33–41.

3   M. Aruch testimony, HVT, 3007. I am indebted to his daughter, Nelly Aruch, for additional information and explanations.

Jews escape to Euboea. In September 1943, he and seven other Jewish doctors went to the mountains. There he served as a doctor in the Second Company of the Thirty-Fourth Regiment and also took part in battles. He estimates that around 300 Jews fought in Central Greece.

* * *

The young Jews Yakov Koumeris, Markos Botton, David Aharon, and Maurice Florentin, as well as Dick Benveniste, succeeded in escaping from Salonika to the mountains. David Broudo, Moise Eskaloni, and the brothers Yitzhak and Dario (David) Amir escaped from forced labor camps. To understand their decisions, we need to reconstruct the course of their flight and the events associated with it, considering what they knew or imagined at the time about the fate of the Jews. We must understand their concrete options and the circumstances of their escape as well as their motivations, but we must also consider the personal commitments that deterred them from fleeing. In addition, we must examine the social networks and the options for action that were available to these Jews in general. To narrate the various stages of such paths, we must also shed light on their social determinants, without losing sight of the fact that such a daring enterprise entailed the very real prospect of death, both for them and for their loved ones.

Jews from Salonika mainly began to join the ELAS at the beginning of 1943, when discriminatory measures against the Jews were introduced. Others joined shortly after the deportations to Auschwitz-Birkenau began. What did these Jews, who decided to risk their lives and take up arms, know about their futures at that time? Today we know that despite the strict Nazi adherence to secrecy, and in spite of the misleading language and tactical deceptions that they systematically used, in the summer of 1942 the Polish resistance movement and radio disseminated detailed information about the mass murder of Jews in extermination camps using poisonous gas, in trucks and subsequently in chambers constructed especially for this purpose.

Yet we also know that this information was not taken seriously at the time, even when it was published in newspapers such as the *New York Times* and broadcast by official radio stations, such as a BBC broadcast in December 1942. The "unbelievable" message was considered excessive or even deliberate anti-German propaganda. Two Slovak Jews who had escaped from Auschwitz in April 1944 brought with them the "terrible secret." Moreover, the Allies had been aware of the "details" of the extermination in Auschwitz since 1943;[4] however, as Annette Wieviorka notes, this news may well have been lost in the volumes of information relating to Poland, and it may not have been associated with, or credibly reinforced by, the deportations of Jews from other countries.[5] Some certainly had access to this "information," but it remained unconfirmed and difficult to act upon in such a state of uncertainty. Adam Rayski, a Jew and an active member of the French resistance, described how the illegal Yiddish-language press, run by Jewish Communists, struggled to decide whether to share the "unconfirmed news" regarding the implementation of the Final Solution in Poland with the Jewish community in France.[6]

All the testimonies of Greek survivors agree that the victims misjudged the nature of the extermination camps and the fate of the deportees. Gradually, they became accustomed to a life under the conditions of an "abnormal normality," within which the coherence and the consequences of events were lost and the boundaries between good and evil often blurred. People focused their efforts on coping with the present day, and their ability to look to the future was drastically limited. Over a long period of time— even after that Black Sabbath of July 11, 1942, when the male Jews

---

4 See also Eugen Kogon, Hermann Langbein, and Adalbert Ruckerl, *Les chambres à gaz secret d'État* (Paris: Editions de Minuit, 1984), as well as Richard Breitman, *Official Secrets: What the Nazis Planned, What the British and the Americans Knew* (London: Hill and Wang, 1999).

5 Annette Wieviorka, *Auschwitz: 60 ans après* (Paris: Robert Laffont 2005), p. 206.

6 Adam Rayski, "The Jewish Underground Press in France and the Struggle to Expose the Nazi Secret of the Final Solution," in Michael J. Berenbaum and Abraham J. Peck, eds., *The Holocaust and History: The Known, the Unknown, the Disputed, and the Reexamined* (Bloomington: Indiana University Press, 1998), pp. 699–715.

of the city were ordered to gather on Platia Eleftherias in agonizing and degrading conditions to register for forced labor,[7] and until February 1943—Jews and Christians shared the same "abnormal normality" of everyday life under the occupation: terror, fear, hunger, longing for freedom.

Even though the first acts of resistance in Salonika took place as early as November 1941, and a mass demonstration was held in March 1943, news from Athens also probably had a reassuring effect. Indeed, On March 7, 1943, Ioanna Tsatsou joyfully recorded in her diary an announcement that appeared in the morning papers: the withdrawal of the mobilization order.[8]

A few months previously, in October 1942, the Jews had briefly dared to breathe freely. Following intensive efforts and negotiations with the Germans, the Central Committee for the Coordination of the Works of Social Welfare, established by the community in April 1942, had succeeded in relieving the Jews of their obligation to provide compulsory labor, thus saving thousands of them from certain death.[9] However, deception became the norm again after the introduction of anti-Jewish measures: in response to protests by the Jews against their exclusion from all public institutions (professional associations, welfare funds, etc.) and their total separation from the social body of the city, the Germans called upon the community to devise a plan to establish special professional associations, institutions, and funds that would ensure the rule of law within a self-governing community.[10] Adapting to the abnormal conditions through negotiations, ransom, and any other means possible seems to have provided temporary relief for the weak of the community and bypassed some dangers; it eased the suffering

7   That day, around 9,000 Jews from Salonika aged between eighteen and forty-five gathered on Platia Eleftherias. After registration, 3,500 of them were sent to forced labor. Around 12% died as a result of the terrible conditions. The German orders for the gathering on Platia Eleftherias were given by the general governor of Macedonia, Vasilios Simonidis. See Andrew Apostolou, "The Exception of Salonika: Bystanders and Collaborators in Northern Greece," *Holocaust and Genocide Studies*, 14:2 (2000), pp. 165–196.

8   Ioanna Tsatsou, *Diary during Occupation* (Greek) (Athens: Estia, 2000).

9   Molho and Nehama, *In Memoriam*, pp. 60–67.

10   Yakoel, *Memoirs*, pp. 117–119.

of the people, but at the same time this played a disastrous role, contributing to the game of delusion orchestrated by the Nazis. Of course, we know this only today, with the advantage of our *a posteriori* knowledge.

Fragiski Ambatzopoulou rightly notes that the diary entries made by Yomtov Yakoel (who, having acted as a legal councilor for the Jewish community in Salonika and having served on the central committee that assisted the Judenrat, tackling all the problems that the needy faced, especially the provision of food, subsequently fled to Athens) between the summer and fall of 1943 included not a scrap of "precise information." Although the Jews of Salonika had already been deported, and he himself was highly familiar with community affairs—just as he knew that this was no "ordinary pogrom"—at the time he was clearly unaware of the fate of the deportees and the nature of the concentration camps. In short, the Jews of Salonika had no idea what happened to the transports that arrived in Poland, and whatever "information" circulated was not considered accurate **knowledge** and was thus repressed.[11] Despite this, a few young Jews did not feel that they needed more information before taking their fate into their own hands. Let us take a closer look at some of them.

When the Germans invaded the country, Yakov Koumeris, born in 1920, had already completed his grammar school education at the French, Italian, and Higher Commercial Schools and was in the process of completing his military service. He fought in the Battle of Crete. There, together with another Jew serving as an army interpreter, he fell into the hands of the Germans and became a prisoner of war. Yakov managed to escape, arriving in Euboea on a fishing boat and from there traveling to Athens. He stayed with an uncle in the city for a few days, before returning to Salonika at the end of 1941. In July 1942, when the male Jews were ordered to gather at Platia Eleftherias, he reported. However, a few months later, in February 1943, he refused to obey the order to wear the yellow star and decided to flee. His father, who, according to Yakov, sympathized with the Socialist movement and the EAM, succeeded in putting him in contact with a Jew who worked for

11 Fragiski Abatzopoulou, "Introduction," in Yakoel, *Memoirs*, pp. 23–27.

the community and allegedly collaborated with the Germans but at the same time was involved in the resistance. When the latter was accused of being a collaborator after the war, Yakov defended him. In his testimony, Yakov recalled that he left Salonika on Saturday, March 20, along with Dick Benveniste, Johnny Mano,[12] Michel Broudo, and three others (including a pair of brothers) whose names he had forgotten. They did not wear the yellow star when they met somewhere in Vardaris, at the entrance to the city. There a contact person was waiting for them. They left the city and hid in a ditch. A second contact person then led them to Veria, and from there to a village in the Vermio Mountains. Yakov later recalled how the partisans held a parade in the village on Independence Day (March 25).

However, Yakov seems to have confused the date of his departure together with Dick Benveniste: in reality, they left a month earlier. On February 25, 1945, Dick noted in his diary: "It's been two years since I left, and I still have not heard from my sister." And, according to his ELAS discharge certificate, he served from February 20, 1943, meaning that he left Salonika around this time. Thus, Yakov Koumeris and Dick Benveniste fled Salonika before the deportations began yet after the establishment of the ghettos.

Saltiel Gatenio (probably the person mentioned in Dick Benveniste's diary as Sam Gatenio), who fled the ghetto together with Yakov and Dick, was one of the first to give testimony (in 1959) regarding his experiences.[13] He recalls that he joined the resistance together with his brother David and friends Isak Emmanuel, Angel Saltiel, Michel Broudo, Raul Frances, David Benveniste, Raul Mano, and a few other Jews from Salonika. Before leaving, he met a supposed friend to whom he entrusted his stationery store; the latter subsequently embezzled his entire fortune. Interned in the ghetto, Saltiel and his brother were forced to decide whether to

---

12 For Johnny Mano's story (in Greek) see Christos Kavvadas, "Joseph (Johnny) Mano: A Jewish Volunteer in the War of '40, Then Guerilla ELAS and, finally, a Soldier in the Greek Army during the Civil War," *Lefkas Island* (blog, Greek), July 14, 2014, http://www2.puresight.com/blcp.html?ps895prm=1633079701 (accessed July 20, 2014).

13 Novitch, *Le Passage des Barbares*, pp. 64–67.

Dick Benveniste's discharge certificate from the ELAS , February 19, 1945

"fight the Nazi plague" or remain with their mother and protect her. They ultimately decided to contact the resistance only when several good neighbors promised to look after their elderly mother. They formed a fifteen-member group of young men and left the ghetto one afternoon at 5:00 P.M., one after the other, arriving at the appointed meeting place, which was located some distance from the city, in a valley. At first they were guided by a farmer, later by a young boy. They only moved about in the dark and the whole march lasted four nights. On the way, others joined them, including some Jews, until the group numbered about thirty-five people. In a village, a farmer took them home and offered them food and shelter. As soon as they had rested, they set off again to reach their destination: Mount Paiko, on the summit of which a partisan camp was located. Among the 300 partisans in the camp, according to Gatenio, there were about seventy-five Jews. Yet they had a mere twenty or so old rifles, and thus retreated higher into the mountains when they learned that the Germans were approaching. The retreat on the mountain slopes was difficult and dangerous, surrounded by Germans on all sides. Saltiel himself was cut off from the group, along with his brother, forcing them to hide in the thorny undergrowth. They were rescued by a young shepherd, found the right path again, and, after a long march, reached the partisans. Military units were formed at Tsotyli on the Pindus mountain range.[14] Those who were not fit to fight were sent back to Athens to fulfill other roles for the resistance.

Moisis Bourlas was born in Cairo in 1918. His father was from Volos, his mother from Chios. His family returned to Greece in 1928, settling in Salonika a few years before the war. Moisis had worked since his schooldays and in 1935 became a member of the Communist youth organization. He served as a soldier on the Albanian front in the Greco-Italian War and came into contact with the resistance movement during the withdrawal. Later, he opposed the racist laws, refused to wear the yellow star, and tried to convince young Jews to enlist in the resistance. "We went to fifty-three houses," he says, "but we left Salonika for the mountains with only thirteen men." Among them were some who returned home as soon as they left the city because they could not bear to leave their relatives. The group Moisis refers to here is probably the same as that described by Yakov Koumeris and Saltiel Gatenio. Moisis

14 According to Kapetan Fotinos, there were mass uprisings on February 26 and 27 in Tsotili. See Dimitris (Fotinos) Kyriazopoulos, *Western Macedonia: Free Greece during the Occupation. Memoirs from the National Resistance, 1940–1944* (Greek) (Thessaloniki: Kodikas, 2004), p. 311. Dora Raban Eliahu, who joined the partisans in Kastoria after leaving Salonika to work in Florina, also mentions seventy Jews who found safety together with her among the partisans, adding that in Tsotili they were split up and sent to different areas of Free Greece YVA, O.3/3564261.

remembered that Dick Benveniste was the last to join this group of escapees. Their march, he continues, lasted three days and nights. They arrived at a destination near the city of Giannitsa. Ten of them were taken to Mount Paiko and the Vermio Mountains. Moisis and Dick spent their initial days in the mountains together, became friends, and parted when Dick was transferred. The entire Bourlas family joined the partisans: Moisis' father, his younger brother, and even his two sisters served as fighters,[15] while his mother remained in a village under the protection of the partisans.

Solomon (Tsitso) Cohen fought alongside another two of his brothers in the mountains. His oldest brother, a doctor who had studied in Germany, decided to remain with his parents. He believed that his profession would enable him to help others. He never returned from Auschwitz. Four other brothers in hiding were saved thanks to the help of kindhearted Christian citizens. Tsitso, who, like his brothers, had attended the Lycée Français, returned from the Albanian front to Salonika. He worked as a sales representative and scraped together life's necessities on the black market during the occupation. Neither he nor his brothers reported to Platia Eleftherias in July 1942. "We were courageous enough not to go," he recalled. Yet he placed the yellow star on his clothing. Seeking to avoid possible arrest by the Germans, he generally slept in the homes of friends and not at the apartment on Miaouli Street in the ghetto. He himself was not politically active at the time, although his family had a close friendship with Alexandros Kallidopoulos (the son of General Kallidopoulos), who was a member of the EAM. The young Kallidopoulos facilitated the contact with the resistance. The two brothers remained in hiding for three weeks. They were then instructed to go to meeting point, from which a comrade would lead them and a group of twenty or thirty young men by night to Mount Paiko, and from there to the Vermio Mountains.

Simantov Razon found his way to the partisans alone and was perhaps one of the first Jews recruited by the ELAS. He too had fought on the Albanian front. Unlike his father and brothers,

15 Yolanda Bourlas testimony, YVA, O.3/3555336.

he preferred not to report to Platia Eleftherias. A shoemaker by profession, as were all the men in his family, he was a Communist, like Moisis Bourlas. When the people of Salonika suffered from extreme hunger, he went to nearby villages to obtain flour on the black market. There he made acquaintances and, very early on, in 1942, he came into contact with the partisans and procured a forged ID card in the name of Simon Diamantopoulos. In his unit, he recalled later, there were about fifteen Jews. After joining the partisans, he returned to the city in 1943 and went to his family home to try to convince his relatives to follow him and join the partisans. One of his brothers threw a glass in his face: "Yes, you again with your Communist ideas..." His father was also not convinced, and his other brother obeyed his father. Razon's family perished in the Nazi extermination camps in Poland.

Many sought to flee Salonika, both as individuals and as groups. When the war broke out, Markos Botton happened to be in the area of Rodolivos, near Serres. Born in 1921, he had attended Greek elementary school and French Catholic School, and studied at the Faculty of Agronomy at the University of Salonika. When the economic crisis of 1930 ruined his father's business, the Jewish charitable organization Bnei Brit took over the financing of his studies. Following the confiscation of farmers' animals by the Greek army during the Greco-Italian war, he was made responsible for allocating livestock and work to the peasants.[16] At the time of the German invasion, in addition to his studies, Markos was working in the port as a warehouse keeper. He did not report to Platia Eleftherias, deciding instead to observe this spectacle of violence and humiliation from a safe distance. Years later he recalled: "Whatever the Germans say, I will not go. I said to my mother, 'I will not go to Poland.'"[17]

---

16 Other students of agronomy were also sent to help in the villages during the Greco-Italian war. At the outbreak of the war, the agricultural directorate of Salonika dispatched Stratis Anastasiadis, then in the third year of his studies, and some other students to help with sowing and field cultivation in central Macedonian villages. See Anastasiadis, *From Resistance*, pp. 25–26.

17 The story of Markos' brother is extremely interesting: a student in Athens, he was denounced and held in Haidari. Deported in September 1944, he succeeded

One of his contacts at the university told him about the EAM. "We were about twenty young Jews looking for a way to go to the mountains." While waiting to make contact with the partisans, Markos went in and out of the ghetto, donning and removing the yellow star accordingly. As time passed, a few of the young men changed their minds and decided to stay with their families. Finally, a middleman took Markos and two comrades to an apartment outside the ghetto, where they spent the night. That same night, the Germans rounded up Jews for forced labor. The next day, the fugitives made their way to the western exit of the city, where they met up with other Jews. The first liaison man handed them over to a second, and thus they crossed the River Axios, arriving at Mount Paiko. For two weeks they marched day and night, their armaments consisting of a few old rifles. They reached the Vermio Mountains where they met 200 armed partisans, with whom they spent two weeks. There was much excitement, they ate well and sang.

In May 1941, OKNE, the federation of Communist youth organizations, formed the first resistance cell at the University of Salonika, with students from all four faculties boosting its numbers by the end of the year.[18] Like Markos Botton, Maurice Florentin was a third-year student at the Faculty of Agronomy when he decided to go to the mountains. Together with his brother, he had appeared for registration on Platia Eleftherias, but shortly before the establishment of the ghettos, his brother fled to Mandatory Palestine. Thanks to a Christian friend who provided him with a job near the Faculty of Agronomy, Maurice was released from forced labor. On March 20 or 21, 1943, three weeks after being interned in the ghetto in the Faliro/Agia Triada area, Maurice managed to escape. His political views tended toward the Left, but he was not a member of any party.

in escaping from the train taking him to Poland. He found himself on the Slovakian border and, when he was arrested, passed himself off as an Italian. He was taken to the border and liberated by Soviet soldiers. Returning to Salonika, he found out that his entire family—with the exception of one brother who had joined the partisans—had been killed in the camps (Henri Botton, HVT, 3017).

18 Kaftantzis, *The University of Salonika*, p. 27.

By now, the EAM exercised considerable influence in Salonika, especially among the students. When Maurice learned about the partisans and their struggle, he wanted to follow their example. "Why don't you scram now that the Germans are after you?" one of his friends asked him. He thought about it briefly and made a decision. His neighbor, Johnny Beza, agreed to join him. So, one day, wearing their work clothes, they took off the yellow star and left the ghetto, without the guards noticing. A liaison led them out of the city. They spent two nights in a house waiting for other escapees, but the latter never arrived, perhaps having changed their minds at the last moment. On the third day, they left for Giannitsa. Near the bridge over the Axios River, a stranger, realizing that they were Jewish, saved their lives by preventing them from entering a coffee house that was full of Germans. Their first stop was Mount Paiko. From there they proceeded to Mount Kaimaktsalan, going from village to village, crossing Macedonia, and avoiding Germans at all costs because they had no military training. On the way, they met, as Maurice recalled, about ten Jews from Salonika.

David Aharon was born in 1914, the son of a porter who worked in the port of Salonika. He had fought on the Albanian front and suffered the deprivations of the occupation, and he later recalled how he was forced to sell everything he possessed for a bit of food. He too was called up for forced labor. At this point he decided to look for a middleman who would help him and a few other comrades to join the partisans. His first attempt failed. Indeed, as soon as the man who presented himself as a mediator received the money, he betrayed David to the Germans. At the last moment, David managed to escape from the clutches of the Germans.

In the meantime, Jews were only allowed to live in certain parts of the city, in ghettos, from which they were gradually transported to the Baron Hirsch district and from there to the camps. David put his fate in the hands of a student from Elassona, who one day gave him a piece of bread accompanied by information about the EAM. This friend, together with a comrade, liquidated the traitor who had betrayed David. From that moment, David waited for a signal. One evening there was a knock at his door. After half an hour, he was to open the door and wait for a man in a blue coat. Between

6:30 and 7:00 P.M., the man appeared. David followed him. About fifteen more men were also following this man, maintaining a distance of 20 meters between them. Near the city exit, they had to pass several Greek police officers. One of them whispered to them, "Be well. Until freedom comes!" After a three-hour walk, they left the city borders, never losing sight of the man in the blue overcoat. At one point this man changed places with another, who suddenly emerged from behind a tree. Later, a twelve-year-old boy became their guide, leading them on a narrow path on the edge of a precipice. David's shoes were full of holes by this time, and one of his companions gave him some pants that he used to wrap his feet. They made their way laboriously into Free Greece, where the partisans ruled and the Germans barely dared set foot. David recalled that weapons were handed out to them in the village of Vlasti, which was "famous for its cheese production."

Jacques Serror was born in 1917 in Salonika. During the Greco-Italian war, he served as a paramedic in Salonika and with the Red Cross. He recalled reading an article in French, "Les trains de la mort marchent encore" (The death trains are still rolling), and this motivated him to flee. He made contact with the ELAS, which, he noted, was not very difficult. He paid a truck driver who transported food for the Red Cross to take him and his sister to the mountains.

Yakov, Dick, Sam, Moisis, Tsitso, Markos, Maurice, David, Jacques, and many others made contact with the resistance either after the Jews were forced into ghettos or shortly before or immediately after the deportations began. The timing was inevitable: at this moment the resistance became organized and manifested itself. The fear of betrayal or arrest and family ties always posed obstacles. However, the young were willing to take these risks. Indeed, one partisan, Leon Matalon, returned to Salonika in April 1943 from the mountains to marry his fiancée, Fanny Florentin, subsequently taking her to the mountains with him.[19] All these young people left in smallish groups organized

19 See Yael Feldman and Steven Bowman, "Love and War on Mount Olympus: Jewish Participation in the Greek Resistance," *Thetis*, 4 (1997), pp. 253–257.

by EAM liaisons. Some of them had gained experience fighting on the Albanian front, others were carrying weapons for the first time in their lives. They walked to Mount Paiko and the Vermio Mountains. There they parted ways, relocating in accordance with operational planning and the logistical requirements of the war.

Some of these young Jews from Salonika, such as David Broudo, the brothers David (Dario) and Yitzhak Amir, and Yitzhak Mosse, escaped from forced labor camps and encountered the partisans in areas far from Salonika. Escape, which was risky enough for them, could have potentially led to fatal consequences for their families at home.

The winter of 1941–1942, which was characterized by extreme cold, hunger, and epidemics, hit the Jewish community particularly hard, above all its poorer members (the overwhelming majority).[20] Saby Saltiel, the first chairman of the community appointed by the Germans, sought to ameliorate the situation by setting up a large central committee that was tasked with alleviating the plight of the people: it established soup kitchens and other social-welfare services, and it informally took over administration of the community. Months of relative calm ensued, until a notice appeared in the *Apogevmatini* newspaper ordering all adult Jews between the ages of eighteen and forty-five to gather on Platia Eleftherias on Saturday, July 11, 1942, to register for forced labor in areas of military significance, under the auspices of the Müller and Todt organizations. The scenes that unfolded on that Saturday and the following day—scenes of martyrdom, torment, and humiliation under the burning sun and the gaze of passersby—are well documented in stories and gruesome photographs.

"Notably," said Yomtov Yakoel, "during this collective registration and forced enlistment of 8,000 to 9,000 Israelite

---

20 Kavala, *Salonika during the Occupation*. On the hunger crisis, see Violetta Hionidou, *Famine and Death in Occupied Greece, 1941–1944* (Cambridge: Cambridge University Press, 2006); Maria Kavala, "Hunger and Survival in Occupied Greece," in Vasilis Panagiotopoulos, ed., *History of Modern Hellenism 1770–2000, Greece at War 1940–1949*. vol. 8 (Greek) (Athens: Ellinika Grammata, 2004), pp. 49–62.

Greek citizens for labor, there was not a single reaction—neither from Greek society nor from the local or state authorities."[21] Two thousand workers were sent to construction sites in various regions, to Katerini, Litochoro, and Leptokaria, to the quarries of Sedes, Nares, Mount Olympus, and Halkidiki. From the very outset, the central committee, which included Yakoel, assumed responsibility for the care of the workers; in addition, a corresponding protocol was also signed according to which the community would pay the ransom to liberate the workers—this was viewed "in Israelite circles as a very successful action."[22] Given the exhausting and humiliating nature of the forced labor, the weakest soon collapsed, and death took a toll in the workplaces, where every family had a loved one.

The community worked intensively: first to free the heads of families with many children and students, then introducing a tax on wealthy members to raise ransom monies to free its members from forced labor. The community also ensured the provision of medicines and food, in addition to caring for the families of the laborers. Community doctors visited the workplaces. As the mortality rate rose in October, the Judenrat began negotiations with the Wehrmacht war administration councilor for the Aegean-Salonika region, Max Merten, regarding the possibility of buying themselves out of forced labor obligations via ransom monies. After lengthy efforts, an agreement was reached and the Jews were released from forced labor for a ransom of 2 billion drachmas, payable by December 15, 1942.

The news of the agreement spread quickly, and the Jews breathed a collective sigh of relief. Meanwhile, the Germans downgraded the chairman of the Judenrat to a simple employee and transferred the community leadership to Rabbi Koretz.[23] The

21 Yakoel, *Memoirs*, p. 59.
22 Ibid., p. 66.
23 Molho and Nehama, *In Memoriam*, pp. 69–72. Solomon Uziel, who took part in negotiations as a member of the central committee, spoke out after the war and confirmed the success of the mission: "We managed to halt the German plague with the help of 2.5 billion drachma." He made it clear that it was not wise to hand this huge sum over to the untrustworthy chairman, Saby Saltiel,

sum demanded was colossal, but Merten promised that no further action would be taken against the Jews. The Central Committee and the Judenrat under Koretz's leadership worked hard to draft a wealth-based taxation plan for members of the community in Salonika, as well as those based in Athens, to raise the ransom money. The first installment was paid, and 3,000 workers returned from different parts of the country.

In 1959 Miriam Novitch recorded the testimony of Peppo Cohen, a professor of mathematics.[24] He remembered the events that occurred on Platia Eleftherias, the registration, and the assembly of the first 2,000 workers: "I decided to escape forced labor and flee. I asked my family and friends to do the same. I sought to make contact with the resistance. However, in 1942, resistance in our area was still in its infancy. The mountains and forests were, alas, far away." Cohen fled to Athens with the help of a railroad worker, where he survived the occupation using false papers.

Apart from all those who experienced the tragedy of forced labor firsthand,[25] an outside observer also saw the images of horror. The poet Giorgos Vafopoulos, a native of Salonika, who worked as an employee at the public library during the years of the occupation, described in his memoirs a train journey to Athens in the summer of 1943:

> A few miles from Lamia the train stopped again, in a desolate spot where my soul was tested by terrible scenes out of Dante's hell…Down below in the small ravine, in front of the place where the train stopped…there were several barracks, which a few months ago might have

whereupon the chief rabbi was asked to take on this role, which he did. See Steven Bowman, ed., *The Holocaust in Salonika: Eyewitness Accounts* (New York: Bloch Publishing Company, 2002), p. 243; see also Isaac Aruch's testimony in Novitch, *Le Passage des Barbares*, pp. 18–24.

24 Novitch, *Le Passage des Barbares*, pp. 13–15.

25 The nineteenth and last transport left Salonika for Auschwitz-Birkenau on the night of August 9, arriving on August 18. The 1,800 Jews on the train had survived until then by working in forced labor. Of these, 1,529 were taken directly to the gas chambers. See Danuta Czech, *Auschwitz Chronicle: 1939–1945* (New York: Henry Holt and Company, 1990), p. 465.

housed some "labor battalion" of distressed Jews. There were now a few ragged figures who, it seemed, had at some point been human. Emaciated bodies shrouded in tatters, barely able to move they were so weak. The dehumanized faces resembled the anguish of wounded animals...These living dead were devoid of everything human, the apathy of the animal had become their mask, their natural "decorum," which knows instinctively how to resist, had died...I crouched in a corner of the carriage, eyes closed, shamed and pained. I felt that I, too, was complicit in this great crime because I did not have the strength to speak out against this murder of humanity, because I did not have the courage to follow these fellow human beings into the tomb of shame.[26]

Some, nonetheless, managed to escape this hell.

One example was David Broudo. David was born into a large family in 1924. Like many Jews of Salonika, he learned French at school, while at home he spoke Judeo-Spanish and Greek. When he told his story, he could not explain why, but he did not obey the order to report to Platia Eleftherias. For a short while he stayed in the ghetto—he could have left, he said, but what would have happened to his parents?—until he was sent to forced labor in Karya, near Lamia. From late April to early June, he endured extremely harsh conditions. When, one day, he was dispatched to fetch supplies, he seized the opportunity to flee, together with another Jew, a young medical student named Robert Mitrani,[27] even taking the Germans' money with them. From Lamia the two ran 10 kilometers, reaching the village of Agoriani in Parnassos, where they encountered a gathering of partisans: "I was not a Communist. I said that I wanted to fight the Germans." They spent two weeks learning how to use weapons. Shortly thereafter he happened to meet his brother, who had fled to the partisans before him.

26 Giorgos Th. Vafopoulos, *Pages of an Autobiography: Resurrection*, vol.2 (Greek) (Thessaloniki: Paratiritis, 1971), pp. 180–182.
27 Also known as Kapetan Makavaios, see Bowman, *Jewish Resistance*, pp. 54–60.

Brothers Yitzhak and Dario Amir were twenty-seven and seventeen, respectively, when the anti-Jewish measures were introduced. They came from a well-to-do family that had been hit hard by the economic crisis of the early 1930s. Yitzhak was a self-taught musician and played trumpet, while David was enrolled at the agricultural school. Yitzhak came home one day with a backpack on his shoulders and announced that he had decided to join the partisans. His father burst into tears. The departure was postponed, and when the Germans sent the brothers (and their third brother) for forced labor shortly thereafter, the parents had already been taken to the Baron Hirsch transit ghetto, from which they were subsequently deported to Poland. For forty days, the Amir brothers endured the hard labor. Then the eldest, Yitzhak, announced his escape plan. He did not include the third brother, whom he considered too frail to endure the hardships of the escape. Yitzhak and David agreed and put their plan into action. They managed to get through the fence, hid for one night, and then walked until they reached a village where they encountered partisans. "Do you want to stay with us, or should we send you to Athens?" the partisans asked them. The two brothers put on uniforms of the ELAS and followed a leader northward, through a series of villages. David watched over the weapons and food while Yitzhak continued to play the trumpet and organized a partisan band...!

Moise Eskaloni was born in 1920, the child of a working-class family. He had been working in factories since the age of sixteen, and one of his uncles, he recalled, was among the founders of the Communist Party. When the war broke out, Moise was in military training in Tripoli. He was released provisionally and returned to Salonika. He, too, preferred to observe the gathering on Platia Eleftherias from a distance. Already a member of the Communist youth organization, he initially refused to follow the order for conscription into forced labor, but he changed his mind when he learned that the Germans possessed lists of names. He was subsequently sent to do heavy road construction work in Halkidiki. Together with another prisoner, he drafted an escape plan, in the course of which a German guard was killed. Using safe trails, which black marketeers showed them, the two returned to Salonika. There, Moise was forced to go underground and decided to "disappear," taking his mother, sister, and brother-in-law with him. At first, they hid in a farmhouse near Salonika, not far from the Oraiokastro sanitorium. A little later, Moise undertook secret missions for the resistance using false papers. When this became too dangerous, he left his family and joined a partisan unit. He spent four months training to carry out sabotage missions.

Yitzhak Moshe (Kapetan [Captain] Kitsos)[28] was born in 1919 in the poor Jewish Baron Hirsch quarter; his family was involved in the Socialist movement. He attended the French and German schools and in the years of the Metaxas dictatorship (Ioannis Metaxas, prime minister of Greece 1936–1941) was a member of an anti-Fascist organization that had close ties to the Communist Party. In March 1940, he was called up to the army; at the beginning of the war, he found himself billeted on the Albanian border. After the surrender, Yitzhak and many other soldiers made their way home on foot. Arriving in Salonika, he found his house occupied by the Germans. He sought refuge, joined the Communist Party, and soon became involved in resistance actions. In the summer of 1942, he was sent to Tembi for forced labor. However, he managed to escape and join the partisans in Vermio, near Naoussa.

* * *

After the war, an article published in *Israilitikon Vima* (Jewish Tribune),[29] entitled "Memories of the Persecution: The Evacuation of the Inhabitants of Regie," described the "evacuation" of the population of Regie Vardar to the Baron Hirsch ghetto:

> This neighborhood, which had been the happiest, most heroic, and liveliest of Salonika's neighborhoods, lay in

28 Ibid., pp. 17–30.
29 S. Levi, "Memories from the Persecution: The Deportation of Regie Inhabitants," (Greek), translated from the Ladino by G. Mavros, *Israilitikon Vima*, May 7, 1947.

deep silence. No sound came from the speakers at the two coffee shops located at the beginning of the main street. Only the terrible footsteps of the militiamen rang out, as sinister as the calls of crows. Now and then the barking of a hungry dog…Outside, a rumor was circulating that they'd be taken away at dawn. The poor inhabitants were nervous. A nightmare had come upon them. The militia endeavored to dispel their concerns, but the people's soul intimated the catastrophe. Each and every one of them went to prepare a backpack and a bundle of clothes for their fateful journey. Some young couples organized their escape to "the sacred mountains of Greece," as the rabbi of Volos said. Others, less resolute, who didn't know the way, who had no connections, or no money, contented themselves with exchanging their ghetto for a night and going to the ghetto of Sygrou to delay their demise a while longer (rumors were spreading everywhere that the inhabitants of the neighborhood were going to be taken away because they were… Communists). Around four o'clock—it was a beautiful spring morning, when nature stood in stark contrast to the fate of our relatives—the nocturnal rumors and fears began to become reality.

The "way," "connections," "money,"—there were many factors to be taken into consideration when young Jews, among them many women, decided to leave their families and city and go to the mountains. Some risked their lives (and those of their families) and escaped forced labor. It seems that for most the decisive moment came in early 1943, when the anti-Jewish measures intensified and the noose around their necks grew even tighter. Many had acquired experience on the Albanian front. They came from different social and economic backgrounds, and not all of them had any connection with the leftist movements, although such relationships made it easier to make connections. In any case, there was a crucial moment for each one, as well as certain dilemmas that they later addressed in their accounts: Should they report to

Platia Eleftherias or not? Should they wear the yellow star? Should they stay in the ghetto? Should they report for or avoid forced labor? Should they leave their families behind? Should they trust someone who offered to lead them out of town in exchange for a sum of money? Should they take the route of violence or not? Their answers were not all the same, nor did they necessarily lead to the same next steps.

During the first weeks and months of 1943, the resistance networks organized themselves and the ELAS army strengthened its presence. Those who had relations with the movement in the prewar period had the necessary contacts, but in principle anyone could reach it. Social background seems to have played no greater role than family obligations. Yet to save an entire family—the old, women, and children—one needed money; and for a future partisan to escape, boldness and the gifts of youth were required: determination; the strength to endure life in the mountains; readiness and the will to take up arms. As has often been stated, family ties were frequently an obstacle that could not be overcome. The remorse felt by those who left their families behind often proved difficult to bear. In the end, it was all a matter of character: to accept the reality or to rebel, to be timid or reckless, independent or responsible for others?... These are questions that my depiction cannot take into account at this point.

CHAPTER 3

In the Mountains: From Mountain Range to Mountain Range, from Battle to Battle

B efore the capitulation of the Italians in September 1943, the rules of the partisan struggle were dictated by the light armaments they possessed. In western Macedonia, some mountain ranges are more than 2,000 meters high, with an average altitude of around 500 meters, and in the wooded mountain ranges the partisans were able to find refuge almost everywhere. They used the tactics of guerrilla combat, surprising the opposing forces by attacking their positions, supply lines, and communication routes, followed by withdrawal to inaccessible heights. The liberation of the mountain regions from opposing positions was designed to expand the "Free Zones." As soon as the Germans resorted to purge operations, the partisans withdrew into inaccessible areas, securing their supplies, and attempting to defeat the rearguard of the enemy. When the Pinerolo Division surrendered following the Italian capitulation, the partisans took possession of heavy weapons. This enabled them to carry out frontal attacks and to expand their troop movements.

In March and April 1943, the growth of the rural partisan groups was marked by clashes between units of the ELAS and the YVE/PAO[1] in Imathia, Pella, Pieria, and western Macedonia; in

---

1 The YVE (Defenders of Northern Greece) was formed by Greek officers in the summer of 1941 to fight against the traditional "danger from the north." Its main activity was the surveillance of Bulgarian propaganda. Later, its only role

the summer, the conflict worsened. By the summer of 1943, the partisans constituted a considerable force: the ELAS conducted hundreds of attacks and destroyed dozens of kilometers of railway, while at the same time battling armed groups that colluded with the Wehrmacht. In the areas of western and central Macedonia, the Germans used collaborators against the partisans. They also recruited Colonel Georgios Poulos' armed forces, which were active around Ptolemaida and Kozani, along with the Comitadjis (slavophone gunmen who followed the commands of Bulgarian propaganda) and the PAO militants in the Kilkis region. In August 1943, the PAO attacked the ELAS in the Vermio Mountains and the city of Katerini. In the area of northern Kilkis, in the districts of Serres and Halkidiki, and in the triangle formed by Kozani, Grevena, and Kastoria, Turkish-speaking Pontian Greeks and Germans attacked the EAM.[2]

The partisans emerged victorious from these struggles, and by the summer of 1943, the ELAS dominated large parts of the country. Free Greece stretched from the Albanian-Greek border to the area surrounding Athens. It included the Pindus Mountains, reaching as far as Giona, Parnassos, Elikona, and Parnitha in central Greece, and encompassing the areas of Olympus, Kissavos, Pilion, and Chasia in Thessaly and the mountains of Epirus, Pieria, and Vermio in central Macedonia, the areas of eastern Macedonia and

was anti-Communist. It was dissolved in March 1943 and replaced by the PAO (Panhellenic Liberation Organization), whose goal was "the liberation of the fatherland and the creation of a greater Greece according to the historic law of the nation." It provided the Greeks and Allies with emergency aid from the Middle East and operated radio stations for the transmission of information. After initially growing closer to the EAM, the groups paths' diverged in the summer of 1942. The EAM accused the YVE/PAO of "Fascism and cooperation with the occupiers," while the latter accused the EAM of "attempting to seize power to establish a dictatorship of the proletariat." From 1943 onward, the conflict worsened. See Papapolyviou, "Resistance intra muros."

2   Nikos Marantzidis highlights that Turkish Pontic Greeks felt their identity was threatened by the new realities created by the EAM. They joined Nazi collaborators fighting against the ELAS. See Nikos Marantzidis, *Yaassin Millet/ Long Live the Nation: Refugees, Occupation and Civil War, Ethnic Identity and Political Behavior among the Turkish-Speaking Orthodox Greek of Western Pontos* (Greek) (Heraklion: University of Crete Press, 2001), pp. 109–194.

Thrace, Crete, Euboea, and Samos. By the end of 1943/early 1944, the Germans, in collaboration with paramilitary units, such as the Tagmata Asfaleias (Security Battalions), Organization X (from the Greek letter Chi, members of which were known as Chites), and some armed gangs, unleashed violent attacks in the countryside and in urban centers, and carried out concerted purges in areas controlled by the ELAS. Nevertheless, in January 1944, the ELAS succeeded in crushing the PAO, and in the summer of the same year it quashed the plans of the Germans to appropriate all agricultural production.

* * *

The testimonies of the Jews of Salonika who fought in the western and central Macedonian regions describe these clashes with the German armed collaborators during the spring and summer of 1943.

Yitzhak Moshe escaped forced labor in the summer of 1942. He subsequently joined the partisans, but he fought in only a few operations prior to March of the following year. On March 30, 1943, he recalled, they were ordered to go to a grain store and distribute wheat to the peasants. The next day, they attacked the Germans, capturing four of them, together with a large number of weapons. The Germans started the counterattack two days later. At the time, Yitzhak recalled, numerous young Jews from Salonika joined the partisans, around 500 by the end of April/beginning of May. In May, they retreated from the Naoussa area via Grevena to the Vermio Mountains. Following clashes with the Germans in the summer and in September 1943, the partisans were forced to retreat further to Kastoria, Kozani, into the area of the River Aliakmonas and from Neapolis and Grevena. Yitzhak, a.k.a. Kapetan Kitsos, led the fight against the collaborators in the Kastoria area and even tried to kill the German commander of Aridea. He took part in the battles of Kostochori (September 1943), Kastania (near Kozani), and Kerassea, which cost the Germans heavy casualties. He then turned to Veria. In April 1944, significant clashes took place with the collaborators in Edessa. The fighting continued in the summer to ensure control over the harvest. In July 1944, the partisans fighting under Kapetan Kitsos retreated to Grevena; their commander, Papaflessas, was killed in battle. In Pelargos, Yitzhak was involved in battles against Turkish-speaking collaborators.

Spring 1944 was a difficult time.[3] On May 1, the report of the German South-East military command included the following statement: "Northern Greece, especially the mountain ranges of Vermio and Paiko, is subject to repeated attacks by the partisans against the strategic positions of the Security Battalions and our supply centers." And on May 25: "In northern Greece, most of the partisan forces have retreated westward after escaping our purges. The operations took place in the mountain ranges of Vermio, Paiko, and Kaimaktsalan."[4] Of course, these operations also included massive reprisals against the civilian population.

The German retreat in October 1944 was the scene of the last heavy fighting. In the course of one of these battles—led by Kapetan Kitsos—Moisis Bourlas' younger brother lost his life. Moisis also mentions ambushes and sabotage along the roads to Salonika, Giannitsa, Veria, and Skydra, actions that forced the Germans to concentrate forces and carry out attacks on Mount Paiko. In the following major clash, about 700 partisans moved from place to place to deceive the enemy, giving the latter the impression that it was dealing with a large number of fighters. Afterwards, the partisans retreated to Mount Kaimaktsalan and from there to the Vermio Mountains, where they encountered larger, well-organized, and armed (but also many unarmed) formations, including Jews. Since many had no weapons, they withdrew from the Vermio Mountains back to the Ptolemaida plain, although without encountering any Germans, whose ring around them was tightening.[5] Moisis remained in place with a rearguard at the

3 Kapetan Fotinos mentions ten-day long operations in the Vermio Mountains in April 1944. See Kyriazopoulos, *Western Macedonia*, pp. 530–535.

4 *Nazis and the National Resistance in Greece: Seven Secret Reports of the General Military Staff*, with an introduction by Michalis Lyberatos (Greek) (Athens: Dromon, 2012), pp. 40–41.

5 The memoirs of Kapetan Fotinos offer detailed reports of military events: "The Germans mustered strong forces from Salonika and the other garrisons in Macedonia, gathered together 10,000 men, air force, artillery, motorized units,

foot of Mount Siniatsiko, where the Germans found them. He recounted that he shot at the enemy in an "intoxicated spirit of revenge" until, wounded in the hand, he was forced to retreat. The ensuing battles, reported Moisis, took place on the Kilkis plain. They sought to force the Security Battalions and the PAO men to leave the Kroussia Mountains. In local villages, which had suffered under the Security Battalions' reign of terror, the partisans received a warm welcome and good care. Other villages, as he reported, were administered by "reactionaries" and were therefore often the target of partisan attacks, as the latter sought to free the plain of Giannitsa from reactionary clutches. The Security Battalions were driven toward Kilkis. Reinforced by ELAS reserve troops, the partisans crossed the plain and conquered Kilkis, where they not only took prisoners of war but also appropriated a stash of weapons and farm animals. The ELAS then prepared for a frontal attack on the retreating Germans.

Yakov Koumeris received his baptism of fire in the spring of 1943 in the town of Naoussa, where the partisans had previously equipped themselves with blankets and khakis from the Lanaras factory. The partisans defeated the Germans and retreated to the mountains as the enemy reinforcements arrived, taking with them a prisoner of war. The latter was ready to desert, but the Germans threatened retaliation if he did not return. Despite his concern for the fate of his family, this prisoner signed a letter saying that he had decided to remain with the partisans of his own free will. Indeed, he fought by their side until the end of the war. As clashes with the Germans continued, the partisans had to retreat ever higher into the mountains. Acute appendicitis forced Yakov to take the train from a station near Larissa to Athens. There he received false papers and continued his activities for the resistance under the name Konstantinos Koumeridis. However, realizing that he was

and on April 25 they began operations in Vermio, which lasted for about ten days...With the full strength of their troops, the Germans hunted down our forces, which had withdrawn to Kaimaktsalan, to the plain of Giannitsa and [Mount] Paiko. The forces of our platoon undertook a new maneuver over Vermio/Siniatsikos in the face of the new situation, passed through the Voio, and reached the liberated areas." Kyriazopoulos, *Western Macedonia*, pp. 530ff.

under surveillance, the resistance sent him back to the mountains. An Austrian officer, whom he had met in Salonika through black-market connections, agreed to help. He handed Yakov over to a platoon commander, who in turn hid him in the baggage car. In Salonika he again had severe problems with his appendix and underwent surgery in a private clinic. For a few days he recovered in the house of a Jewish doctor who was married to a Catholic (most probably Isaac Matarasso, although Yakov does not mention his name in his testimony), before returning to the mountains. He was involved in many subsequent battles.

The Sixteenth Regiment of the ELAS (three battalions under Captains Mavros, Papaflessas, and Kolokotronis), based in the Vermio Mountains, drove the Germans out of the area of Grevena. This was Free Greece, where the Germans could not set foot. Here Yakov met Dick Benveniste, Johnny Mano, and Michalis (Michel) Broudo. The latter was in charge of the money dropped by British aircraft, which was used to buy groceries in the villages. The Jews, Koumeris recalled, were warmly received by the partisans. Some, like his brother, were unfit to fight and stayed to work in Naoussa. They hid in villages under the protection of the partisans. Partisans not actively engaged in fighting "spent the day doing nonsense or mindlessly running around." They relocated from one place to the next and walked for up to twenty hours at a time, singing partisan songs and listening to the news on the radio.

In the Vermio area, Saltiel Gatenio was initially responsible for the weapons that the British dropped on an almost weekly basis. Six weeks later, he was transferred to a sabotage and combat squad. They blew up bridges and railroad tracks. In this context, two Jewish comrades are often mentioned: Dick Benveniste and Jacques Katan, who were characterized by their great courage.

When he arrived at Mount Paiko, Tsitso Cohen still had no weapons. Having served as a captain in the Greco-Italian war, he was given a rifle, and he began to use it immediately. He remembered the respect he earned for being so fearless; he was admired by everyone. Before daybreak, the partisans would set off for a place which they knew the Germans would be passing. The most memorable battle took place in Leptokaria in July 1943 and cost the Germans numerous lives. A battalion set out to climb the mountain. "The wisdom of Kapetan Mavros was that he commanded the partisans to retreat." The Germans turned around and went back to Pineios to bathe. The partisans surprised them with an attack, crushed them, and took prisoners of war. Mavros said, "Take the officer and do whatever you want with him." They did nothing to him. "The German officer began to cry, said that he knew Jews, and so on." He was interrogated. "All day we walked from one mountain to the next," related Tsitso, in the Naoussa area, in Chasia, Konitsa, Epirus, Veria. They slept in stables, in farmhouses, or outdoors. They spent two winters in the mountains, able to keep warm only if the British dropped clothes for them.

His brother served in another unit, with the young resistance fighters of the EPON (United Panhellenic Organization of Youth). In Grevena he carried out acts of sabotage against German trucks. Tsitso later said that Aris Velouchiotis liked him and called him "*Yehudi*" (Jew). Everyone knew they were Jews and behaved very well toward them. When Tsitso learned that his brother, Maurice, was sick somewhere in Trikala, Kapetan Petros, "who looked sinister but had a heart of gold," took care of the matter and brought him a letter from his brother. "The Greeks thought we Jews were cowards. In the mountains, we showed them what was what," Tsitso said, recalling Jacko Cohen, who had been wounded in a battle and was back on the battlefield a week later. He also mentioned a young officer who was killed in action, Albertiko Karasso (the son of a well-known Communist, his father was one of the first to be shot by the Germans). He remembered two or three others who were killed, as well as Solomon Allalouf, who served as an interpreter, and the nurse Fanny Florentin.

David Broudo, as we saw above, was in the area of Parnassos to conduct sabotage operations further south. Moise Eskaloni began his work in the area around Salonika, on Mount Hortiatis, between Panorama and Asvestochori. From there he moved together with 170 comrades to Livadi in the Halkidiki region, in the leading unit of the battalion. For four months he trained in sabotage and later participated in numerous operations. "I wanted to dispel the reputation we had at that time, that we were cowards," he said, relating how he struck down a captured German major who spoke Greek and was responsible for tracking down the remaining Jews. The latter taunted him, saying "none of them will ever return." When he arrived in Salonika to carry out a mission, he found the city empty, without Jews, but avoided anyone who might recognize him. The farther the Germans withdrew, the more the partisans advanced toward Salonika, until they received instructions from the Middle East to disband the battalion and form shock troops.

Tsitso explained that everyone knew about his Jewish identity. His words, as well as those of Moise Eskaloni and other Jewish partisans, testify to their pride. Not only because they had survived—often heroically—but because they preserved their identity, which they were in danger of losing.[6]

In the summer of 1943, Markos Botton heard gunfire in the Vermio area for the first time: it was the German purges. On a steep path, Markos and his mules slipped, separating him and two comrades from their unit. They climbed a slope and waited for nightfall to reach the foot of the opposite mountain, where they spent the night in a house in the village of Thymaria, from there making their way to Veria. Later, Markos was sent as group commander to the area of Halkidiki, leading a unit of over fifteen members. In the summer of 1943, he became a member of the Communist Party. "How did you become a member?" he was asked in an interview. His answer: "Quite unexpectedly. Just before we went to the Halkidiki." In Halkidiki he took part in battles against Georgios Poulos' men, the latter "dressed as Germans," and there, he went on, he met no other Jews.

Simantov Razon took part in the battles from early on. "At first we were about 100 to 150, most of us Communists," he said. Since he had already served in the army, he was immediately given a weapon. A German prisoner of war who had proved trustworthy and was involved in all operations fought at his side. Simantov was often sent to the city on a mission: he was instructed to meet a

---

6   See also James M. Glass, *Jewish Resistance during the Holocaust: Moral Uses of Violence and Will* (New York: Palgrave Macmillan, 2004), p. 2.

certain person (he was given a description in advance) who then handed over medications for the partisans. While he was in the mountains, he had only one thought in his head: "**If** I get out of here alive, then I'll go home again...**If**..." (Simantov emphasized the words in bold in his oral testimony). The Englishmen who were with them "did not even get their hands dirty...they did not fight, they sat in the sun, ate, drank." When the partisans were not fighting, they cleaned their weapons, deloused themselves, and chatted. In the evening, they rested by the fire and sang partisan songs, not knowing what to expect the following day. Perhaps a messenger would surprise them with the news that "the Germans are coming!"

Once they had to cross a river to escape the Germans. A scout preceded them; the last to cross was a Jewish partisan who had fallen asleep, exhausted, putting the lives of 500 men at stake. He was only forgiven, Simantov recalled, because he was a Jew. Simantov was involved in heavy fighting when the Germans carried out their purges in 1943. Wounded, he was taken to Giannitsa, where a family of Communist Party members took him in and treated him like one of their own children. He spent three months recovering in their home.

David Aharon was active in Free Greece and beyond (reaching, he said, the Chasia Mountains) and estimated that he encountered about 400 to 500 Jews. He speaks only briefly about life in the mountains: "We went from village to village, fighting the Germans." He spoke in more detail about the battle in which 650 Italians, fighting on the side of the Germans, were taken prisoner but then deserted, preferring to stay with the partisans. Some of them, David recalled, proved to be extremely useful later, when the partisans received weapons from the British, because they knew how to repair the weapons. David was responsible for the weapons' storehouse. The weapons were dropped by the British from airplanes, together with money, with which the partisans in the villages could buy medications, food, and all they required for their daily needs. Of course, the Germans retaliated, destroying the villages that supported the partisans. In his testimony, David talked in great detail about a battle in which several partisans stayed behind to cover their comrades who were bringing the weapons to safety. The Germans captured a young Jew named Carlos, whom they executed in Kilkis as a deterrent.

Jacques Serror served as a cook in the area of Grevena. In this capacity he could, he said, protect his sister, who made shirts and pants for the partisans. His brother Chaim was a fighter and was killed in a battle west of Grevena (near Spileo). When Jacques himself was in mortal danger after being bitten by a rabid dog, the partisans transported him to Salonika, where he was treated and saved thanks to the help of a Christian friend. When he was well again, he returned to the mountains. The relative ease with which the sick or wounded, such as Yakov Koumeris and Jacques Serror, were sent to the city to recover and then returned to the mountains is quite remarkable.

Maurice Florentin also testified that the partisans were constantly on the move. If a village was liberated, they slept in houses or schools. Sometimes they were well received, with villagers having no choice but to give them food. Usually, the British guarded the hills, while specially trained partisans blew up the railroad lines. Maurice was a commando fighter. He recalls the battle of May 6, 1944, near Rapsani, at the foot of Mount Olympus, when they surprised the Germans as the latter were washing themselves in the river. Many German soldiers were killed and those who were able to flee left their weapons behind.[7]

---

7   The diary of a (Jewish) partisan, which was published in the *Israilitikon Vima* (in Greek) on May 17, 1945, and shared by Matsas (*The Illusion of Safety*, pp. 274–277), offers a description of the same battle against the Germans on May 6, 1944. The battle started when the news arrived that a group of about twenty Jews from Larissa, hiding under the protection of the partisans at the foot of Mount Olympus, had been betrayed by German collaborators. Sons of these Jewish families conveyed the news to the partisans. A group of 150 partisans surprised the Germans, and a battle, known as "the Battle of Karalakos," ensued. The partisans killed 242 Germans, and eight partisans lost their lives. Most of the Jews, apart from the first three runners who had sought to notify the partisans, were saved. According to this version from the diary of a Jewish partisan, the partisans embarked on the battle to help the Jewish families. M. Matsas draws further on the testimony of Iosif Matsas, a partisan and eyewitness, adding that one of the leaders involved, together with his men, in the battle of the partisans was Markos Karasso, a student from Salonika. His father was Albertos Karasso,

Maurice was seriously wounded in the leg during this battle. He hid until his comrades returned to carry him away. From then until liberation, he was taken from hospital to hospital, receiving treatment for the severe leg wound and its repercussions. This experience, as well as Dick Benveniste's illness, led Maurice to reflect on the many hardships the partisans had to endure. Dick, he reports, became ill with diphtheria—without doctors or medication, let alone a hospital.

Daily diary entries attest to the purpose their author ascribes to events at the very moment they occur. They complement memories of everyday life in the mountains, the struggles, and the universe of war. Dick Benveniste was a stickler for accuracy and pedantically noted place names and dates. His diary describes a long journey, from August 24, 1944, until his release on February 20, 1945: from the Kamvounia Mountains to Pieria, Vermio, to the area south of Lake Giannitsa, then the area around Salonika, Vodena, Karatzova, Kaimaktsalan, through Florina, on the Kozani plateau, and finally to the area around Veria and the city itself. War also has a "physical dimension," and the way it is depicted in this case is characterized by the strains to which the body was subjected: strenuous marches, fever, injuries, cold, hunger. The partisans stayed in the villages, lodged in schools or in houses. While the Germans were in the

one of the leaders of the labor movement in Salonika, who had been executed by the Germans. Markos Karasso was killed in a battle in July 1943 near Edessa; see Matsas, *The Illusion of Safety*, p. 303. Iosif Matsas gives the names of the three boys who tried to inform the partisans and were killed, as well as the name of the boy who finally succeeded in doing so. The same battle is also described by Andreas Kedros, but with other emphases and without mentioning the Jewish partisans: "In the meantime, clashes and fighting continued between the ELAS and the German commandos in the mountains and along the entire length of the main traffic routes, which were reinforced by security battalions. In the north of the country, between May 3 and 10, for the first time, there were real military battles between the Germans on the one side and the Greek and Albanian partisans on the other. On May 6, the ELAS managed to encircle and destroy a complete SS battalion near Olympus. The enemy lost 230 people, and the ELAS captured fourteen prisoners of war. The booty was considerable: twelve guns, twenty-five machine guns, eighty rifles, twenty revolvers, eight binoculars, etc." Andreas Kedros, *The Greek Resistance, 1940–1944*, vol. 2 (Greek) (Athens: Themelio, 1983), p.186.

surrounding area, the partisans remained outside the villages. They were always moving from place to place.

Dick's diary begins as the partisans are making their way to Kozani, near Deskati. Upon reaching Rymnio, they realized that the Germans had left the area. Nothing remained but scorched earth: "Smoke from a fire rises from a nearby village." Dick was ill, suffering from a headache and a fever, when they moved from South Pieria to Vermio: "Heavy head, and I'm lying flat. Now we are in Pieria making the terrible climb to Vermio…Last night we took a path that no goat would take. The Haliacmon River rushes beneath us. Our path is less than 2 feet wide and the abyss yawns below us. The animal on which I ride tries to throw me off. The animals with the guns slip. At two we finally arrive in Polyfytos."[8]

Like Maurice Florentin, Fanny Florentin-Matalon[9] also remembered Dick's illness (just before he began writing his diary):

> I offered my services as a Red Cross volunteer with Free Greece and helped the doctor. The hospital was housed in schools; instead of beds we had a blanket as a mattress. In the spring of 1944, Dick was taken to Spileo, near Grevena, in a very poor state; we were all very weak. Doctor Atzemis examined him and told me that it was diphtheria, a serious illness in an adult. We separated him from the others. When I saw Dick, I was happy that he was with us, but I was worried. The doctor went to Grevena and found a vaccine that saved Dick. When the fever subsided, he could not move and was very weak, unable to stand on his feet. With hot foot baths and massages, he recovered, then returned to his unit.

8   I thank Spyros Karavas, who many years ago helped me identify the place names mentioned in the diary and sketch Dick's march through the mountains.
9   Letter from Fanny to the author (Seattle, November 11, 1997). On Fanny see also Feldman and Bowman, "Love and War on Mount Olympus." From our correspondence: "In June, forty-four Germans entered the villages. I was with several sick people in a forest near Ioannina. The Germans caught us. We were in several jails in Ioannina and later in the Pavlos-Melas camp in Salonika. The Red Cross saved me. When the partisans marched into Salonika at the end of October 1944, I was there."

Lice were a constant plague, diseases were common, wounds from battles were sometimes very hard to care for, and chilblains were extremely painful, all making the exhausting marches unbearable. Indeed, in December, Dick, sick again, arrived at a hospital in Florina. A month later he was suffering from severe frostbite.

Dick Benveniste's route in the mountains, as described in his diary entries, August 18, 1944–February 2, 1945

From the summer of 1944, the Germans suffered defeats on all fronts, but they engaged in heavy rearguard actions, while the Security Battalions continued to operate and the partisans increased their activities. The troop relocations and strenuous marches in the mountains continued. As they retreated, the Germans left a trail of blood and dead bodies, burning down entire villages.[10] Advancing toward Vermio, Dick Benveniste noted: "Friday, September 8. At 8 we arrive in a village where the fires are still burning. The Germans came here the day before yesterday. The village is called Goules." Monday, October 10, seemed at first to be relatively quiet, but Dick writes: "In the afternoon we are eating when the salvos and thunder of gunfire lets loose. We leave the village [Paleo Skylitsi] and move to our positions. Shortly thereafter the news arrives. The Germans in two tanks have attacked Neo Skylitsi. We sleep outside that night."

On their march toward Kilkis, they stopped in Mikrokampos. There Dick became sick again: his fever rose and the doctor gave him injections of quinine and camphor. Two days later he noted: "Sudden panic in the village. Two thousand PAO men showed up in a neighboring village. All disappear. I too leave the village, but soon afterwards we return. Luigi is shaking with fear." Two days later, the partisans captured 450 PAO fighters. As they crossed the Gallikos, they were struck by a horrible sight: "Everything has been destroyed by the Germans, everywhere."

Although the PAO was dissolved in 1944, in central Macedonia almost all the armed units of this organization (or those using its name) continued to work with the Germans in various ways. This is also evidenced by official documents of the PAO. The acronym "PAO" was used by a large part of the Macedonian population as a synonym for the insulting *tagmatasfalitis* (Security Battalion tramp).[11]

Food was a constant worry: scarcity and rising prices caused real fear. Dick noted down in his diary every crumb of bread. The specter of hunger affected everyone and everything. In January 1945, "The only topic of conversation is bread and the political situation." Yet everything was somehow tied up, he says, with a

10 See Kyriazopoulos, *Western Macedonia*, pp. 531–532.
11 Papapolyviou, "Resistance intra muros," pp. 65–66.

certain nostalgia: a restaurant in Naoussa where he once ate, a huge pie, a homemade pita, good wine in a villager's home...

Most of the Jewish partisans who fled Salonika went to the Vermio Mountains and Mount Paiko. Those who came from other cities or escaped forced labor found themselves fighting in other areas. Jewish partisans held positions of responsibility and participated in battles. Sometimes they were sent back to the city to deal with an illness and then returned to their units. In their testimonies, the Jewish partisans often call other Jews by the names they were assigned. In his diary, Dick Benveniste mentions many of the Jewish partisans he met: Maurice Chaim, (Yakov) Koumeris, Dassa, Oskar Kapon, Lazar, Sam Gatenio, David Broudo, Tsitso (Cohen), Henry Pipano, Salvator, Jacques Katan...

CHAPTER 4

The End of the War: Liberation and the Difficult Return

For the Jewish partisans from Salonika, the end of the war meant an ostensible return to "normal life." About two months after the liberation of the city, they were released from their units. Many of them learned that they were the only survivors of large families, that their homes were inhabited by strangers, and that all their possessions had been stolen. Many would subsequently fight in a civil war, and many would learn about the torments of exile, imprisonment, and renewed persecution.

* * *

Although early in September 1944 the leaders of the EAM and KKE urged the ELAS to draw up a plan for the occupation of Salonika, when the Caserta Agreement (an agreement signed in Caserta, Italy, between the Greek government-in-exile, the British Command in the Middle East, EAM/ELAS, and EDES) was publicized on September 26, the ELAS forces were placed under the command of the British. On the orders of Lieutenant-General Ronald MacKenzie Scobie, the Macedonia Divisions of the ELAS were quartered in Veria, and the British forbade the ELAS units from crossing the River Axios and approaching the city of Salonika. Nevertheless, the ELAS forces in Central Macedonia started preparing to liberate Salonika on October 20. In addition, the Greek residents of the city demonstrated against the Germans from the middle of the month.

Gradually, the German occupying forces withdrew to the western outskirts of the city, under the protection of an informal ceasefire. On October 26, the day of the patron saint of Salonika, 150,000 people demonstrated in the city center, with armed ELAS reservists present yet remaining in the background. The same night, forces of the Eleventh Division of the ELAS crossed the Thermaic gulf, reached Halkidiki via Pieria, while at the same time units of the Tenth Division approached the city from the River Axios.[1] The following evening, Kapetan Markos Vafiadis installed his team in the Upper Town, and on October 30 the withdrawal of German troops, escorted by the men of Georgios Poulos, Greek colonel and Nazi collaborator, and members of the Security Battalions, was complete.[2]

The partisans landed rapidly and successfully, surprising the Germans, who, as Kapetan Sarandis Protopapas-Kikitsas of the ELAS writes in his memoirs, perhaps believed that the Allies had arrived. Fighting took place on the hills of Sindos and around Chalastra, and, shortly after noon, Salonika was under the control of the ELAS.[3] Vafiadis's telegram states: "Our units took Salonika today at three o'clock in the afternoon. People are jubilantly running through the streets of Salonika and embracing the partisans."[4]

All those who experienced these moments described the same celebratory atmosphere: "The Germans had not yet made it out of the city when all the bells began to ring. A flood of liberated slaves spilled out onto the streets. They kissed, danced around, sang, decorated their houses, courtyards, and balconies with Greek flags and the flags of the Allies...The first partisans arrived in the

---

1 Papapolyviou, "Resistance intra muros," pp. 86–87.
2 Protopapas-Kikitsas estimates that around 12,000 collaborators followed the Germans when the latter withdrew from Greece. See Sarandis Protopapas-Kikitsas, *The Tenth Division of ELAS: National Resistance in Macedonia, 1941–1944* (Greek) (Athens: N. Margaris, 1978), p. 409.
3 Ibid., p. 414.
4 Ibid., pp. 415–416.

city from the east."[5] After describing people's fear upon hearing the explosions from the harbor as the Germans blew up the quays, the poet Vafopoulos continued:

> And when everything had calmed down, when the last German was gone, and as the whole city began to feel the agony of the uncertain future, the voice of freedom could suddenly be heard. The first English soldiers appeared on the streets along with the first partisans from the Greek mountains. And the people were overwhelmed with joy and spilled out onto the streets, strangers hugged strangers, greeting them with the Easter message, "Christ has risen." How come so many blue-and-white flags appeared so suddenly?[6]

Dick Benveniste arrived in the city for the first time some days after its liberation. The news of its liberation had reached his unit somewhat belatedly on October 31, 1944:

> Around 10 o'clock in the morning, having just drunk tea, we receive the news that Salonika has fallen. We leave the pots and pans of food standing and go. We pass the following villages: Palia Kavassila, Nea Kavassila, Episkopi, Loutro, Niseli, Niseloudi, Megalo Alambro, Klidi, Malgara, where we arrive at one o'clock in the morning after a strenuous fifteen-hour march through the mud. In Niseloudi the whole village came out to meet us. In Tsinaforo triumphal arches had been erected. In Klidi we sit for about an hour and eat. Generally, in all villages an enthusiastic reception. We stay over in Malgara.

On November 1, they set off across the River Axios, finding the bridge blown up. In the evening, they crossed the river, but the next

---

5   Drosaki, *In Salonika*, p. 129.
6   Vafopoulos, *Pages of Autobiography*, pp. 230–231.

day they were ordered to march rapidly toward Kilkis and walk all night. "Situation unchanged. I'm starting to worry and want to leave," noted Dick on Sunday, November 5, when panic ensued after PAO fighters appeared in a neighboring village. Finally, a message arrived from his battalion about the situation in Nea Koukloutza. On the night of November 9, 1944, they decamped— in the distance they could see the lights of Salonika. Around noon the next day they continued to Oraiokastro, where they stayed overnight "in a beautiful villa with beds and every comfort." The wind howled eerily all night; it was very cold. It was also cold on Saturday, November 11, and the summits of Mount Olympus seemed to be "painted white." Dick's impatience heightened, "We run back and forth and do not reach Salonika." But finally,

just as we are done with the hot drinks, we are told that we have leave to [go to] Salonika. On the way I fly. I enter the town and go to Platia Vardariou. My heart is tightening because I don't see any familiar faces? I go to my shop, and everyone is alien to me. Finally, I go to Lakis and have lunch there. No news from Nikos. After eating, I go to Marc Assael. Very warm welcome. I also go to Fanny's house[7] and see her. In the evening, I eat and sleep in Assael's house.

Sunday, November 12. Beautiful day. In the morning I go and find Jackito, the son of Uncle Moise, who had been hiding in Salonika. From there [I] walk to the market square. I also go to Joe's house, find Stavros, and collect valuable information. My sister is in Athens. At around eleven, [I am] on the way to Oraiokastro. On the way I stop a car and arrive not tired at all.

That was Dick's first day in Salonika. There were no Jews in the city, apart from those who had been in hiding: cousin Jackito, friends Assael and Fanny (Florentin-Matalon). The latter was

---

7   When Dick later married, he insisted that Fanny sit with his family during the wedding, as she recalled many years later in a letter.

his childhood girlfriend and his nurse in the mountains; she had returned to Salonika after a series of adventures. His heart contracted...the deportations—silence. Prior to his return, he had held on to the hope that the disaster was not total. Less than two months later, on December 27, now back with his unit, Dick noted: "Today we learned that 4,000 of our men have returned to Salonika." The news was too good to be true.

* * *

The political scene became increasingly complicated, and the war continued. Yet certain things reminiscent of remnants of a civilized past began to return hesitantly to the partisans' harsh daily life. On December 8, 1944, Dick was in Florina, carrying out his new role as a secretary in the command headquarters. His new job entailed a great deal of work and he remained in the office until late at night. He took some money and explored the city, jotting down notes as if he were a tourist in peacetime: "Florina is a very beautiful, well-planned city with beautiful buildings." A few days later, the first snow fell. He continues:

> At Kato Vevis station we take the exit to Amyndeon. The route leads into a gorge, with the railway tracks beside us. We reach the Amyndeon plateau. To the right of us is a Slavic-speaking village, Xynonero [sour water]. There we set up camp. The village really deserves its name. The water is like soda. All day we march without eating anything; in the evening we eat potatoes and sweetened cornbread in village homes.

The Germans were leaving, the country was liberated. On January 27, 1945, Dick arrived in Veria and joined the Kikitsa Division as an interpreter. He had been informed of his transfer only two days previously:

> In the afternoon, they call me to the battalion headquarters and tell me I am being transferred to the

division. It was like being hit by a bomb. What kind of work will you have me do in the division? I soon find out. On the one hand, I'm glad because I'll get a bit of peace and quiet, but I'm worried too because I'm moving away from the company.

In Veria, idleness made time pass slowly: "Afternoon walks. Veria is a barren city. There is a street where everyone strolls and nothing else. Although there are tavernas and coffee houses, you need money for that." On Wednesday, January 31, he noted:

This month too is over. Exceptional frost. The usual all day long. I walk around the streets without finding any place to stretch myself out. In the afternoon I met a very likeable girl from here, Lora Azaria. In the evening, the whole gang meets up and goes to visit her at home.

On Sunday, February 4, the weather was "wonderful" again:

From three o'clock until the evening we stroll around. All the girls are outside today. There are quite a few pretty girls in Veria, and it is not hard to seduce them, but it's hard to approach them because of the uniform. In the evening we go to a tavern and from there home.

Three days later he noted:

In the afternoon we go to the cinema. An old American film, but after two years of such uncivilized living I enjoy it, because I feel that I am becoming civilized again. In the cinema I met Lora Azaria. I really like her very much. In the evening we went to the home of a Jewish friend, and we were invited to dinner tomorrow.

The weather was good again on February 15:

Rarely is the weather so good in February. Right now, the thought bothering me is the question of [what will happen during my stay in Salonika]. Until now we went around with our plates and bowls and somehow got something to eat. But now we have to fight for our food. Every night, before I go to sleep, I make a lot of plans about how to secure my livelihood.

Two days before Dick's release from duty, when his impatience reached a peak, he received a letter from his friend Dassa, who wrote to him "that the suit…which Jacky's fiancée kept still exists." What else had survived? What things remained from his prewar life?

* * *

The survivors—those who had returned from the camps, those who had stayed behind and hidden, and those who had fought in the mountains—took on the job of rebuilding the community. Based on the pages of the *Israilitikon Vima* (Jewish Tribune) newspaper, which was published in Salonika from November 1945 to October 1947, Albertos Nar eloquently depicted the climate of the harsh winter of 1944–1945.[8] On December 6, 1944, 137 Jews

---

8 See the chapter "The Jewish Community of Salonika through the Columns of *Israilitikon Vima*, 1945–1947," in Albertos Nar, *Seated by the Sea…Studies and Articles on the Jewish Community of Salonika* (Greek) (Thessaloniki: University Studio Press, 1997), pp. 257–280. Sadly, I found very few pages of this valuable newspaper, on which Nar draws, in archives and libraries. Since the first Greek edition of my book, a book by Leon A. Nar appeared based on this material, *In Salonika Again: The Hesitant Return of Greek Jews to the Native Place (1945–1946)* (Greek) (Athens: Polis, 2018). On the rebuilding of the community, see Joshua Eli Plaut, *Greek Jewry in the Twentieth Century, 1913–1983: Patterns of Jewish Survival in the Greek Provinces before and after the Holocaust* (Madison: Fairleigh Dickinson University Press, 2000); Bea Lewkowicz, *The Jewish Community of Salonika: History, Memory, Identity* (London: Vallentine Mitchell, 2006); Katherine Elizabeth Fleming, *Greece: A Jewish History* (Princeton: Princeton University Press, 2008), pp. 166–189; Rena Molho, "La reconstruction de la communauté juive de Salonique après la Shoah," in Esther Benbassa, ed., *Salonique: Ville juive, ville ottomane, ville grecque* (Paris: CNRS, 2014), pp. 117–138. For recent work on the return of Greek Jews after liberation see the contributions in Evanghelos Hekimoglou and Anna Maria

who had hidden in the city and its surrounding area gathered in the Monastir Synagogue on Syngrou Street and chose representatives for the first provisional postwar community council.

A year later, on January 20, 1946, in a letter[9] to Isaak Safan, who had contacted the Jews in Salonika from New York regarding his search for relatives, the community reported that it had about 2,000 members: around 1,000 of these had returned from the death camps and perhaps another 150 to 200 were expected to return; 1,500 Jews from Salonika were still in Athens, many of them had been there since the beginning of the occupation. Toward the end of the same year, on December 23, a letter addressed to Sam Levi,[10] editor of the *Cahiers Sephardis*, mentions, among other things, 2,500 survivors (*rescapés*), of whom several hundred were in Mandatory Palestine by this stage. The community now amounted to around 1,800 souls.

At first, the main problem was how to accommodate these few returnees. Indeed, they found their homes inhabited by strangers, be it other unfortunate refugees or unscrupulous war profiteers. Families shared rooms in apartments or slept on the cement floor of the synagogue on Syngrou Street. Accommodation, food, and clothing—nothing was easily obtained in those days. In the minutes of the community council meetings, we read that in April 1945, "by order of the military governor and commander… those returning from the mountains and who lack clothing"[11]

Droumpouki, eds., *The Day After the Holocaust* (Greek) (Thessaloniki: Jewish Museum of Greece, 2017); Rika Benveniste and Pothiti Hantzaroula, "After the Tempest: The Post-Holocaust Years in the Netherlands and Greece," *Historein*, 18:1–2 (2019), https://ejournals.epublishing.ekt.gr/pfiles/journals/14/editor-uploads/issues/776/main776.html?1=776&2=18605 (accessed September 5, 2021); Dellopoulou Hari, "1945: The First Trials against Jewish Collaborators in the Special Court in Athens: A Peculiar Source of Information," *Ta Istorika* (Greek), 62 (2015), pp. 189–200; Tzafleris Nikos, "Rebuilding the Jewish Communities after the Holocaust: The Relief Programme of the American Joint Distribution Committee in Post-war Greece," *Historein*, 18:2 (2019), https://doi.org/10.12681/historein.14583 (accessed October 1, 2021).

9   Foreign Correspondence, 1945, HAJCTh, folder 00162.
10 Foreign Correspondence, 1946, HAJCTh, folder 00189.
11 Book of the Proceedings of the Community Council, session of September 9, 1945, HAJCTh, folder 02667.

were to be given 160 jackets and pairs of trousers. Some of the survivors from the camps still wore the characteristic striped prisoner trousers or military boots. Along with a lack of clothing, the returnees also suffered from physical and mental illnesses of all kinds, including tuberculosis, which resulted in many broken bones. The highest priority was accorded to taking care of children: a hug, a song, education.

All eyes were on the community. The survivors pinned all their hopes on it, they were angry with it, they offered it their services. Yet the community, which had to rebuild the charitable committees from scratch, now needed help[12] from the United Nations Relief and Rehabilitation Administration (UNRRA), the American Joint Distribution Committee (JDC), and other communities abroad, as well as individuals, relatives, and Sephardic Jews outside Greece. Apart from the problems arising from undeniable material loss and daily need, we cannot understand those years without considering the experience of a never-ending war and spiritual crisis: values and social fabric dissolved, with ramifications for the sense of community and the common good. Even the very young suddenly found themselves fighting a war, forced to take responsibility for themselves and others.

The former partisans contributed to the reorganization of the community. In February 1946, during a meeting of members of the Resistance Movement, those present received a report about the JDC's activities. In *Israilitikon Vima* we read, "The members of the resistance movement, as a justification for their behavior, cite their complete neglect by the JDC, and until the Welfare Committee takes up its work, are in need of support so that their requirements can be met."[13] On the same page, another column reported on a gathering of "deportees": "It is true, and we need to acknowledge, that until now all those deportees have not received the loving attention that people who have miraculously been saved

---

12   A report of the Jewish Committee for Relief details the living conditions of the surviving Jews in Athens and Salonika, concluding with evidence of their desperate situation and disappointment. The Wiener Holocaust Library, 849/1 (April 1946).

13   *Israilitikon Vima*, February 22, 1946.

from death need...Those deportees and all the Jews of Salonika consider the community alone their protector."

The first community elections were held on April 14, 1946. In January 1946, letters from the Theodor Herzl Zionist Association, the Union of Hostages of Poland ("hostages" was the official term for deportees), and the EAM Israelites were read out during a meeting of the community council by their representatives, who chose representatives for the electoral committee.[14] Those who had been incarcerated in the concentration camps—the "Poles," as they were called—received the majority vote; they were followed by "those who came from the mountains," meaning the members of the resistance, while the "Zionists" won third place, and of course there were also "Independents." At the first session of the fifty-member community assembly, scheduled for May 8, 1946, a council was to be elected. Despite some mutual distrust,[15] a unifying spirit eventually outweighed any dissent. Thus, an article published on January 25, 1946, in the *Israilitikon Vima*, entitled "Unity," read, "Today the old camp mentality is no longer viable for us. There is only one principle: unity, brotherhood, solidarity, mutual help. And, according to this principle, we have to elect a community assembly and a community council of national unity."

The assembly elected Paul Tazartes as chairman with thirty-nine out of forty-four votes, and Leon Carasso was chosen as vice-chairman with thirty-eight votes.[16] The former had survived in hiding while the second had been under the protection of the partisans. The protocols (written in Judeo-Spanish) reveal that the community represented fewer than 2,000 Jewish survivors, a tiny number compared to the 52,000 prior to the war (*la assemblea presente representa solo 2,000 djidios al lugar de 52,000 y que eyos son los survivientes de una florisciente communitad que vinia*

14 Book of the Proceedings of the Community Council, session of January 21, 1946, HAJCTh, folder 02667, pp. 180–182.

15 *Israilitikon Vima*, January 26, 1946.

16 Among the participants at the first meeting, I note fifteen survivors of the camps, eight resistance fighters, as well as eleven people who had been in hiding. I have been unable to discover any information about the remaining fourteen persons.

entre las primas del mundo).[17] The assembly met once or twice per month. As early as the second session, it proposed that a memorial be erected to the victims of the Germans: an imposing monument in memory of the Jews of Salonika murdered in the course of the German persecution (*un monumento imposante al beth ahaim en memoria de los djidios de Salonico desparecsidos del causo de las persecutiones allemanas*). During the session of September 14, Baruch Schiby, a former partisan, insisted: "The work being done at the children's center is not adequate; we need systematic educational programs for the youth!" He also requested the establishment of a community museum, which would educate people about the Jewish community of Salonika prior to the catastrophe (*ke se organize un museo communal para informar la posteridad sovre loke fue la communidad de Salonico antes de la catastrofa*).

On April 1, 1947, handouts of food for the poor were discontinued; it seems that the immediate goal of the social measures had been achieved. Of course, some survivors remained in sanatoriums,[18] yet many others, deemed to be in good health, in fact remained broken until the end of their lives. The survivors now had to confront the state,[19] dealing with those who had appropriated their possessions, who were protected by the

---

17 Book of the Proceedings of the Community Council, HAJCTh, folder 02520.
18 On November 3, 1946, the general assembly of the community discussed the cases of those with tuberculosis (see HAJCTh, folder 00157). See also the archive of pulmonary doctor G. Karamanis, in which he discusses the newly established Pilion-Sanatorium: K. I. Gourgoulianis and A. Kortatzi-Prasa, *The First Mountain Sanatorium: One Struggle, Many Lives* (Greek) (Volos: General State Archives, University of Thessaly, 2013), as well as Kostas Michalakis, "The Jews and the Sanatorium" (Greek), *Sanatorio Archive* (blog), October 2010, http://sanatorio-archives.blogspot.gr/p/blog-page_28.html (accessed June 19, 2014).
19 For a comparison to other countries, see David Bankier, *The Jews Are Coming Back: The Return of the Jews to their Country of Origin after World War II* (Jerusalem and New York: Yad Vashem and Berghahn, 2005). More recently, David Weinberg focused on the reconstruction of Jewish communities in France, Belgium, and the Netherlands in *Recovering a Voice: West European Jewry After the Holocaust* (Liverpool: Littman Library of Jewish Civilization, 2015).

government, and collaborators, who went unpunished[20] (while so-called Jewish traitors were brought to trial and convicted). They also faced bureaucracy that placed obstacles in their way, and a government that initially ordered all Jews to vote in separate polling stations in the national elections of March 1946, while the resistance fighters were being hunted down...

* * *

Many of the returning Jews were homeless; various families lived around a shared courtyard, under one roof. Although the cancellation of the laws enacted during the war should have meant an immediate return of Jewish assets, in reality lengthy procedures were required. These dragged on for years due to the hostility of the local, judicial, and political authorities. Even worse, with the usual perversions of logic, the demand for the restitution of Jewish assets resulted in poison and bile regarding alleged Jewish avarice, creating the impression that all Jews were rich and possessed hidden treasure. Alarmed, the provisional community council, at one of its sessions in October 1945, discussed a piece published by the daily newspaper *Proini Ora* (Morning Time), describing it as "the beginning of antisemitic propaganda."[21] The antisemitic publications led a columnist in the newspaper *Evraiki Estia* (Jewish Hearth), which was published from March 1947 in Athens, to note:

> The Jews returned from incarceration and did not receive any care from the official state. Yet, even worse, they have always faced, and they still face, insurmountable difficulties in the recognition of their rights, and in any case, these difficulties, along with state

---

20 See Stratos Dordanas, *The German Uniform in Mothballs: The Survival of Collaborationism in Macedonia, 1945–1974* (Greek) (Athens: Estia, 2011), as well as Dimitris Kousouris, *Trials of the Collaborators, 1944–1949: Justice, State Continuity and National Memory* (Greek) (Athens: Polis, 2014).

21 Book of the Proceedings of the Community Council, session of October 23, 1945, HAJCTh, folder 00157.

indifference, are responsible for ensuring that so many Jews are still homeless, and that tuberculosis has spread so much among them in the time since their liberation; the number of those infected today is eight times higher than it was in 1945.[22]

And even though the war had long since ended, desecration of the Jewish cemetery continued. In 1947, day after day, the tombstones were taken from the Jewish cemetery, transported in wheelbarrows to various parts of the city, ending up in the courtyard of the Demetrios Church. Later, they were used to pave the street that connects Boulevard Vasileos Georgiou with the Straitigio.[23]

Between 1945 and 1947, the communities in Salonika and Athens, as well as various smaller towns, contended with the challenges that their reconstruction entailed. When the first elections for the community assembly took place, the bitterness and anger of those who had returned from the concentration camps, the hostages, were evident. In November 1947, the first assembly of representatives of the Israelite communities was convened in Athens, "in an atmosphere of mistrust and suspicion," as the reporter of *Evraiki Estia* noted. The two Jewish newspapers, *Israilitikon Vima* and *Evraiki Estia*, reported on the international political stage, with particular emphasis on issues concerning Jews. The defining themes were of course the question of migration to Mandatory Palestine and the process of establishing the State of Israel. Yet the everyday life of the communities during the painful process of their reconstruction was also on the agenda. In 1947, topics pertaining to everyday life included the restoration of the inner doors of Salonika's one remaining synagogue, the distribution of "unleavened bread imported from America" for Passover (2.5 or 2½ kilograms per person), the replacement of the rabbi of Athens, who had left for Egypt, and the journey of the Athenian *mohel* to Salonika "to circumcise ten babies."

22 *Evraiki Estia*, July 18, 1947.
23 When Jewish gravestones were used in the restoration of the Demetrios Church, the community sent a letter of protest to Ephor of Antiquities Pelekanidis, see HAJCTh, folder 00157 (November 14, 1946).

There was general agreement that looking after children was a top priority: a children's center was opened in Salonika, and summer camps in Agia Triada were inaugurated in the summer of 1947. In two phases, seventy-two children spent "twenty days in the clean sea air," which many of them urgently needed. There, able to be children once again, all dividing lines slowly disappeared, and the joy of life gained the upper hand.

"Normal life" also meant compromise: for some in marriage, for others at work, and for some deciding to give up their studies. Yet in its simplicity, life could still be enjoyable: the youth rediscovered love and dance. Black and white photos eternalize a Sunday trip to the sea, to Peraia. Young men and women meet in a pastry shop in their neighborhood and dance at any opportunity. Victims struggle to find the strength to stop reenacting their victimhood and to return to normal life. Some people seem to have been able to leave the recent past behind, focusing on the future. Others cannot stop relating gloomy stories of suffering and horror. Some seem to be proud that they were able to bear the suffering, even strengthened by their resilience. Yet others simply seek to forget. Begetting children becomes a miracle that inaugurates "normal life." Weddings become frequent occurrences, with survivors preferring to marry someone who can understand; a partner to whom one does not need to explain the crimes a human being is capable of committing and the good he is able to perform; a partner who himself has incredible stories to share, tales of humanity and solidarity, of hate and betrayal; a partner who, like everyone else, copes with the demands and trade-offs of postwar life but also has to contend with the loss of loved ones and unbearable pain.

Indeed, behind the facade of "normal life"—work, family, and all kinds of distractions—there was also **mourning**. One day of collective mourning was the Day of Remembrance for the Dead of the Concentration Camps, commemorated on March 20, 1947: all Jewish businesses were closed, and the announcement concerning the memorial service for the dead was affixed to their doors. The synagogue was crowded and darkened, the chandeliers covered, and hundreds of candles burned. The service began at 10.00 A.M., and Christian friends were present in addition to the "officials." Rabbi Michael Molho, Council Chairman Albert Menache, the lawyer Sam Nahmias, and the "older historian" Joseph Nehama spoke, and the crowd burst into tears.[24] For some, "normal life" was lost forever.

As early as August 6, 1945, the community began to register its members:[25] "Any incorrect statement will result in withdrawal of the right to receive welfare services." The first two to register had survived the occupation in hiding; the next four as resistance fighters. The first registration of a survivor from the camps took place on August 20, 1945, and, as witnesses say, pertained to a person who had already left for Mandatory Palestine.

As one of the first to register, Dick Benveniste was recorded as head of his family on August 7, 1945:

Name of father: Iakovos
Name of mother: Henriette
Place and date of birth: Salonika, 1921
Date of arrival: February 21, 1945
Former and current occupation: Employee
Food card no.: 365089
School education: High School (6)
Health status: Good
Return of house? No
Rooms occupied before the persecution: 6
Rooms currently occupied: 1/3
Return of business: No, I owned 12% of a confectionery shop at 89 Tsimiski Street, but the business was disbanded, the stock was plundered and taken by the owner of the property.
How were you rescued? I joined the resistance forces.

---

24 *Evraiki Estia*, April 11, 1947.
25 Nine of the sixteen books in which the community members were registered according to heads of their families are extant. In these surviving volumes, 232 heads of families declare that they survived in the resistance. In the last volume, the final entry carries the serial number 1,500, dated May 6, 1946. However, the last volume (with the serial numbers 1,501 to 1,600) has not survived.

The undersigned declares that during the persecution by the Germans from February 25, 1943, to October 30, 1944, he sustained the following damage:
Property ownership: None
Movable assets: 1.) Valuables and money: 1 stamp collection worth 50,000 drachmas as well as various pieces of gold jewelry; 2.) Merchandise: 12.5% of the confectionery shop on Tsimiski Street, i.e., goods today worth 200,000 (two hundred thousand) drachmas; 3.) Furniture and appliances: One complete bedroom, bathroom, and kitchen utensils, and a library of 450 books and dictionaries; 4.) Clothing: Four suits with matching underwear; two chests with my mother's dowry.

Already at the first meeting of the Provisional Community Council on March 11, 1945, "after a thorough investigation and discussion" regarding employing a staff member, "the matter was approved and decided upon." If the preferred candidate among the four applicants would not accept the position, "David Benveniste wishes to be recruited for a salary of 8,000 drachmas." On November 16, 1945, it was decided that a "head of department for the services of the community" would be appointed, with a basic salary of 40,000 drachmas—to increase according to inflation—plus an additional allowance of 30,000 drachmas.[26] At the end of 1946, Dick Benveniste, by now community director, signed the community correspondence with official offices, organizations abroad, as well as individuals. Of course, much of the community correspondence at the time concerned searches for relatives, issuing certificates, and the crucial issues of housing and caring for the survivors. From 1945, the restrained response to anxious letters searching for relatives is a more or less stereotypical formula (in Greek, French, or Judeo-Spanish): "The person named does not appear registered on the list of returnees...despite all public announcements...In all likelihood, he has suffered the fate of so many unfortunate Israelites."

---

26 Book of the Proceedings of the Community Council, January to December 1945, HAJCTh, folder 00157.

Tsitso Cohen returned to Salonika at the end of December 1944. He did not want to go to Athens, which had turned into a battlefield: "*Basta* [Enough]!" he said in an interview, as if talking to himself. Yet for many partisans, their adventures were not yet over. For some—like Moise Eskaloni, and especially for Markos Botton, David Broudo, and Moisis Bourlas—the commitment to the Left was integral to their lives and did not end with the conclusion of the war. This decision was anything but easy. Indeed, very soon the persecution of the Left began.

More than 80,000 people were arrested in Greece in 1945, with or without charge, and the vast majority of them belonged to the Left. While collaboration with the enemy went unpunished, anyone suspected of being a leftist was condemned by judges, many of whom had also been in office during the occupation. With the elections of 1946, Greek politics moved clearly to the Right, and the gendarmerie, the army, and the police became active against all those who had "been involved in the struggle of the rebels against the state since the beginning of the occupation."[27]

Moise Eskaloni was among the first partisans to arrive in Salonika on October 28, 1944. Shortly before, his family had miraculously escaped the massacre in Chortiatis, the village in which they had been hiding (this was a violent reprisal conducted by the collaborationist Security Battalions and Wehrmacht troops following an ambush by the ELAS). He himself escaped arrest thanks to the timely intervention of his comrades. The people of Salonika, he recalled, received the partisans with tears of joy in their eyes and carried them on their shoulders. They spent the first night at the German School, and Moise, who had not been ill once

---

27 Mark Mazower, "The Cold War and the Appropriation of Memory: Greece after Liberation," in István Déak, Jan T. Gross, and Tony Just, eds., *The Politics of Retribution in Europe: World War II and its Aftermath* (Princeton: Princeton University Press, 2000), pp. 212–232; see also Mark Mazower, ed., *After the War Was over: Reconstructing the Family, Nation and State in Greece, 1943–1960* (Princeton: Princeton University Press, 2000), and above all Eleni Haidia, "The Punishment of Collaborators in Northern Greece," in Mazower, *After the War*, pp. 42–61; see also Kousouris, *Trials of the Collaborators*.

throughout the previous two years, collapsed, exhausted, with a high fever. He related:

> Later, the December events took place…The partisans of the ELAS decided not to leave the government to the royalists…At that time, we did not yet know that the world had been divided at Yalta and that we had been condemned…We were ordered to move 45 kilometers from the urban centers.

As many partisans, Moise was traumatized by the Treaty of Varkiza (an agreement signed in Varkiza, near Athens, on February 12, 1945, between the Greek minister of foreign affairs and the secretary of the Communist Party, representing the EAM/ELAS) and the surrender of weapons. "How did everyone give up his weapon, a part of himself…We felt that to be a betrayal, but we could do nothing else." Moise witnessed the mutual mistrust and a series of incidents in the ranks of the ELAS, including charges of high treason and executions. He returned to Salonika and found his surviving relatives. The Jewish community provided temporary accommodation, and he himself secured some makeshift furniture with the help of the partisan administration. However, the government unleashed an unprecedented hunt for Communists, and Moise, who lacked a "social conscience certificate" (according to this measure, which was introduced in 1938, the police authorities or the army issued a document certifying that a citizen was neither a Communist, nor sympathetic to the Communist Party; those who did not possess it, as well as their relatives, were excluded from working in the public sector) remained without work.

An old friend of the family, a tailor, came to Moise's aid. He bought several sets of linen and sewed him a suit. The EAM office contacted him and asked for his help in procuring food and the weapons that the partisans had hidden. Moise, who had witnessed the internal party confrontations up close, hesitated, but finally agreed on condition that he be "left in peace afterwards." In fact, he took on various assignments, and he was once caught by the police, although he managed to escape. He succeeded in identifying those who had betrayed him, including an ungrateful Jew whom Moise had once saved. Now that he was known to the police and thus could no longer help the organization, he was left alone: "Yes, I acted loyally, but I did not want to fight anymore....How should I say it...I was tired...Everyone went to the mountains, but I stayed in Salonika...We took the normal route.... One day I was called to do my military service. Should I fight my comrades?"

Moise decided to report—otherwise he would face the accusation of desertion, the punishment for which was the death sentence—hoping not to be sent to a fighting unit. At the same time, he was preparing to go to France or Spain using forged papers. Yet he was lucky: the army sent him to a technical school in Athens, and, as the civil war drew to a close, he was able to use certain contacts to extract himself from military service. He returned to Salonika, worked hard, married, had children, and built his own house, making sure that his "children receive a good education and don't live in poverty."

At the time of the liberation, Markos Botton was in Salonika. "People cried for joy...But I did not know where I could go," he recalled. His house had been occupied by refugees from East Macedonia and Thrace. Markos was one of those who saw the December events and the bitterness of defeat. "Everyone was fighting there. We in Macedonia stayed where we were. We were astonished. Why did we not go to help [the ELAS partisans against the government]?...We were not given any explanations. Later we learned that Aris [Kapetan Aris Velouchiotis, leader of the ELAS] had insisted."

Following the Treaty of Varkiza, the partisans left the cities. Markos' battalion transferred its prisoners of war to the town of Aridea, and in early 1945 its members gave up their arms in Edessa. From there, Markos returned to Salonika. He remembered the persecutions of the leftists, the tense atmosphere, and the panic spread by the newspapers. In Greece, he said bitterly, "the prisoners of war held by the ELAS [who had collaborated with the Germans] were released and partisans were hunted down." In Salonika he came into contact with the organization and fled to avoid joining it again, this time to Yugoslavia, to Tsesovo, and then to Bulkes (modern-day Maglić),[28] the famous village in Serbia, which was abandoned by its ethnic German inhabitants when the Wehrmacht began their retreat and turned into a small people's democracy by young Communists.

Markos remained in Bulkes for two years, together with some comrades from Salonika. In 1947, he received instructions from the Communist Party to return to Greece and join the Democratic Army, first in the Belles area, later in the region of Halkidiki. He would be serving in the Second Office, tasked with contacting people in the villages to gain information, but he would also be involved in battles and ambushes. In the spring of 1949, the ruling body of the mountain forces appointed him lieutenant colonel of the DSE (Democratic Army of Greece). After defeats at Vitsi and the Gramos Mountains, the Democratic Army laid down its arms. In August, Markos went to Bulgaria, settling first in Berkovitsa and later in Sofia. From there, however, he returned to Belles, armed and tasked with "raising the morale" of his comrades. From September 1949 to the formal end of the civil war in August 1950, Markos, together with about twenty comrades, roamed the Kerdyllia Mountains, always on the lookout for food, hunted by the National Army and gendarmerie. During a battle he was wounded in the back; in August 1950, the party sent someone to replace him, and Markos returned to Bulgaria. In Sofia he studied chemistry and worked at the radio station, where he also met the woman he would marry in 1954. He pursued an academic career at the University of Sofia, where he

28 After the conclusion of the Varkiza Treaty in February 1945, thousands of ELAS supporters fled Greece for Yugoslavia, others went to Bulgaria or Albania. Among them were "Slav Macedonians." Bulkes was a largish village in Yugoslavia, not far from Novi Sad, near the Danube. Its German inhabitants were displaced toward the end of the war. Refugees founded the "Greek Communist Community" (the first refugees arrived in the village in May 1945, and in June a total of 2,702 people lived there; the population then increased to between 3,000 and 3,500 people). It was a social self-government experiment led by the Communist Party, with collective work and cooperatives. The Greek community of Bulkes was at the center of a propaganda battle between Athens and Belgrade, and later between Yugoslavia and the Soviet Union, and in the summer of 1949 the community was dissolved.

taught metallic chemistry. Markos remained without citizenship and only returned to Greece after the fall of the colonels in 1976, "for family reasons"...

The pages of the *Israilitikon Vima* of January 25, 1946, contain a report from Thessaly, in which we read, among other things, the following:

> Solon Chatzis from Volos, a modest, ever popular, and brave young man, was murdered a few months ago by the anti-Communist guerrillas led by Grigoris Sourlas. Many others are still in custody, others have been forced to leave their homes, and all are suffering from the daily attacks and harassment of the authorities, the henchmen, and collaborators who have seized properties and possessions.

The times were difficult, but, while the civil war still raged, on October 3, 1947, the *Israilitikon Vima* published a statement that was also a request to the government authorities:

> The exiled Israelites are to be released. Minister of the Interior Rentis has repeatedly asserted that all those who were deported as part of the mass arrests carried out by the Zervas Ministry without trial by the security committees should be immediately released. As a result, certain people who fall into this category have already returned from the islands. However, not a single Israelite has returned, though most of them belong to this category...The Israelites urge Mr. Rentis to put his statements into practice and to order an immediate return of the Israelites deported without trial and a review of the judgments imposed on the others. They were deported simply because they had taken part in the resistance movement.

In those days, many found the combination of Jew **and** leftist unbearable. On another page of the same newspaper, a contributor to the column entitled "From a Jewish Perspective" wrote an ironic piece entitled "Courteous Inaccuracy" about the insurmountable bureaucratic obstacles placed before a former camp inmate who wanted to return to his confiscated house. At the end of the piece, the author reveals the reason for these struggles: "Because his wife's brother, instead of going to the crematorium, went to the mountains and fought the Huns, and the brother who committed this crime once slept in his house."

David Broudo was one of the first to register with the community—he was the thirty-fifth member—stating that he arrived in Salonika on June 20, 1945. He also found strangers in his house and soon learned that he had lost two brothers and four sisters, in addition to his parents. After the Treaty of Varkiza, he offered his commander, General Dimitriou, refuge in Salonika and even traveled to Lamia and Athens on Dimitriou's behalf to renew contact with his relatives. In January 1945, David was recognized in Livadia and the police arrested him.[29] On June 18, he sent a request to the community:

> As a Jew from Salonika, I was taken away by the
> Germans to the Karya forced labor camp; from there
> I escaped and joined the partisans. When I came to
> Athens, I was arrested and imprisoned on the pretext
> of various false charges. I stayed in jail for three months
> and was temporarily released on bail. Today I received a
> telegram requesting that I appear in Athens on the 21st
> of the month…On the basis of the above, I ask that you
> grant me a loan of 30,000 drachmas…At the same time,
> I request that you write to the Athenian community on
> my behalf, so that they might provide me with food and
> a lawyer to assist me.[30]

29 See the testimony of General Dimitriou about this affair, which resulted in David Broudo spending around a decade in Greek jails. See Dimitrios N. Dimitriou, "The Participation of the Jews in the National Resistance," *Chronika* (Greek), 104 (1989), pp. 3–6.

30 Letter from David Broudo to the Jewish community of Salonika, HAJCTh, folder 00154: 00143–00144.

Some months later, on March 4, 1946, he dispatched another letter from the Lamia prison, this time to the lawyers of the Salonika community: no lawyer had visited him yet, although he had received 30,000 drachmas from the community. He continued:

> Of course, I know that I'm not the only one asking the community for help, but I was in the mountains for three years, and barely had I come back on June 27, 1945, when I was put in jail on various charges. After five months, I was released for two and a half months, to be arrested again in early October of the same year. I would ask you to be more diligent about my case, because I am all alone and far from those friends of mine who remain alive.[31]

The community responded immediately, "We have the honor to inform you that we are doing everything we can in your case. As far as the clothing items are concerned, we must inform you that your brother has already received them."[32] The police was in possession of his file, and he was accused of having taken part in people's courts (courts introduced by the EAM in the villages that meted out severe punishments to those who stole or killed livestock as well as Nazi collaborators and traitors). David was sentenced three times and spent eleven years in prison and exile. "They wanted me to sign a confession," he explained in an interview conducted many years later, and then listed the places of his martyrdom: the Averof prison in Athens, detention centers in Thebes, Chalcis, Livadia, Lamia, Corfu, then exile to the island of Gioura and Crete…He wrote to Ben-Gurion, and the Israeli ambassador visited him in prison. In 1955, following the agreement reached between the governments of Israel and Greece, David and several other Jewish partisans, who were either in prisons or in exile, boarded a plane to Israel. After arriving in

---

31 Letter from David Broudo to the lawyers of the Jewish community of Salonika, HAJCTh, folder 00195: 00159–00160.
32 Letter from the Jewish community of Salonika to David Broudo, HAJCTh, folder 00195: 00158.

Israel, David wandered around Tel Aviv all night before going to visit a friend.

Moisis Bourlas likewise escaped prison and exile, flying to Israel in exchange for relinquishing his Greek citizenship. His story is quite similar to that of David Broudo, but the tone of his narrative is more epic: "When the conquerors had left and the valley was peaceful again, we rested for a few days and then set about going to Salonika on foot. We reached the top of Oraiokastro, cleaned our boots, shaved as well as we could, and readied ourselves for the parade." Moisis, like Dick Benveniste, was given a few days to spend in the city. However, before he managed to take his leave, he was ordered to move south to participate in the fighting in Athens. They reached as far as Atalanti, where they turned back and returned to Veria. There, shortly afterwards, Moisis was released from service.

Upon his return to Salonika, Moisis, a former Communist, immediately contacted the EAM. Very soon, as early as the summer of 1945, the police began to harass him—he was arrested, beaten, tried in a military court, and eventually exiled to the islands for almost six years: Ikaria, Makronisos, Agios Efstratios. Moisis went to Israel in 1951 following the aforementioned agreement and settled in Haifa. In the following years, he led an adventurous life and moved around a lot, spending periods in Israel, Bulgaria, and the Soviet Union. He returned to Greece in 1990, remaining there until the end of his life in 2011.

The Jewish partisans who were no longer involved with the Left during the Greek Civil War faced the same question as all other survivors: Should they stay in Greece or emigrate? If they decided to leave, to where should they go? Mandatory Palestine, that is *Eretz Israel* (the Land of Israel), America, or another country? Whatever their response, they were generally called to military service in the National Army and, albeit with a heavy heart, answered the call.

Yakov Koumeris and Jacques Serror took the first opportunity to leave for the United States. Yakov returned to Salonika for the first time in November—Dick would meet him later in Veria—and then again after his release from the partisan units. He was fortunate enough to find his house untouched, but very quickly learned about the fate of the Jews of his city. In 1945 he was called to join the ranks of the National Army to fight in the "second partisan war." "Just how much I've fought only I know," he said in a somewhat enigmatic tone in an interview given many years later. He remained with the army until 1948, after which he worked on the stock exchange and, together with his brother, as a sales representative. In 1950, he married and moved to Chicago. "At that time there was a wave of migration to America, and we wanted to try it." As a migrant, he first worked in a factory producing cameras and later in a sewing-machine factory. He returned to Greece in 1986 to be near his brother.

After the liberation, Jacques Serror set out from Grevena and, after a march that lasted thirteen or fourteen days, reached Salonika. He had lost two brothers, one in the Greco-Italian War, the other in the resistance. Due to the death of his first brother, he was not called up for military service. Since he too could not return to his house, now occupied by strangers, he survived with the help of the community. He found work in a British canteen, where he met his future wife. He worked there until 1949. In 1951 they received the much-coveted visas and left for America.

When the war ended, Simantov Razon did not know where to go. Upon his return to Salonika, he was warmly received by his shoemaker colleagues, and yet he went back to Giannitsa, to the family of leftists that had nursed him during the war. He stayed with them until all of them were killed—under false pretenses— by representatives of the government. He escaped that fate only because it was known that he was a Jew. He returned to Salonika and took a job in the community-run canteen, a kitchen for the former hostages. He feared that traitors would take revenge on the partisans. One day, he saw the name of his sister on a list of those who had returned from the concentration camps: he was incredibly disappointed when he discovered that it was not her but rather another woman with the same name. After a few months, he decided to go to Mandatory Palestine. He talked about his intention with a soldier of the Jewish Brigade, who put him into contact with *hachshara* people who coordinated preparations for immigration to Mandatory Palestine, and he traveled by ship to Piraeus, from where he left for Israel.

When Salonika was liberated, the Amir brothers took leave, walking for three days from Larissa to Salonika. They stayed in town for a month. They had lost their parents and two sisters in Auschwitz, as well as their brother, whom they left behind at the forced labor camp: "We've seen what we've seen," they told the interviewer. In December, both boarded a small trawler and made it to Volos. The answer to the question posed by the interviewer comes naturally: "We belonged to the Left, they saved our lives." They were already near the Isthmus of Corinth when they learned from the British about the Treaty of Varkiza. In mid-1945 they returned to Salonika. They reported to a British Intelligence Service officer and told him that as partisans they had rescued British soldiers who had been captured by the Germans.

The older brother, Yitzhak, found work as a musician and married. On June 20, 1945, Dario Amir submitted an application to the community:

> Gentlemen, I have the honor to inform you of the following: As a student at the Faculty of Agronomy of the University of Salonika, I had to suspend my studies because of the persecution by the Germans. I know how to type. In the absence of other skills, I am without work and completely destitute. Therefore, I ask you to look favorably on this application and to accept my request to serve your community. Most humbly, the applicant.[33]

David eventually found work in a canteen, at the recommendation of the community, and, thanks to a scholarship, he was even able to resume his studies and graduate. Then, "the strangest thing happened," David said, referring to the fact that, in the midst of the right-wing climate of terror, he was forced to fight against his comrades. Indeed, he was drafted to serve in the National

---

33 Letter from Dario Amir to the Jewish community of Salonika, HAJCTh, folder 00159 (Documents I, 1944–1945): 00182.

Army. During his service, he worked in a warehouse. An excerpt from a letter in which he thanked the Union of Hostages for a package it had sent him during his military service was published in the *Evraiki Estia* in March 1948.[34] Almost as soon as he was released from military service in 1949, he left for Israel, where he immediately joined the IDF, serving in its orchestra as a trumpet player! David followed him in the winter of 1950, in time for the *Hanukkah* festival. He worked on a kibbutz in the Negev desert and completed his doctorate in agricultural science.

"When the Germans left, we started to move down to the villages." David Aharon became quite laconic when it was time to describe the last part of his life with the partisans and the negotiations that preceded the Treaty of Varkiza. "The English came...Should we leave the guns or not? Yes, no, no, yes..." Despite everything, he remained in Athens and participated in the December battles. "In Athens we stopped the English tanks." David returned to Salonika. "I did not know anything...On becoming a partisan, I heard that the Jews did not go to work but to the crematoria...When they came back, they began to tell us, but we did not believe them." He found nothing left of his house but debris, it had been taken over by a German collaborator, and the Greeks had blown it up. "I met my wife, who had just returned from the camp...You are alone, I am alone, let's marry."

However, Salonika held little appeal for the couple. In 1946 they boarded the ship *Haviva Reik*, which was destined for Haifa. After a month in the British camp at Atlit and two months on a kibbutz, David moved to Haifa and then to Tel Aviv, where his wife had already found employment. He worked as a construction laborer and later in a bakery. During the British Mandate, he was active in the paramilitary Jewish organizations, the Haganah and then the Etzel. He fought in the War of Independence, during

---

34 "You cannot imagine the joy and, above all, the moral satisfaction I felt when I received the parcel that you had the kindness to send me. I sensed that I was not alone in the troubled moments of my soldier's life, but that good friends, who understood each other's needs, supported me. You've proven with your work that the goal of your organization is not just to help your own members, but to help each member of our Israelite community." *Evraiki Estia*, March 12, 1948.

which, as he proudly explained, he instructed soldiers in the use of weapons.[35]

Seriously wounded in the leg, Maurice Florentin spent the first summer after being released in hospital in Salonika. He did not have a home to go to, so he stayed with friends for some time. Finally, he found work with the Greek Department of the British Intelligence Service. When he tried to get a passport to visit his brother in Israel, he was required to renounce Communism. He refused, saying, "I am not a Communist, and I deny absolutely nothing. I do not need a passport."

All these testimonies highlight the climate that prevailed in the country after liberation from the Germans and during the years of the civil war. They vividly demonstrate how the joy of regaining freedom was poisoned by the sadness of mourning those lost, by financial difficulties, and, not long after, the shadow of right-wing terror and persecution. The state seemed to be hostile to the Jews who survived. All these testimonies allow us to comprehend the common problems that each individual faced, as well as the various responses and choices made by the survivors. Inevitably, the witnesses in part rationalize their decisions with the benefit of hindsight or remain silent about certain things. However, a diary from that period helps us to understand not only the dilemmas but also the ambiguities surrounding desires and decisions. The climate of political uncertainty, the fluctuations, and the daily highs and lows in the days after the

---

35 Eliau Avraham from Kastoria, a former partisan, explains his own trajectory. He fought—from village to village—in the Grammos Mountains, in Epirus, and in Olympus. He describes surprise attacks against the Germans and clashes with their collaborators in Thessaly (EASAD) and in the Turkish-speaking villages of Olympus, whose inhabitants were fanatical anti-Communists. In an interview, he explained what led to the civil war: "Allegedly, Greece was liberated by the English. In fact, it was liberated by the partisans. The English interfered and brought the king...The partisans said no...We fought for three years..." In 1946, Eliau Avraham went to Athens to join the *hachshara*, because "...we saw that the Jews were fighting British imperialism." The police arrested him for desertion from the National Army. He was forced to perform his military service at the Army Technical School in Athens, but by the end of 1948 he managed to escape and boarded a ship carrying illegal immigrants to Mandatory Palestine. Eliau Avraham testimony, YVA, O.3/5248097.

liberation also left their mark on the last part of the diary kept by Dick Benveniste while he was in the mountains. When the partisans were ordered to leave the cities, his unit began a march westward, to an unknown destination:

> Friday, November 17: Koumeris went on leave. I myself am not taking leave, because the effort is not worth it for twenty-four hours. I have a fever, a bad cold.
> Saturday, November 18: Unchanged.
> Sunday, November 19: I'm not moving from my mattress. In the evening we learn that we are leaving. Rumors circulate, but no one knows where we are going.

They finally set out on the morning of November 21, and two days later they crossed the River Axios; they continued their march without much sleep, at times walking, sometimes running, sometimes on carts. On November 26, they marched into Edessa. The next day, Dick learned that they would not be staying there long. "They say we're going to Aridea. I cannot stand it anymore and have lost my courage." Three days later, he noted, "Aridea is a big, muddy village, with nothing of interest. My heart has contracted since we got here." On the evening of December 2, he added that "life here is of no interest." A few messages arrived: "The ministers have given up on us because the government wanted to liquidate the ELAS. The situation is getting worse."

On the following day, December 3, tens of thousands of people demonstrated in support of the EAM on Syntagma Square in Athens. They were shot at from the rooftops of the police headquarters and the Old Palace. On that day, Dick noted: "This morning we were brought to the rally, and then we marched ahead of the people. The people of the periphery had gathered, and everyone was shouting slogans for the ELAS and against its dissolution. A village sent us gifts and pastries." The following accounts reflect the drama and the course of events, the political and military instability as conveyed by the news, but also Dick's feelings and personal torments:

Monday, December 4: The situation is getting worse. In Athens, blood was spilled yesterday. It seems to me that we are on the way to a civil war. Around noon, there was a general assembly of the unit, which lasted until midnight. I was meted out five days' arrest, because I poured out the soup in Vrysaki, when we went to Veria.

Tuesday, December 5: Today we leave. Our first destination, Florina. We are heading for a civil war.

They passed through Mount Kaimaktsalan and continued their march, completely exhausted and often without food. Yet on December 6, he noted in his diary: "The news is very pleasing. Papandreou [who had joined the Greek government-in-exile and was appointed prime minister by King George II, with the support of the British] has resigned and the ELAS prevails everywhere." On December 9, the mood changed: "The war with England is now a fact. A hard fight awaits us." On December 10, Dick was admitted unconscious and feverish to hospital; he recovered there for three days and noted: "Today we did not feel so bored, we were preparing a general assembly of the hospital." However, the same evening he learned that they would be leaving Florina the very next day for Kozani.

Dick spent the days of December marching through the snow and unbearable cold. A few kilometers before Kozani, he burst into tears and was transported the rest of the way by cart. "When I consider that we have to get to Epirus, I feel on the verge of going insane." In Kozani, despair overcame him: "May God hear our cries and make it that we will not have to go to Epirus. If we go there, it will end in tragedy. The political situation is unchanged. In the evening I sat with Dassa and Kitsos from the seventh division in front of the stove, and we discussed the events of the past." At noon on December 23, he learned that the radio station had announced the reaching of an agreement and that all hostilities should cease. "I hope that's what happens, so that we can settle down." On Christmas Eve, "the weather remains disgraceful," and bread was scarcer than ever. He did not venture outside but sewed the soles back onto his boots. In Kozani it was really cold, fifteen degrees below zero. The whole regiment gathered, and the Jews too. On New Year's Eve, Dick was on the move again, crossing the Haliacamon River. They spent New Year's Day in Velventos, sleeping in the houses of the villagers. They ate their fill, and despite the pain in his injured leg, Dick once again took up his pen: "In the evening I eat a greasy pie with pork...an excellent wine...roast pork and canned meat."

Over the next few days, the news and the mood changed:

January 5, 1945: Today we had little sun. The news is not good. No agreement was reached.

January 8: There is good news today. The British are withdrawing their demands, and it seems that an EAM government is being formed.

January 11: The news is better. Signing of a ceasefire and the talks will be continued.

January 12: Another EAM/ELAS victory. Signing of a definitive ceasefire on our terms. The weather today is wonderful.

January 15: The only topics of conversation are bread and the political situation.

January 19: This morning we have discussions between the Communist Party and executive members, and another EDA [committee for the education of the partisans] meeting in the afternoon, and so the day goes by very quickly.

They left Velvendo on January 22, and Dick was in Veria five days later. On February 2, new negotiations began between the EAM, the government of Nikolaos Plastiras, and the British, and on the following day, February 3, Dick noted: "In the afternoon I go to listen to the radio. The talks in Athens have begun. People are waiting eagerly for the results." His diary continues:

February 4: After noon on the radio. The news is very good. The EAM delegation agreed to disarm the ELAS. I hope that an agreement will be reached.

February 9: Every day my concern is growing as

to whether the war will end. Today it is said that our dissolution is now a settled thing.

February 11: The news is not good tonight. There are disagreements again.

February 12: I wake up late in the morning. The first thing I know is that an agreement has been signed. Overall relief.

The Treaty of Varkiza was signed on February 12, 1945, between the government and the EAM. On February 18, the day before his release, Dick, along with another Jewish man and several others, went from tavern to tavern, getting pleasantly drunk...

In contrast to David Broudo, Moisis Bourlas, Moise Eskaloni, and others, Dick Benveniste—like many Jewish partisans—was not active in the Left in the prewar years. Nevertheless, his hopes in the mountains were identical to those of the members of the EAM: he was a fellow fighter for freedom, and he wanted to see fair government representation for the EAM and the resistance in the postwar years. He participated in assemblies and organized discussions among the members of the Communist Party, and he expressed his desire to see the ELAS become a well-organized and disciplined army. Above all, he longed to be reunited with his family; the more time passed, the greater his fear and impatience became. What he wanted more than anything else was for the war to end, as he wrote on Thursday, February 1, 1945: "I wholeheartedly request that [the talks between the EAM and the government] lead to something that gives us some peace and quiet."

Like most, he too did not find peace very quickly. He accepted work with the community, found a few of his friends, but in 1948, as if he had not fought enough, he was called up for military service in the civil war, fighting against his former comrades. On April 3, 1948, he arrived in Corinth to enlist in the National Army. By this time, he had met his future wife, a young woman who had returned from Bergen-Belsen and was now working for the children's center run by the community and the JDC. They married in 1949, shortly before he was released from the National Army.

* * *

Hannah Arendt showed little or no interest in resistance in general and Jewish resistance in particular because she thought it too weak, too insignificant, and too bland in relation to the Nazi machinery. Raul Hilberg saw the weakness of the resistance as a characteristic feature of the extermination process. And yet the Jewish partisans in Europe took an offensive against the Germans, just as they defended their communities as far as they could. Fighting against the German occupiers, taking up arms against oppression, released an energy that pulled the self out of an imploded psychological universe, giving it individual dignity and a sense of solidarity with others.

In the case of Greece, we can say that the resistance was successful,[36] at least with regard to thwarting German plans to exploit the country's resources for the German military machine, as well as the casualties that the occupying forces suffered, and the number of Jews saved. As far as the involvement of Salonika's Jews in the resistance is concerned, we have found that their contribution, in the circumstances of the implementation of the Final Solution and the development of the EAM/ELAS, should certainly not be overlooked.

Did the experiences of the Jewish partisans of Salonika differ from those of their non-Jewish comrades? The answer to this is resoundingly positive. The circumstances under which the Jews made the courageous decision to "go to the mountains" were altogether different and more urgent. And even if, as true comrades, they shared the pains and hardships in the mountains, they separated ways again toward the end of the war. If the hardships and problems of poverty and civil war were common to all, in addition the Jewish partisans returning from the mountains found their community devastated and countless relatives murdered.

"I did not meet any Jews from the resistance who considered themselves victorious," writes Annette Wieviorka in her beautiful

---

36 Polymeris Voglis summarizes this in *Greek Society during the Occupation, 1941–1944* (Greek) (Athens: Alexandria, 2004), pp. 173–178.

book about Jewish fighters in the French resistance.[37] This observation applies equally to Greece. The degree of their modesty was similar to the extent of the tragedy suffered by their families and the unfair treatment they received after the war at the hands of the Greek state. How could a partisan who had lost his parents and siblings in the death camps feel victorious? How should he overcome the unwarranted feelings of guilt that plagued him because he had left his kith and kin, because he had not been able to convince them to follow him on his uncertain, yet by no means hopeless, trajectory? The partisans put up a strong resistance but could not prevent the tragedy, and for all of them the joy of victory had a bitter aftertaste. Many placed their survival in the hands of fate—they were no different to the camp survivors—and it required good fortune to stay alive in the mountains, to endure the hardships, and to escape the enemy's bullets. The partisans' words bespeak fear, determination, and camaraderie. Focusing on the discourse of the partisans themselves, we can understand the dilemmas and difficulties of that epoch; and if we listen carefully to their accounts of returning home, of the postwar years, and of the civil war, we will be better equipped to understand the complexity of their choices and their solitude.

37 A Wieviorka, *Ils étaient juifs*, p.13.

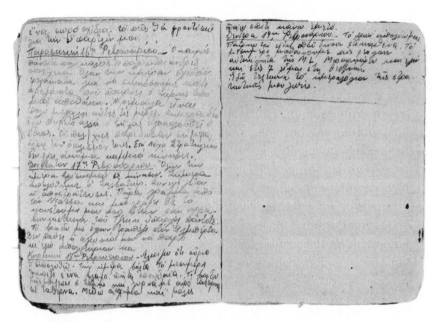

The last pages of Dick Benveniste's diary, February 11–19, 1945

PART TWO

"What Is There for Us in Greece? Who Is Waiting for us There?"

Chapter 5

Jews from Salonika, Displaced Persons in Bavaria

Luck, chance and freak are the stones with which every road from Auschwitz is paved.

Göran Rosenberg[1]

Difficult Return and Starting Anew

Salonika, October 30, 1944: "A day that started cloudy and grew sunnier hour by hour," Salonika-born writer Nikos Bakolas recalled.[2] Since early afternoon, partisan units had been arriving in town; two or three days later, the British landed. The Jews too returned to the town. First those who had hidden in Salonika itself emerged, followed by some Jewish partisans, and then those who had found hiding places in the mountains, in villages, or in Athens: in total seventy to eighty people. After the first survivor from Auschwitz arrived in Salonika on March 15, 1945, the terrible news regarding the fate of the Jews quickly spread...How could anyone believe him? Until the end of spring, survivors from the concentration and death camps constantly streamed into the city. We sometimes forget that in the spring of 1945, a sea of people spilled out of the camps, prisons,

---

1   Göran Rosenberg, *A Brief Stop on the Road from Auschwitz* (London: Granta, 2014), p. 106.
2   See the documentary "October 30, 1941: The Liberation of Salonika," Archives of Greek Radio and Television (ERT), https://archive.ert.gr/4787/ (accessed June 20, 2014).

and factories or from hiding places, beginning to make the long journey home. They often wandered for months. Many of the former prisoners felt they had no home. In small or large groups, or alone, Greek Jews traveled via complicated routes through the cities of Czechoslovakia, Hungary, Holland, Belgium, France, Yugoslavia, and Italy.[3] Many of them spent some time in military hospitals or sanatoriums, alone.

The options open to the Greek survivors were closely linked to their family histories, the desperate search for loved ones, chance encounters, the difficulties of leaving for the "New World" of America or *Eretz Israel*, and the return to Greece. Sometimes the survivors returned to Salonika via Athens; more often they came by rail, alighting at the terminus Sidirokastro on the border with Bulgaria. They were received by the Red Cross and UNRRA and taken to the Pavlos-Melas camp in Salonika. Some found relatives or friends waiting for them. Others returned to their homes or received support from an old friend or neighbor.

For many, however, the only support came from the Jewish community, which sought to help all those who had returned from the ashes: partisans, those who had been in hiding, and survivors from the camps. All were enveloped in a disturbing strangeness. Having coped entirely alone with their fates, they were strangers to the seemingly remote and unburdened people around them, banished from everything they had once trusted, estranged from everything in which they had once believed. They were alienated from their own lives. The nightmare that plagued and tormented Primo Levi became their reality: hunger, cold, pain, fear, exhaustion, despair, and constant, all-consuming death—who could possibly believe that? Even if they wanted to talk about it, they quickly realized that anyone who had not lived through it, not seen it with their own eyes, had no desire to hear about it. Worse still, an unjustified, deep mistrust weighed heavily on them.

---

3   Nathan Massarano, a survivor of Auschwitz, was one of those who returned alone to Salonika. He survived by relying on certificates issued by the military authorities in the countries through which he passed. I am indebted to his daughter Ida Massarano for information and for sharing these documents with me.

Those who had not experienced the camps were ready to believe that only criminals could have survived, or at best those who became criminals. Or even that the camps could not have been all that dreadful, as proved by those who had survived and returned... Sometimes the distrust was even apparent in relationships with loved ones, in a hierarchy of torment and pain that suddenly came to the fore and poisoned the desire for a normal life. What did "normal life" mean anyway? Anger, pain, loneliness, guilt, and hope—all these feelings alternated in an endless merry-go-round.

The List

On November 13, 1946, Dick Benveniste, by this time director of the Jewish community in Salonika—now located on Vasileos Irakliou Street—wrote to the Jewish community in Athens confirming receipt of a letter from the latter that included a list of "coreligionists who had survived and were housed in Feldafing (Germany)."[4] The original list of names had been sent to Athens on August 27, along with the following letter (in French):[5]

Feldafing 27.8.46

To the
Jewish Community of

Athens,
Mitropol. Nr. 2

We, Greek Jews deported from Salonika and still in Germany, wish you a Happy New Year on the occasion of the New Year 5707, "May the year end with all its curses and may the year begin with all its blessings." Amen.

Enclosed you will find the list of names and surnames of all Greek Jews in Bavaria, you can publish them in the newspapers of your country so that our

---

4 Foreign Correspondence, 1947, HAJCTh, folder 00188: 0005.
5 List of names, Foreign Correspondence, 1947, HAJCTh, folder 00188: 0007 and 00008–00009.

relatives know that we are alive and that our address is the following:
DP Camp FELDAFING-BAVARIA-GERMANY
UNRRA TEAM No. 109   U.S. Zone

With many greetings and blessings and in expectation of your answer.

your brothers and sisters
Samuel Moise[6]

The list includes the following names: Azriel Mosse, Solomon Amar, Isaac Amar, Nissim Almalech, Haim Almosnino, Mair Almosnino, Samuel Allalouf, Sabetay Acounis, Jakob Algava, Peppo Aruch, Angel Benozilio, Pinhas Beleli, Samuel Beja, Isaac Benjamin, Moche Barouch, Nahama Benzamen, Peppo Barouch, Avraham Belleli, Solomon Belleli, Isaac Cohen, Ovadia Cohen, Isaac Shialoum, Jakov Kalvo, Isaac Schiby, Moritz Dassa, Abram Mano, Matheo Israel, Nathan Massarano, Leon Mazliah, Eli Mallah, Sam Moche, Moritz Naar, Lazar Nahmias, Daniel Nahmias, Moise Samuel, Abram Saias, Salvator Saporta, Semtov Sevi, Jakob Salem, Isac Senor, Peppo Sedaka, Samuel Yechaskel, Simantov Hadayo, Leon Hadayo, Markos Hanoka, Samuel Haim, Vital Pesso, Haim Pardo, David Pardo, Salomon Osmo, Ezra Hayat, Samuel Ventura, Simtov Ventura, Eli Yakar, Eli Albagli, Sabetay Hanania, Sabetay Hanoka, Rachel Franko, David Levy, Alberto Mordoch, Salomon Acounis, Salvator Mosche, Moise Mosche, Solomon Barouch, Solomon Yani, Leon Simcha, Menachem Simcha, Moise Litchi, Isac Tiano, David Nachama, Senor Levy, Michel Levy.

6   For the original French see the appendix.

Feldafing 27.8.46

A la
Communauté Juive de

Athènes
Mitropol.Nr.2

Nous,juifs grecs,déportés de Salonique et demeurant ici en
Allemagne,en occasion de la nouvelle année 5707,nous vous souhaitons bon an " que l'année termine avec sa malédiction et qu'il
commence avec beaucoup de bénédiction,Amen "
     Ici inclus,vous trouverez une liste complète avec les noms et
prénoms de tous les juifs grecs de la Bavarie,et nous vous prions
de la publier dans les journeaux de votre pays,pour faire savoir
à nos parents que nous sommes vivants et que notre Adresse est la
suivante:
          D.P.Camp FELDAFING -BAVARIA-GERMANY
          UNRRA TEAM Nr.109   U.S.Zone

Avec beaucoup de salutations et bénédictions,nous restons en attendant votre réponse.
               vos frères

                    Samuel Moïse

Letter from the Greek Jews in Feldafing to the Jewish community in
Salonika, August 27, 1945. Courtesy of the Historical Archives of the
Jewish Community of Thessaloniki

LISTE DES JUIFS GRECS DEMEURANT AU CAMP DE FELDAFING				
NOM	PRENOM	NOM DU PERE	NOM DE MERE	DATE DE NAISSANCE
Mosse	Azriel	Mosson	Recoula	1917
Isaac	Amar	Yeouda	Perla	1914
SALOMON	MAR	ISAAC	DODOUN	1917
NISSIM	ALMALECH	JACOB	RACHEL	1917
HAIM	ALMOSNINO	DAVID	LOUNA	1917
MAIR	....			1920
7 SAMUEL	ALLALOUF	ELIAOU	REYNA	1922
8 SABETAY	ACOUNIS	NATHAN	ELEONORA	1918
9 JACOB	ALGAVA	SALOMON	SARA	1921
10 PEPPO	AROUH	HAIM	SINIORA	1922
11 ANGEL	BENOSIGLIO	DAVID	REYNA	1926
12 PINCHAS	BELLELI	JOCHANAN	POLINA	1916
13 SAMUEL	BEJA			
14 ISAAC	BENIAMIN	YEOUDA	GRASSIA	1918
15 BAROUCH	MOCHE	PINCHAS	LOUTCHA	1909
16 BARSION	MOCHE	DAVID	KLARA	1919
17 BINIAMIN	MACHAMA	MOSCHON	ESTREA	1915
18 PEPPO	BAROUCH	ISAAC	LOUTCHA	1927
19 ABRAM	BELLELI	MORDEHAI	BELLA	1915
20 SALOMON		DAVID	JULIA	1921
21 ISAAC	COHEN	YEKMIA	SOULTANA	1927
22 ISAAC	SCHALOUM	PINCHAS	MIRIAM	1918
23 OVADIA	COHEN	ISAAC	SARA	1923
24 JACOB	KALVO	ISRAEL	RIVKA	1923
25 ISAAC	SCHIBI	SCHALOM	PALOMBA	1908
26 MORITZ	DASSA	BENIAMIN	MATHILDE	1925
27 ABRAM	MANO	JACOB	BOUENA	1919
28 ISRAEL	MATHEO	SCHALOM	DOUDOUN	1923
29 NATHAN	MASSARANO	SALOMON	DOZNA	1924
30 LEON	MAZLIAQH	ABRAM	PALOMBA	1912
31 ELIE	MALIAH	SALOMON	ORO	1928
32 SAMI	MOSCHE	JOSEPH	RACHEL	1920
33 MORITZ	MAR	ISAC	LEA	1909
34 LAZAR	NAHMIAS	ELI	ESTREA	1922
35 DANIEL		SALOMON	ESTHER	1926
36 MOYSE	SAMUEL	ABRAM	DOLSSA	1900
37 ABRAM	SATAS	MOSCHON	SOL	1912
38 SALVATOR	SAPORTA	HAIM	ESTELINA	1923
39 SIMTOV	SEVY	JACOB	DODOUN	1925
40 JACOB	SALEM	ELIAOU	HANNA	1919
41 ISAC	SENOR			
42 PEPPO	SEDAKA	BENSION	KLARA	1916
43 SAMUEL	YECHASKEL			
44 SIMANTOV	HADAYO	YLOUDA	DZAMILA	1909
45 LEON				1912
46 MARCOS	HANOKA	ABRAM		1919
47 SAMUEL	HAIM	LEVY	TAMAR	1913
48 VITAL	PESSO	JACOB	ROZA	1922
49 HAIM	PARDO	JACOB	NAOUMI	1922
50 SALOMON	OSMO	ELIAOU	MITRO	1923
51 DAVID	PARDO	YLOUDA	IDA	1925
52 EZRA	HAYAT	MAHEL	DJAMILA	1920
53 SAMUEL	VENTURA	SALOMON	ESTREA	1914
54 SIMTOV				1917
55 ELI	YAKAR	MENACHEM	REYNA	1928
56 ALBAGLI	ELI	JACOB	SOULTANA	1912
57 SABETAY	HANANIA	SABETAY	REYNA	1915
58 SABETAY	HANOKA	MANOUEL	RACHEL	1927
59 RACHEL	FRANKO	SALOMON	REYNA	1926

The list of names of Greek Jews at Feldafing included with the letter of August 27, 1945. Courtesy of the Historical Archives of the Jewish Community of Thessaloniki. Some of those on the list later altered the spellings of their names. The spellings they adopted are used in the following discussion.

Moise Samuel, born in 1900 in Salonika, was rabbi of the Greek Jewish community in Germany and became treasurer of the federation they founded a few months later. He sent a list containing the names of the survivors of the concentration camps who originated from Salonika, requesting that it be published so that relatives could take note of surviving family members. Naturally, he ended his letter with the traditional greetings and blessings for the Jewish New Year. Shortly thereafter, the list, which contained seventy-three names (first and last name, name of parents, date of birth), was published under the title "Israelite Community of Salonika: An Interesting Announcement" in *Israilitikon Vima.*[7]

Of course, the community did not fail to respond to Samuel. On November 13, its director wrote a letter[8] in which he expressed the great joy caused by the news that nearly a hundred fellow Jews had been saved "from the clutches of the German barbarians" (*Barbares Allemands*). He responded with hopes that the New Year would bring "the liberation of our land and the restoration of the people of Israel" (*la libération de notre pays national et le rétablissement du peuple d'Israel*) and that "the New Year will be a time of peace and prosperity for our people who suffered such trials in the last war."

It was not the first time that the Salonika community had corresponded with survivors in Germany. A few months earlier, in June 1946, the community had received a letter written in broken French from Landsberg, signed by Eli Cohen, the son of Moise Cohen, who had been supervisor of Salonika's railway station (*chef de gare de chemins de fer de Salonique*). It was addressed to the president of the community.[9] On the occasion of the anniversary of liberation "from the Nazi enslavement," Eli wrote, on May 16, 1946, "in the name of all the Jews of Salonika," sharing news of those compatriots who had stayed in Germany and intended to go to Palestine. He sent greetings from all the Jews who originated

---

7   *Israilitikon Vima*, 42, October 25, 1946.
8   Foreign Correspondence, 1946, HAJCTh, folder 00195: 00890.
9   Foreign Correspondence, 1946, HAJCTh, folder 00195: 00223–00224.

from the city asking on their behalf for a list of the names of those Jews still living in Salonika, so that the survivors might "learn something about their family members." He also informed the community that many people had gone to honor the dead near Landsberg, "where Hitler unleashed antisemitism and wrote *Mein Kampf*." He signed off with the hope of meeting the revered president in the future "in our free Jewish state," where they would hoist aloft the "white-blue flag of Israel." The letter closes with thirty-seven names. A letter in French was dispatched on behalf of the community, expressing the immense joy caused by the news that "other coreligionists managed to escape the clutches of the barbaric Germans." It expressed the wish for a speedy return to *Eretz Israel* and the conviction that "you will be able to settle there and begin a normal life."[10]

Who were these Greek Jews that—more than a year after their liberation from the death camps—remained in Germany? How many of them were there? Tracing their trajectories, one is confronted with a history that can be illuminated from different angles and described on different levels, the history of people known euphemistically by the postwar humanitarian bureaucracy as Displaced Persons, DPs. This is the story of several hundred thousand people, a story that was hardly known until a decade or two ago, and that includes Jews from Greece. To tell their story, we must return to the time of liberation and even earlier, to the years of exile to the camps in Poland and Germany.

Liberation: The Logistics of the Deportees

In the icy winter of 1944–1945, half-naked, exhausted, and hungry people wandered incessantly on corpse-covered roads. Death marches from camp to camp—sometimes on trucks, sometimes on trains, but always under the threat of bombings—lasted for days and seemed endless. People died from cold, hunger, typhus. Some left the columns to flee, others found freedom when the dreaded

10 Foreign Correspondence, 1946, HAJCTh, folder 00195: 00222.

guards were not looking; the luckiest among them met liberators wearing the uniforms of Soviet, American, or British soldiers, men who looked at them with a mixture of pain and disgust.

At the time of the liberation, millions of people, mostly from Eastern Europe, found themselves far from home. It is often forgotten that in the spring of 1945, hundreds of thousands of former prisoners poured out of the camps, prisons, factories, and hiding places, a "flood of nomads" that began to make its way home by train or on foot: prisoners of war, slaves in the factories and forced labor camps, political prisoners, concentration camp prisoners, and extermination camp survivors. They often wandered for months, many of them not knowing where or how to pick up the severed threads of their lives. This wandering may be known to some from Primo Levi's book *The Truce*.[11]

Ten days after the German capitulation, on May 18, 1945, the London *Times* published a headline that read, "Europe Is on the Move. The Exiled Peoples Are Going Home."[12] A few days later, *The Palestine Post*, a Palestine-based newspaper, called on those Greeks who had come to the country as refugees and wished to return to Greece to report to UNRRA offices.[13] In Germany, in the months that followed, travel by rail was virtually impossible, while the streets were flooded with automobiles, trucks, bicycles, horse-drawn carts—anything that those wishing to return home could use for travel. Some stayed in Germany for a few months or a few years. Let us look at the big picture for a moment before concentrating on the Greek Jews among the returnees.

With the end of the war, a new chapter began in the history of expulsion, migration, and the practical administration of huge numbers of people. After the liberation, more than 7 million people poured through the streets of Western Europe, another 7 million were found in countries controlled by the Red Army, 140,000 were in Norway, 95,000 in Italy, and we must not

11 Primo Levi, *The Truce* (London: Abacus, 1998).
12 *The Times* (London), May 18, 1945.
13 *Palestine Post*, May 30, 1945, p. 4.

forget all the thousands of people not recorded by the statistics. These "liberated" persons were given a new name, one coined in the US as the political and military authorities tried to foresee the problems that the end of the war would entail: DPs. The definition of this term in 1944, in the context of a plan for postwar reconstruction, was primarily military: it referred to persons who, because of the war, were found in areas outside the national borders of their country of birth. The remit of the International Refugee Organization (IRO, a United Nations organization tasked with facilitating people's return to their home countries or the regulation of those residing in host countries) restricted the DP designation to persons displaced by the Nazi or Fascist authorities, while anyone who was outside their home country and could not or would not seek protection from the land of which he was a citizen was considered a "refugee."

In reality, the Allied powers did not completely agree regarding the interpretation of these concepts. In addition, there were constant movements—official and illegal—of large numbers of people, and the refugees often resorted to false declarations to speed up or delay repatriation.[14] Furthermore, the concept of citizenship in an area with frequently changing borders was rather murky. In the context of the Cold War and the increase in refugee flows from Eastern Europe and the Baltic states, the term DP became a synonym for "political refugee" and was used in IRO terminology from 1947/1948 onward as a universal appellation for refugees of all kinds. If DP *stricto sensu* originally meant "refugee due to war," later all "new refugees" were labeled as such.

After the war, in the years 1945 to 1951, **a nation was born**, a "nation of refugees": this group was formed—even if its constituent members did not wish to belong to it—because the authorities, although they classified the refugees according to the criterion of nationality, failed to distinguish between them in terms of the help that they required.[15] As Hannah Arendt, who

---

14 Georges Malignac, "Personnes Déplacées," *Population*, 3:4 (1948), pp. 737–741.
15 Gérard Daniel Cohen, "Naissance d'une nation: Les personnes déplacées de l'après-guerre européen," *Genèses*, 38 (March 2001), pp. 56–78.

considered the problem of DPs deeply political and not merely a humanitarian or practical issue, remarked, "Citizenship is no longer regarded as something immutable, and nationality is no longer necessarily identified with state and territory."[16] Moreover, she highlighted that the neologism was also a means of avoiding the real problem of the postwar period and ignoring the existence of stateless persons, insofar as the authorities insisted that the ultimate goal was to return them to their countries of origin, even if they were not recognized as citizens there or if their return was desired only in order to punish them.

The DPs represented a challenge to the "natural order of things," which tends to presuppose that the maps of nation, state, and territory roughly coincide.[17] So where does their history belong? The policy of the military authorities and UNRRA, which had participated in discussions at Allied headquarters since November 1943, sought the immediate and mass return of refugees to their countries of origin. Indeed, most of the approximately 8 million DPs in Germany had returned to their homeland by the end of 1945: about 5,700,000 people.[18] Apart from the case of Soviet citizens and a group of war criminals, after the war, political practice in the repatriation of displaced people deferred to the will of the victims themselves, in accordance with the UN resolution of 1946. In addition to UNRRA, from the summer of 1946 the "humanitarian bureaucracy," as Gérard Cohen aptly termed it, included the IRO and the JDC.

16 Hannah Arendt, "The Stateless People," *Contemporary Jewish Record*, 8:2 (1945), p. 147.

17 Lisa Malkki, *Purity and Exile: Violence, Memory, and National Cosmology among Hutu Refugees in Tanzania* (Chicago: University of Chicago Press, 1995).

18 According to UNRRA, 1,488,000 DPs remained in Germany, Austria, and Italy, of which 53,322 were Jews (3.6%). On the UNRRA statistics, see Malcom Proudfoot, *European Refugees, 1939–1952: A Study in Forced Population Movement* (Evanston: Northwestern University Press, 1956); see also Vincent E. Slatt, "Nowhere to Go: Displaced Persons in Post-V-E Day Germany," *Historian*, 64:2 (2002), pp. 275–294. For an overview of the breakdown of DPs in the postwar era, see Anna Holian, *Between National Socialism and Soviet Communism: Displaced Persons in Postwar Germany* (Ann Arbor: University of Michigan Press, 2011), pp. 37–42.

By the end of 1947, there were three subcategories of DPs, Jewish and non-Jewish:[19] (1) 300,000 Polish workers (out of 3 million who had been sent to forced labor in the Reich territory). In 1947 an additional 700,000 Polish or Ukrainian-Polish people left their homelands for political or economic reasons to go to the American zone of occupation; (2) 190,000 refugees from the Baltic States, mostly opponents of the Soviet regime, fleeing the military authorities that were searching for collaborators and war criminals; and (3) more than 250,000 Jews.

The central core of the last group consisted of 40,000 Jews from the concentration camps in Germany and Austria. There were also Jews from the Soviet zone of occupation who survived the Nazi concentration camps in Poland and then the terrible death marches, which continued the extermination process as the Soviet army was approaching.[20] Many more perished in the chaos that prevailed until the total capitulation of Germany on May 8, 1945—of hunger, typhus, and exhaustion. In total, there were about 200,000 Jewish survivors at the time of the liberation. Yehuda Bauer calculated that around 70,000 of them returned to their countries of origin[21] in Western Europe, Hungary, and Romania, but also to Poland and Czechoslovakia, while 10,000 went to Sweden, where they received medical care. In addition to this core of former inmates of the Nazi camps were Jews who found themselves the victims of antisemitism, leading them to flee from Silesia, Czechoslovakia, Romania, and Poland. These included the 75,000 Jews who fled Poland in the months following the Kielce pogrom that took place in the summer of 1946.[22]

* * *

19 Cohen, *Naissance d'une nation*. See also Françoise Ouzan and Manfred Gerstenfeld, *Postwar Jewish Displacement and Rebirth: 1945-1967* (Leiden: Brill, 2014).

20 Daniel Blatman, *The Death Marches: The Final Phase of Nazi Genocide* (Cambridge: The Belknap Press of Harvard University Press, 2011).

21 Yehuda Bauer, *Flight and Rescue: Brichah* (New York: Random House, 1970).

22 See Jan Gross, *Fear: Antisemitism in Poland after Auschwitz: An Essay in Historical Interpretation* (Princeton: Princeton University Press, 2006).

The mass human movements continued. Jews left Eastern Europe in large numbers: 80,000 Polish Jews who had survived in hiding, another 150,000 to 200,000 who had returned from the Soviet Union, and 120,000 who wanted to return to their homes after liberation but encountered aggressive antisemitism in their home countries. From the fall of 1945, the Bericha ("escape")—an organization that facilitated illegal immigration to Palestine which was still under the British Mandate—coordinated this exodus.[23] Six weeks after the liberation, 80,000 to 90,000 Jews found themselves in Germany,[24] their number increasing significantly with the arrival of Eastern European Jews: following the arrival of Polish Jews, the total rose to 230,000 at the end of 1946 (180,000 in Germany), and in 1947, as mentioned earlier, other Jews arrived from Hungary, Czechoslovakia, and Germany, bringing the total number of Jewish DPs to over 250,000.[25]

There were more men than women. They had all witnessed the terror and violence of persecution, torture, killings, and constant danger; a third of them were survivors of forced labor and death camps. Among them were a few children and elderly persons, their families nearly wiped out. Regardless of the various origins of the DPs, contemporary observers generally described them as the "human fallout of war," as victims of the reorganization of large sections of the population and the exploitation of their labor power. Their situation led to political

---

23 A famous trick used by the members of the Bericha, the "Greek trick," was to furnish Polish Jews crossing the Czechoslovakian border with fake documents confirming that they were Greeks seeking to return to Salonika or Athens. The trick failed because the authorities encountered real Greeks on their way back to their homeland. See Mark Wyman, *DPs: Europe's Displaced Persons, 1945–1951* (Ithaca: Cornell University Press, 1998), p. 147.

24 Hagit Lavsky, *New Beginnings: Holocaust Survivors in Bergen-Belsen and the British Zone in Germany, 1945–1950* (Detroit: Wayne State University Press, 2002), pp. 7–28; see also Kurt R. Grossmann, *Refugees, DPs, and Migrants* (New York: Institute of Jewish Affairs and World Jewish Congress, 1962). Grossmann fled from Germany in 1933 and was active in helping refugees. He was responsible for providing relief supplies on behalf of the World Jewish Congress and authored numerous articles and essays for the press.

25 Lavsky, *New Beginnings*, pp. 32ff.

discussions about international justice, human rights, United Nations humanitarianism, and ways to administer migration.[26]

However, from the very beginning, from 1945 onward, there was an urgent need to find a way to ensure the survival of this vast group of people, a task that, as it turned out, was not merely a temporary one. In a shattering testimony, in which the present and the past collide, Ruth Klüger says:

> We had been the first DPs in Straubing. The others came by and by, if they didn't live in special DP camps. Hardly a one was older than thirty, and most were Jews. Each had his own tale of suffering and survival. The normal fate had been death; every one of us was an exception. The military government and various international organizations, including the United Nations, saw to it that they had a place to stay and fed them. The Germans hadn't lost their hatred and contempt of Jews... It simmered on, as stew in a high-quality saucepan continues to simmer after the gas has been turned off.[27]

They were accommodated in the homes of Germans, some of whom had only recently been their persecutors, and in former military barracks, in hotels, monasteries, or hospitals. Between 1945 and 1948, even certain concentration camps (such as Bergen-Belsen or Dachau) were converted into camps for DPs. In 1946, when the number of Jews living in the American zone had quadrupled, the ratio between DPs living inside and outside the camps had not changed fundamentally: only one in four lived in a city.[28] In 1947, there were still 762 DP centers in operation, 416 in the American

---

26 Gérard Daniel Cohen, *In War's Wake: European Refugees in the Postwar Order* (Oxford: Oxford University Press, 2011), p. 6.

27 Ruth Klüger, *Still Alive: A Holocaust Girlhood Remembered* (New York: The Feminist Press, 2001), p. 151.

28 Eva Kolinski, *After the Holocaust: Jewish Survivors in Germany* (London: Pimlico, 2004), pp. 131–132. See also Anna Holian, "The Ambivalent Exception: American Occupation Policy in Postwar Germany and the Formation of Jewish Refugee Spaces," *Journal of Refugee Studies*, 25:3 (2012), p. 6.

zone and 272 in the British zone (there were no DP camps in the Soviet zone). Those camps operating in cooperation with the relief organizations as reception centers were able to develop into self-governing communities. If this had not been the case, the existence of these camps would have signified nothing less than the extension of the DPs' unbearable imprisonment.

To prevent collaborators, traitors, or even ordinary adventurers from obtaining access, candidates were necessarily "filtered." For their part, the survivors tried to provide evidence of how much they had suffered in order to qualify for care, protection, and accommodation, hoping that their DP status might allow them to emigrate. The potential immigrants to the New World also had to prove that they were useful workers and had training in technical professions.[29] The JDC provided a great deal of care for Jewish DPs in the camps. In general, the camps were experimentation grounds for new humanitarian practices, and their democratic administration was a novelty in the field of humanitarian aid in the postwar world. The general treatment was a symbol of the residents' liberation from Nazi enslavement.[30] Those who had survived the camps were in a dire state of health and most required urgent medical treatment.[31]

Many of the Jewish DPs moved back and forth between Germany, Austria, and Italy. From 1947, the IRO made UNRRA the administrative authority responsible for them, and, with the

---

29 ORT (Association for Vocational Crafts) created new possibilities for vocational training. See Leon Shapiro, *The History of ORT: A Jewish Movement for Social Change* (New York: Schocken Books, 1980).

30 Gérard Daniel Cohen, "Between Relief and Politics: Refugee Humanitarianism in Occupied Germany 1945–1946," *Journal of Contemporary History,* 43:3 (2008), pp. 437–449, as well as his book *In War's Wake;* see also Jessica Reinisch, "Preparing for a New World Order: UNRRA and the International Management of Refugees," in Dan Stone, ed., *Post-War Europe: Refugees, Exile and Resettlement, 1945–1950* (Reading: Gale Cengage Learning, 2007); Silvia Salvatici, "Help the People to Save Themselves: UNRRA Relief Workers and European Displaced Persons," *Journal of Refugee Studies,* 25 (2012), pp. 1–24.

31 The reports by all the relief organizations are full of details regarding the need for care and assistance; see the report by JDC doctor Dr. Joseph Shapiro: "Study of Health Conditions in Jewish Communities in the Third Army Area," dated December 22, 1945, JDC Archives, NY-AR 45-54-00031-00986.

help of the Red Cross, relocation instead of repatriation became the established aim. Prior to 1948, a total of 40,000 Jewish DPs left Germany. There were two key moments that brought significant changes in the number of those leaving: in 1948, immigration to the US was made easier by the new Displaced Persons Act. In the same year there was also significant immigration to Mandatory Palestine following the United Nations' decision to partition the country, which was reached on November 29, 1947. The hard core of the DPs were those Jews who could not or did not want to be repatriated, and they soon demanded (and were granted) accommodation in separate camps from other DPs.

It is worth noting that until September 1945 the Jews were not granted any special victim status or privileges by the Allies; rather they were classified by their nationality. Only toward the end of the summer did it become clear that the Jews refused to be accommodated together with other Germans, Poles, or citizens from the Baltic States, compatriots perhaps, but often also antisemites who had been involved in their persecution. Over time, the military authorities understood the specific problems of the Jewish survivors, and the Americans introduced a special status as well as separate camps for the Jews. The situation was different with the British, who feared that autonomous Jewish camps could become breeding grounds for Zionist activities. The survivors, for their part, did not stop reminding the authorities that they had not been sent to the crematoria as Poles, Lithuanians, or Germans but rather as Jews. Survivor and president of the Jewish Landsberg camp, Samuel Gringauz, once remarked that the Nazis created a kind of "ecumenism" that had not existed before the war.[32] When they met other survivors from the camps, the rescued Jews waiting to immigrate to America or Mandatory Palestine realized very soon that the new order was not intended to be transient.[33] As Samuel Gringauz writes, "The Jewish community of Europe has ceased to promise a future for

---

32 M. Wyman, *DPs: Europe's Displaced Persons*, p. 134.
33 Juliane Wetzel, "Les camps pour personnes déplacées juives en Allemagne de 1945 à 1957," *Vingtième siècle: Revue d'Histoire*, 54 (1997), pp. 79–88.

Jewish culture. The latter will in the future have to base itself on two centers of Jewish life: Palestine and America."[34]

This was a crucial turning point in political history and in the history of migration. The JDC's proposals to the Committee for Problems of Peace[35] in February 1946 anticipated emigration from Europe, especially to Mandatory Palestine. In this context, the historian must ask the following questions: What factors influenced the decision regarding the DPs' final destinations? How were external difficulties, the issuing of visas, the search for relatives, etc. related? Here we directly encounter the history of political exile, a history of the problematic relations of exile with every type of humanitarian institution, and the history of discourses concerning humanitarian aid and human rights. Likewise related is the history of the Zionist movement. From another perspective, we are also dealing with a complicated international political history and its many facets in the early years of the postwar era and the Cold War period.[36] Specifically, we must consider the history of British politics: questions about oil, the road to India, the desire to contain Soviet expansion and cooperation with the Arab states, the British Mandate in Palestine and the obstacles to Jewish immigration; the history of American politics: how to deal with victory, including Middle Eastern policies, the Cold War, and restrictions on immigration, but also racism and antisemitism, which had by no means been overcome in America in those years;[37] the history of countries such as France, Italy, and Greece, which at least tolerated the illegal movements of Jews who ventured to immigrate to Mandatory Palestine at a time when the British

---

34 Samuel Gringauz, "Die Zukunft der jüdischen Kultur," *Jüdische Rundschau* (May/June 1946), cited by Wetzel, "Les camps," p. 84.

35 *Vers la paix et l'équité: Récommendation du American Jewish Committee* (New York: The American Jewish Committee, 1946).

36 See Arieh J. Kochavi, *Post-Holocaust Politics: Britain, the United States and the Jewish Refugees, 1945–1948* (Chapel Hill: The University of North Carolina Press, 2001); Wyman, *DPs: Europe's Displaced Persons*; Ben Shepard, *The Long Road Home: The Aftermath of the Second World War* (New York: Anchor, 2011).

37 Leonard Dinnerstein, *America and the Survivors of the Holocaust* (New York: Columbia University Press, 1982); Beth B. Cohen, *Case Closed: Holocaust Survivors in Postwar America* (New Jersey: Rutgers University Press, 2007).

prohibited it; and the history of the Soviet-influenced countries, which, like the Soviet Union itself, facilitated emigration because the Jews, at least according to the British, intended to undermine the British position in the Middle East.

Prior to the immigration reforms of 1948 and 1950, a few Jewish survivors had made their way to the US. Illegal immigration to Mandatory Palestine is another important chapter in Jewish history. After the end of the war, about 51,000 of the 70,000 illegal immigrants were arrested and sent to camps in Cyprus or back to Germany, for example the famous ship *Exodus*. Considering that these movements, repatriation, and even return to the camps were constant hallmarks of the world of Jewish DPs, it is difficult to formulate a precise statistical picture of this population group. Nevertheless, the following figures give a general picture of emigration destinations: by the end of 1948, 12,349 Jews had immigrated to the US and 36,664 to Mandatory Palestine; in the period between July 1, 1947, and June 30, 1949, approximately 200,000 Jews immigrated to Israel.[38] Between 1946 and 1954, the US accepted 140,000 Jewish DPs.[39] Thus, by 1948, approximately 400,000 Jews had emigrated from Germany. After the founding of the State of Israel and the implementation of the new immigration law in the US, the flow of migration changed. Two-thirds of the migrants sought to go to Israel. The number of DPs in Germany had fallen to 55,000 by the beginning of 1949, and by the end of the same year, only a hard core of 27,000 Jews remained in the country.[40]

In Jewish historiography, the *She'erit Hapletah* (the surviving remnant) forms part of the controversial history of Zionism and the role of Holocaust survivors in the establishment of the State

---

38 In addition, before 1948, 7,169 left for Canada, 15,131 for South America, and 6,453 for Australia. See Bauer, *Flight and Rescue*, pp. 319ff.

39 Dinnerstein, *America and the Survivors*. Of course, this increase occurred after the act of 1948, which was ratified in 1950. See also Francoise Ouzan, *Ces Juifs dont l'Amérique ne voulait pas: 1945–1950* (Paris: Complexe, 1999). Other destinations in the same period were: Great Britain (82,000), Canada (69,000), Australia (55,000), France (35,000), Argentina (27,000), Belgium (27,000), Brazil (20,000).

40 Lavsky, *New Beginnings*, p. 36.

of Israel.[41] The first modern mention of this term, which is of biblical origin, is found in a leaflet published in the winter of 1944 in a subcamp of Dachau by the former head of the Kovno ghetto. The Jewish DPs in Germany used this term to refer to themselves, thus expressing their own identity as well as the feeling that they represented the most dynamic element of Jewish life in Europe.[42] For the Zionist movement, the DPs were also a political instrument in the fight for independence and a tool to generate positive public opinion. The 1946 film, *These Are the People*,[43] produced to publicize the DPs' cause and raise money for them, shows Jewish DPs walking around the streets of a camp: conversing, reading newspapers, talking, pushing babies in prams, and "waiting, waiting, and waiting," as the narrator's voice intones, for the world finally to take heed of them...

Yet it would be wrong to consider the DPs as passive. This perception is often suggested, first by the miserable state in which they found themselves and from which they could only extricate themselves with supreme effort, and likewise, of course, by their position as recipients of humanitarian support, which was crucial if they were to recover, and even to stay alive. Despite all this, these people began to rebuild their lives, sought solutions for the most urgent problems of economic survival, faced their difficult past and uncertain future, and often opted for solutions that would take them on the rocky road of comradeship, education, and the founding of a family.[44] In other words, their beliefs, the sense of

---

41 Israel Gutman and Saf Avital, eds., *She'erit Hapletah, 1944–1948: Rehabilitation and Political Struggle: Proceedings of the Sixth Yad Vashem International Historical Conference, October 1985* (Jerusalem: Yad Vashem, 1990); Idith Zertal, *From Catastrophe to Power: Holocaust Survivors and the Emergence of Israel* (Berkeley: University of California Press, 1998); Ephraim Dekel, *Brichah: Flight to the Homeland* (New York: Herzl Press, 1973); Bauer, *Flight and Rescue*; Tom Segev, *The Seventh Million: The Israelis and the Holocaust* (New York: Picador, 1993).

42 Zeev W. Mankowitz, *Life between Memory and Hope: The Survivors of the Holocaust in Occupied Germany* (New York: Cambridge University Press, 2002), p. 286.

43 *These Are the People*, The Steven Spielberg Jewish Film Archive of The Hebrew University of Jerusalem, H00304.

44 See Avinoam J. Patt and Michael Berkowitz, eds., *We Are Here: New Approaches*

belonging to a community, participation in self-government, and the ability to cling to hope all disprove the image of the "surviving remnant" as completely passive, as though they were absent from the course of their history when attempts to emigrate failed.[45]

Beyond political history, there is also the extraordinarily interesting social and cultural history of a people in a transitional state, on the move and waiting, with no state and no central authority, a story that we have only begun to hear in the last two decades.[46] In their daily lives, these people spent countless hours waiting in lines, at training centers, administrative offices, and post offices, staring at bulletin boards in the hopes of coming across a loved one's name among the lists of the survivors. These people waited, but they also fell in love, ironed clothes, and gave birth to children, they were furious, they cried, they hoped, they satisfied their hunger, they bought and sold…

In the end, there were only 250,000 to 300,000 Jewish DPs, and eventually they moved on to one "promised land" or another. The last DP camp, Föhrenwald, near Munich, closed in 1956. A law passed in 1951 transferred responsibility for "Homeless foreigners" (*Heimatlose Ausländer*) to the new West German state. The history of the DPs, and the remaining Greek Jews among them, calls into question our view of peoples rooted in their lands; Jewish people, and the DPs among them, were on the move. Who were they? How many of them were there? And what did they want? How did they organize their lives in Germany, and on what did they base their decision not to return to Greece? What stories did they have to tell about the war or their past? How did they imagine their future? How were their lives entangled with the threads of history?

to *Jewish Displaced Persons in Postwar Germany* (Detroit: Wayne State University Press, 2010).

45 Mankowitz, *Life between Memory and Hope*, esp. pp. 285–303.

46 See also Atina Grossmann, *Jews, Germans, and Allies: Close Encounters in Occupied Germany, 1945–1949* (Princeton: Princeton University Press, 2007); Mankowitz, *Life between Memory and Hope*; Margarete Myers Feinstein, *Holocaust Survivors in Postwar Germany, 1945–1957* (Cambridge: Cambridge University Press, 2010).

As pointed out above, the displaced persons were in a state of constant flux and statistics are inaccurate for many reasons. A document from the World Jewish Congress mentions 300 Greeks in Feldafing on August 1, 1945.[47] A confidential document bearing the date January 9, 1945, speaks of twenty-five Greeks among a total of 3,596 displaced persons in Feldafing.[48] A JDC report concerning the Landsberg camp dated October 1, 1945, mentions seventy-one persons who had lived in Greece before the war (of whom fifty-eight were born in Greece) out of a total of 4,976 Jewish DPs.[49] The aforementioned letter sent by Eli Cohen from Landsberg to the community of Salonika in May 1946 refers to thirty-seven Greek Jews,[50] while the list that the community received from Moise Samuel in August 1947 includes the names of seventy-three Jews living in Feldafing and its environs.[51] A letter of June 8, 1948, from the same sender mentions sixty Sephardic Jews from Greece in Feldafing and 200 in the American zone.[52] Another letter from September 1948 states that twenty of them had since left the camp.[53] In the pages that follow, I try to approach the reality behind these elusive numbers.

47 This document, entitled "List of Greek Jews in the Camp of Feldafing. Block 4/6," dated August 1, 1945, lists 300 names of men housed in Block 4b in Feldafing. In fact, there were also two Italians, two Yugoslavs from Sarajevo, and two men from Athens with Christian names. In addition, 218 of them provided information about their place of birth, their age, and their desired destination. The vast majority (187) of the men were from Salonika. Of these 218 survivors, just over half were between the ages of twenty and thirty, thirty-eight were under twenty, and fifty-one were over thirty (of whom only six were older than thirty-five), World Jewish Congress London Records, Hf. 197, 5 pages. I am grateful to Nikos Tzafleris, who provided me with a copy of the document from the USHMM (Catalog No.: ITS 422).
48 JDC Archives, NY-AR 45-54-00031-00894.
49 JDC Archives, NY-AR 45-54-00029-00793.
50 Foreign Correspondence, 1948, HAJCTh, folder 00195: 00223–00224.
51 Foreign Correspondence, 1947, HAJCTh, folder 00188: 00005–00009. This is exactly the same list that is also in the WJC archive, dated December 15, 1946 (catalog number ITS 421). At that time, the remaining persons on the list of August 1, 1945, had already been repatriated.
52 HAJCTh, folder 00233: 00078–00079.
53 HAJCTh, folder 00233: 00072–00073.

CHAPTER 6

Following the Traces of the Greeks on the
Feldafing List: Spring 1943 to May 1, 1945

I decided to try to track down and trace the seventy-three people named on the list of Greek Jews who were still in Bavaria in the fall of 1946. In many cases, I was able to find testimonies, most of which were recorded in the 1990s.[1] I wanted to hear firsthand their own memories of those

---

1 The testimonies come from the following archives: YVA, VHA, HVT, USHMM, as well as transcriptions of oral testimonies. Specifically, I relied on the following testimonies: Aaron Abraham, VHA, 51861; Jack Azous, VHA, 36740; Shlomo Akounis, VHA, 3397; Nissim Almalech, VHA, 1258; Dario Angel, VHA, 44545; Albert Cohen, VHA, 50326; Isaac Cohen, VHA, 3651; Ovadia Cohen, VHA, 38127 and YVA, O.3/3558750; Daniel Yechiel, YVA, O.3/3564489; Yehudah Eliezer, VHA, 46193; Sabetai Hanoka, YVA, O.3/3559485; Gavriel Kamhi, VHA, 3396; L. Herman, HVT, 3127; Yakov Levi, YVA, O.3/3558580; Henry (Erikos) Levi, VHA, 22659; Leo Mallah, VHA, 10027; Avraam Ben Yakov Mano, YVA, O.3/5419589; Yehuda Leon Markus, in Shmuel Refael, ed., *Benetivei She'ol. Yehudei Yavan Bashoah: Prakei Edut* (Hebrew) (Jerusalem: Institute for the Study of the Jews of Salonika and Organization for Greek Survivors of the Concentration Camps, 1988), pp. 346–350; Menahem Shabbetai, in *Benetivei She'ol*, pp. 332–336; Jack Mordoki, VHA, 34096; Eli Benyakar, VHA, 15115; Moshe Salvator, Wisconsin Historical Society, Oral Histories, Wisconsin Survivors of the Holocaust; Avraam Mosse, VHA, 13463; Sam Moshe, VHA, 146; Alfred Naar, USHMM, RG-50.120*0110 Aaron Dassa, VHA, 41280; Harry Perez, VHA, 48687; Moshe Pessah, YVA, O.3/4027240; Gabi Petilon, VHA, 23914; Raphael Raphael VHA, 17637; Salvator Saporta, VHA, 22913; David Sevi, VHA, 14549 and YVA, O.3/3559896; Irving (Isaak) Senor, VHA, 51365 and HVT, 1404; Yakov Sides, VHA, 12027 and YVA, O.3/3561515; Yitzhak Tiano, VHA, 4723; David Tchimino, VHA, 32833 and YVA, O.3/3740888; H. Simon,

years, or at least their view of those times. I made a discovery: all of them, as well as many others that I came across later (and who were not on the list but spent a short time in Feldafing), shared the same special story following their deportation from Salonika and transport to Auschwitz-Birkenau, a story that we— as with all stories connected to the concentration camps and the death marches—can only understand with the help of survivors' testimonies. As I followed their narratives, I noticed that their paths included specific stations:

1. Deportation from Salonika to Auschwitz (spring/summer 1943)
2. Transport to Warsaw and forced labor in the ruins of the ghetto (August to November 1943)
3. Evacuation from Warsaw and death march to Dachau (July 1944)
4. Forced labor in Mühldorf, a subcamp of Dachau
5. Evacuation of the camp by train in the direction of the Alps
6. Liberation by the Americans (April 30, 1945)
7. DP camp at Feldafing (May 1, 1945)
8. Emigration

The protagonists of this story are men from Salonika. More than two-thirds were between the ages of eighteen and thirty in 1946, that is, they were fifteen to twenty-seven years old when they were deported to Auschwitz, which is consistent with the data we possess concerning the demographic profile of DPs.[2] Their socioeconomic position seems to reflect the diverse structure of the Jewish population of Salonika in the prewar period: we find children of wealthy families (the father of one was the director of a tobacco factory, the father of another the owner of a paper-bag

HVT, 218; Solomon Hagouel in Kounio-Amarilio and Nar, *Oral Testimonies*, pp. 396–410.

2   According to a report by the JDC regarding Bavaria, the ratio of men to women at the start of 1946 was 2:1, and 81% of survivors were between eighteen and thirty-nine years old. See Lavsky, *New Beginnings*, pp. 31–32.

factory), middle-class families (prosperous merchants, one's father was a pharmacist, another a wool exporter and importer), alongside many who lived in the city slums and came from working-class families or whose fathers were simple craftsmen.

All these people were deported from Salonika to Auschwitz I and Auschwitz II-Birkenau between March and August 1943, together with more than 40,000 other Jews from the city.[3] They represent the few Jews who were not immediately taken to the gas chambers. These Greeks, along with some 3,680 other Jews from Auschwitz (Belgians, French, and Dutch), were transported to Warsaw in four transports between August and the end of November 1943, tasked with clearing the ruins of the ghetto following the uprising that had taken place in April.[4] A previous transport to Warsaw had arrived from Buchenwald in July 1943, including 300 non-Jewish political prisoners. Most were Communists, but there were also a few homosexuals. The latter built the camp (erected on the ruins of the ghetto) in which those arriving in Warsaw on the subsequent transports from Auschwitz were then accommodated. The first transport, with 503 Jews, of which 500 were Greeks and 3 were Poles, left Auschwitz on August 31, 1943. This was followed by three more transports on October 7 and 8 (with 1,151 and 1,032 prisoners respectively) and the last on November 27 (with about 1,000 prisoners).[5]

---

3 According to a document compiled by the Jewish Community of Salonika dated July 4, 1945, in a response to a request by the Red Cross for information about the number of deportees, 42,300 Jews were deported from Salonika (Documents I, 1944–1945, HAJCTh, 00159). According to German archival sources, nineteen transports with a total of 48,533 Jews from Salonika arrived in Auschwitz between March 20, 1943, and August 18, 1943. See Czech, *Auschwitz Chronicle*.

4 Jewish resistance in Warsaw was not organized until 300,000 people had been deported or murdered and only 55,000–60,000 Jews remained in the ghetto, facing certain deportation. The initial successes of the resistance, which had virtually no resources, led to the temporary suspension of the deportations. The Germans had estimated three days for the dissolution of the ghetto, but the resistance lasted for over a month. See Israel Gutman, *Resistance: The Warsaw Ghetto Uprising* (New York: Houghton Mifflin, 1994).

5 Czech, *Auschwitz Chronicle*. On the transport of August 31, see p. 475, on the transports of October 7 and 8, pp. 501– 502, and on the transport of November 27, p. 535. I thank Johannes Houwink ten Cate, who confirmed my own research

The journey in cattle cars must have taken about two days. Unsurprisingly, the witnesses do not remember the exact dates and the numbers of those transported with them. Salvator Saporta recalled that he was transported to Warsaw along with 300 other Greeks; Irvig Senor with another 350; and Nissim Almalech reported that his transport took place in August or September and that there were about 500 Jews from Greece on the train. Dario Angel remembered that he, like others, did not touch the piece of bread he had been given for the journey so as not to break the fast of Yom Kippur. Most of them thought that the Greeks had been chosen for Warsaw because they knew no Polish and therefore were unlikely to be able to escape. However, as was customary given the camp conditions, where one was sent was always a matter of chance.

In 1943, Daniel Yechiel was nineteen years old and lived with his family in the slums of the Baron Hirsch neighborhood, which the Germans had converted into a ghetto and transit center for all transports to the camps. Daniel was deported to Auschwitz with the first transport, which left Salonika on March 15, 1943. Together with others, he worked in the Kanada *kommando* in Auschwitz-Birkenau, where he sorted through the belongings of the prisoners, their clothes and possessions, as soon as they arrived at the camp. He said that he voluntarily signed up for labor in Warsaw because he knew about the selections awaiting the prisoners, which ended with death in the gas chambers. Yakov Sides wanted to escape work in the crematoria of Birkenau. One day they were told that 500 Greeks were to be taken to Warsaw. They did not know the kind of work they would be given, but Yakov was also chosen. Upon his arrival in Auschwitz-Birkenau, fifteen-year-old Eli Benyakar was separated from his brother, who ended up in the Buna camp (Auschwitz III-Monowitz). Eli was thus alone in Birkenau, but he was saved from selection in August by the Block Elder, who told him: "Get lost, go to Warsaw, there are no gas chambers there." Within forty-eight hours they were taken from Birkenau to

concerning the Greeks in Warsaw and gave me comparable information about the approximately 1,000 Dutch Jews, as well as the 1,000–2,000 Hungarians, who were also brought to Warsaw.

Auschwitz, where they received civilian clothes marked with a red stripe and wooden shoes that discouraged any thought of escape, even though the camp in Warsaw was not surrounded by electric fences. The nineteenth transport from Salonika to Auschwitz on August 10 included 1,800 Jews who had been drafted into forced labor at the end of March. Those who were not immediately sent to the gas chambers were taken to Warsaw.[6] In total, about 1,000 Greek Jews were transported to Warsaw.

In prewar Warsaw, a Polish military prison was located at 24 Gęsia Street (the Pawiak prison). In 1939, under the German occupation, this prison was converted into a labor and education camp run by the German Security Police and in 1943 into a concentration camp for prisoners from other regions. Although only ruins remained, the camp was equipped with a crematorium; however, it was no longer functioning by the time the Greeks arrived. In Warsaw, Alfred Naar encountered a bombed-out landscape; he describes the property in Gęsia Street that he guarded, which was surrounded by a wall. Inside were two or three buildings, and further inside were five large barracks in which three-tiered beds had been set up.

In Warsaw, the prisoners received new numbers that differed from their Auschwitz numbers. Aaron Dassa was given the number 1,770. The Greeks initially worked building a camp near the cemetery, close to the Pawiak prison. The first batch of workers, including Eli Benyakar and Yakov Levi, slept in the open air until they had set up the barracks that would serve as their lodgings. The Greeks were housed in Blocks 2 and 3.[7] Across from them they could see the destroyed buildings, but at that point they knew nothing about what had happened there. They learned only later about the ghetto uprising, as Yakov Levi recalled. He himself only found out about the uprising when some Jews of Polish descent arrived from France and, in discussion with Poles, were informed about what had happened. In the sewers the Germans were still

6 Bowman, *The Agony*, pp. 91–92.
7 Concerning conditions in the work camps see also: Browning's chapter "Survivor Testimonies from Starachowice: Writing the History of a Factory Slave Labor Camp," in *Collected Memories*, pp. 27–59.

looking for Jews and killing them, reported Yakov Sides. One day, Alfred Naar discovered a boy and a sick girl hiding underground. When he returned to the spot the next day to bring them some food, the boy had disappeared, and the girl was dead.

Work in Warsaw included collecting all the objects found on corpses and in the ruins, clearing the ruins, and collecting metal, wood, and bricks to be used as building materials by the Germans. The materials were transported by cart by Poles. The working conditions were intolerable. One of the first and most shocking testimonies regarding forced labor in Warsaw was given by David Lea, who was interviewed by David Boder a few months after liberation in August 1946 at the JDC offices in Paris.[8] First in broken German and later in fluent Judeo-Spanish, David, the only member of his family to survive—he lost thirty-seven relatives in the crematoria—explained how he was brought to Warsaw on Yom Kippur 1943 and worked as a "young and healthy man" in the ruins of the city, "with hoe and spade…without food and with only 150 grams of bread a day, at noon 1 liter of water…forty hours of work."

The working conditions were deplorable, and the food was never enough to satisfy the prisoners' hunger. Eli Benyakar thought himself lucky because he said he was a baker: consequently, he did not have to work in the cold but was assigned the task of cleaning potatoes in the kitchen. The same applied to Peppo Salem and Aaron Dassa. Yitzhak Tiano weighed 29 kilos when he arrived in

---

8   David P. Boder was a psychologist at the Illinois Institute of Technology in Chicago. We are indebted to him for the first tape recordings of survivors' testimonies and an archive comprising 120 interviews with a total length of 200 hours. David P. Boder, *Topical Autobiographies of Displaced Persons: Recorded Verbatim in DP Camps with a Psychological and Anthropological Analysis* (Los Angeles, D. Boder, 1957). "David P. Boder Interviews David Lea, August 12, 1946, Paris, France," Voices of the Holocaust, https://voices.library. iit.edu/interview/leaD?search_api_fulltext=david%20lea (accessed September 12, 2021). Lea returned from Warsaw to Auschwitz, where he worked in the *Sonderkommando* from the summer of 1944 until the liberation of the camp in January 1945. We encounter him again when, now working for the JDC in Paris, in August 1946 he exchanged letters with the community of Salonika to find out what had become of his houses in Mavili Street (HAJCTh, folders 00195: 00644 and 00645).

Warsaw. "We were all skeletons,"[9] he reported. Nissim Almalech believed that he managed to survive because he was able to steal from the kitchen: "The squeamish did not survive. The rich from Greece did not survive." Daniel Yechiel was caught pilfering some potatoes from the kitchen; he was saved only thanks to the help of his comrades: "We were a close group of Greeks and cared for each other." On Sunday afternoons they sang for the Germans and secured themselves an extra ration of bread. They played Greek songs or tunes that the Germans knew, like "*Mama so tanto felice…*"

However, the surest way to get some food was naturally to get things from the Poles on the black market, exchanging coins or objects that they had found in the rubble for something to eat. After describing how they gave the Poles everything they found in the ruins—a piece of wood, a gold tooth—in exchange for a little food, Moshe Pessah added that one day he had the good luck to discover several jars of jam: "We had a veritable market." And he concluded: "Man gets used to anything, the eyes get used to… man is garbage." He also remembered how he warmed himself by wrapping himself in the cover of a *Sefer Torah* that he found in the ruins. Alfred Naar was likewise lucky: he found a box of jewelry in the rubble. He traded it for zlotys, which he then used to buy bread, vodka, and salami. He shared his booty after a dream in which his father had appeared to him, saying: "I brought you bread to give to your brother as well." Daniel Yechiel remembers that the Jews from Hungary were even weaker on arrival.[10]

9 The term *Muselmann*, Primo Levi writes in *If This Is a Man*, was used by veteran camp inmates to describe the extremely weak who were destined for "selection" and death in the gas chambers, see "The Drowned and the Saved," *If This Is a Man* (London: Penguin Books, 1988), pp. 93–106.

10 Not only the Greeks but also other groups experienced the Warsaw camp and the march to Dachau. Between 1,000 and 2,000 Hungarian Jews arrived in Warsaw after the Greeks. One of those who came from Munkács (Mukačevo), then part of Hungary, was in Auschwitz (in May 1944) for only eight days before being brought to Warsaw. He describes the hunger in Warsaw, the thirst during the five-day march, and the last stop of the transport to Landsberg in unbearably full wagons, in each of which thirty to thirty-five people died. See S. N. testimony, born 1927, http://degob.org/index.php?showjk=2 (accessed June 20, 2014).

Even when the news arrived that the Russians were approaching and the prisoners had the opportunity to escape, they knew that they would not get far without being able to speak Polish, recalled Yakov Sides. Nevertheless, some attempted to escape and contact the partisans. A handsome boy named Saul, the brother of Irving Senor, went with the Germans to deliver the laundry for washing. A young Polish woman fell in love with him, and the partisans wanted to help him escape. However, a soldier shot and arrested him. As soon as the young man had recovered from his injury, he was hanged to deter further attempts at escape.[11] Alfred Naar took aside his brother (Isaac or Irving), who was about to faint at the sight, and poured some water over his face. Two other Greek Jews were luckier:[12] In the spring of 1944, Gabi Benozilio escaped, together with a Frenchman named Weinstein and a man from Salonika named Matalon. For weeks he wandered around in Poland, hiding with a Polish family, but was betrayed and brought back to Auschwitz. There, fate smiled on him again: while awaiting trial and certain execution, he managed to get hold of the civilian attire of a political prisoner and in this manner was able to survive. Together with his cousin Baruch Almaliah, Moshe Benozilio escaped through the sewers and later met up with Polish partisans.

Even though in Warsaw there were no selections, meaning the weeding out of the weakest to take them directly to the gas chambers, prisoners died in their hundreds from typhus. According to Henry Levi, 450 Greeks were diagnosed with typhoid fever.[13] In total, between 1,000 and 1,300 prisoners died from a three-month long typhoid fever epidemic that broke out in Warsaw. Many tried to hide their illness and avoid the hospital barrack because they

---

11 In his recently published memoir, *I Did Not Want to Die: From Norway to Auschwitz* (Jerusalem: Yad Vashem, 2021), pp. 160-161, Robert Savosnick recounts the story of Saul Senor. I want to thank Rebecca Wolpe for bringing this to my attention.

12 Yitzhak Kerem, "New Findings on Greek Jewish Heroism in the Holocaust," *Sephardic Horizons*, https://www.sephardichorizons.org/Volume2/Issue2/kerem.html (accessed September 23, 2020).

13 Johannes Houwink ten Cate, who studied the Dutch Jews in Warsaw, estimates that 1,000 to 1,300 of them died of typhoid fever, meaning that about ten people died daily in an epidemic that lasted for three months. The associated fall in productivity may explain why the Hungarian Jews were brought to Warsaw.

knew that the Germans would execute them rather than take pity on them. Yakov Levi managed to leave the infirmary. Two weeks later, when the Russians were only 40 kilometers away, the Germans killed about 300 sick prisoners and began preparing for the evacuation of the Warsaw camp.

On July 27, the Germans gathered the prisoners on the square. "Those who cannot walk should step out of line," they announced. Nobody stepped forward. "They knew the trick," remembered Yakov Sides. Maurice Moshe recounted the episode somewhat differently in his book dedicated to Salonika, which was published two decades later in Tel Aviv. He talks of a certain "interpreter who acted as a savior."[14] They lined the prisoners up on the square and ordered them to lie down on the ground as soon as the partisans appeared. They also announced that they would start a march: during the day they would march and at night they would stop. If anyone felt too weak, they should step forward, and they would then be transported by car. The interpreter, a fellow prisoner by the name of Raul Leon, who was "pious, educated, intelligent, and diplomatic," did not translate the commands of the Germans literally but rather according to his own understanding: "*Ermános* [Spanish for "Brothers"], *móko* ["Shut up!"], don't move!" The German officer waited for two minutes, and when he saw that no one was coming forward, he exclaimed, "Bravo! You are all well." Everyone answered, "Yes indeed!" Then a Jewish-Hungarian doctor translated the commands word by word. "Maybe he was scared, maybe he had not understood...Who knows?" As soon as he stopped talking, a group of Hungarians stepped forward and the Germans lined them up and executed them. On that day, 180 prisoners were executed.

The Germans evacuated the Jews from the camp in Warsaw. About 300 prisoners were left to clean the camp and the barracks and collect the corpses. On August 1, the Polish partisan revolt broke out. On the fifth day of the uprising, the prisoners in

14 Baruch Uziel and David Benveniste, eds., *Saloniki: Ir Va'em Be'Israel* (Hebrew) (Jerusalem and Tel Aviv: Institute for the Research of Salonikan Jewry, 1967), pp. 311–312.

Gęsia Street were freed, among them 348 Jews—Polish, Greek, Hungarians, Czech, Romanian, and others. Despite their exhaustion, they joined the partisans.[15] Among them were seventeen Greeks, including the brothers Alberto and Dario Levi.[16] In 1959, another Jew from Salonika, Isaac Aruch, who had remained in Warsaw, remembered the uprising: "In August 1944, a real uprising broke out in our camp. We fought in Starowka— the old town—and in the streets...Unfortunately, we did not have enough weapons. We were sent to very dangerous points. Most were killed in the unequal fight. After our defeat, I reached a bunker with my two friends, David Cohen and Isaak Moshe, and a few other Jewish and Polish fighters, where we remained until liberation."[17]

Yakov Sarfati met the partisans in the summer of 1944. He stayed with them for some time and then came to a village where, until his liberation by the Soviets, he pretended to be mute because he could not speak Polish. Six more Greeks (Baruch Almaliah, Sam and Yakov Arditi, Joseph Nahmias, and Yakov Mallah) left Warsaw, circumvented the German checkpoints, and fled to the forests.[18] In September 1944, Abraham Giladi escaped from the city through the sewer system, crossed the frozen Vistula, and managed to reach the Russian positions.[19]

As the Red Army advanced at the end of July 1944, the Warsaw prisoners were driven in a grueling march toward the German border. The march lasted three days. More than anything else, the survivors remembered their terrible thirst. They scratched

---

15 Gunnar S. Paulsson, *Secret City: The Hidden Jews of Warsaw, 1940-1945* (New Haven: Yale University Press, 2002), p. 184.

16 Refael, *Benetivei She'ol*, pp. 261–276.

17 Novitch, *Le Passage des Barbares*, pp. 18–25. The title is inspired by an interview in which Isaac Aruch told Novitch, right after describing how the Soviets liberated him in a bunker, "I have never returned to Salonika, where everything speaks to me of the passage of the barbarians and of our great grief." See the story of Isaac Aruch in Andreas Kedros, *The Greek Resistance, 1940-1944* (Greek), vol. 2 (Athens: Themelio, 1983), p. 39.

18 Edward Kossoy, "The Gęsiówka Story: A Little Known Page of Jewish Fighting History," *Yad Vashem Studies*, 32 (2004), pp. 323–350.

19 Kerem, "New Findings."

the earth for a drop of water. Henry (Erikos) Levi recalled that Poles spat at them or threw stones, while the German soldiers shot anyone who collapsed from exhaustion and could no longer get up. Aaron Dassa recalled how a Greek boy, who answered to the name Aboav, tried to hide. The Germans' dogs tracked him down and the soldiers executed him. When a few of the thirsty fell into the Vistula and held up the march, the Germans opened fire, and the victims' blood colored the water red. The salty meat, the only food they were given, made them even thirstier. Near the border, a train bound for Dachau awaited them; eighty men were squeezed into each wagon.

In August 1944, they were in Dachau, not far from Munich.[20] The showers did not frighten them. "Who was still alive?" Dario Angel said to himself. They were given civilian clothes with a red stripe on the back. Some, like Erikos Levi and Jacques Mordoki, spent only a few days in Dachau, others a few weeks, including Salvator Saporta and Yitzhak Cohen. Later they were divided into the nearby satellite and subcamps of Dachau: Mühldorf with its own subcamps, Waldlager, Kaufering, Landsberg, and Allach. All these camps had been built when the German arms industry required secure production facilities. Near the first factories, a complex of hundreds of satellite camps was built in 1944–1945. For example, the Luftwaffe aircraft factories, which initially employed the elite of the German workforce, were converted into forced labor camps.[21]

In these camps, the Jews were given the most difficult and

---

20   In this context, the testimony of Iosif Karasso, given in the postwar trial of Vital Hasson, Jacques Albala, and others is also relevant. Karasso left Salonika on the transport of August 7/8, 1943. He remained in Auschwitz for fifteen days before being transferred to Warsaw. He made the following statement: "[I arrived there with] about 500 Greek Jews to salvage the bricks from the ghetto and clean the place. From September 1 to January, my two brothers died of untold torments, hunger, and hardships...In addition, the activities of the Polish partisans had increased, and the Germans took us to Dachau, where we were detained for several days in labor camps. Our job was to haul huge tree trunks, and when we resisted, they beat us. Every night four or five died of the agony and hard work." Trial of the Traitors, July 1946, HAJCTh, folder 00190.1: 00002-00340.

21   See Daniel Uziel, *Arming the Luftwaffe: The German Aviation Industry in World War II* (Jefferson: MacFarland, 2012), esp. pp. 194–235.

dangerous jobs, such as hauling cement (they often almost fell into the cement) and construction work. Since 1942, the German armament industry warehouses had been strategic targets of Allied air raids. Moreover, starting in September 1944, in addition to the exhausting work, survival became even harder due to the chaotic communication and the distribution of food through a ration card system. In any case, production continued until the last months of the war. In 1944, these camps resembled the Tower of Babel: Russian prisoners of war encountered Jews, men and women alike, workers from Belgium, France, and Italy. Although the armaments industry was under strict SS supervision and constituted part of the camp system, the prisoners had somewhat greater chances of survival there.

There were also some Greek Jews in these camps who had not come from Warsaw. From mid-1944, an increasing number of Jews were sent to the war industry camps because more and more workers were needed for construction and in the underground factories. Depending on the need for labor, the prisoners were transported from one camp to another. Alfred Naar was initially sent to Munich to repair damage to the road caused by bombardments, and he was later taken from Dachau to Mühldorf, where he worked together with Hungarian Jews. From there he was transported to Mühlhofen and then back to Mühldorf. There was an aircraft factory with underground facilities near an air force base. Some prisoners even believed it was a facility for manufacturing a nuclear bomb!

Salvator Saporta and Marko Chanoka have never forgotten the Christmas they spent in Mühldorf in 1944, when they received bread in exchange for singing Greek carols to the German officers. To demonstrate how pleased they were with the Greeks' songs, the following day the Germans assigned them work in a particularly favorable place, outside the camp, Dario Angel relates. The other prisoners, however, regarded the Greeks as thieves. Their memories are always connected to the search for anything that would satisfy their hunger and help to keep them upright.

In Mühldorf, Moshe Pessah, having learned that one needed a vocation in order to survive, claimed to be an electrician and thus got more food. An elderly German officer, who had a son on the front, kept a protective eye on him. Yakov Sides, who worked in a factory in Mühldorf, was also an electrician. When an electrician was needed in Landsberg, he installed a lamp in each barrack for an officer who gave him something to eat. Eli Benyakar was sent to the Waldlager camp in the Mühldorf camp complex, which was also underground. The work there was tough; he hauled cement. Yet he too was lucky. His friend Zakinos fell ill, and although they were friends, the Polish Kapo did not help him. Eli took over Zakinos' work. He even managed to steal some soup and distribute it to other Greeks. Finally, a Greek Kapo noticed and helped him: he brought Zakinos to the Red Cross, and thus he survived. When the Allied planes bombed a sugar factory, sugar was scattered everywhere! "We ate until we got sick," Erikos Levi recalled.

At the end of April 1945, the noise of gunfire and the Allied bombers was heard for days. Some Greek Jews from the Warsaw group were released. On May 2, Isaak Senor saw an American tank at the camp gate. Leon Benmayor and Leo Mallah had not been in Warsaw but in Auschwitz and various labor camps. In April 1945, they were in Dachau, and on April 25 they were loaded onto a train that constantly changed direction. One evening, Leo Mallah recalled, they were forced to disembark into the snow outside. It was chilly, and three or four of them decided to stay awake all night and talk, so as not to be overwhelmed by sleep and thus freeze to death. Only 200 people survived that night. They were in Mittenwald when a German officer told them that the war was over. "Where should we go? We did not know where we were... We started to run. We were starving...A soldier on a bicycle came to us and said, 'You are going in the wrong direction...Run and hide.'" They spent the night in a barrack. The next day was May 1: they heard the noise of tanks and saw the American flag...

Given the lack of raw materials, production in the camp factories had stopped in the previous weeks. Nevertheless, the massive evacuation of the labor camps did not begin until the Allies had penetrated the heart of the Third Reich. The SS ordered the evacuation of about 3,600 prisoners from Mühldorf. Many of the Greek Jews who had previously been imprisoned in Warsaw now boarded a train for 2,500 to 3,000 passengers; its destination was unknown. "They were planning to kill us in some place where German citizens would not see what was happening," Salvator Saporta said. "There was a rumor that the destination was the Tyrol," Nissim Almalech recalled.

With the Allies bombarding them, the prisoners fastened a striped prisoner's uniform to the roof of the train as a signal for the pilot. While still being bombed by American planes, on April 27, the train stopped at the small station of Poing, 18 kilometers from Munich. An officer (according to Yitzhak Tiano) or the stationmaster (according to Nissim Almalech) told them, "You are free!" The SS soldiers were gone. The prisoners left the train and started running madly in the direction of the fields and the city to look for something to eat. However, soon air force soldiers returned to restore "order." They opened fire on the prisoners and forced them back on the train. There were 402 dead, including two Greeks. One of them was Nissim Almalech's brother. They collected the dead and put them in two wagons, but no one knows where they are buried.

Maurice Moshe wrote about the same incident after the war:

> I was with Salvator Moshe, who now lives in America, and the daughters of Rabbi Mordechai Saias, who today also live in Israel. We flung ourselves to the ground to avoid being hit and approached the train. I helped them climb into it. When it was my turn, I heard a noise behind me. I turned and saw an SS man ready to shoot me. Then a miracle occurred: a Wehrmacht officer told him not to shoot, and he told me to get on the train."[22]

The train made its way to Munich, but it never arrived. On April 28, the train, with its 2,000 prisoners, stopped on a hill southwest of Munich, at Tutzing. This time everyone was afraid to leave the train, even after they understood that the German guards had long since fled.

---

22 Maurice Mosse, "Episodes in the Camp," in Uziel and Benveniste, *Saloniki: Ir Va'em be'Israel*, p. 312.

While the train stood motionless, a group of Polish Jews who had been interned in the Kaufering camp met for a meeting that Zeev Mankowitz considered the founding act of *She'erit Hapletah*. Among them were those who would become the leaders of the DPs in Germany: Samuel Gringauz and Zalman Grinberg. The latter, a doctor, hurried to the next village to seek help for the injured. Two days later they saw in the distance armored vehicles with a white star—Americans. The American army freed the prisoners on April 30 near Tutzing.

"The best day in our lives was when we saw the Americans coming," Eli Benyakar recalled.[23] Ernest Landau, a Viennese Jew on the same train, described the moment of liberation: "Then all of a sudden American officers and soldiers appeared. Forgotten were hunger, exhaustion and despair...The American soldiers were thronged, embraced, kissed, and hoisted on people's shoulders."[24] The Greek Jews spoke Spanish with some American soldiers. The Americans offered them food: chocolate and jam in abundance, which were eaten on the spot and caused dysentery among the starving group. "You can go anywhere you want, but kill no one," the Americans said.

Together with seventeen other Greeks, Yitzhak Tiano went to a house where he found food and clothes. The German residents of the area put bowls of soup in front of their houses so that the former prisoners would not enter their homes. According to Daniel Yechiel, this prevented neither theft nor acts of revenge. The wounded were taken to the nearby monastery of St. Ottilien, where, under the direction of Dr. Zalman Grinberg, a hospital was set up for the survivors.

Just a few weeks later this doctor gave a shattering speech in German, which had become the common language of the

---

23 Robert Antelme describes in graphic detail the liberation of the camp, *L'espèce humaine* (Paris: Gallimard, 1957), pp. 269–306, as does Charlotte Delbo, *Auschwitz et après II: Une connaissance inutile* (Paris: Editions de Minuit, 1970), p. 174.

24 Angelika Königseder and Juliane Wetzel, *Waiting for Hope: Jewish Displaced Persons in Post-World War II Germany* (Evanston: Northwestern University Press, 2001), p. 11f.

survivors. He wondered at the logic of the fate that had left them alive while millions of others had been wiped out, exclaiming,

> We belong in the common graves of those shot in Kharkov, Lublin, and Kovno. We belong to the millions gassed and burnt in Auschwitz and Birkenau; we belong to the tens of thousands who died under the strain of the hardest labor; we belong to those tormented by milliards of lice, the mud, starvation, the cold of Lodz, Kielce, Buchenwald, Dachau, Landshut, Utting, Kaufering, Landsberg and Leonsberg...We are not alive—we are dead...We are free now, but we do not know how or with what, to begin our free yet unfortunate lives."[25]

At the same place, in St. Ottilien, three months later, on July 25, the first meeting of the surviving Jews in Germany was held.

On May 1, 1945, all those who were not wounded were taken by American Commander Smith to Feldafing, near Munich. In July 1945, 14,000–15,000 Jews lived in Bavaria; in the course of 1946, the Jewish population quadrupled,[26] and by the end of 1947 about 78,400 Jews lived in the greater Munich area, of which two-thirds lived in DP camps (Landsberg, Feldafing, Föhrenwald) and a third in private homes.[27]

25 Grinberg's speech can be found in Robert H. Hilliard, *Surviving the Americans: The Continued Struggle of Jews after Liberation* (New York: Seven Stories Press, 1997), pp. 11–22.
26 Kolinski, *After the Holocaust*, pp. 131–132.
27 Holian, "The Ambivalent Exception," p. 6.

CHAPTER 7

In Bavaria: The Search for Kinsmen, Food, Weddings, and the Black Market

F eldafing is a picturesque little town 15 kilometers from Munich. In 1945, it housed a Hitler Youth academy made up of seven two-story buildings, a dozen temporary structures, and six or seven large villas. The core inhabitants of Feldafing included the survivors from the aforementioned train.

Erikos Levi was ill for eight days after trying to satisfy his hunger in one fell swoop. At that time, he weighed 35 kilos. Of those who had been in Warsaw, 386 survived, he recalled. "Feldafing is on the shores of a lake, it's beautiful, almost paradisiacal... carpets, chandeliers, pianos, fabulous food," Nissim Almalech explained fifty years later. In the villas they found clothes, they went swimming in the lake. The former prisoners were housed in twin rooms, in buildings separated by nationality. They finally slept in beds again and wore regular shoes.[1] Sam Moshe found an accordion. They formed a band that played every afternoon. Alfred Naar remembered that they took down curtains and gave them to women who knew how to sew: thus, all the women got to wear beautiful clothes.

---

1   In *Night* (first published 1958), Elie Wiesel describes the moment when he first looked at himself in the mirror: "I had not seen myself since the ghetto. From the depths of the mirror, a corpse was contemplating me." Elie Wiesel, *Night* (New York: Hill and Wang, 2006), pp. 199–200.

The military administration, but also the aid organizations, or, in short, all those who were responsible for the management of the refugee problem, produced numerous documents containing information about the world of the DPs from the perspective of the military or humanitarian bureaucracy. Rarely did the displaced people keep diaries themselves or record their feelings: at that time, their main concern was physical recovery and finding their relatives.

In May 1945, American soldier and journalist Robert H. Hilliard traveled around the Munich region.[2] On streets surrounding the city he met survivors: skeletons in striped uniforms, wandering around, their feet wrapped in rags or barefoot, in search of food and a place to sleep that was safe from the Germans, who often seemed to be just waiting to bring Hitler's Final Solution to a conclusion. He also noted that those who participated in the Nazi crimes were the first to deny everything. Those who were not Jews but simply workers at least had a home to which they could return.

At first, Hilliard encountered small groups of refugees, but over time these groups grew larger and larger, seeming to come from everywhere and go everywhere. They were omnipresent on the streets outside the cities, carrying their belongings in a worn suitcase, in a cardboard box wrapped in twine, or in a piece of cloth, its four corners knotted at the end of a stick. Some pushed a packed stroller or baskets to which they had attached wheels. Others had absolutely nothing. Some pulled a piece of bread out of their trouser pockets and chewed it while they were walking. Anyone with a DP identification card could make a stop in the cities, where there might be some office that would give them a portion of food. They would put the food in their pockets or in a paper bag to eat when they were back on the road…

For the military authorities, the DPs were a potentially dangerous mass. Having suffered terrible torments, they were considered a threat to public safety, order, and health. The military

---

2　Hilliard, *Surviving the Americans*, pp. 15–16 and 26ff.

did not treat the Jews among the displaced with much sympathy,[3] failing to understand that their experiences did not allow them to behave like the other DPs. The suffering and humiliation that they had suffered had created a huge gap between them and the rest of humanity. Unlike other exiles, they did not have families to help them, they were alone, quick-tempered, and disappointed. The DPs welcomed the protection and segregation offered by the camps but at the same time they demanded freedom of movement within the zones of occupation. These competing desires framed the emergence of **spaces of exception**, as Anna Holian describes the refugee camps in the territories officially regarded as Germany.[4]

Earl G. Harrison's famous report, presented to President Truman on July 20, 1945,[5] caused a considerable stir after its publication in August. It sharply criticized how the military authorities dealt with the exiles, especially the Jews. The authorities, Harrison wrote, could not understand the passionate insistence of the Jews on finding family members; their desire to eat—and not just for calories; the catastrophic lack of sanitation that caused children to die of typhus; their need to live apart from others; the psychological problems caused by their traumatic experiences; their desire to be allowed to immigrate to Palestine; and more…From Salonika, Joseph Nehama[6] described matters in the same way:

> In the reception centers…they were treated like unwanted persons, like war criminals. The unruly and chaotic mass was regarded as a mishmash of outcasts,

3 Michael R. Marrus, *The Unwanted: European Refugees from the First World War through the Cold War* (New York and Oxford: Oxford University Press, 1985). See also thirty-four letters that the commandant of the Landsberg camp sent his wife in the US between September and December 1945, in Irving Heymont, *Among the Survivors of the Holocaust, 1945: The Landsberg DP Camp Letters of Major Irving Heymont* (Cincinnati: American Jewish Archives, 1982).
4 Holian, "The Ambivalent Exception," pp. 452–473.
5 Earl G. Harrison, *The Plight of the Jews in Europe: A Report to President Truman* (New York: Reprinted by the United Jewish Appeal, 1945).
6 The author of the second part of *In Memoriam* (revised edition, 1974), pp. 345–346.

outcasts whose destruction or death is of no great interest...The overseers of these camps, who had been tasked with their care, were soldiers who had waged wars and had difficulty distinguishing the Germans from their victims. In their minds, they confused the exiled and the defeated Nazis. Their language was cheeky and arrogant...They insisted on imposing an iron discipline on those thirsting for freedom...Some even reached the point of believing that the food distributed was an act of generosity, the gesture of rich people who were dipping into their own personal wealth.

The writer Tadeusz Borowski, who was liberated from Allach on May 1, 1945, wrote in a letter from Munich dated February 1946: "I am writing in a chaotic manner, but that's precisely how I live."[7] Then, some months later, on October 6, 1946, he explained in another letter to former a schoolmate:

> I'm writing this letter to you from Munich. But I didn't get from Auschwitz to Munich by the shortest route. I went through several camps, sometimes on foot, sometimes in open cattle wagons, unable to get much sleep and completely without eating. You probably haven't got the slightest idea how long a person can live without eating...Were it not for tremendous homesickness and uncertainty, life would be tolerable, pleasant even, there are wonderful books even in Germany...[8]

The DPs were almost exclusively preoccupied—in a compulsive way, one could say—with food. Yitzhak Cohen recalled that the Greeks in Feldafing had a habit of stealing. When 10,000 eggs disappeared, you could see Greeks making omelets everywhere! They walked around in pairs or threesomes, bought for three and stole for five; on trains they emptied out the contents of

---

7   Tadaeusz Borowski, *Postal Indiscretion: The Correspondence of T. Borowski* (Evanston: Northwestern University Press, 2007), p. 39.
8   Ibid.

Germans' suitcases and threw what they did not want out of the train. Abraham Mano told the same story: A few Greeks who had cleared out a food store were sent to another camp near Munich as punishment.

Of course, although the provision and distribution of food has a symbolic and ritual character, it also served a psychological and military function, too. For the US military authorities and for UNRRA, for the Jews as well as for the Germans, food was a way of making sense of issues of guilt, rights, and victimhood. Access to food stocks reflected to a certain extent the classification of groups or individuals into victims, perpetrators, and bystanders, and the corresponding conflicts focused on to what and how much each group was entitled. Indeed, for the survivors of Nazism, privileged food supplies were an urgent need and represented political recognition and some form of compensation. The Germans protested against this type of preference, even though they themselves had other sources of fresh food beyond the ration cards. For each survivor, UNRRA set the (generally unattainable) target of 2,500 to 2,650 calories, while the food cards for the Germans provided 2,000 calories, the same as for citizens in the liberated countries like France or Belgium.

After returning to Greece from Munich, a correspondent for *Evraiki Estia* reported on August 15, 1947: "The food that is distributed to displaced persons in Germany is constantly being reduced and now stands at 2,000 calories per day. There is a shortage of sugar and fat." As Atina Grossmann[9] remarked, "food politics" was part of the "arithmetic of standards" typical of the welfare state and humanitarian activism in the second half of the twentieth century. The prevailing language spoke of grams, fats, total daily calories, vitamins, coffee, and cigarettes. The calories separated the foods from their cultural weight, making the various foodstuffs comparable and interchangeable. The humanitarian aid organizations created registers of American cigarettes, canned meat, milk powder, jars of jam and sardine cans, bread, flour,

9 Atina Grossmann, "Grams, Calories, and Food: Languages of Victimization, Entitlement, and Human Rights in Occupied Germany, 1945–1949," *Central European History*, 44:1 (2011), pp. 118–148.

biscuits, coffee, chocolate etc. The IRO was preoccupied with statistical analysis, transforming refugees into abstract categories with no historical peculiarities. The black market was a way for the displaced to take affairs back into their own hands. They sought to break free of the role of the child into which they had inevitably been forced by their dependence on the distribution of food and on account of the authorities' inability to understand cultural and religious customs, Grossmann aptly noted.

* * *

In the first years after the war, the black market was one of the main engines of the economy. We are familiar with the figure of the "Greek" in Primo Levi's *The Truce*.[10] The narrator explains how, at the end of the war, together with a group of former prisoners and accompanied by the Soviet army, he wanders through Central Europe. He meets heroes, traitors, thieves, and intellectuals. Among them, the figure of the Greek stands out, a multilingual and omniscient Jew from Salonika. He is a jack-of-all-trades, probably once a merchant, now an expert in the art of the black market, which was essential for survival.

Reports on the black market and clashes with the German police are found in the archives of the American military administration.[11] The black market was a means of survival in Feldafing and one of its most important occupations. "There was no money at that time," says Dario Angel. "You put down a watch and got a bicycle." In the postwar world, the shortage of goods and uncertainties surrounding Allied policy, as well as the ration card system, turned the black market into a completely natural phenomenon. In 1945, when the Reichsmark no longer had any value, cigarettes were the best of all currencies.

Like other former prisoners, Salvator Moshe preferred to live in a house together with its German owners outside Feldafing,

---

10 Known in the US as the *Reawakening*. See Primo Levi, *The Truce* (London: Abacus, 1998).

11 Jay Howard Geller, *Jews in Post-Holocaust Germany, 1945–1953* (Cambridge: Cambridge University Press, 2005), p. 41.

in Waldheim.[12] Contact with Germans was quite typical of the survivors' everyday lives,[13] especially when they decided to live outside the camp for some time. Salvator brought food, and the owners of the house cooked for him. He made it clear that all this was done with ration cards, that it was impossible to buy anything in the shops without cards, be it shoes or groceries. Salvator walked a distance of 80 kilometers (trains barely functioned), introducing himself as a representative from Feldafing and in this way exchanging coffee, sugar, and cigarettes from the Red Cross for toothbrushes and toothpaste. Then he returned to Feldafing with his bag full and sold what he had bought for a small profit. On the black market, one dollar was worth 300 marks. Every week Salvator took the same route, accompanied by his brother-in-law, bringing diverse products to Feldafing, for example shoe polish. Once, his girlfriend, who usually helped him avoid the military police, failed to do so, and he ended up spending a night in prison for illegal activities.

Yitzhak Tiano also stayed in Waldheim for two years, during which time he came to Feldafing on and off as the needs of the black market dictated. He sold products that the Joint had procured for him and with the proceeds bought gold in Frankfurt. However, the roads were dangerous: police and military police patrols, but also bands of "free workers" who no longer had any work, made trips risky. This new way of managing one's vital needs explains why many deportees who had lost their entire families stayed in Germany and waited for an exit permit. When asked in 1995 why he stayed in Germany after he had been liberated and spent a year in the hospital, and what he did there, Shlomo Akounis replied, "Business." "Black market?" the interviewer asked. "No, white…" he replied, ironically.

For most DPs, black-market dealings were an absolute necessity. Indeed, Germans often refused to sell them food or

---

12 See the novel by Ghita Schwarz, *Displaced Persons: A Novel* (New York: William Morrow, 2010).

13 Atina Grossmann, "Entangled Histories and Lost Memories. Jewish Survivors in Occupied Germany, 1945–1949," in Patt and Berkowitz, *We Are Here*, pp. 14–30.

clothing. The Germans, who were also involved in the black market, regarded the Jews' business dealings as immoral. Reporting on his trip to Germany in the fall of 1948, Kurt Grossmann noted that the Jews were undoubtedly active on the black market, largely as a consequence of the chaotic economy, but that they did not amount to more than 3 percent of such "entrepreneurs." In the circumstances, he commented, even angels, and not just mere humans, would have participated in this kind of activity.[14] Grossmann also described the emerging antisemitism, commenting that relations in Bavaria and around Munich were very tense.

The Germans saw the black market as a means to torment them, invented by the Allies and displaced people. They did not want to admit that the illegal business was a consequence of the war they themselves had started, preferring to consider themselves victims of the occupying powers and the Jews.[15] The Jews, who never amounted to more than 10-20 percent of the total number of DPs, were no more active on the black market than any other group. Yet, even if the Germans avoided the use of openly racist language, they regarded the Jewish survivors as criminals or as individuals inclined to criminal activity. According to the questionnaires of the American military administration in 1946, 39 percent of the German population were strongly or moderately antisemitic and longed to bring annoying discussions about the past to an end. They ascribed to the displaced Jews all manner of historic stereotypes: criminals, Communists, privileged, powerful. They at once feared and despised them.[16]

The displaced Jews were well aware of the moral complexity of the problem and rationalized their involvement in an illegal but

---

14 Kurt Grossmann, *Report on Germany* (September 5, 1948), JDC Archives, NY-AR45-54-00029-00793.

15 Laura Hilton, "The Black Market in History and Memory: German Perceptions of Victimhood from 1945 to 1948," *German History*, 28:4 (2010), pp. 479–497.

16 Michael Berkowitz and Suzanne Brown-Fleming, "Perceptions of Jewish Displaced Persons as Criminals in Early Postwar Germany: Lingering Stereotypes and Self-fulfilling Prophecies," in Patt and Berkowitz, *We Are Here*, pp. 167–193; see also Wolfgang Benz, "Germans, Jews and Antisemitism in Germany after 1945," *Australian Journal of Politics and History*, 41:1 (1995), pp. 118–129.

common practice. In addition, many of them had already become familiar with the practices of the black market during the time of the German occupation, and they regarded it as a temporary means of survival. The war determined in its own way what was legal and what was not. We should not forget that many of them survived the Nazi camps only because of their lack of obedience, which enabled them to preserve their humanity. Tricking the authorities and disobedience had become a way of life. Moreover, the war had shown them that many law-abiding governments were unwilling, or simply unable, to protect their Jewish citizens, and even now the British authorities considered their attempts to migrate to Mandatory Palestine criminal. In short, it was difficult for the Jewish DPs to accept that their disobedience or participation in the black market was in any way reprehensible, and attentive observers noted that the Jews systematically refused to accept the restrictions imposed on them by the Allied powers.[17]

A historian who served in the US army and also worked hard to help the refugees noted in 1947:

> For the Jewish DPs the war has not yet ended, nor has liberation in the true sense really come as yet. Their problems still unsolved, their future not in their own hands, they still consider themselves at war with the world and the world at war with them, and they feel they must maintain a totalitarian conception of unity at all costs. In many ways they have become totalitarians. All cultural activity must have only one aim, to make propaganda for Palestine. The leaders do not trust open discussion of intellectual problems. They are cold and at times arrogantly indifferent to pleas for tolerance, intellectual freedom and the like.[18]

Why waste energy creating order in a camp that you want to leave

17 Ralph Segalman, "The Psychology of Jewish Displaced Persons," *Jewish Social Service Quarterly*, 23 (1947), p. 362.
18 Koppel S. Pinson, "Jewish Life in Liberated Germany: A Study of the Jewish DP's," *Jewish Social Studies*, 9:2 (1947), p. 114.

soon? Why work hard when until only recently hard work could cost you your life? Why obey when until yesterday obedience meant submission and there was no other option? Who had taken care of them until now? In a narrative from *This Way for the Gas Ladies and Gentlemen*, Tadeusz Borowski describes how survivors of the camps destroy everything they see because they are so furious.[19]

In the summer of 1945, the DP camps were characterized by apathy and disorder. Military and UNRRA officers tried to persuade the displaced people to maintain cleanliness and order. The psychological complexity of liberation manifested in a series of fast-changing sensations: insatiable hunger, overwhelming joy, the desire for revenge. Those responsible referred to them as suspicious, mythomaniac, lazy, lethargic, and apathetic. The survivors suffered from mental health problems: posttraumatic stress disorder. The authorities, however, did not even see the faces of the displaced persons, viewing the world of the camps only as statistics and calculations concerning vital calories and the need for medical care. No measures were taken to deal with mental and physical violence in an environment with a seldom friendly German population. The need for schooling and vocational training or sex education was ignored. Among the children and adolescents who spent their puberty in the camp, the experts discovered a maturity resulting from the struggle for survival, but they also noted extreme immaturity resulting from the loss of parents. After the end of the war, hundreds of thousands of orphans entered this stage, including tens of thousands of children of Jewish parents who had perished in the Nazi camps.

Alfred Naar recalled that in the first period after the liberation a "war" broke out between the Greeks and Ukrainian prisoners of war, who had molested some Greek women. To protect the honor of their women, the Greeks organized a dance evening in which they "put the violent Ukrainians in their place." The Americans, he said, considered them real heroes and rewarded them with gifts.

19 Tadeusz Borowski, *This Way for the Gas Ladies and Gentlemen* (London: Penguin Books, 1976).

Francesca Wilson, a British social worker who became acquainted with the Balkans during the war years, had been in the service of UNRRA since January 1945. Her description of the Greek Jews at Feldafing sheds light not only on what she saw but also on her own Orientalist outlook:

> Wherever I went I heard it said that the Greek Jews were to blame. They were the worst in the camp. There were less than three hundred of them, but they were worse than all the rest put together…the sergeant on guard said sadly, there had been three complete orchestras in the school, but the night that they had come in, the Greek Jews had rushed into the place and broken them all up… The Greeks were too lazy to pull the plugs and stuffed down all sorts of rags and waste …Other Greeks began crowding round me, talking to me in fluent French. Many of them were quite young men and, in spite of their hollow cheeks, not unhandsome. Their large sad, dark eyes made them look appealing and innocent, like half-tamed animals. They had all come from Salonika… They smiled at this and swore that it was the finest town in Greece. Some of them had had shops and cafés there, others were barbers and tailors, and some students. One had studied science for six months, another had just entered the university as a medical student. "Do you know Greece?" they asked. "Do you like Greeks?"…They liked the bit about being Sephardim—it was obvious that they felt superior to Yiddish Jews. "We don't speak Yiddish," they said proudly. "We speak Spanish, Greek, French, and Hebrew."…"Why did you break the musical instruments?" I asked. "Because they were German," they said. "We had to smash things when we were freed. Never mind, we can sing to you without instruments. We have the best choir in the camp…"[20]

20 Bowman, *The Agony*, pp. 223–226.

Amidst this chaos and the ruins of the war, love stories blossomed, and weddings took place. Many of the Greek survivors of Auschwitz, Warsaw, Mühldorf, and the death marches met their future spouses in Bavaria. These marriages were often "mixed marriages": for example, when a Jew from Salonika fell in love with a Jewish woman from Central or Eastern Europe. The files preserved in the JDC archives testify that in most cases the "mixed" couple did not return to Greece.[21]

Salvator Saporta met a Polish woman, married her, and stayed in Germany with her for several years. In 1946, in Landsberg, Yakov Levi met a woman from Czechoslovakia. They waited for a year until they managed to immigrate to Mandatory Palestine. Ovadia Cohen told his future wife about the medical experiments he had to endure. She agreed to marry him, and their daughter was born in Feldafing, where they remained for three years. Magda Altman came from Hungary. She met her husband Isaak Salum, from Salonika, in Feldafing and emigrated with him to America in 1950.[22]

Sam Moshe also married in Feldafing, under a *chuppah* (a canopy under which the bridal couple stand during the marriage service) and only after having signed the *ketubah* (the marriage contract) as befits a Jewish wedding. His eldest daughter was born in the camp. Isaac Senor met his wife three or four weeks after liberation. She was from Vilna. They lived in a small village, and scarcely a month had passed when they stumbled across the town hall. They married there on June 20, summoning two witnesses

21 In the JDC Archives (JDC Archives, Jewish Displaced Persons and Refugee Cards, 1943–1959) I found forty-five identity cards (index cards) of Jews from Salonika. These are "family papers" in which the spouse or brothers are identified as escorts; they were issued as identity cards for persons who had registered with the JDC's Department of Migration in the Munich area or in Austria because they wished to travel to Mandatory Palestine. The date, their profession, and their desired destination were recorded. Many of them, such as Shlomo Akounis, Marko Chanoka, or Abraham Mano, eventually immigrated to Israel.

22 For their testimony, see Magda Altman Schaloum, Seattle Stories, Jewish Women's Archive, https://jwa.org/communitystories/seattle/narrators/schaloum-magda-altman (accessed June 20, 2014); Magda Schaloum, Survivors Voices, Holocaust Center for Humanity, https://www.holocaustcenterseattle.org/survivor-voices/magda-schaloum (accessed September 12, 2021).

and receiving a small document as a certificate. When they learned about Feldafing, they moved there. Their eldest daughter was also born there.[23]

Nissim Almalech regained his strength when he met Bella. She had beautiful big eyes that enchanted him. "Are we going to dance tonight?" he suggested. She was his first girlfriend. Because he did not speak Yiddish, many thought that he was not Jewish. To Bella's delight, Nissim found a school where she could study graphics; he even rented a room for her in Munich with the money he had earned on the black market, while at the same time working for the camp police. Bella received a visa for America and waited for him in New York.

Salvator Moshe's girlfriend, who had gone to Mandatory Palestine before him, did not wait for him, instead marrying another man. The archives of the Jewish community of Salonika contain a handwritten *ketubah*, signed in Feldafing on August 5, 1945,[24] which testifies to the marriage of Moses Allalouf of Salonika and Esther Mendelson of Romania. Shortly thereafter, the couple arrived in Salonika. There, the marriage was confirmed on September 18 by Rabbi Michael Molho. The couple later went to Canada.

There were many marriages and weddings in the world of the DPs, some of them quite strange. As is known, fewer women than men survived the Nazi camps,[25] and most of them were between the ages of sixteen and forty. Two out of three DPs were male. Reports by UNRRA or the JDC rarely dealt specifically with women's issues, and, of course, women were also underrepresented in the committees of the DPs.[26] Nevertheless, women in the DP

23 As their daughter (Lyne Farbman, a psychologist, lives in Maryland) told me by phone in November 2013.

24 Marriages, HAJCTh, folder 00774: 00353–00354 (August 5, 1945).

25 At the first selection in the extermination camps, the "incapacitated"—women, old people, and children—were selected for immediate murder. While the Nazis did not regard women as unfit for hard labor, they did not want to separate them from the children, because this would "distract" them from their work. The chances of women surviving were extremely low.

26 Judith Tydor Baumel, "DPs, Mothers and Pioneers: Women in the She'erit Hapletah," *Jewish History*, 11:2 (1997), 99–110.

camps showed enormous emotional and physical strength; they gave birth to children, studied, and were also politically active.[27] Traumatized girls met partners as young as them, or others who had lost their children, people who had spent the war years in hiding or had survived in the vicinity of the crematoria. All of them felt a strong desire to marry, to overcome their loneliness, and to return to "normal life."

Marriages soon ensued and motherhood followed, with anticipation and sometimes anxiety. In the spring of 1946, one in three women was either pregnant or pushing a stroller.[28] A baby boom was regularly mentioned in documentation of the American Jewish philanthropic organizations in 1945 and 1946. In 1948, the birth rate among DPs was twice as high as that in the USA.[29] Beyond the need to look for any psychoanalytic explanation, Grossmann points out[30] that these weddings, marriages, and births were a conscious and ideological statement. These people, happy to be photographed pushing their strollers, declared their presence to the world. This statement also implies a kind of symbolic revenge, a revival of the dead, and a possible end to the past that so haunted the victims. Women were determined to assert their reproductive role, to proclaim their fertility, to confirm that they had survived. Childbirth was a way of emphasizing their admirable reentry into the human world.

As early as the summer of 1945, the former inmates of the Nazi camps converted the reception centers into self-governing

27 Margarete Myers Feinstein, "Jewish Women Survivors in the Displaced Persons Camps of Postwar Germany," *Shofar: An Interdisciplinary Journal of Jewish Studies*, 24:4 (2006), pp. 67–89.

28 Baumel, "DPs, Mothers," p. 102.

29 Of course, the "baby boom" is characteristic of the entire postwar period in general and of the rebuilt Jewish communities in particular. A letter from Salonika written in 1946 to the editor of the *Cahiers Sephardis* noted, among other things, that since the liberation 200 weddings had taken place, three babies were born every fifteen days, and an increase was expected in 1947 (see HAJCTh, folder 00189). The many births led to demands for the presence of a *mohel* to circumcise the newborns in various communities.

30 Atina Grossmann, "Victims, Villains, and Survivors: Gendered Perceptions and Self-Perceptions of Jewish Displaced Persons in Occupied Postwar Germany," *Journal of the History of Sexuality*, 11:1–2 (2002), pp. 291–318.

communities, even though they hoped that they would not have to stay there for more than a few weeks. They talked about their experiences, expressed their opinions. They knew what they had suffered under the Nazis and tried to discern what would become of them. Between their prewar past and their plans for the future, they developed cultural activities that helped them begin to heal the wounds of the recent past:[31] theaters, newspapers, schools, as well as bodies that represented them vis-à-vis the authorities. The sense of belonging to a community was closely related to responsibility for self-government and representation in dealings with the army, UNRRA, and Jewish charities. The Anglo-Jewish Association reported in 1946 that "national consciousness among European Jews is more widespread and perhaps stronger than ever." In occupied Germany, the Jews were granted the status of an "extraterritorial collective" with political rights and a special right to emigrate.[32] In April 1945, Hannah Arendt wrote that the Jewish people were on par with the other forty-four members of the United Nations and had the right to participate "in the organization of victory and peace."[33]

---

31 Jacqueline Giere, "We're on our Way, but We're Not in the Wilderness," in Berenbaum and Peck, *The Holocaust and History*, pp. 699–715.
32 Cohen, *In War's Wake*, pp. 128–129.
33 Quoted in ibid., p. 131.

CHAPTER 8

Self-Organization

The Federation of Sephardic Jews (1947–1949)

In a somewhat paradoxical way, a unique exilic Jewish culture emerged in postwar Germany. Communities of survivors organized their own institutions: schools, hospitals, courts, political parties, and committees. The more time passed, the more obvious it became that the displaced not only lived to eat but also to make music[1] or to play sports.[2] Dario Angel recalled boxing matches in Feldafing, and Jacques Azuz described watching his brother Mordechai fight against a Hungarian boxer in the ring. Theater performances assumed a therapeutic function for the survivors.

As early as July 25, 1945, representatives of the surviving Jews in Germany met in St. Ottilien. Ninety-four representatives met on behalf of 40,000 Jews from forty-six centers in Germany and Austria. In the second half of that year, the "Central Committee of the Liberated Jews of Bavaria" (in Yiddish: Tsentral Komitet fun di

---

1   Shirli Gilbert, "'We Long for Home': Songs and Survival amongst Jewish DPs," in Patt and Berkowitz, *We Are Here*, pp. 289–307; see also Lavsky, *New Beginnings*, pp. 157–161; Ruth Gay, *Safe among the Germans: Liberated Jews after World War II* (New Haven: Yale University Press, 2002).

2   Philip Grammes, "Sports in the DP Camps, 1945–1948," in Michael Brenner and Gideon Reuveni, eds., *Emancipation through Muscles: Jews and Sports* (Lincoln: University of Nebraska Press, 2006), pp. 187–212.

bafreite Yidn in Daytshland, known as ZK) was also formed.[3] It represented 18,000 Jews from Bavaria, who were later joined by the Jews arriving from Eastern Europe. Its offices were originally located in Feldafing but subsequently moved to Munich, where they were initially housed in the offices of UNRRA and then the JDC. At the end of January 1946, a large gathering of Jewish DPs took place, and on August 8 of that year, the Central Committee elected a new board chaired by Dr. Samuel Gringauz. The Central Committee represented the displaced Jews vis-à-vis the authorities: the American military administration, UNRRA, the Red Cross, the international Jewish organizations, and the local authorities. It petitioned, as previously mentioned, for separate housing, internal autonomy, and improved services. In addition, it coordinated the search for relatives as well as schooling and vocational training. Finally, it launched a campaign to lift the British ban on immigration to Mandatory Palestine and sought to influence public opinion by disseminating information.

In November 1945, the Jewish DPs formed a Central History Commission that coordinated the collection of testimonies from the persecuted. In addition, this commission gathered songs and works of art originating from the camps or among the partisans.[4] It collected early forms of **oral history**, emphasizing the testimonies of every Jewish survivor, even children,[5] and closely following a carefully designed questionnaire.[6] Among

---

3   Mankowitz, *Life between Memory and Hope*, pp. 101–130.

4   Laura Jockush, "Memorialization through Documentation: Holocaust Commemoration among Jewish Displaced Persons in Allied Occupied Germany," in Bill Niven and Chloe Paver, eds., *Memorialization in Germany since 1945* (London: Palgrave Macmillan, 2010), pp. 181–191; Orna Kenan, *Between Memory and History: The Evolution of Israeli Historiography of the Holocaust, 1945–1961* (New York: Peter Lang, 2003), pp. 19–35.

5   Boaz Cohen and Rita Horvath, "Young Witnesses in the DP Camps: Children's Holocaust Testimony in Context," *Journal of Modern Jewish Studies*, 11:1 (2012), pp. 103–125.

6   Laura Jockush, "A Folk Monument for Our Destruction and Heroism: Jewish Historical Commissions in Displaced Persons Camps in Germany, Austria, Italy," in Patt and Berkowitz, *We Are Here*, pp. 31–73; see also Laura Jockush, *Collect and Record! Jewish Holocaust Documentation in Early Postwar Europe* (Oxford: Oxford University Press, 2012).

the testimonies is that of Moise Samuel of Salonika, who was, as he himself declared, a rabbi and one of the leaders of the Greek Jewish community in Bavaria. His photograph—accompanied by the caption, "Mr. Moise Samuel, former chairman of the Zionist Association Max Nordau, Salonika,[7] Auschwitz survivor, currently the head of the 180-strong Greek-Jewish presence in Feldafing camp in Germany"—was published on February 27, 1948, by the newspaper *Evraiki Estia*. His testimony, found in the archives of Yad Vashem and consisting of twenty-six typewritten pages in Yiddish, was recorded on December 17, 1947.[8] The witness did not write his own testimony; rather, he dictated it to a commissioner who had previously received training in how to ensure the account was as detailed as possible, including experiences, events, dates, the names of Germans, etc. The testimony is signed by both the witness and the transcriber. Samuel dictated, probably in French, a brief history of the Jews of Salonika and their persecution by the Germans, which the transcriber then translated into Yiddish.

At that time, a lot of committees and associations were founded in Bavaria to represent the DPs and their interests. Anna Holian speaks of a "mania" for founding committees, but also emphasizes that these committees did not serve as a mouthpiece for collectives. Rather, they focused on trying to solve current problems.[9] As we have already seen, correspondence between the Greek Jews in Bavaria and the Jewish community in Salonika began in May 1946, and this too sought to respond to specific needs, such as the acquisition of documents, raising money, and so forth.[10]

---

7 In 1935, a young leader of the left Zionist Poalei Zion (Workers of Zion) movement visited Salonika. Thus, connections were established with the Socialist Zionist Max Nordau Association, which became a branch of the World Union of Poalei Zion. The Max Nordau Association participated in all demonstrations of the Left and ceased their activities in the years of the Metaxas dictatorship. See also Baruch Schiby's contribution to Uziel and Benveniste, *Saloniki: Ir Va'em be'Israel*, p. 133.

8 YVA, M.1E, file 1621. I thank Nikos Tzafleris for drawing my attention to this document.

9 Holian, *Between National Socialism and Soviet Communism*, p. 12.

10 The communal and private correspondence was conducted in Greek, French, or Judeo-Spanish, with one exception: in April 1946, David Sevi and Albert Mordoch, who were searching for relatives, approached the community. The

At the end of April 1947, the Greek Jews in Bavaria or in the US zone of occupation founded the Federation of Jews of Greece and Latin Descent (Fédération de Djidios de Grèce i de origine Latina), headquartered in Villa No. 1, Feldafing. The Federation was recognized by the Central Committee, and, on May 15, 1947, the Greek Jews of Bavaria informed the community of Salonika of its foundation. Their letter, written in Judeo-Spanish, bears the following letterhead: *Federation Sefaradischer Juden aus Griechenland und Latinischen Staaten der amerikanischen Besatzungszone Deutschlands.* The letter also informed the community of the composition of the council chosen at the April 26 elections: Azriel Moshe (chairman), Maurice Moshe (secretary general), Moise Samuel (treasurer and rabbi), Haim Almosnino and Simantov Hadayo (members).[11] Raul Benozilio was named honorary chairman.[12] From this point onward, Moise Samuel signed much of the Federation's correspondence, which was conducted in French or Judeo-Spanish. Since his time in Auschwitz, he had been known as *nono* (grandfather) and had gained a reputation

> good news that Mordoch's brother was alive and ready to leave for Mandatory Palestine was accompanied by a request that letters be written in another language, not German, in the future, so that their content would be better understood and the community could respond appropriately, see HAJCTh, folder 00195: 00935 and 00936.
>
> 11 Letter of May 15, 1947, Foreign Correspondence, 1947, HAJCTh, folder 00213: 00127. Ten days later, on May 25, the Federation announced its creation to the WJC in London, which forwarded the message to New York: "Having survived the awful German concentration camps and lost the most precious in the world (our families, position, property) we are living here, a very small minority compared with the other Jews whose languages we do not understand." They therefore sought to restore communication with their brothers (correligionists) and offered the traditional greeting "Shalom!" On July 17, an answer arrived from New York, expressing willingness to help. It asked for a list of the members of the association and brief information and concluded with the hope that it would be possible to "find a group of people in this country [America]" that will meet their needs (American Jewish Archives, Ohio (AJA), World Jewish Congress Collection, Box D69, File 6).
>
> 12 From Munich, Raul Benozilio was able to put the Greeks in contact with the Central Committee, see letter of July 20, 1947, Foreign Correspondence, 1947, HAJCTh, folder 00213: 00131. He himself then set out for Paris, as we will later see (Foreign Correspondence, 1948, HAJCTh, folder 00233).

for giving good advice, which in some cases contributed to saving lives.[13] DPs from Salonika spoke of a future exchange of useful

Greek Jews begin to organize themselves. Letter from the Federation of Sephardic Jews to the Jewish Community of Salonika, August 21, 1947. Courtesy of the Historical Archives of the Jewish Community of Thessaloniki

13 Moise Samuel immigrated to Israel in 1948, dying there in 1966. He was honorary director of the Association of Greek Survivors of the Holocaust, see *Saloniki: Ir Va'em be'Iisrael*, p. 356.

FEDERATION SEFARADISCHER JUDEN

aus Griechenland und Lateinischen Staaten in der Amerikanischen Besatzungszone Deutschlands

IN FELDAFING

19 IX 47

Jewish Communitie of Salonica
Vassileos Herakliou 24

Signores i caros correligionarios!
Ressevimos vouestra estimada lettra del 19 Agosto , en la quoi
iala mos avisach ,que es empossible de obtener certificatos de nasse-
nsia para nouestros miembros. Tenemos el grandissimo regreto de avisa-
rvos , que estos certificatos son sin ningouna emportansa para noué-
stros miembros , siendo aquellos que los tenian de menester, pensavan
partir para la Amerika quon la Quota Grega. Or d'après renseignamie-
ntos de Athèna i del Consolo Americano en München es que la Quota
Grega ya esta yena por 5o anios. Dounque i el plano de estos maloro-
sos caye en el agoia.
    Ala occasion de Roch-Achana transformimos nouestro local
en queila -Beth-El, Grassias al arivo de ounos quoiantos livros a
ouzo Sefaradi de parte del Grand Rabbino de New-York, sou Emminenssia
Dr Alkalay, nouestro Rabbino Samuel Moise podo recitar las orasiones
quon oun succes bastahte grande. Aparte los djidios gregos que se
izieron oun dover de assestir en viniendo de differentes lougares
de la Zona Amerikana, moutchos ermanos Eskenazis attirados a titro
de couriosita , se quedaron asta la fin de las orasiones , siendo
estavan mouy satisfetchos del resiento de nouestra orasion , ansi
que de la harmonia de nouestros cantes. Nouestro presidente Azriel
Moschè, en ouna avla antes dela lectoura de la Thora, exposo los
boutos de nouestra Federation , el lavoro que tenemos etcho en este
courto tiempo, las relationes quon nouestros correligionarios del
moundo, los ayoudos que ressevimos del estraniero, etc. La assistenssia
entousiasmada i ezmouvida , izo diversos donos para nouestros hazinos
(tbc) ansi que al fondo national Djidio. (Moutchos Eskenazis tanbien
izieron donos a los hazinos gregos)
    A nombre de todos los gregos vos adressamos nouestros por
vouestra particitation de oun million ala souscription que avrio la
Communautè Centrala de Athénes en nouestra favor. Es verdad que el
montante que metitech ala disposition de Athèna es mouy grande par ra-
pport a vouestras fouersas. Ya touvimos la occasion de meldar siertos
journales de Gréce, i vimos la endiferensia de los Djidios ricos de
Athènes a nouestro igoiardo,.... ma non mos toca a mozotros a criticar
lo solo que pouedemos dezir es que , el Central Comitè de München
mos da el derito de tomar ouna Ration cada mes, la quoiala la metemos
graciosamente ala disposition de los gasinos. Grassias al Dio , que la
situation de todos los miembros del Comitato es mas o menos bouena,
por las diversas fonctiones que tenemos en el lager, de sorta que todo
lo que mos dan de München como paga se va para los proves i hazinos.
Enfin non quieremos alargar sovre los sacrefipios personales que aze-
mos quon nouestros miembros, siendo nouestro dover mos ouvliga.
    Moutchas grassias tanbien por el encorajamiento en lo que
concerna la question cultural, grassias que ya ressevimos del Central
Comitè de München todas las direktivas i lo menesterozo a este sujeto.
Esperando en ouna noueva añada de regmision , quiered
agradeser caros correligionaries, nouestras mijores salondes fraternel

El Secr. Gen. /Moschè Moritz/   El Presid./Azriel Moschè/

Greek Jews begin to organize themselves. Letter from the Federation of Sephardic Jews to the Jewish Community of Salonika, September 19, 1947, Courtesy of the Historical Archives of the Jewish Community of Thessaloniki

information and announced that they would prepare a list of the names of survivors from Greece. Indeed, as was noted above, this was produced a month later.

Letters took at least a month to reach Greece, but a response from Salonika addressed to the "gentlemen and dear coreligionists" (*signores y cros coreligionarios*) came speedily: the Jews in Salonika sent their brothers and sisters who had survived the torments of the concentration camps heartfelt wishes for success. Enquiries were made, of course, into the "intentions of the Federation and its work plan" (*los butos de vuestra federation ansi que vuestro plano de lavoro*).[14] In response to this inquiry, the Federation sent an interesting letter.[15] The first paragraph briefly explains the necessities that led to the foundation of the Federation: most of the members, on account of their age or work, were not highly educated, rendering contact with their coreligionists who spoke other languages rather difficult. Likewise, because most planned to immigrate to Palestine or the US, it was decided that they should form a federation to ensure their rights, to help the sick, and to raise the morale of their compatriots.[16] The letter concludes by explaining that they had already begun to organize Hebrew and English lessons, and that the most difficult problem remained the support of the poor and the sick. After two years in the concentration camps, many were still seriously ill, and five members were being cared for in sanatoria. Even small relief measures were expensive, and it was necessary to purchase everything on the black market. Athens (through the KIS, the Central Jewish Council) had promised to

14 Letter of June 23, 1947, Foreign Correspondence, 1947, HAJCTh, folder 00213: 00126.
15 Ibid., letter of July 7, 1947.
16 In Judeo-Spanish: *Malhorozamente la mas grande partida de nuestros miembros non trouvieron la chance de possedar ouna instruction mas o menos suffisiente – sea a cauza de sous tierna idad, sea por sous position materala precaria – lo que rende el contacto difficile quon nuestros conermanos de otra lingua, I pensando que eyos dezean emmigrar en Palestina—la mas grande parte—o en USA, tambien poueer revendiquar nouestros deritos, por pueder ayoudar nouestros hazinos, i enfin relevar el moral de nouestros consiyadinos detchedimos de fondar la Federation.*

send support. Finally, the letter requested that the community of Salonika dispatch a prayer book according to the Sephardic rite to be used on *Rosh Hashana* (New Year) and *Yom Kippur* (the Day of Atonement) 5708.

The community replied,[17] congratulating the Federation on its activities. The letter also mentions that despite its financial and material difficulties, and the need to care for its own members, the community had already sent 1 million drachmas to the KIS: altogether a total of 12 million had been raised and food would be sent to Germany. Furthermore, some Jews from Salonika had also made private donations for the same purpose. The letter continued by mentioning that the prayer book would be sent as soon as possible, but that the situation with respect to the requested documents (birth certificates, military certificates, and so forth) was somewhat complicated. Indeed, the mayor's office did not send documents to Jews living abroad, and consequently the application had to be processed through the Greek consulate in Germany. The letter closed with the usual greetings for *Yom Kippur* and the New Year.

Rabbi Moise Samuel responded in the name of the Federation, sending greetings written on a typewriter in Judeo-Spanish with Hebrew additions by hand.[18] The letter was accompanied by a message that the rabbi issued on the occasion of the high holy days, two and a half years after the liberation.[19] In it, he indicted the British policy that blocked immigration, detaining pregnant women and children in camps in Cyprus, and called on the UN to end their suffering: "Where are the governments that want to be called liberal and democratic doing? Where is humanity?" The rabbi also addressed the Sephardic Jews in Bavaria, calling upon them to observe *Yom Kippur*, to refrain from working, and to do what they could for the sick, especially those suffering from TB.

---

17 Letter of August 19, 1947, Foreign Correspondence, 1947, HAJCTh, folder 00213: 00129–00130.
18 Letter of August 21, 1947, Foreign Correspondence, 1947, HAJCTh, folder 00213: 00126.
19 Letter of August 21, 1947, Foreign Correspondence, 1947, HAJCTh, folder 00213: 00127.

And indeed, a few months later, in one of their few reports about the Greek Jews in Bavaria, *Evraiki Estia* published a strong call to the communities and Jews of Greece in the hopes of inspiring feelings of solidarity:[20]

Brothers, a few months ago, the Central Jewish Council received a letter pertaining to your hundred coreligionists from Greece, survivors of the Auschwitz killing machine, who are still in the camp for displaced persons in Feldafing in the American zone in Germany. In this letter, these wretched brothers describe their tragedy in the darkest hues, their martyrdom, and the circumstances of their life in exile. In moving words that testify to their pain and longing for life as it was before the war, they ask us to send them some food, and above all a few Greek products and cigarettes, to complement their inadequate diet and help them remember their beloved Greece. After the Central Jewish Council succeeded in obtaining permission from the authorities to send over these products, the sum of 8 million drachmas is needed for their delivery. They approached twenty-five of the wealthiest Jews in Athens, to whom copies of the correspondence with the exiles were also sent, requesting that they contribute to the collection of this relatively insignificant sum. Of the twenty-five people approached, only THREE responded and offered a total of 900,000 drachmas. Despite our repeated appeals and exhortations, the others refused to contribute. In view of this unspeakable lack of human sentiment for and solidarity with people to whom fate has dealt the most severe martyrdom in Jewish history, the Central Jewish Council has decided to appeal to Jewish communities across the country and to Greek Jews in general, rich

20 "Call upon the Jewish Communities and the Jews of Greece," *Evraiki Estia*, May 30, 1947.

and poor, requesting that they give whatever they can, however little, so that the products mentioned above can be acquired and sent to the exiles who are waiting for them. No offer will be accepted from those who previously refused to contribute. Offers can be made to the communities or directly to the Central Jewish Council.

As we have seen, the community of Salonika and certain individual Jews responded privately to the request for help. The angry appeal had an effect. In the following issue of the newspaper, on July 4, a list of donors was published, along with the sum they had raised for the displaced Jews: 4,710,000 drachmas had already been collected, and "the contributions continue to arrive."

The Jews of Greece sent 73,000 Greek cigarettes to their brothers and sisters in Bavaria. Nevertheless, on May 7, 1948, *Evraiki Estia* noted that:

> Our coreligionists from Greece, rescued from the crematoria and remaining in Feldafing, have resorted to activities to procure the release of the cigarettes sent from here and confiscated by the American authorities. They also announced that they held a moving service on March 20, the anniversary of the arrival of the first transport in Auschwitz, in which all members of their organization in the American zone participated.

In September 1948, the displaced persons returned again to the matter of the cigarettes:[21] the American authorities had still not released them. The cigarettes were not only intended for smoking; they could also be exchanged on the black market that the Americans were trying to bring under control. Indeed, 73,000

---

21 Letter and message from the rabbi for the New Year, September 12, 1947, Foreign Correspondence, 1948, HAJCTh, folder 00233: 00072–00073.

cigarettes amounted to an invaluable commodity in the hands of the Greek Jews.

Another letter from the Federation, dated September 19,[22] informed the Jewish community of Salonika that the documents requested were useless because "the **quota** for America is filled," and the plans of the wretched displaced people were thus shattered. In addition, the letter reported on the financial situation of the members. Through the press they knew that the rich were indifferent toward them. Fortunately, they themselves were free to make use of everything they had received for the poor and sick from the Central Committee in Munich. With great satisfaction they explained that the New Year had been a great success, partly thanks to the prayer books they received. The famed rabbi Dr. Alkalay from New York was present and sang psalms with Moise Samuel. Out of curiosity, many Ashkenazic brothers attended, and Rabbi Samuel spoke with them and explained to them the aims of the Federation and the work it had already done in such a short time.

Many years later, when Samuel was in Israel, he remembered this visit by the Ashkenazim, but also, as will be discussed later, the often difficult relations with these "Yiddish Jews." He was even inspired by these memories to relate the following ostensible incident: "What happened on the *Simchat Torah* festival[23] you would not believe...Don't think that only the Hasidim can celebrate. We from Salonika do so too, in our own way. Only one of us was sad in Feldafing. Do you know who that was? A middle-aged tailor from the Lodz ghetto who was dumb already before the war...And he now sees that we from Salonika are celebrating, singing and dancing on *Simchat Torah*...And do you know what I saw with my own eyes and heard with my own ears?...When this tailor from Lodz saw us celebrating, dancing and singing on *Simchat Torah*, he came over and danced and sang with us. But when the dance was over, he could no longer get any sound out of his mouth."[24]

22 Letter of September 19, 1947, Foreign Correspondence, 1947, HAJCTh, folder 00213: 00128.

23 *Simchat Torah* celebrates the end of the yearly cycle of Torah readings.

24 Uziel and Benveniste, *Saloniki: Ir Va'em be'Israel*, p. 313.

Of particular interest is the last letter sent by the Federation in the year 1947,[25] dated November 23. A copy of this letter was also sent to Athens and to the Union of Hostages,[26] as the former deportees were known, in Salonika. The Greek DPs reported that the infamous Max Merten had settled in the Munich area and recounted what was common information: Merten gave the order for forced labor in 1942; he issued the orders to confiscate Jewish homes and businesses. The Jewish community of Salonika was therefore asked to send documents that would prove his guilt, to help bring him to justice. Furthermore, they informed the community that a fellow coreligionist, M.B., was with them in the camp. They had recently been told how cruelly he had treated his fellows in the Baron Hirsch ghetto. He had even been a member of the Hasson gang.[27] They all had to be punished, the letter urged; better late than never. All the more so because his behavior was anything but correct today. So, they awaited instructions and documents from Greece.[28]

They wrote to the community in Salonika with more information on May 3, 1948: The Merten case was being reviewed by Minister Auerbach, thanks to the documents sent by the Central Board of the Jewish communities in Greece and thanks to the book *In Memoriam* by Michael Molho. Four or five more copies of the book were requested: these would be sent to Greeks in other cities. This book proved to be very important when Merten was brought to trial. On July 4, the community responded that, unfortunately, they had no way of sending material that would lay blame on M.B. Indeed, an investigation by the Union of Hostages had concluded that "this person was one of those whose actions led to the destruction of all our loved ones; but we cannot prove it

---

25 Letter of November 23, 1946, Foreign Correspondence, HAJCTh, folder 00233: 00033.

26 For a discussion of the term "hostages," as used by both the state and the survivors themselves, see Rika Benveniste, Luna: An Essay in Historical Biography (Greek) (Athens: Polis, 2017), pp. 84–86.

27 Vital Hasson was a Nazi collaborator, a member of the Jewish police, and was particularly violent toward his fellow Jews. After the war, he was arrested, condemned to death, and executed.

28 Letter of May 3, 1948, Foreign Correspondence, 1948, HAJCTh, folder 00233: 00075–00076.

in concrete terms." The community, grateful for the information they had received about the murderer Merten, sent out two copies of *In Memoriam*, expressing their assurances that they would do whatever possible to ensure that the man responsible for the deaths of their loved ones would be brought to justice. On September 12, there was still no significant progress in the matter.[29] Two weeks earlier, Auerbach had written explaining that the steps he had taken in the military administration in Munich had failed; one had to be patient because the Americans investigated every case before doing anything.

The cases of the suspected traitor M.B. and Max Merten are characteristic of the activities of the Jewish DPs in Germany: longing for retribution, they made efforts to convict and punish all those who had been involved in the extermination of the Jews, be they camp Kapos, Nazis, or traitors from within their own ranks. In 1948, on the anniversary of the first transport from Salonika to Auschwitz, the Salonika Jews held a memorial service, as they had done in the previous year. The choice of this date is significant: they commemorated not when the first deportation left Salonika (March 15) but when it arrived in Auschwitz (March 20). The former prisoners had left Salonika forever, their common reference point was now Auschwitz, meaning death rather than origins. Many years later, the survivors in Salonika would choose to commemorate the day on which they were wrested from their birthplace.

One year after its foundation, the General Assembly of the Federation met and expressed confidence in its board.[30] Moise Samuel's letter of June 8, 1948, to the community of Salonika,[31] is rich in information, but it also assumes an apologetic tone when he reports on Sephardic life in Feldafing. The reasons for this

29 Letter of September 12, 1948, Foreign Correspondence, 1948, HAJCTh, folder 00233: 00072–00073. On the history of the Merten case in the postwar era, see Susannne-Sofia Spiliotis, "An Affair of Politics Not Justice: The Merten Trial (1957–1959) and Greek-German Relations," in Mazower, *After the War*, pp. 293–302.
30 Letter of May 3, 1948, Foreign Correspondence, 1948, HAJCTh, folder 00233: 00075–00076.
31 Letter of June 8, 1948, Foreign Correspondence, 1948, HAJCTh, folder 00233: 00034–00035.

will become clear below. Samuel wrote in his letter that 4,000 Ashkenazim and sixty Sephardic Jews from Greece resided in Feldafing: "Like them, we too have our own little community, because we do not speak their language. We have a synagogue, a club with all amenities, attend all official ceremonies, participate in national and religious events, have a fund to help the weak, especially those who are going to Palestine, and also have a number of sick who count on us (unfortunately we have eight cases of TB). The communities in Greece, Palestine, and America support us," he continued. The letter went on:

> The Americans seized 75,000 cigarettes sent to us by the Greek communities eight months ago. Recently, we held a party and offered the revenue from it to the Haganah.[32]…From Feldafing alone, four Sephardic Jews went to Palestine, and everyone between the ages of seventeen and thirty-five has signed up for military service[33] and is waiting for the order to go to Palestine. There are about 200 Jews from Greece in the American zone, headquartered in Feldafing, and all of them belong to the Sephardic Federation. We are in contact with the Sephardic communities around the world…the Canadian Jews from Munich gifted us a *Sefer Torah*… In 1947/1948, twenty-six children were born to Greek parents, two children died at the age of six months, and a young man of twenty-two died in a car accident.

32 Haganah, Hebrew for "defense," was a paramilitary organization active in Palestine from the 1920s. During the British Mandate, it undertook ventures against the British and supported the illegal immigration of Jews into the country. After the founding of the State of Israel, it became part of the official army, the Israel Defense Forces.

33 *Giyus*, Hebrew for "recruitment, engagement." In February 1948, representatives of the Haganah, the Jewish Agency, and the Bericha met with inmates from the DP camps in Paris to discuss *giyus*. The aim was to recruit men and women between the ages of seventeen and thirty-two, who were to be prepared for *aliya* (immigration to Israel) and to integrate into the army. See Avinoam J. Patt, *Finding Home and Homeland: Jewish Youth and Zionism in the Aftermath of the Holocaust* (Detroit: Wayne State University Press, 2009), pp. 237–258.

The Salonika Jews in Bavaria were still waiting for permission to immigrate to Palestine or to the US.

The Jewish year came to an end with the letter of September 16, which included the New Year's message for the year 5709 from the Sephardic Rabbi Moise Samuel.[34] After mentioning the memorial service for the souls of the six million victims, and a special mention of Salonika, a city praised "for its glory, for its past, for its charity, and excellence" (*por sous nisim, por sou pasado, i por las ovra de bien por exelensia*), Samuel officially thanked the JDC for its interest and help, ORT for offering vocational training, and Sephardic Jews both in America and in Israel, as well as those still in Greece. Thanks were given for financial help but also for the encouraging letters received. Finally, he asked for a few more copies of Molho's book, but also for some or other "book for engineers in Greek."

In these years, the correspondence between the Salonika community and the Federation of Sephardic Jews highlights some typical characteristics of the world of the DPs in general, and the Greeks in particular. Out of the ruins of the extermination camps, in an international climate of uncertainty, those who experienced terror, humiliation, and the death of all their loved ones rose up once again thanks to their courage, beginning to organize themselves. After the collapse of the world as they knew it, they took their lives into their own hands. Who else could they trust? They reestablished contact not only with the community in Greece but also with international organizations. Initially, they encountered the Jewish employees of the JDC, who were there to help them and yet came from a completely different world, with ambiguous feelings: the JDC employees were alien to them, had no idea what they had experienced, and wore military uniforms.

Some sought the security of the camp, some preferred to live outside, and some came and went. Some of the Ashkenazic Jews saw them as just "Greeks," not real Jews. Yet they certainly regarded themselves as Jews, often as "Salonikans" from Greece, but the

34 Letter of September 16, 1948, Foreign Correspondence, 1948, HAJCTh, folder 00233: 00049.

official designation they choose for their union was "Sephardic Jews." Sephardic Jews from Greece "and from other Latin states." What did this mean in reality? Were there any French, Italian, or Dutch Sephardic members of the Federation? If so, we have no idea of their names. In Germany, confronted with the suspicious looks of the Ashkenazic Jews and one of the only languages that they, fluent in so many languages, had not mastered, the Greek Jews became "Sephardic" and discovered that their own customs (*minhagim*) differed from those of their counterparts. "We live here, a small minority, in contact with other Jews whose languages we do not understand," stated the letter informing the World Jewish Congress about the establishment of the Federation.[35] Weddings and marriages alone broke down borders, and these were not always without obstacles.

The DPs realized that they were living in a provisional space but had no idea how long this would continue. These people, compelled to adapt, found themselves once again living a "normal life," in which, apart from some pleasant surprises and unpleasant turns, there was one very specific and constant concern: the search for loved ones and relatives. On December 28, 1947, a letter was written from Weilheim in the name of Daniel Salamo Nahmias, who lived in Feldafing and sought information about his relatives. It was almost two months before the community replied, having taken time to verify the bad news: the relatives' names were not on any of the lists, and unfortunately nobody had responded to the announcements.[36] In June 1949, Salvator Saporta from Munich wrote a letter to the community in search of his younger brother. In 1943, five-year-old Muziko was with his father in Sochos, Langadas. The father was arrested and deported, but Salvator had been told that the child had stayed in Sochos, hidden somewhere, and then rescued. Before leaving Europe forever, Salvator went in search of his little brother, and the community made every effort to make enquiries with the

35 See above, the announcement of the foundation of the Federation.
36 Letter of December 28, 1947, Foreign Correspondence, 1948, HAJCTh, folder 00233: 00105.

authorities, communities, and gendarmerie in Sochos, Langadas, and Lachanas. Unfortunately, the answer was not positive: they knew of the child and assumed that the little boy had followed his father. The search would continue as soon as the circumstances of war permitted it.[37]

A report by the JDC, dated June 21, 1948, informs us that the evacuation of Feldafing had begun in the previous April.[38] The evacuation of sick people from the sanatorium and the establishment of a kosher kitchen are mentioned, but the report also notes that all these changes and the mobilization of the people led to tensions between the inhabitants of the camp. On May 4, 1949, Solomon Sasson of Landsberg wrote to the community of Salonika requesting the documents needed for his emigration.[39] The community asked him to resubmit his application from Feldafing using paper with the Sephardic Federation letterhead, which would confirm his identity (and also that he is alive). On June 1, Sasson replied that, due to immigration to Mandatory Palestine and America, the association no longer existed, but that he himself had been a member. He agreed to provide his membership card with a photograph to convince the community to help him leave Germany.

The Sephardic Federation was active in Germany for over two years. Much has been forgotten from that time because it did not seem worth mentioning, or because it was deliberately kept secret or suppressed by the survivors. Yet one incident disturbed the relative calm of everyday life in Feldafang, even assuming the status of a diplomatic incident. Therefore, although it left barely any trace in recollections, its details were recorded in the Federation's official correspondence with the community in Salonika and with the World Federation of Sephardic Communities and the World Jewish Congress. It is our duty to recount this incident, which involved the Greek Jews of Feldafing, to reflect on its significance, and to estimate its weight at the time.

---

37 Foreign Correspondence, 1949, HAJCTh, folder 00248: 00181–00194.
38 Report, June 21, 1948, JDC Archives, NY-AR45-54-00028-00819.
39 Foreign Correspondence, 1949, HAJCTh, folder 00248: 00146–00152.

Greek Jews in Feldafing, date unknown. Courtesy of the Jewish Museum of Thessaloniki

Pesah 5708 en Feldafing
espartiendo paquetos de
kare de America, 6 personas i paq
queto.adientro dela keilla

Moise

On the back of the above photograph, Moise Samuel noted that it was taken in 1948 on the occasion of the Passover festival, during the distribution of aid packages from America. Courtesy of the Jewish Museum of Thessaloniki

Greek Jews in Feldafing, including a key indicating the names of those present. Courtesy of the Jewish Museum of Thessaloniki

Greek Jews in Feldafing. Courtesy of the Jewish Museum of Thessaloniki

All for a Can of Shoe Polish...

Before a concert, which was given just three weeks after liberation, the doctor Zalman Grinberg, later the publisher of the Yiddish newspaper *Undzer Veg*, spoke on behalf of the survivors from the "venerable and old communities in Europe," including "Budapest and Prague, Warsaw, Kovno, and Salonika." "We are not alive yet—we are still dead," he began and continued by expressing his fears that no one would understand what they had endured.[40] The Jewish DPs from Greece, as well as some of the Polish, Czech, and other Jews from Central and Eastern Europe, shared common experiences of the Nazi camps. Nevertheless, there were internal differences between members of the *She'erit Hapletah* in terms of class and culture. These cultural differences, in the eyes of the small Sephardic minority, justified the need to create their own body. Of course, there were moments of agreement and solidarity, and the Zionist movement—as well as "mixed" marriages—also had the effect of crossing the dividing lines.

In addition, the "Kapo trials" brought together the various groups of Jewish DPs, united by the shared experience of the camp. The trial of a Kapo from Salonika was followed by trials of Jews from elsewhere in Greece, Poland, and Lithuania. Samuel Gringauz, chairman of the Landsberg Council, reported that the observers of the trial unanimously voted for the death sentence. He saw this consensus as a promising sign of an emerging Jewish national consciousness.[41]

However, at the same time observers were troubled by the lack of solidarity between the different nationalities. After the author of a report from the Landsberg refugee camp noted that the refugee population of about 5,500 in October 1945 included Jews from Poland (74%), Lithuania, Hungary, Russia, and Greece, he added that the camp leadership was almost entirely controlled by the Lithuanians, leading to internal political disagreements,

---

40 Hilliard, *Surviving the Americans*, p. 11.
41 Margarete L. Myers, "Jewish Displaced Persons: Reconstructing Individual and Community in the US Zone of Occupied Germany," *Leo Baeck Year Book*, 42 (1997), pp. 314–315.

particularly in light of the fact that the majority of the block elders were Poles."[42] Hannah Arendt, by contrast, recognized that all groups of refugees or DPs had developed their own collective consciousness and stood up for their rights as Poles, Jews, Germans, and so on. She criticized their inability to recognize that what they all shared was a lack of fundamental "human rights."[43]

In fact, the DPs often stood out not only due to their demanding and aggressive nature but also as divided among themselves. In his testimony, Abraham Mano recalled certain problems vis-à-vis the Ashkenazic Jews. He even decided to change his name to Abraham Klein! Mano's memories are weighed down by the pain of the continued failure to recognize the Sephardim as Jews, even after liberation, and similar feelings probably persisted after immigration to Israel. Following the liberation by the Americans, Solomon Chaguel remained in Munich, where he rented a house together with several other Jews. They had decided to settle in Germany, he says, and to start a business. After all these years, his testimony about that time remains rather cryptic:

> All of us were gathered at the Feldafing camp, which had been a school for Hitler's officers, and all the different nationalities lived in luxury, including Greek Jews, but also Christians and Russians. We were fine, we were given food, and I remember two incidents. The first was that the Greek Jews were constantly arguing with everyone else. I could not live with them and went to live with the Poles, who included three or four people whom I had rescued in the camps and who felt they owed me something, and so everything was fine.[44]

Efforts to cope with the problems of everyday life and emigration often pushed existing tensions, caused by professional, national, or

---

42 Report on Camp Landsberg and Activities of the JDC, September 1–October 10, 1945, JDC Archives, NY_AR45- 54_00031_00881.

43 Hannah Arendt, *The Origins of Totalitarianism* (New York: Harcourt Brace Jovanovich Publishers, 1973), p. 292.

44 Kounio-Amarilio and Nar, *Oral Testimonies*, pp. 408–409.

228 • Those Who Survived

cultural conflicts, to extremes. It is not surprising that in the postwar period, be it in Israel or in the Diaspora, these tensions were kept silent, especially since talking about them would mean recognizing the problem and trying to achieve reconciliation. Consequently, the information we can gather from *Evraiki Estia* is also quite scant. "Sad Events," is the title of a brief statement published on September 24, 1948, which reads as follows: "The World Union of Sephardic Jews based here has asked the World Jewish Congress Council to support the restoration of peace and good relations between the displaced Sephardic and Ashkenazic Jews living in a shared camp in Feldafing in Germany. These relations have been shaky for some time, and the World Jewish Congress is considered the most appropriate organ for their normalization." On November 5, 1948, the same paper also cautiously announced: "The matter between Sephardic and Ashkenazic Jews is over." Readers were informed that the incident in question had been provoked by the camp leader's decision to relocate ten Sephardic Jews to another camp to "ensure order." What event so shook the order in Feldafing and led to the desire to remove ten Sephardic Jews? The correspondence between the Sephardic Jews and the community of Salonika and between the World Union of Sephardic Jews and the Council of the World Jewish Congress unveils the mystery.[45]

In June 1948, Moise Samuel dispatched to the community of Salonika copies of a letter that he had sent to the Cultural Committee of the Central Committee of Displaced Persons, as well as an article sent to the *Journal of Displaced Persons*.[46] The letter, written in Judeo-Spanish with handwritten additions in Hebrew, contains several references to the holy scriptures and was signed by him as rabbi. It protests that the DP Central Committee talks about events without having checked exact details. In the name of the "holy law, justice, and humanity," Samuel calls upon the members of the Central Committee to take over the investigation personally.

---

45 AJA, World Jewish Congress Collection, MS361, Box D69, Folder 6.
46 Letter of June 27, 1948, Foreign Correspondence, 1948, HAJCTh, folder 00233. The pages are torn and the correct order is: 00085, 00089, 00084, 00090; see also the article entitled "Pogrom en Feldafing," ibid., 00083, 00092, 00084, 000091, 00082.

The letter continues in a dramatic tone. "In 1932, I witnessed a pogrom," writes Samuel (probably referring to the pogrom in the Jewish Campbell district of Salonika on June 26, 1931), and "in Feldafing in 1948, for the second time, I saw a pogrom—carried out by the Jews of one nation against the Jews of another nation, small in number but large in history; in Torquemada's days in Spain, our ancestors preferred to be slaughtered under Queen Isabella than deny their sacred law" *(I en Feldafing en el 1948 asisti por la segounda of the pogrom de parte de Djidios de ouna nation contra Djidios de autra nation moy tchika en noumero ma grande en la estoria; en la Espania de Torquemada nouestros agouelos somportaron el quemadero de la reyna Isabela, por non renegar nouestra santa ley).*

Samuel himself was not present at the incidents, having gone to Weilheim for religious reasons.[47] However in an article bearing the title "Pogrom en Feldafing" he details the following: On Wednesday, June 7, at 7 P.M., twenty-five-year-old Polish Jew Janek Schneider was selling shoe polish *(vendia boyas de condorias).* David Pardo, a Greek Jew and one of his regular customers, inquired about the price of a can. The Pole replied contemptuously, "I do not sell to Greeks because they are robbers and thieves" *(Ladrones y bandidos).* The Greek protested, "I'm honest, and you've always sold to me! I was honest before and not now?" The Pole remained stubborn: "All Greeks are alike." The verbal attack led to a physical assault. The Pole grabbed an iron bar to beat the Greek, but at that moment Salvator Vivande passed by and ripped the bar out of his hand...Panic ensued...Salvator Saporta also arrived on the scene, beat the Pole over the head and immediately took him to the hospital. Then other Poles arrived, and, to incite the crowd *(por exitar al pouevlo),* they spread the story that Janek had died, then he began to beat the two remaining Greeks.

One of the Greeks jumped out of the window; the other, Salvator Vivande, was handcuffed, beaten, and left half dead. The

---

47 He had, as he explained in another letter, been attending the giving of a *get* (the ceremonial dissolution of Jewish marriage) by the Feldafing Greek Pinhas Beleli to his wife Sarah, who was in Athens.

Poles then went to the barracks of the Greeks. Using petrol, they set fire to the isolated home of Rabbi Moise Samuel, and then the home of Abraham Mano. They stole items worth 90,000 to 100,000 marks and destroyed the houses of the Greeks Ovadia Cohen, Isaac Amar, Leon Majado, Peppo Sedaka, David Pardo, Vital Pesso, Samuel Beza, Isaac Cohen, Meir Almosninos, and Leon Masliah. Subsequently, they proceeded to the homes of other Greeks, first that of Salvator Saporta, who was absent, beating his wife and child and stealing their clothes. They then went to Jacques Salem's house, stole money, hurled the radio out of the window, smashing windows and doors...They went to the house of manager Azriel Moshe, took his Greek flag and his typewriter and dragged him into another room where they began to beat him over the head with iron bars and knives...At 2:00 A.M., the American police was called to enforce order. However, Janek's brother, who was in Föhrenwald, marched up with forty armed friends, as if going to war; he did not encounter a single Greek. Around 9:00 A.M., Janek's gang hunted down Peppo Sedaka, a policeman, and, finding him at the police station, beat him remorselessly around the head, leaving him unconscious. The American police intervened.

Janek, who was said to be dead, came home from hospital three days later, while Azriel Moshe, Salvator Vivande, and Peppo Sedaka, severely wounded, spent twenty-four days in the hospital. Property damage was estimated at half a million marks, including clothes given by the JDC, supply packages, and three years' worth of work. Without checking what had happened, the Jewish press described matters inaccurately, and the US military administration assigned a rabbi and officer to handle the situation. At first, this rabbi acted in an unbiased manner, but then he changed his mind and wanted to evict the guilty from Feldafing. Indeed, he intended to send 90% of the Greeks to another camp, and only after numerous protests was he persuaded to send only nine of them to another camp, 90 kilometers from Feldafing. They hoped that the Polish perpetrators (*pogromistas*) would be brought to justice.

This, in a few words, is the deplorable situation of the Sephardic Jews of Feldafing, wrote Samuel. So far, those affected by the pogrom have not been compensated. The article ended

with the words: "To date, pogroms were organized by non-Jews…
After all that has happened, after so many sacrifices, every Jewish
soul is a valuable commodity, and all our efforts are needed for
the Haganah in [Mandatory] Palestine and not for differences
between us. Hitler sent the Jews to the crematoria without
worrying about whether we were Lithuanians, Poles, Greeks…
Jews of the whole world, let us all come together under the flag
of Israel and set aside our differences and look after our own. If
I am not for myself, who is for me? And if not now, when?[48] (*El
Rey Salomon dicho en sous canticas, me metieron a gouadrar las
vinias, ma mi vinia non gouadri.*)[49]

A few days later, Samuel, in his next letter to the community,[50]
again addressed the events of the "pogrom," describing the "fanatical
mass of Polish robbers and thieves," and adding, "For the sake of
honesty, I must say that we have four or five members among us
about whose behavior a lot could be said, but these people were
already a problem in Salonika, and now cause trouble for all the
rest of us." On July 19, seething with anger, Samuel returned to
this matter:[51] "We hope you received the protest about the pogrom
we sent to all Sephardic communities around the world." He
proceeded to offer some revealing clarifications:

The Ashkenazim have never shown us even the
slightest sympathy. We observed that as soon as we
arrived in the concentration camps. For the idiotic

48 This well-known saying attributed to Hillel is found in *Pirkei Avot* 1:14.
49 "My brothers were angry with me and made me work in the vineyard. I had
    no time to care for myself" (Song of Songs 1:6). At first glance, the use of this
    quotation is puzzling, but its interpretation may have been familiar to scholars.
    Samuel compares the behavior of the Ashkenazim with that of the young
    girl's relatives who treated her so harshly by assigning her the heavy work
    of supervising the vineyard; at the same time, he recognizes that the Jews of
    Salonika had not been careful, just as the young girl had not been cautious about
    the sun that had burned her face, and now she stands before the king. Perhaps
    he also wants to say that even as a rabbi, he cannot protect them from bad deeds.
50 Letter of July 5, 1948, Foreign Correspondence, 1948, HAJCTh, folder 00233:
    00080–00081.
51 Letter of July 19, 1948, Foreign Correspondence, 1948, HAJCTh, folder 00233:
    00078–00079.

reason that we did not speak Yiddish, they did not even regard us as Jews. Even after the liberation, this antipathy did not fade. All the efforts of our culture committee proved futile. And if we convinced the dear gentlemen, it was only temporary...I have referred to a "business incident." The Polish Jews have shown that they are capable of a pogrom against the Sephardic minority, and of doing all that the antisemites in Kishinev and in other cities of Poland did previously. This gang included men of the lowest instincts, without dignity...Many men, women, and children fearfully sought refuge in other camps and took days to return... They were deeply shocked, no one had thought Jews capable of conducting a pogrom...The newspapers were quick to write of "hooligan actions by Jews from Greece," but no journalist came to find out what had happened. Only the newspapers *Unsere Weg* [Undzer Veg] and *Ibergang* wrote a week later (in Yiddish) about the *pogromistas* and described them as robbers. But no one had the courage to publicize the decision of the Feldafing management committee to enforce a collective punishment (in the sense of the Nazi system) whereby all Sephardic Jews should be thrown out of the camp. After our intervention, the chairman removed only five...Those who stayed are in poor condition. Some worked together in a Sephardic detachment, which the camp leaders thought it best to disband. Others worked in their homes, which have now been destroyed by the Ashkenazim, and they are doomed to die of hunger. Responding to our demand that an investigation take place and the guilty parties be found (including the Sephardic Jews), those responsible responded: "We cannot find those responsible among 2,000 to 3,000 Polish Jews." It is significant that except for Poles, no Jews of any other nationality were involved...We who read in our birthplace supplications because of their pogroms, we who helped them as they set off for [Mandatory] Palestine, see it now...Because, unfortunately, we are only few in number, we have no representative in the Central Committee in Munich to defend our rights...We hope that you will appeal to the Central Committee and to the leadership of Feldafing for an investigation, to punish those responsible and to get them to pay compensation...The open letter that we sent to all Jewish newspapers in Germany has not been published. We assume that they do not want the truth to come to light, and that they have come to an agreement with the leaders of the camp, but we are always the victims. However, we hope that through your mediation...

The Jewish community of Salonika, which had always responded in a friendly manner to requests from its kin in Germany, now remained silent. There was no fallout from this delicate diplomatic incident. These were hard years, between the hammer of moral and material reconstruction and the sickle of the civil war, between the dilemmas and differences of daily and political life, between the idea of migration to a promising America or to the utopia of Israel and the decision to stay in the city of one's birth.

Yet, as it turned out, the Sephardic Jews of Feldafing were determined not to let the incident sink into oblivion. A month later, they sent a protest note to the World Federation of Sephardic Communities (WFSC), which corresponded exactly to the letter sent to the community in Salonika. This was followed by intensive correspondence and diplomatic activities.[52] An English translation of the letter sent by the Salonikan Jews was sent to the World Jewish Congress, and in August its chairman, Leon Kubowitzki, instructed DP expert Kurt Grossmann to investigate. He turned to two people: David Treger at the Central Committee of the Liberated

---

52 The last letter concerning this matter sent from Munich (from the Central Committee) is dated January 27, 1949; the last letter of K. Grossmann to the "World Union of Sephardic Communities," dated March 9, 1949.

Jews of the American Zone and William Haber, Representative for Jewish Affairs in the European Council.

Haber was the first to respond, saying that the military authorities had intervened immediately and conducted an investigation, and that reports of the story were exaggerated. While granting that the incident was very ugly, Haber insisted it was not so bloody. Furthermore, he noted that both the Ashkenazic and the Sephardic Jews were responsible for the incident and, finally, that the removal of the Sephardic rioters did not signal discrimination but was rather a practical measure for their protection. A little later Treger also responded by sending a copy of the Yiddish letter from the Central Committee and a translation into English: In the dispute, which he claimed concerned a financial matter, the Greeks had beaten the Poles. Subsequently, a rumor had led to anger and to the attack...It was the Sephardic representative who had demanded the removal of certain persons from the camp.

Grossmann forwarded the reports, and, on December 1, 1948, received a reply from Simon Nessim, chairman of the WFSC, who could scarcely suppress his anger. Without ruling who was right and who was wrong, Nessim did not want to accept that the attack on a whole group had been provoked by an unconfirmed rumor and that the letter sent on behalf of the Central Committee in Munich attributed no "guilt," as if this "terrible outburst" were the logical result of the rumor. "It seems as if he wants to justify the incident, which is by its nature odious, from the perspective of the history of our persecution." Nessim demanded that attention be focused on the Poles involved, claiming that it was an injustice for a whole group to be punished on account of the actions of one or two people. Grossmann forwarded the letter to the Central Committee, which in turn replied with a letter dated January 27, 1949. An argument was dragged up from the recent past, reaffirming "the old antipathy": the Greeks, housed in a separate block, would frighten the rest of the camp with their behavior and claim privileges and aid packages intended for the workers, while they did not want to work themselves. Once they attacked Lithuanian or Polish butchers, and the military police intervened...There was a bad atmosphere. The letter from the

Central Committee concluded, "We regret it when we hear of comparisons with the pogroms," and "we do not distinguish on the basis of descent between different groups of Jews." In any case, the "unhealthy atmosphere" was now a matter of the past. Once again, Grossmann wrote to Nessim, assuring him that the Central Committee did not recognize "special groupings" and that "the sad chapter was finally concluded to the satisfaction of all concerned."[53]

For certain uneducated Poles, someone who spoke no Yiddish was not a Jew, Primo Levi said in an interview. He added, "We Italian Jews were vulnerable; we and the Greeks were the lowest of the low."[54] The diplomatic incident between the Greek and Polish Jews in Feldafing was considered concluded. The dispute had arisen not simply for "business reasons" or over "a can of shoe polish" (*un koti de boyas de condourias*). In fact, this ugly incident concerned poverty, rage, and a lack of understanding.

---

53 The correspondence can be found in the AJA, World Jewish Congress Collection, MS361, Box D69, Folder 6.

54 "In any case, we were opposed to the Sephardic Jews, the Italians. Because we did not speak Yiddish, we were strangers…'Redest keyn jiddish, bist nit jid' [If you do not speak Yiddish, you are not a Jew]…Most of the Greeks were accustomed to this form of discrimination because there was also discrimination in Thessalonica, many Jews from Thessalonica had become quite thick-skinned there…but the Italian Jews, who were accustomed to being treated like everyone else, they were practically defenseless, naked like a shell-less egg." See Primo Levi, *La zone grise: Entretien avec Anna Bravo and Federico Cereja* (Paris: Éditions Payot & Rivages, 2014), p. 77.

CHAPTER 9

Emigration

America or *Eretz Israel*

We come to the last phase in the history of the DP camps, the phase that at once unites and divides the Jewish survivors in Bavaria. Sometimes they were on the move for years, until the goals they had set became clear or viable. The opportunities for emigration or relocation only gradually became apparent. In the spring of 1947, the Canadian government launched a work program for incoming DPs, and a 1948 bill allowed many to immigrate. In June 1948, the US Congress passed a bill that for the first time allowed immigration on a larger scale, but this act was only amended in 1950, allowing a larger number of Jews to enter the country.[1] The Jewish DPs' euphoria over the United Nations' decision to partition Palestine (November 29, 1947) turned to disappointment when war broke out shortly after. The founding of the State of Israel in May 1948 also marked a turning point, making legal immigration possible. Of the seventy-three persons on the 1947 list whose final destination is known, around twenty-five went to America and as many to Israel, while those who migrated

---

1   Ouzan, *Ces juifs dont l'Amériquene voulait pas*; Dinnerstein, *America and the Survivors*; Haim Genizi, *America's Fair Share: The Admission and Resettlement of Displaced Persons, 1945-1952* (Detroit: Wayne State University Press, 1993).

to Argentina, Canada, and other countries, or returned to Greece, can be counted on the fingers of one hand.

I do not want to become embroiled *a posteriori* in rationalizations and justifications for decisions regarding a particular destination. On the contrary, I insist that at that time many roads were apparently available, none of which was paved with roses. Decisions were determined by objective factors (relatives who were rescued and had already returned or settled elsewhere, financial compensation or expectations thereof), but also by quite random circumstances or encounters. Ideology likewise played a role: for many deportees who had lost their families, Zionist culture offered a connection to a community and a utopian vision that could help with survival and serve as an antidote to despair. Of course, this did not apply to everyone.

* * *

This sense of very different paths and probable destinations is also noticeable in a disturbing interview that David Boder conducted in Paris on August 5, 1946, with a young woman from Salonika.[2] After her deportation to Auschwitz, twenty-year-old Rita Benmayor was interned in the Ravensbrück, Retzow, and Malchow camps; in the last she was liberated by the Soviets. "The Russians were good to us," she said, "they gave us food and soap to wash." Then she set off with another twenty-five fellow victims. For three weeks she stole food on her way back to the American zone. The interview was conducted in Paris, in a home for young adults founded by the American Committee for Jewish Refugees. It reveals that Rita had arrived in Paris a year earlier when she joined two friends whom she had met on the street after liberation. She had taken a train to Paris with them. "I did not want to go to Greece, I have no family." In reality, she had a brother who, after returning to Greece and finding none of his relatives there, managed to reach Palestine.

2   "David P. Boder Interviews Rita Benmayor, August 5, 1946, Paris, France," Voices of the Holocaust, https://voices.library.iit.edu/interview/benmayorR?search_api_fulltext=rita (accessed June 6, 2014).

She herself spoke broken German: "If I had gone back to Greece, I would have seen the house without my mother and father, I could not bear to see that." "And what do you intend to do now?" asked Boder. "I'm going to America." Thanks to an American soldier, she had found the address of an uncle in America and was waiting for the Americans to "open the quota" for Greek immigrants so she could leave. In the meantime, she was working.

* * *

In 1946, hoping to involve the US in the process of finding a political solution, the British proposed the creation of an Anglo-American Commission of Inquiry concerning Palestine. Of the 138,320 Jewish DPs surveyed in the American, British, and French zones (the Soviets refused to participate), 118,570 said Palestine was their preferred destination. Of course, many would have preferred a quiet life in the "Golden Land" (*goldene medine* in Yiddish), but at that time the American option seemed unlikely.[3] Perhaps the answer was also a political statement, even if many of the respondents did not actually intend to go to *Eretz Israel*. Although the Shoah had not turned all survivors into active Zionists, the vast majority of them believed that people could have been saved if there had been a Jewish state.[4] In practice, the DPs cultivated a special kind of Zionism, one shaped both by the ideological and practical needs of displaced persons.[5] The Zionists were the only group with a concrete program that seemed meaningful after the catastrophe. Likewise, the Zionists encouraged the DPs to demand their own rights in Germany and gave the deportees the courage to take their fate into their own hands by electing representatives and supervising the distribution of goods and services, in short:

3 Cohen, *Case Closed*; Marrus, *The Unwanted*.
4 Michael Brenner, "Displaced Persons and the Desire for a Jewish National Homeland," in Dan Stone, ed., *Post-War Europe: Refugees, Exile and Resettlement (1945–1950)* (Gale Digital Collection, 2007).
5 Avinoam J. Patt, "Living in Landsberg, Dreaming of Deganiah: Jewish Displaced Youths and Zionism after the Holocaust," in Patt and Berkowitz, *We Are Here*, pp. 98–135.

by making self-organization and self-government a reality. At the same time, the Jewish DP population could leverage pressure to create a Jewish state. The Jewish leadership in Palestine and Ben-Gurion himself, who in 1945/1946 visited the DP camps in Germany several times, knew that only too well. By the end of 1945, the Zionist movement was bringing the deportees into closer contact with each other in Germany, and it seemed as if the prewar divisions had been overcome. Yet the divisions continued to exist, despite the Zionist dream of unity.[6]

In 1946, the fight for free entry into Mandatory Palestine became a central issue in the life of the DPs, who by then felt trapped on German soil. The campaign to influence public opinion focused on Mandatory Palestine, London, and Washington. It also targeted the ports where ships that transported illegal immigrants were docked and the British camps in Cyprus, to which the immigrants on ships stopped by the British before they reached the shores of Mandatory Palestine were taken.[7]

In the years of recovery from the suffering inflicted by the war, the front pages of the newspapers (except in the US) did not allocate space on their front pages to the DPs.[8] In Athens, *Evraiki Estia*, which had a clearly Zionist orientation, published an article on August 15, 1947, entitled "The United Nations Committee of Inquiry Visits Displaced Persons Camps," with a subtitle that left no doubt: "The only solution is immigration to [Mandatory] Palestine." The article refers to a memorandum written by the DPs themselves: "A ten-page memorandum was submitted to the investigating committee by the Central Conmittee representing the 250,000 displaced Jews in Germany and Austria. It expresses the unalterable determination of the deportees not to agree to any new diaspora, as well as the will of all to migrate to [Mandatory] Palestine and to devote themselves to the restoration of freedom and a stable life for themselves and their children."

A letter from the Sephardic Federation to the community of Salonika dated September 12, 1948, stresses, among other things,

---

6 Mankowitz, *Life between Memory and Hope*, pp. 88–100.
7 Ibid., p. 188.
8 Cohen, *In War's Wake*, p. 9.

that the most important thing was to leave Germany as soon as possible (*lo mas enteresante para mozotros es de abandoner la Allemagna alo mas presto possible*), informing the community that seventeen members had already left for *Eretz Israel* (two on board the *Exodus*), one for Paris, and two for Canada. One of those was Eli Benyakar, "under a different name because he was too young to sign up."[9] The famous *Exodus* was an American cruise ship that left the port of Marseilles in July 1947 carrying around 5,000 Jewish DPs. As the ship approached the coast of Mandatory Palestine, it encountered a storm and was discovered by the British. Initially, the crew and passengers were brought to a British camp in Cyprus, as was customary. However, following the intervention of British Foreign Minister Bevin, the refugees were taken back to Germany as an example. After three months, the ship docked in Hamburg and the refugees were forcibly dragged off it and taken to northern Germany. The incident provoked international outrage, and in Germany many Jewish DPs went on hunger strike in protest.

The route from Feldafing to *Eretz Israel* usually went through Italy.[10] Led by the Jewish Brigade, a unit of Jewish soldiers who had fought side by side with the British during the invasion of Italy,[11] and by envoys from Mandatory Palestine,[12] about 32,000 Jewish refugees crossed the Alps into Italy from the end of summer 1945 until June 1948. The refugees were accommodated in ordinary refugee camps or in *hachsharot*, Zionist camps, which prepared them for immigration. In Italy, however, where their economic situation was unbearable, the military presence of the British was also very strong, and their interests, related to the British Mandate

9   Letter of September 12, 1948, Foreign Correspondence, 1948, HAJCTh, folder 00233: 00072–00073.
10 Zertal, *From Catastrophe to Power*, pp. 17–51.
11 The Jewish Brigade was founded in September 1944 by the British War Office. It consisted of Jews from Palestine and participated in the fighting in Italy. From July 1945, soldiers of the Jewish Brigade were deployed in the British zone of occupation in Germany, where they helped the survivors and were also active in the training of refugees willing to emigrate. The brigade was dissolved in 1946.
12 Bauer, *Flight and Rescue*; see also Zeʼev Venia Hadari, *Second Exodus: The Full Story of Jewish Illegal Immigration to Palestine, 1945–1948* (London: Vallentine Mitchell, 1991).

in Palestine, made it difficult for the thousands of refugees from all over the world to immigrate to Palestine. Hundreds, sometimes thousands, of refugees illegally crossed the border each month. The border guards and Carabinieri deliberately looked the other way, while the position of the authorities, officially neutral but in practice in favor of emigration, could be summarized as follows: "In spite of the unforeseen problems that arise from the arrival of hundreds of refugees, it is not possible to establish a real border, and it is not possible for the Italian authorities to pursue an anti-Jewish policy"[13] (*non e possibile istituire una vera linea di frontira et none possibile per le autorità italiane fare una politica anti-ebraica*). Envoys from Mandatory Palestine chartered ships that secretly took the Jews out of Italian ports, which were not under British military control, with the Italians helping or simply looking the other way.

Of course, Jews who had been liberated from other camps also arrived in Italy via various routes. Moshe Aelion, for example, had been deported from Salonika to Auschwitz, but death marches had taken him to the Mauthausen, Melk, and Ebensee camps, where he remained until his liberation in May 1945.[14] Many years later he told Yakov Schiby how he set out in June 1945 to return to Greece via Italy.[15] Meeting soldiers from the Jewish Brigade was crucial in changing his mind, and he set off for the camp of Santa Maria di Bagni (today Santa Maria al Bagno) instead. There he found that Jews originating from other parts of Europe were given priority in the allocation of places on ships bound for Mandatory Palestine. "We Greeks were considered bullies. Some went to Bari, smacked the table with their fists, and five of us were taken and sent to [Mandatory] Palestine." For the rest, the journey meant constant delays and detours (via Rome and Genoa) until in June 1946 they were able to board a ship. The British stopped the ship just before

13 Susanna Kokkonen, "Jewish Displaced Persons in Postwar Italy 1945–1951," *Jewish Political Studies Review*, 20:1–2 (2008), pp. 91–106.

14 Moshe Ha-Elion (Aelion), *Las Angustias del Enferno: Las passadias de un Djidio de Saloniki en los campos de eksterminasion almanes Aushwitz, Mauthausen, Melk i Ebensee* (Ladino) (Beer Sheva: Centre Moshe David Gaon, Ben-Gurion University, 2007).

15 Lampsa and Schiby, *Life from Start*, pp. 304–306.

it reached the shore of Mandatory Palestine. Moshe Aelion was forced to spend several weeks in the British camp at Atlit before making his way by foot to Tel Aviv.

Dario Angel recalled that he left Feldafing without papers, crossing the Italian border hidden in an American truck. He arrived in Modena via Bologna, where a large refugee camp had been set up in the city's university. Dario sold blankets to the Italians, earning enough money to go to the theater or the cinema. He showed the inmate number tattooed on his forearm and traveled around the city without paying for tickets. In Italy, he learned that his brother was alive. He reached Santa Cesarea via Milan and Florence, waiting there nine months before he was able to board a ship to Mandatory Palestine. The British stopped the boat, forcing him to spend six months in Cyprus before finally reaching Mandatory Palestine, where he had to stay in the Atlit camp for another month. Menachem Shabbetai, who had also been in Feldafing, gave up on the idea of going to the US or the Soviet Union and followed the Jewish Brigade through Italy. His ship was also stopped by the British, and he remained in Cyprus for a year and a half before reaching Mandatory Palestine at Easter 1947.

Dario Sevi recalled that one day he met soldiers from the Jewish Brigade in Munich who were searching for survivors. He showed them the way to Feldafing. "The soldiers spoke of *Eretz Israel* and the Mediterranean." For many refugees, the fighters from Mandatory Palestine who proudly wore the Star of David embroidered on their uniforms symbolized a new Jewish identity. Without much thought, Dario left for Italy with about forty others. They bypassed the border controls and arrived at the refugee camp in Modena, where they celebrated the Jewish New Year and the Day of Atonement, but it never occurred to them to go to synagogue. His brother wanted to return to Greece to look for their sister, but Dario managed to persuade him to come with him instead, fearing that his brother would be called up to the army in Greece. Even those who had escaped the hell of the Nazi camps were not granted any preferential treatment by the Greek government;[16] on

16 See part 1, pp. 69ff.

the contrary, they were ordered to fight on the fronts of a merciless civil war that had broken out in the spring of 1946. Dario Sevi remained in Italy until September 1946; he reached Mandatory Palestine in April 1947, following a forced stay in Cyprus.

Yakov Levi, along with his Czech-born wife, whom he had married in Landsberg, also spent a year in Cyprus. He later recalled Golda Meir's visit to the camp, an event that led to 500 babies being allowed to travel to Mandatory Palestine with their parents! Moshe Pessah, along with thirty other Greeks, decided to return to Greece. After arriving back from Landsberg in Munich, Moshe asked, "Friends, what are we supposed to do in Greece? Who is waiting for us there? Let's go to [Mandatory] Palestine." They returned to Landsberg on an American truck. An emissary from Mandatory Palestine inculcated them with Zionist ideals in a speech that Moshe remembers as follows: "Your parents fought against the Germans, your grandfathers against the Turks, we will fight for Mandatory Palestine." The ship on which he went to Mandatory Palestine was stopped by the British, and he was forced to spend sixteen months in Cyprus. "There was no freedom for us there either. We were in a camp." He married a Czech woman whom he had met in Germany. At first, they were only friends, but in Cyprus they fell in love and married. "Most girls got married to have someone to protect them."

Sometimes decisions changed abruptly: Alfred Naar was in Italy, waiting for the next ship to travel to Mandatory Palestine. He tried to pass the time by having fun in Santa Cesarea, but then changed his mind and decided to go to Rio de Janeiro. He even went to the Brazilian embassy. That same evening, however, he began to be tormented by thoughts and fears: "What should I do if a new Hitler suddenly appears there?" Thus, he left his suitcases where they were and went with merely a backpack straight to the Jewish Agency in Bari, announcing his new decision: "I would like to go to *Eretz Israel.*" Like Yakov Sides, Alfred Naar reached *Eretz Israel* in 1948, following a stay in the refugee camps near Bari and internment in Cyprus.

Emigration options were severely limited by the search for, and the finding of, relatives. When the American rabbi Abraham

Klausner arrived in Dachau in 1945, he set about creating lists of the survivors to help families find each other. The lists of names were posted in the camps and published in Yiddish newspapers. The deportees combed them systematically in the hope of finding a familiar name, a pleasant surprise, or confirmation of a rumor: Someone saw him alive...back then. Very often the tiniest rumors or clues that a relative was still alive were enough for a survivor to cover many miles, only to receive information that the loved one was in fact no longer among the living.[17] For example, David Tsimino had rented an apartment in Munich and was planning to join the American army in order to enter the US. Nevertheless, he did not stop searching for his relatives. One day he came across the name of his sister on a list of Bergen-Belsen survivors. A Jewish American officer helped him get on board a small Dakota-type aircraft, and thus he arrived in Greece. He went to Salonika, managed to get identity papers, but did not find his sister. So, he returned to Germany, stayed there in 1945/1946, and met a woman whom he had once heard singing in Auschwitz. He married her, and in 1947 they left for *Eretz Israel* together.

Likewise, Aaron Dassa lived in Feldafing but looked everywhere for his brother, following a Greek from the Red Cross into the French zone in search of him. He returned to Feldafing, however and, after healing from an injury, joined the soldiers of the Jewish Brigade en route to Italy. With three friends from Salonika, he remained for some time in the camp of Santa Maria di Bagni at Bari, with a circle of Greeks: "What do we have in common with the Ashkenazim?" he said to himself...He traveled on to Rome and Genoa. The real goal, however, was to get to Haifa, where he had an aunt: "I had no other place to go."

* * *

From 1948, the *giyus* campaign offered the DPs in Germany the opportunity to acquire citizen rights and duties in the newly founded State of Israel, including taxation and compulsory military

17 Wyman, *DPs: Europe's Displaced Persons*, p. 133.

service. This gave all those who were still on German soil the opportunity to take responsibility for their own decisions.[18] In June 1948, all Sephardic Jews in the DP camps in Germany between the ages of seventeen and thirty-five signed up in the framework of *giyus* and were waiting to go to Mandatory Palestine.[19]

From Athens, *Evraiki Estia* followed the refugee drama and informed its readers regularly with short pieces about Germany, Italy, and Cyprus, and on the occasion of major events also featured longer articles. On July 1, 1947, the paper published a report from a Jerusalem correspondent: "11,000 Jews detained in the Xylotymbou camp in Cyprus called a twenty-four-hour hunger strike to protest their poor living conditions. The strike also involved 200 children in the camp." On August 15, 1947, a moving photograph of a refugee holding a baby in his arms appeared on the front page. The article was dedicated to the ship *Exodus*: "The adventure of the 'Exodus 1947' continues. The refugees refused to disembark and are being taken to an unknown tropical country." The same page included a brief report from Rome: "Seven hundred Jewish refugees accommodated in the Farma camp have tried to leave with the intention of illegally entering Palestine." The news of the founding of the State of Israel on May 14, 1948, was accompanied everywhere by celebrations and expressions of joy. A few days later, on May 21, *Evraiki Estia* reported, among other things, the following:

In Italy, the 30,000 Jewish displaced persons were seized by a frenzy of joy and organized a festival with dancing and fireworks. Similar events are also reported from the camps for Jewish displaced persons in Germany and Austria, whose number reaches 300,000. The commander of the American troops stationed

18 Avinoam J. Patt, "Stateless Citizens of Israel: Jewish Displaced Persons and Zionism in Post-War Germany," in Jessica Reinisch and Elizabeth White, eds., *The Disentanglement of Populations: Migration, Expulsion and Displacement in Postwar Europe, 1944–49* (Basingstoke: Palgrave Macmillan, 2011), pp. 162–182.
19 Letter of June 8, 1948, Foreign Correspondence, 1948, HAJCTh, folder 00233: 00034–00035.

in Germany, Clay, declared that people should work toward the fastest possible repatriation of these Jews to [Mandatory] Palestine, promising to provide the necessary means of transport.

On October 8, a report from Munich informed readers that the immigration of Jews from Germany to Israel by air had started with the support of the JDC, and that twenty air transports were scheduled per month. And on November 5, it was learned that 530 Jews from the central Italian camps had gone to Israel.

* * *

It seems that the destination of many survivors, like Eli Benyakar or Erikos Levi, was not fixed from the outset. Eli and his comrades followed the Jewish Brigade and, after a short stay in Landsberg, illegally crossed the border into Italy. They were housed in the Academy of Modena. He was accompanied by his friends and remembered dances, girls...And, of course, he was active on the black market: he had taken Hitler Youth clothes from Feldafing, which he now sold. He took the train from Rome to Milan, and the fact that he spoke Spanish made communication with the Italians much easier for him. He said that he was a prisoner of war, showed his number, traveled without a ticket, made money, and bought sugar. He showed his number, said *prisonero di guerra*, and was given something to eat. Once he told his story to a tailor, who then made him a suit. When he returned to the camp, he was informed that his ship had already left for Mandatory Palestine. "It doesn't matter, I'll take the next one," he said.

Until December 1945 he remained in Italy. He earned a little money and decided to return to Germany to buy leather goods and bring them to Italy. However, he was stopped at the border, and thus finally ended up back in the camp of Santa Maria di Bagni. His compatriots were happy to see him alive. The second attempt took him to Innsbruck. He returned to Feldafing, but there he fell ill and was forced to spend four weeks in a recuperation home. When he returned to the camp, his suitcase with all his goods had been stolen. All he had left was the money he had won playing poker during his recuperation...Again he started to work: he bought goods in Munich and sold them in Feldafing. He even opened a shop, the first in Feldafing! "Were not you curious to return?" the interviewer asked him. "To tell the truth, no...I had sold everything before they took us...Everything was gone...I wanted to go to Israel...In Italy, my friend told me to go to Greece...Go and report back to me." He then received a laconic telegram from Greece that said, "Do not come back." Eli stayed in Feldafing and, as we have already seen, went to Canada in 1948, hiding his true age and giving a false name.

Together with five Greek friends, Erikos Levi followed the soldiers of the Jewish Brigade to Italy, where they decided to part with the brigade. They stayed in Italy for eight months and were active in the black market. They sold packages from UNRRA and the Red Cross. Erikos remembered that they did well, but even after all these years he hesitated to tell his wife about his activities... He nevertheless admitted that they never went to bed before dawn and spent the nights in clubs in Rome, Treviso, and elsewhere. Yet when he learned that his older brother was alive, he left everything and returned to Salonika, where he met his future wife, a survivor from Bergen-Belsen. Despite having spent two years in the Nazi camps and losing almost his entire family, he was conscripted into the National Army, and from 1947 until the end of the civil war he was forced to fight against other Greeks. It had been a mistake to return, he said: "The memories, the antisemitism." In 1951, he finally managed to regain his house, which was occupied by strangers. Through a friend, he obtained a document confirming that he had fought against the Communists, and thus received the long-awaited visa for the US.

Two-thirds of the Jewish DPs went to *Eretz Israel*, while 140,000 Jewish survivors emigrated to the US.[20] Of the 218 people on the list of Greeks at Feldafing who supplied a preferred destination on August 1, 1945,[21] sixty-eight stated Mandatory Palestine, nineteen

20 Ouzan, *Ces juifs dont l'Amérique*, p. 145.
21 "List of the Greek Jews in the Feldafing camp Block 4/6 (August 1, 1945)," World

the US, and two South America. Slightly more than half (129) wanted to return to Greece. As we have seen, of the seventy-three people who remained until 1948,[22] about half went to Israel and the other half to America. Sam Moshe remained in Feldafing until 1949, Salvator Saporta and Nissim Almalech until 1951, when they were allowed to enter the US. This process had never been easy. In May 1949, Victor Romano wrote from the Landsberg camp to ask the community of Salonika to send him a birth certificate so that he could go to America, as they had previously done for Leon Veisi, who received an invitation and even an employment contract from an uncle who had lived in America since 1917.[23]

A collection of refugee cards preserved in the archives of the JDC[24] gives us useful data about forty-five Jews from Salonika who lived in Bavaria, especially in Feldafing and Landsberg, but also in Munich, Weilheim, and elsewhere. They show that in September 1949, Viktor Romano was able to go to America. For some of the Jews from Salonika (such as Isaac Amar, Michel Levi, Moise Litsi, Salvator Moshe, Isak Sialum, and Menashe and Leon Simcha), the hour of their long-awaited departure came only months or even years after they had submitted their applications. Many of them were accompanied by a wife who was not Greek and newborns or small children. For others, the file was closed before they emigrated, and their destination changed: in 1946, Shlomo Akounis wanted to go to France and Abraham Mano to the US. The two eventually immigrated to *Eretz Israel*. The file of an "unskilled" twenty-year-old from Feldafing, who wished to immigrate to the US, was closed with the remark "medical rejection."

The lives of the refugees were never a rose garden: in Mandatory Palestine, those immigrants who had come to the

Jewish Congress London Records, Hf. 197, 5 pages. Copy of the document from the USHMM (Catalog No.: ITS 422).

22 "List of the Greek Jews in the Feldafing camp (December 12, 1946)," World Jewish Congress, vol. 1038.

23 Letter from Victor Romano to the Jewish Community of Salonika, Foreign Correspondence, 1948, HAJCTh, folder 00248: 00033–00042.

24 Klüger, *Still Alive*, pp. 171ff.

country before the war greeted the survivors from the camps like lost relatives but then treated them as if they were responsible for the loss of their loved ones. The material conditions were hard, and immigrants were assigned only the basics: an iron bed, a mattress, a shared room, and a little money to get by.[25] Yet on the other side of the Atlantic the realization of the American dream also traversed the desolate path of poverty. Likewise, a city full of immigrants is one in which locals find a way to distance themselves from the newcomers,[26] keeping away from the refugees who, as Hannah Arendt wrote in 1943, had lost their "language, which means the naturalness of reactions, the simplicity of gestures, the unaffected expression of feelings."[27]

In the public perception, America welcomed the refugees, the "newcomers," cordially and triumphantly, thereby extinguishing the stigma attached to being a refugee. The country's primary goal was understood to be the reintegration of the newcomers into working life, showing them how to become productive American citizens.[28] Similarly, the former deportees became *olim* (immigrants) as soon as they set foot in *Eretz Israel*, and their stories were often crushed under the weight of efforts to build up the nascent state.[29] Refugees were recognized as victims of violations of their rights, but in order to escape the negative connotations of "statelessness," they had to submit to the customs of their new home.

* * *

In the end, it seems that deciding whether to return to Greece, to make *aliya*, or to wait for permission to enter the US or any other country depended on another important historical factor: chance.

---

25 Segev, *The Seventh Million*.
26 Klüger, *Still Alive*, pp. 171ff.
27 See Hannah Arendt's essay "We Refugees" in *The Jewish Writings* (New York: Schocken, 2007), pp. 264–274. The quote is from p. 264.
28 Cohen, *Case Closed*. See also Beth B. Cohen, "From Case File to Testimony: Reconstructing Survivors' First Years in America," in Bruce Zuckerman. ed., *The Impact of the Holocaust in America: The Jewish Role in American Life* (West Lafayette: Purdue University Press, 2008), pp. 1–30.
29 Segev, *The Seventh Million*. See also Kenan, *Between Memory and History*.

Salvator Moshe, whom we saw making his living on the black market in and around Feldafing, managed to get everything ready to leave for *Eretz Israel*: a refrigerator, a stove, and a sink. And yet he changed his mind when his girlfriend, who had left before him, married someone else whom she had met in Israel. He subsequently sold everything and enlisted to wait for an entry permit to the US. After many years, and still in broken English, he admitted: "I came to the States not knowing nobody. The only person I knew was my friend, the one who is in California now, was in New York, but my destination was to here. To Milwaukee? Milwaukee, because I declare I know shoes, and a lot of shoe factories in Milwaukee, and they send me direct to Milwaukee."[30]

* * *

In one of Aharon Appelfeld's last books,[31] the protagonist is a one-armed man who escapes from the ghetto and hides in the woods. Toward the end of the war, he finds himself in Italy, where he excels in dealings that are at least initially based on the black market. He acquires a huge fortune and builds an international network of trading partners. He constantly pushes the thought of *aliya* out of his mind. Near Naples he restores a castle, which will house former inmates of the concentration camps, who are now "displaced," stumbling over each other in aid agencies' offices. In the castle, they can listen to music—Schubert, Brahms, Bach— as they drink tea. Indeed, the torment inflicted upon them would accompany them forever and ever, and beautiful words would not help; the chain of disasters had wiped out their consciousness, they did not know what they wanted in this world. Only music could offer them some respite...

* * *

30 Moshe Salvator testimony, transcript, p. 29, https://www.wisconsinhistory.org/HolocaustSurvivors/pdfs/Moshe.pdf (accessed June 20, 2014).
31 Aharon Appelfeld, *Ve Haza'am Od Lo Nadam* (Hebrew) (Or Yehuda: Kineret, Zemorah-Bitan, 2008).

Adorno may or may not believe it, but sometimes the prisoners sang in the Nazi camps—to endure the suffering or to save their lives. And after the catastrophe, in the ruins, they continued to sing. The Greek Jews liked singing songs from the early 1940s. As Eli Benyakar reminisced about his days in Feldafang: "We started to sing old songs, got organized..."

Writing History, Remembering, and Forgetting

How can we understand the relative absence of the DPs from collective memory[32] when these very people played such an important role in setting up historical committees and struggled to collect documentary evidence pertaining to deportation and annihilation, in addition establishing remembrance and memorial days? Were these perhaps the initiatives of but a small elite of intellectuals who were ignored by the majority? Whatever the answer, their daily lives, activities, accomplishments, and failures were lost in silence after immigration to Israel, the US, and other countries. Their embitterment is set down in only a few literary works and testimonies.

Was there some kind of voluntary repudiation of the identity associated with the label DP? It was as though this label sealed their individual and collective prewar existence in other countries. For many, being a refugee was something new, connected to the war. In any case, this label indicated a new kind of refugee, now called "displaced persons" or "deportees," many of whom felt as if they were in exile. Their desire to divest themselves of the label "displaced" was legitimate and in fact universal; other labels, more elegant, more promising, were coined for them: *olim*, newcomers... The period they spent in Bavaria was one of transition, and they wanted it to be that way. Yet, as this transitional period came to last longer and longer, it became a hallmark of normalcy, albeit a very peculiar normalcy, with its very own "provisional" laws and its own provisional options for action.

---

32 See also Kenan, *Between Memory and History*, p. 67.

This applied all the more so to those who were still young. And the displaced persons were young. Memories of their youth might reappear only slowly, if they did not forever fall victim to more pervasive memories of the camps and the challenges of building a new life from scratch in a new country. And when they finally settled in new countries, how could they talk about the "extraterritorial" experience, the time they had spent in the DP camps in postwar Germany Whatever the answer, the absence of the DPs from collective memory is partly due to the attitude of most scholars who did not want to hear their stories. It was not until the 1990s that historians of social history turned to the tale of the DPs, one that transcends territorial boundaries and is dedicated to the lives of people and their diverse experiences, all too often obscured by terms such as "displaced persons" or *She'erit Hapletah*. This sudden interest must certainly be seen in the context of the recent attention to migration research and refugee issues in general.

* * *

As for my own efforts to reconstruct the microhistory of a group of Jews from Greece in the midst of the DP world, I would not venture to say that I have been able to give a definitive answer to the above questions. In trying to grasp the history of a socially heterogeneous group of fluctuating size, I realized that the common basis was the decision not to return home. This decision was based, in part, on shared experiences characterized by both a connection to, and an alienation from, other deported Jews. This shared experience was bound up with common experiences amidst all these unique stories of expulsion, enshrined in the specific route taken: a route that began on the shores of the Mediterranean Sea, in Salonika, continued to Auschwitz-Birkenau, moved on to Warsaw and the subcamps of Dachau, and ended in Bavaria near Munich. These Salonikan Jews felt close to all those other Jews who, like them, had passed through the Nazi camps; there was a kind of connectedness forged by the experience of shared terror. Love, too, provided closeness, or marriage to women from Romania or the Czech Republic...And then there was the connection based on a shared political vision of a new life in *Eretz Israel*. Yet at the same time, there was an alienation created in the postwar period by feelings of mistrust and the coldness of a language they could not understand.

To better understand the decision not to return to Greece, as well as the rationalizations and sentiments that shaped this decision, we must look at their story in the larger context of the emigration of Jews from Salonika in the interwar and postwar years (until the 1950s).[33] This will be the subject of a forthcoming book.

Here I sought to illustrate the complexity of their history— one poised between the Germans and the Allies, between the experiences of the war and the future, and between Greece, Israel, and America. I wanted to understand the strength that allows people to gather up the shreds of their lives so that they can make decisions and determine their individual and collective destiny. I also wanted to demonstrate that there are certain moments in people's lives at which it is largely a matter of chance whether they go one way or the other. In the end, real people do not act according to any impersonal structures.[34] They cannot always change history. Rather, their thoughts, feelings, and dilemmas are part of history.

---

33 On the migration of Salonikan Jews to America in the prewar years, see Devin E. Naar, "From the 'Jerusalem of Balkans' to the Golden Medina: Jewish Immigration from Salonika to the United States," *American Jewish History*, 93:4 (2007), pp. 435–473.

34 See also the considerations of Alon Confino, *Foundational Pasts: The Holocaust and Historical Understanding* (Cambridge: Cambridge University Press, 2012), p. 116.

PART THREE

"Ma Chère Valika": Salonika–Bergen-Belsen–Salonika

In memory of Valérie Tchenio Saltiel, Elisa (Zizy) Saltiel-Benveniste, and Nina Saltiel-Kondopoulou.

A Mom's story was like Braille—it was the gaps that produced the content.[1]
Amir Gutfreund

The people are gone. Their footprints remain. Very strange.[2]
Ida Fink

1 Amir Gutfreund, *Our Holocaust* (New Milford and London: The Toby Press, 2000), p. 49.
2 Ida Fink, *A Scrap of Time and Other Stories* (New York: Random House, 1987), p. 136.

CHAPTER 10

Valérie and Beniko

Background

Valérie, daughter of Sarah and Meir Tchenio, was born in Salonika in 1905 or 1906. The Tchenio family proudly cherished the somewhat vague memory of their noble lineage: they were descended from *conversos* from Aragon. Valérie lost her mother and five siblings in the war: Albert, Peppo, Moise, Oscar, and Regina, a half-sister from the first marriage of their father, who had died in 1928. They were all deported with their families from Salonika to Poland and murdered in Auschwitz-Birkenau. In addition, Valérie lost her husband, Beniko Saltiel. She returned to Salonika from the Bergen-Belsen camp in Germany with her three children, Zizy, Nina, and Dario. Her older sister, Nella, survived the war too, first because of the protection afforded by an Italian passport, later thanks to some friends who offered her family a hiding place in Athens.[1]

The Tchenios were a wealthy family. Valérie's brothers had inherited their father's business: a large men's clothing store on Ermou Street. The oldest of them, Albert Tchenio, was politically active: after the elections of 1934, he became treasurer of the

---

1 Nella was married to Sam Modiano, the famed journalist and publisher of the French newspaper *Le Progrès*. On their experiences during the occupation, see the testimony of their son Mario Modiano, likewise a journalist: http://www.centropa.org/biography/mario-modiano (accessed June 20, 2014).

257

Chamber of Commerce and Industry, and in 1936 he entered parliament as a member of the General Radical People's Union (Geniki Laiki Rizospastiki Enosis).[2] He was active in the charitable arm of the Jewish community, which took care of the needy, was honorary chairman of Maccabi, and deputy chairman of the last elected board of the Jewish community of Salonika.

At the tender age of just twenty, Valérie married Beniko Saltiel, son of Shemtov, who was five years her senior.[3] The Saltiel family maintained a flourishing timber trading company that had been founded by Beniko's grandfather, Moise. Valérie and Beniko had four children, the third of them, little Marcella, succumbed to one of the illnesses that often afflicted young children at that time. In 1933, the birth of a baby boy perhaps offered her parents some comfort. Beniko Saltiel was also an active member of the Chamber of Commerce, and like many wealthy Salonikan Jews, he dedicated much of his time to the welfare committees of the populous community, which included many in need. Beniko had two brothers, Moise and Albert, who worked with him in the family business, and three sisters, all of whom were already married: Emma, Olga, and Elda. The latter lived with her husband and daughters in Belgrade. Only Moise and Elda survived the war.

Valérie and Beniko Saltiel and their children lived a comfortable life in a pretty two-story residential building on the boulevard Vasilissis Olgas in the Exochon (Campanias) neighborhood, surrounded by the wider circle of their many-branched family, Jewish and Christian friends, and social acquaintances. Their

---

2   He was also the sole Jew to be elected to parliament in the last elections before the war, see Dimosthenis Dodos, *The Jews of Salonika in the Elections of the Greek State, 1915–1936* (Greek) (Athens: Papazisis, 2005), pp. 202–203, also Leon Nar, *Jewish Members of the Parliament, 1915–1936* (Greek) (Athens: Foundation of the Greek Parliament, 2011), pp. 134–135, where Albert Tchenio is referred to as an "aristocratic figure, who had sworn to serve the Jewish element in his town of birth."

3   Notification of their marriage was given on June 19, 1924 (vol. 64/Γ/1924, June, HAJCTh Register of Marriages [Kazamientos 1917–1941]), in the presence of witnesses and the rabbi of the Catalan Synagogue, Hasdai David Saltiel, who had conducted the ceremony the day before in the couple's home. Rabbi, groom, and bride signed in French and Hebrew.

children enjoyed a good education, which was sometimes austere, sometimes gentler, as was common in bourgeois families at that time. The parents kept the children away from the discussions and problems that preoccupied adults. These children of wealthy families matured late and were at times abruptly torn from the world of their childish concerns: worrying about being punished for having eaten too many sweets, for a forbidden swim in the sea, or for behaving badly during a piano lesson…When the war broke out, Valérie, who was about forty years old, was still under the "protection" of her husband and her brothers, mistress of a large household, and responsible for the children as well as all family and social obligations. She had an elegant manner and a cultivated spirit, modeled after the French education that she had enjoyed. As in most bourgeois-Jewish houses, Judeo-Spanish was used interchangeably with French.

Valérie Saltiel before the war

In Athens: March to July 1941

From March to July 1941, Beniko sent eight letters to his "dear Valika" (Valérie's nickname in Spanish), who had moved to Athens with their three children for an indefinite period. Through their careful choice of words and what they said, or omitted to say, these letters offer us a unique opportunity to grasp the initial reaction to the occupation, the dynamics of relationships and communication, and decision-making processes. All the letters are handwritten in French on the company's stationery: "Moisis Saltiel Sons & Co. Wood Merchants. New Wood Merchants Neighborhood (at the train station). Salonika." An exception is the first letter, which was written on a typewriter in Greek and bears the stamp of the censorship authority. Beniko's letters shed light not only on the "atmosphere of war" but also the deceptive "climate of normality" in occupied Greece and in a Jewish family. They provide answers and at the same time raise even more questions. The first letter, written in Greek and containing numerous spelling mistakes (Beniko and Valérie spoke good Greek but had a French education), reads as follows:

Salonika, March 19, 1941

My beloved Valika,
I was pleased to receive your telegram, and I hope you met Yiannis at the train station and had a good trip.
We are all doing fine here, thank God. Father has almost recovered, Mama Sarah had a fever of 38 degrees Celsius the day you left, and now seems to be doing much better; today it's only 37.3, and the doctor said that if she doesn't get another bout of pneumonia, she will fully recover.
I hope that you have been well advised in the hotel, in any case you should agree on what you must pay. Or let Yiannis fix it. Yesterday I sent you the money via telegraph, 140,000 via Mr. Tarrazi.
I hope this trip makes it easier for you to manage to find a small cottage, furnished, with three rooms, in

Marousi or Kifisia, and that you also go on holiday in the summer.

You should go early to the restaurant to make sure you eat well and in peace. Last night I was waiting for the general, that's how I passed the time.

The children should be good, take good care of them, and kiss them from me. I kiss you too.

Yours

Beniko

The loving husband and father's instructions to rent a home make it clear that the stay in Athens was to be relatively long. This financial burden caused no particular concern, and a network of social contacts eased the situation. Worry for the family informs this brief letter from beginning to end—from the health of elderly parents to concern for the children. The school year had been abruptly interrupted by the war. It is not clear what motivated the move; the recipients knew the circumstances and thus did not mention them in the letter, especially considering the all-seeing eye of the censor. Athens was probably considered a haven from the bombing raids that plagued Salonika. Emily, Beniko's sister-in-law (she was married to Albert Saltiel, Beniko's brother), who survived Auschwitz, later recalled that she and her husband moved to Arnaia on the Halkidiki, where they had friends, for the same reason.[4]

* * *

Two days later, a telegram arrived at the Hotel Kentrikon: "Meet Mrs. Maragopoulou Kifisia Ikarias 11 Phone: 0-1500 House Kifisia to rent. Stop. Mum good fever free. Benny Saltiel." Valérie followed this advice, as can be seen by the address stated in the next letter, which was delivered to her in person. Beniko too had left Salonika on the day the Germans marched into the city, and on April 10 another telegram was received by a certain Antonakakis

4   Emily (Emilia) Saul testimony, VHA, 37995. After the war the house at 95 Vasilisis Olgas Odos housed the Yugoslavian Consulate.

in Ippokratous Street: "I'm coming tomorrow. In Chalcis. Benis."
Beniko visited the family. We do not know how long he stayed, but
he subsequently returned to work in Salonika, now occupied by
the Germans. The next letter is dated June 1, 1941:

My beloved Valika,

I take advantage of the departure of my friend and
colleague Profil [Porfyrios] Efiliadis to write to you in
detail.

First: I write to you almost every day by post, quite
apart from what I send to you via couriers, friends, etc.
I have received nothing from you to this day and am
troubled.

Yiannis sent me a letter about Mr. Avramidis and
Leonidas and told me that his wife Eftychia came to see
you, and that reassured me; I hope you are all in good
health.

Here the family is all together. The Saltiels and the
Tchenios are wonderful, Father is getting better and
better. Yesterday, he got up and sat in the chair, lucky I'm
here, because he wanted to see me.

As for me and the old friends from our community,
we are all quite calm, there is no reason for you to be
worried. The storm has definitely died down.

I'm staying with Aunt Rachel, I lunch with Mother
and the Camchis at Olga Saltiel's place, sometimes
with Maurice Molho, and in the evening with Uncle
Isak. Aunty takes care of everything. I have the best
room, bath, etc., and Moise and Uncle Isak bend over
backwards for my sake.

Through Mrs. Eftychia, the wife of the doctor, who is
staying in Athens, phone 84233, with her aunt…I have
sent you a suitcase full of various things; if you have not
got it yet, call and send someone to pick the case up.

My beloved Valika, we do not lack for anything apart
from coffee…oil, soap, and clothes. The rest is abundant.
It worries me very much that you have no bread…etc. to

eat. And I wonder if it wouldn't be preferable for you to come back here.

Aunt Rachel is at our disposal, but I'm sure you will not want to stay here. Impossible. In fact, we could rent a house, but without furniture, beds, etc. That's why I think it's best to stay there. Besides, traveling is very difficult. Father thinks we should stay in Athens for the winter. I will, God willing, be in Athens in ten days.

I'm writing to make sure that you buy clothes, shoes, and everything that you and the children need for the winter immediately and without hesitation, because there is nothing here and I'm sure there will be nothing in Athens.

The furniture, crockery, beds etc. remain in the house—the *Musaffirs* are not thinking of leaving. Everything I could take with me, I packed in two chests. Emma carried the lot, poor thing, and left many of her own things behind.

As far as I could see, there is no clothing here, neither the children's nor yours.

Likewise in our other house…and in the house of Olga Molho as well as in the offices, but why worry yourself about that since it's generally the case here.

I hope you got the money from the bank.

If Mr. Ephiliadis finds something on the way, he will buy it for you. Please thank him and pay him for it.

My friendly greetings to Mrs. and Mr. Mavrakis and Nikos Ekaterinis. Yiannis should write to me whether Mr. Antonakis has recovered from his illness and where he is staying.

Greetings to Mr.…to Mr. Charalambos and his wife, to Mr. and Mrs.…

Take good care of the children, Zizy, Nina, and Diko, and hug them. I kiss you tenderly,

Your

Ben[5]

5 For the original French, see the appendix.

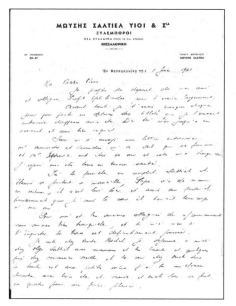

Letter from Beniko Saltiel to Valérie Saltiel, June 1, 1941

The letter barely mentions the dramatic events unfolding in those days, and the correspondence is only incompletely preserved. The letter focuses on things that affect the city of Salonika, the Jews, and Valérie's family. As already described, the German invasion of Salonika on April 9, 1941, meant the immediate closure of the Jewish newspapers and the looting of their municipal offices. On April 15 and 18, the Germans arrested and detained several community officials, as well as community leaders and prominent members of several committees such as the Matanot Levyonim (Gifts to the poor),[6] including Valérie's brother, Albert Tchenio. Chief Rabbi Koretz, who was in Athens at the time, was arrested there on May 17. The Gestapo invaded the community offices and plundered their archives. The synagogues were also looted. On April 21, bilingual (German and Greek) signs were hung up in Salonika's restaurants: "Jews unwanted."

With the war and the German invasion, the schools closed too; they would not open again until June. The school attended by the Saltiels' oldest daughter, the American Anatolia College, became the German headquarters. Many citizens who had relatives in Athens or had other possibilities to live there left Salonika.[7] On April 12, the beautiful Saltiel home on Boulevard Vasilissis Olgas was seized by the Germans. The letter of June 1 is silent about so many things.

What does it make clear? Above all, Beniko's constant efforts to maintain communication in any way possible are evident. We also hear of a network of people with Christian names, such as the timber merchant Ephiliadis, who seem willing to assist. Without hesitation, even joyfully, the family—including siblings, uncles, and aunts—offers its immediate help and assistance: an aunt takes

---

6 The members of the council, the board, and well-known personalities were arrested: Charles Beraha, Albert Arditi, Solomon Uziel, Saltiel Cohen, Saby Saltiel, Rafael Menache, Isaac Sciaky, and Albert Tchenio (see Molho and Nehama, *In Memoriam*, pp. 48–49). Solomon Uziel also mentions Yomtov Yakoel (Bowman, *The Holocaust in Salonika: Eyewitness Accounts*, p. 241). Jacques Revah mentions Jacques Mochee, Michel Sarfatis, Saul and Meir Molho as well as Rachel Schimsi in Novitch, *Le Passage des Barbares*, p. 26.

7 Kavala, *Salonika during the German Occupation*, p. 135, cited from Virginia Zanna, *Diary of War, 1940–1941* (Greek) (Athens: Ermis, 1979), pp. 152–159.

care of lunch, an uncle dinner…Valérie at least need not worry: the Tchenios and Saltiels are doing very well! Papa Saltiel's illness is improving, and he now enjoys spending time with his son. There is no word of Albert Tchenio's imprisonment. Perhaps they told Valérie nothing about this to avoid worrying her. Also, what the letter says about the community is reassuring: "We are quiet, do not worry, **the storm has definitely died down!**" This would later prove to be a tremendous illusion. People, even the most far-sighted and realistic, need to be optimistic; their realism is thus limited to confronting the difficulties of everyday life: *À la guerre comme à la guerre* seems to have been the accepted refrain.

Beniko notes with bitter humor that the *Mussafirs* (a Turkish word for guests, used to refer to the German occupiers) who have taken possession of his house apparently do not want to move anymore, and that belongings were missing from the two chests that he had managed to salvage, which is why clothes and shoes needed to be bought for the winter in Athens. He says that the situation is the same for everyone! In those days, the inhabitants of Salonika had already learned about the bombing, they had mourned their first victims, and suffered damage. Of course, they also felt the absence of certain goods, but the shortage in Athens was far more dramatic. In Salonika everything was available! Everything except coffee, oil, soap, clothes…Beniko will take care of everything. Repeated newspaper articles and the constant reports in official and unofficial texts bear witness to a considerable shortage of bread and cereals, sugar, oil, and soap during the entire summer of 1941.[8]

The letter also addresses a difficult question, a dilemma: to remain in Athens or return? And if one returned, where to live? Beniko's father advises that they should stay in Athens! Self-protection, preference, the desire to adapt to the new realities, and the illusion that a return to daily life is possible despite the war—these are the elements that characterize this correspondence.

The third letter, dated June 21, was mailed immediately after Beniko's return from his trip to Athens, which he took in mid-

8   Kavala, *Salonika during the German Occupation*, p. 179.

June, just as planned, according to his previous letter. Again, it has a calming effect, especially with regard to the health of the family. He even mentions his meeting with Albert and worries about Valérie's painful arm. A bruise maybe or an infection? The letter is unclear. There are two new points: first, he mentions the purchase of a product from Mrs. Nitsa's brother, Mr. Takis; and secondly Valérie should try to find out if and at what price the house next to that of Mr Charalambos is being sold. The idea of a move back to Athens is now being considered more seriously.

The next letter, the fourth in the series, begins with equal concern for Valérie's arm, even imparting the advice of a physician to apply hot compresses and take pills. He expresses concern about the children. Are they alright? Do they go to school? Is Diko studying? In Salonika it is very hot, especially in the evening: you lock the doors at 9.30 P.M. and can hardly breathe in the heat! His aunt cares for him a lot, his father is better, and at his mother-in-law's home he met Nella, Valika's sister, "Everyone is wonderful. The Karayanides are still staying with us" (*Les Karayanides restent toujours chez nous*). This refers to the Germans who seized his house, referred to in a previous letter as *Mussafirs*. The letter then expresses his feelings and plans for the future:

> Valika, darling, today I complete my fortieth year and I thank you for your wishes…next time…we will celebrate together.
>
> The month of June has passed, there is still a month to pass and then with luck we will be together. If things are going well, you will come here and stay at Emma's house, otherwise I will probably go and stay in Kifisia until September, then we will take a furnished house in Athens, because for several reasons I may have to go there. In any case, write to me and tell me if you're managing to buy enough to eat and your opinion of what I wrote you.[9]

9   For the original French, see the appendix.

He continues: "On Saturday I'm going to eat at Emma's, yesterday [I ate at] at Maurice's, and today at Moise Saltiel's place." He sends greetings to all their acquaintances and kisses to the children. They have not yet decided where they will live in the future, and hunger seems to be encroaching, even for the affluent. Valérie's opinion is given considerable weight; any decision is apparently to be made together. Finally, the postscript addressed to the generous Valérie is revealing: "I hope you are not still extending dinner invitations" (*j'espere que tu ne fais plus d'invitation a manger*).

The fifth letter is actually a short note sent via their friend Kostas Gavrielidis. Beniko, as he himself notes, wrote almost every day, sending the letters by mail, but fears that they do not arrive. At any rate, the situation is not looking good, and the balance seems to be tipping in favor of Athens. The Germans were removing furniture from many houses, and the situation had become "unbearable":

> Here things are proceeding as I already wrote you. The *Karayanides* are still looking for houses and furniture that they take away, and many are left without a bed; as a result, life becomes unbearable and you understand that the question of coming here is impossible for the moment. On the other hand, I repeat to you that in barely twenty days I'll be there...[10]

And yet, the decision was overturned before the next detailed letter of July 9 for one simple reason: in Athens "the issue of the stomach" was far more pressing than in Salonika, where one could still drum up fish, meat, and vegetables, albeit at high prices:

> My beloved Valika,
> At last, I have heard from you by the letters of the third and fourth of this month, which afforded me as much pleasure as pain. A pleasure to know the children are healthy and to know that my darling wife thinks a lot

10   For the original French, see the appendix.

about me, unpleasant to know that you are suffering a lot on account of an empty stomach.

I sent you a letter via Mr. Gavrielides, and despite what I have written so far and what he will tell you, after your letters I changed my mind and think that it is preferable that you come here because I would be very angry if you suffered needless hunger.

Here, as I have told you several times, there is meat, fish, expensive but attainable, plentiful vegetables and fruits, almost no sugar or coffee, rice and pasta are in short supply and very expensive, there's a shortage of bread and we have ration cards for it, like in Athens. Still, we eat well and with friends, and, even if we have to pay dearly for it, we have everything.

If you suffer from a lack of food there, it is better to come here or to go elsewhere, together of course.

I wrote to Maurice in Volos to ask him if it is possible to eat well there and if we would be able to find a furnished house there.

In any case, as soon as you receive this letter, please tell me if you are prepared to go to Volos, only, of course, if Maurice writes and tells me that life and accommodation are possible there, or if you would prefer to come to Salonika. I too want us to be together. It is up to you to tell me if life there has become impossible because of the food situation.[11]

Thus, he waits for Valérie's answer. Five days later, the die was cast. This would be Beniko's last letter, because *con bueno* (with luck) they would soon all be together again. The journey would not be very comfortable, but at least it should not be too strenuous. They would miss the good climate of Kifisia and a few other things, but having decided to return, he does not want to delay…He himself cannot come, but he wrote that he is sending Azarias to pick her up because the journey is "complicated." When they arrive,

11 For the original French, see the appendix.

they will live at Uncle Isak's place or with Emma and later rent a small house.

He also gave the following instructions: 1.) She should withdraw the remaining 42,000 drachmas from the bank, a sum that would be needed for the journey. 2.) A journey by train—in carriages with animals—would be very unpleasant. Therefore, she should take the bus, which is fast, safe, and enables her to take all the luggage and the trunk with her! The price does not matter! Otherwise, she should take a taxi, the main thing is to be safe. The advantage of a taxi is that it is even more comfortable, but it cannot hold all the luggage. She should resolve the problem as she pleases, so long as she ensures that the journey is not too frustrating. They should take provisions but no fruit! Cookies. The thermos flask should be filled with tea or with water and cognac. All for two days! She should also take two blankets with her on the bus or in the taxi to put on the seats. She should keep the money on her at all times, it would be needed in Salonika. If they leave Athens in the morning, they should sleep in a hotel in Larissa…Azarias will help. 3.) If luggage is left behind, Yiannis should see to it that it is forwarded with the transport company Shenker & Co. Beds and mattresses should be left with the Mavrakis family. 4.) She should pay Mavrakis for electricity, telephone, etc. 5.) All this should be done calmly, without overexerting herself, because the journey is exhausting and so that she should be in good shape on arrival.

After all these loving, extremely precise, and excessively caring instructions, an order follows: soap, soap for washing laundry, a kilo of cigarettes, that is, 100 packets, ten boxes of Corona cigars, and five packs of matches. Under the extraordinary conditions of the occupation in the summer of 1941, citizens at least tried to preserve certain "traces" of their upscale lifestyle, which distinguished them from the others…Beniko also wrote letters to Yiannis, Mavrakis, and Charalambidis. The letter ends with kisses for the children. In the postscript, Beniko asks Valérie to tell him her exact departure date.

On July 15, 1941, shortly before Azarias left to accompany Valérie and the three children on their return journey, Beniko added two more pages of final instructions: he had just learned that the trains are functioning regularly. Thus, if she leaves Athens in the morning, she should go to Gravia and continue by bus to Lamia. From there, a train goes to Salonika, traveling through the night and arriving in the morning. Of course, the first and second class is not possible, but the journey is much safer, and one avoids a night in a hotel. And he repeats: "Bring cold food and water" (*Prends manger froid et prend de l'eau avec*). He also notes that Uncle Isak and Aunt Rachel were waiting for them. "Nothing more, I'm waiting impatiently, good journey, many kisses, your Ben." And then another P.S., written in pencil at the last moment: "Wear your oldest clothes on the journey..."

How useless, how futile this seems in hindsight. How strange the advice regarding a comfortable and safe journey sounds to people who two years later would be dressed in rags and yearning for a piece of bread. What was this painful arm compared to typhoid fever? Yet such thoughts, as unavoidable as they may be, do not help us understand the history of this family nor the Jews of Salonika. We must not forget that this was one year before the "Black Saturday" of July 11, 1942. People adapted impressively to the conditions of war. At that time, Jews, like everyone else, suffered from a lack of food and from the requisition of homes. In addition, "money did not matter" because Beniko Saltiel's family was rich. It was possible, at least at this point in time, to make do. Moreover, a comprehensive network of friends, relatives, and acquaintances provided great protection. Under these comfortable conditions, emotions were articulated, decisions were made, plans changed.

Two things are certain. Firstly, Valérie's family returned from Athens in July 1941 because the lack of food in Athens cast a heavy shadow even on the well-to-do. The Germans stole food and other goods from warehouses as spoils of war, blaming the Allied blockade for the lack of provisions.[12] In Salonika, things

---

12 Kavala, *Salonika during the German Occupation*. See also Violetta Hionidou, *Famine and Death in Occupied Greece, 1941–1944* (Cambridge: Cambridge University Press, 2006). Had the blockade not come to an end at the close of 1941, the summer harvest would have been insufficient to prevent a situation of starvation like that which occurred in the first year of the occupation. See Polymeris Voglis, "Surviving Hunger: Life in the Cities and the Countryside

seemed to be better, and there were always aunts, uncles, and siblings who could offer aid. Second, there was total ignorance of the singular danger that threatened the Jews. "The storm has finally passed," Beniko wrote, as the clouds were already looming large on the horizon...

during the Occupation," in Robert Gildea, Olivier Wieviorka, and Anette Warring, eds., *Surviving Hitler and Mussolini: Daily Life in Occupied Europe* (Oxford and New York: Berg Publishers, 2006), pp. 16–41.

CHAPTER 11

Return to Salonika: July 1941 to August 1943. The Judenrat

The Judenräte

As mentioned earlier, only a few days after they invaded Salonika, the Germans arrested the members of the community council: Charles Beraha, Albert Arditi, Solomon Uziel, Saltiel Cohen, and Albert Tchenio, community chairman Saby Saltiel (not related to Beniko), the Rabbi's secretary, and, a little later, Yomtov Yakoel the community attorney. Chief Rabbi Koretz and Dr. Alevi were in Athens and thus escaped arrest. After his release, Saby Saltiel took over the leadership of the community. Michael Molho later wrote of him that he ruled over the Jews like a dictator, but that he was despised and seen as inferior by the Germans, while Yakoel described him as a "petty-minded accountant." The qualification that determined his appointment was probably that he had been a supporter of Metaxas' party.[1] Appointments to the position of community leader on the basis of links with the Germans aimed to make the appointees cogs in the machinery. At the same time, it gave the impression that the traditional autonomy and self-government of the community would be at least partly preserved.

---

1   Dodos, *The Jews of Salonika in the Elections of the Greek State*, p. 203.

Before discussing how Beniko Saltiel was involved in the community leadership, it is important to understand the context of the extensive debate concerning the Judenräte (Jewish Councils), their character, and the role they played. These councils, established in the countries occupied by the Germans, constituted a focal point of discussions among survivors immediately after the war. The talk of "sheep led to the slaughter"[2] became a sort of refrain in the effort to describe and explain the process of annihilation. Of course, this sentence had very different meanings depending on who said it: the "bystanders" tried to deny their own responsibility by blaming the victims themselves; the survivors, by contrast, either accused the heads of the communities and tried to respond to the accusation that they themselves had behaved "passively," or, in their grief over lost relatives, they sought to place the blame in their immediate vicinity. After the end of the war, many Jewish communities—in the Netherlands, Hungary, Poland, Romania, and Greece—carried out "honor trials" in which collaborators, members of the Jewish police, and members of the Judenräte were brought to justice. The public indignation found a counterpart in early research into the history of the Shoah. Historians of the Shoah confronted accusations such as those formulated by intellectuals like Hannah Arendt or Raul Hilberg, whose writings contributed to the Judenräte becoming a central historiographical problem.[3]

2   This phrase might derive from the diary of Emmanuel Ringelblum, who took part in the Warsaw Ghetto Uprising in spring 1943: "Because we allowed ourselves to be led like sheep to the slaughter." See Jacob Sloan ed., *Notes from the Warsaw Ghetto: The Journal of Emmanuel Ringelblum* (New York: McGraw Hill, 1958), p. 310. Nehama Tec cited the use of this term as early as 1942 in a revolutionary manifesto published on New Year's Day that asked the Jews of the Kovno ghetto not to submit to the orders of the Germans, see Tec, *Resistance*, p. 6.

3   Their theses are discussed in the first part of this book in connection with the dichotomy "passivity/resistance." It should only be added that Gershom Scholem wrote in private correspondence with Hannah Arendt (June/July 1963), published in English in the journal *Encounter* in 1964, "Which of us can say today what decisions the elders of the Jews—or whatever we choose to call them—ought to have arrived at in the circumstances?...I do not know whether they were right or wrong. Nor do I presume to judge. I was not there." See David Kaposi, "Judge or Not to Judge: The Clash of Perspectives in the Scholem Exchange," *Holocaust Studies: A Journal of Culture and History*, 14:1 (2008), pp. 93–116, quote from p. 100.

The Polish Jew Philip Friedman, himself a survivor and one of the earliest historians of the Shoah, blamed the heads of the communities of Lodz and Vilna, although not for being traitors. He accused them of having been consciously or unconsciously influenced by some kind of "messianic," fascist delusion, trying to become saviors of the people in ways that were foreign to the Jewish spirit.[4] At the same time, some historians have rightly noted that Hannah Arendt's view blurred the distinction between perpetrators and victims. Some even spoke of a vilification of the dead. Arendt, they argued, overlooked the fundamental contribution of Jewish self-government and did not understand what maintaining medical care and procuring medicines and food under the conditions of occupation in the ghettos entailed. Finally, she underestimated the fact that the leaders themselves believed they were fighting for the community. Raul Hilberg seems to acknowledge the last point with the paradoxical formulation that the members of the Judenrat "both saved and destroyed its people."[5]

A key moment in the development of historiography concerning the Judenräte was the 1977 international conference on "Patterns of Jewish Leadership in Nazi Occupied Europe" at Yad Vashem.[6] By then, significant monographs[7] had already underlined the complexity of the phenomenon and the diversity

4 Philip Friedman, "Pseudo Saviors in the Polish Ghettos: Mordechai Chaim Rumkowski of Lodz," in Philip Friedman and Ada June Friedman, eds., *Roads to Extinction: Essays on the Holocaust*, 2nd ed. (New York and Philadelphia: The Jewish Publication Society of America, 1980), pp. 333–378.
5 Hilberg, *The Destruction*, 1985, vol.1, p. 218.
6 Gutman and Haft, *Patterns of Jewish Leadership*.
7 See especially the groundbreaking study by Trunk, *Judenrat*. Although limited to the communities of Eastern Europe, it is the most comprehensive work to date. Of equal importance is Aaron Weiss's *Jewish Leadership*, which assesses east Galicia as well as northeastern Silesia and stresses the positive role played by the councils in the preservation of the communities in a situation of persecution; see also Weiss's essay "The Historiographical Controversy Concerning the Character and Functions of the Judenrats," in Israel Gutman, ed., *The Historiography of the Holocaust Period: Proceedings of the Fifth Yad Vashem International Conference, March 1983* (Jerusalem: Yad Vashem, 1988), pp. 679–696; see also Dan Michman, "Judenrat," in Judith Tydor Baumel and Walter Lacqueur, eds., *The Holocaust Encyclopedia* (New Haven: Yale University Press, 2001), pp. 370–377.

of the reactions among the Judenräte and their individual members. The spectrum of behaviors ranged from full support of resistance groups and their own heroic collectives or individual resistance actions against the Germans to behavior that bordered on collaboration with the enemy. Certainly, there was no "one single Jewish governance" in occupied Europe; rather, there were different approaches in different communities. In addition, the sense of belonging to these communities, which in general were very heterogeneous in terms of culture and class, was not necessarily self-evident. Summing up the results of Yad Vashem's conference, Yehuda Bauer emphasized that the Judenräte had tried to act for the benefit of their communities. They did this according to how they perceived reality and under conditions that did not leave much room for maneuver. The investigations carried out since then seem to support his assessment.

Jan Gross notes that what made the entanglement with the German occupying power so unique was the gap between initial commitments and the final outcome, to which those who swam with the "German current" unwillingly contributed. The course of events was by no means clear initially.[8] Historians draw our attention to the lack of alternative ways out and the dedication of Judenrat members to the interests of their communities. In addition, they emphasize that the fate of the Jews was ultimately not determined by the Judenräte. In other words, though the Germans thought of the Judenräte as tools of annihilation, they did not contribute decisively to that goal. This observation can be verified both in the case of the apparent cooperation of Chaim Rumkowski in the Lodz ghetto and in those cases in which there was resistance: in Warsaw, where Adam Czerniaków killed himself, or in Bialystok and Minsk, where the Judenräte were easily bypassed.

In many cases (in the Soviet Union and the Baltic States) the Final Solution was also the work of the German *Einsatzgruppen* and their willing enforcers on the ground, while elsewhere (for

8 Jan T. Gross, "Themes for a Social History of War Experience and Collaboration in the Politics of Retribution in Europe," in István Deák, Jan T. Gross, and Tony Judt, eds., *The Politics of Retribution in Europe* (Princeton: Princeton University Press, 2000) p. 29.

example, in Serbia) this task was assumed by the Wehrmacht itself. In Croatia, Italy, and Denmark, there were no Judenräte. In Lithuania and Hungary (with the exception of Budapest) the Judenräte were bypassed. In Brussels, where the Judenrat as well as the local authorities refused to distribute yellow stars, the German administration completed the job itself. In France (as well as in Holland and in Romania, but also in the Reich itself), where a national Jewish council had been formed, the Jewish community did not have to bear the heavy burden (the French bureaucracy willingly assumed it) and the activity of the Central Council was limited to welfare work. There is one further "paradox": sovereign and German-friendly governments gave the Jewish leaders more opportunities to maneuver in favor of their community. The Germans' Finnish collaborators gave the Nazis only "Jewish criminals and Communists" but not the entire community, while the Hungarians deported "foreign Jews" prior to the country's occupation in March 1944, but not Hungarian Jews.

The idea of forming Judenräte dates back to Reinhard Heydrich's order of September 21, 1939, at a time when the Nazis had not yet decided to annihilate the Jews but planned to send them all "to the East" or elsewhere. In some cases, such as in Vilna or Minsk, the community leaders were appointed by the Germans. In many cases, such as in Kovno, the leaders of the community had to convince the Judenrat members to take on this role. Mostly, however, the Judenrat was formed by the self-organization of the traditional leaders of the community, following the orders of the Germans or the local authorities that were working with the Germans. In other words, in most cases, the Judenrat was made up of the members of the secular and spiritual leadership of the community.[9]

As we will see in more detail below, the case of Salonika followed a similar model: after the arrest of the community council, an employee, namely the director of the community, was appointed by the Germans as head of the Judenrat. This council acted in

9   Randolph L. Braham, "The Jewish Councils: An Overview," in François Furet, ed., *Unanswered Questions: Nazi Germany and the Genocide of the Jews* (New York: Schocken Books, 1989), pp. 262–263.

parallel to a wider committee made up of members of the traditional community leadership as well as philanthropic bodies. Thus, under the new conditions, which became increasingly oppressive, a degree of self-government was maintained. The members of the committees were mostly wealthy and socially respected individuals with many years of experience and knowledge of all community affairs, members of the affluent bourgeois middle class. One and a half years later, that governing senior executive who had suddenly been turned into a community leader—albeit without much power and manipulated by foreign hands—was replaced by Chief Rabbi Koretz, who was appointed by the Germans to carry out their orders. According to Joseph Ben, the beginning of the Judenrat dates to this moment, December 1942.[10]

Koretz cooperated with the members of the traditional secular leadership, although given his strong-willed character, relations were not always amicable. In addition, the pace of anti-Jewish measures was already accelerating. The Germans constantly made new demands, to which the community had to respond at once. Koretz tried to coordinate the members of the council to follow German orders, believing that in this way they would avoid the worst, until the moment that his initiatives annoyed the German administration. At this point he was replaced by community employee Jacques Albala, a puppet of the Germans, who had no relation to the members of the traditional community. We will return to these events in more detail below, but for now we confine ourselves to certain general characteristics of the Judenräte, as they are known to us today.

Part of the plan for the Final Solution was the annihilation of the members of the Judenräte, albeit only at the very end. Indeed, due to their loyalty, their members were held captive to a network of deceptions and illusions. Even the humanitarian, philanthropic activities to which the dignitaries of Salonika devoted themselves ultimately served the plans of the Germans and were of economic benefit to them. If someone resigned, somebody else would take his place, and in all likelihood there

10 Joseph Ben, "Jewish Leadership in Greece during the Holocaust," in Gutman and Haft, *Patterns of Jewish Leadership*, pp. 118–123.

would be no "power vacuum" or "anarchy." Perhaps the new recruits were vicious and corrupt, and perhaps the "old ones" sought to prevent these newcomers from taking over. Perhaps, by contrast, Hannah Arendt's idea is not so absurd: it was precisely these discredited leaders who helped the masses of the people to become more aware of the reality of the situation and see more clearly. Yet that too is not certain. Whatever the case, the existence of the Judenrat depended completely on the decisions of the Germans regarding the course of the deportations.

Members of the Judenrat lived with the illusion that **their** community could survive the plans of the Nazis, the dramatic details of which were unknown to them. The idea of "gaining time" seemed so plausible. The Nazis successfully used the illusion of Jewish autonomy and the exemption from forced labor or even death to deceive the Jews of Europe in general and those of Salonika in particular.

Research in recent years, in contrast to that in the first decades after the war, has tended to suggest that "the road to Auschwitz was twisted"; it did not lead directly to disaster but followed a path of ups and downs, successes and failures. These deviations were determined by the various decision-making centers operating on Hitler's orders.[11] It should also be recalled that the idea of attacking the Jews as a collective through representatives and under the supervision of the Security Service of the *SS-Reichsführer* (the infamous SD, in which Adolf Eichmann also served) was closely connected with initial plans to force the Jews to emigrate. A first attempt to implement this plan was made in Austria after the country's annexation in 1938, fourteen months before Heydrich's order to form Jewish councils. Under the stranglehold of the persecutors, the institutions of the Austrian Jewish community tried to organize themselves to ensure welfare work as well as escape routes abroad.[12]

11 Dan Michman, "Jewish Leadership in Extremis," in Dan Stone, ed., *The Historiography of the Holocaust* (Basingstoke and New York: Palgrave Macmillan, 2004), p. 326.

12 Doron Rabinovici, *Eichmann's Jews: The Jewish Administration of Holocaust Vienna, 1938–1945* (London: Polity, 2011).

The Judenrat in Salonika

In a searching article, Minna Rozen explains the circumstances under which the image of Chief Rabbi Koretz as a German collaborator was cultivated.[13] Zvi Koretz, an Ashkenazi Jew born in Poland in 1888, became a rabbi in Vienna. He was fluent in several languages and held a doctorate in Philosophy and Semitic Languages from the University of Hamburg. When the congregation of Salonika was looking for a rabbi to carry through its vision of modernization, Koretz seemed the ideal candidate. On August 19, 1933, the rabbi took office in a ceremony held in the Beth Saul Synagogue, attended by all the city's dignitaries. Discussions concerning the role of the community council during the occupation period usually focus on the personality of Koretz: as a "foreigner" and as an "authoritarian figure" he was regarded as the culprit par excellence, responsible for the huge and unfathomable losses. Perhaps it is worthwhile shifting the focus from Koretz, from his personality and his relationship with the Jews of Salonika, to the totality of people who were more or less actively involved in the fate of the community.

Beniko Saltiel was one of them. We have two testimonies, one contemporary—Yomtov Yakoel's diary[14] (see also Part 1)— and one from the postwar period—the memorandum of Solomon Uziel,[15] the only survivor of the Judenrat that surrounded Koretz, comprised of Beniko Saltiel, Jules Naar, Isaac Benveniste, and Albert Arditi. So let us look into the history of the founding and working of the Judenrat. Another survivor from this circle, Isaac Aruch, also gave testimony to Miriam Novitch not too long after the events.

One often reads that the Jews of Salonika lived until July

---

13 Rozen, *Jews and Greeks Remember Their Past*, pp. 111–165.
14 Yakoel, *Memoirs*.
15 This Judeo-Spanish leaflet was distributed as Solomon Meir Uziel, *Savuni gam sevavuni beshem Adonai ki amilam* (Ladino) (Salonika, 1953) and translated into English "They Encircled and Encompassed Me," in Bowman, *The Holocaust in Salonika*, pp. 237–280. The text was translated into English by Isaak Benmayor.

1942 in an atmosphere of "relative calm";[16] Yakoel also speaks of a "period of fifteen months of indifference" on the part of the German authorities, adding that most of the Jews who had fled to Athens returned to their hometown. This also applies to the family of Beniko Saltiel. Certainly, the antisemitic measures had not yet been thoroughly implemented. Nevertheless, we must question this "relative calm" when we consider the phrasing of Maria Kavala, which refers to both the Jews and the Christians: "Old laws and regulations were overturned, but new ones were created."[17]

People's ability to adapt to a new routine of daily life while overlooking its "abnormal" character was truly impressive. "Abnormal," for example, in that the schools—with the exception of private schools—were as good as closed until the spring of 1942; inasmuch as any pleasure experienced while watching a movie was inevitably accompanied by the Nazi newsreel propaganda; because automobiles with loudspeakers drove through the streets and proclaimed German victories; because the newspapers were censored and only antisemitic slurs could be published freely and in abundance; because it was forbidden for more than three people to walk or talk together on the street; because the radio transmitted German longwave transmissions; because executions were announced at regular intervals, reminding people of the foreign occupation and creating a climate of terror; because radio equipment was confiscated by the Germans from the end of September (the Saltiels also had to part with their *Blaupunkt* on April 29, 1941); because wealth evaporated, jobs were lost, careers and years of study were in vain; because the Rosenberg Commando had already fulfilled the plunder order on November 15, 1941; and because even in Salonika, which is said to have been spared the great food shortage, 8,190 people died of hunger, fatigue, and malaria in 1942, four times as many as in 1941 and twice as many as in the two following years. It should be noted that the Jewish population had a much higher mortality rate from malnutrition

---

16 Ben, *Jewish Leadership*. I too discuss this, see Rika Benveniste, "The Leadership of the Jewish Community of Salonika during the Nazi Occupation," *Ianos* (Greek), 2 (1982), pp. 118–123.

17 Kavala, *Salonika during the German Occupation*, p. 152.

and malaria compared to the Christian population: food deliveries to the community were considerably delayed, and about half of the victims of the famine were poor Jews from the Régie-Vardar district.[18] Hagen Fleischer remarked with striking sarcasm that "the Germans at the time were content to decimate the undesirable minority by starving them during the first inexorable winter under occupation."[19] For almost all inhabitants of Salonika—with the exception of course of the "nouveaux riches" who profited from the occupation—the main concern up until 1943 remained acquiring food. This was the "abnormal normality" of the first year under German occupation.[20]

Certificate of surrender of a radio receiver by the Saltiel family, April 29, 1941

* * *

18 Ibid., p. 232.

19 Fleischer, *Crown and Swastika*, vol. 2, p. 303.

20 In her interesting lecture entitled "Jews' Assets during the German Occupation," Stella Salem demonstrated that the total real property of the Jews of Salonika during the first nineteen months of the German occupation, paradoxical as it may seem, remained constant and was not transferred (to non-Jews). This was probably because in Salonika until July 1942 there was no "Jewish race question" and only a few expropriations of Jewish assets. See Stella Salem, "Jews' Assets during the German Occupation and afterwards (1940–1949)," in M. Kavala, ed., *Modern Greek Jewry: Dynamic Presence, Painful Absence, the Present* (Greek) (Salonika: University Studio Press, 2020), pp. 183–224.

The main issues facing the Jewish community were hunger and the diseases that plagued its least resilient members—the poor and children. Before the war, the Jewish community of Salonika was stratified according to class, with considerable socioeconomic disparities between its members, which have not yet been sufficiently researched. In addition, it was infused with conflicting ideologies.[21] In the prewar period, the community had been led by a council that worked with several committees or independent foundations overseen by respected community members. These were responsible for community activities in the fields of social welfare, education, religion, sport, etc. To fully understand matters, however, we must return to the point at which the now-defunct members of the prewar community council, along with several other wealthy Jews active in the committees, decided to take matters into their own hands.

One of them, Yomtov Yakoel—originally from Trikala, he studied in Athens and later worked as a legal adviser to the community (he too had been arrested in April 1941 along with members of the community council)—considered Saby Saltiel's tall stature and closeness to Metaxas his only qualifications. He thought him incapable in all other respects. However, according to Yakoel, someone convinced him to replace the dissolved committees and foundations of the community with new ones.[22] The hunger that had plagued Salonika since the end of 1941, which especially affected the lower classes, forced Saby Saltiel to turn to the people who were involved with the charitable organizations of the community, and especially with the philanthropic Matanot-L'evyonim Foundation. The committee collected the necessary contributions for the soup kitchens in the form of donations, and in April 1941, with the support of the Red Cross, ensured the provision of 2,000 cooked meals for children.

Solomon Uziel, then fifty-five years old, was active in the welfare committee and the community assets management

21   See Maria Vasilikou, "Politics of the Jewish Community of Salonika in the Inter-War Years: Party Ideologies and Party Competition" (PhD diss., University College London, 1999).

22   Yakoel, *Memoirs*, pp. 50–52.

committee. He later stated that this was at his own initiative and that after meeting two community doctors, he explained to Saby Saltiel the need to take action to protect the poor from hunger and illness.[23] In this way, a kind of parallel community structure was created, an extended committee of persons familiar with community affairs, known as the "Central Committee." According to Uziel, this committee comprised ten members: Isaac Angel, Isaac Amarilio, Shemtov Allalouf, Yomtov Yakoel, Abraham Levi, Eliko Molho, Chaim Benrubi, Saby Pelossov, Albert Frances, and himself. Yakoel speaks of an eleven-member committee and mentions Albert Arditi, Sam Arditi, and Jules Naar as members, while omitting Abraham Levi and Chaim Benrubi. Isaac Aruch, the treasurer of the Matanot-Levyonim Foundation, speaks of an extended twenty-member committee of notables, including Alberto Molho, Jules Naar, and Beniko Saltiel.[24] Michael Molho mentions thirteen members, the ones noted by Uziel as well as those added by Yakoel. Whatever the composition, everyone spoke sympathetically about the work of the committee, two members of which—Jules Naar and Alberto Molho—had also served on the last prewar board of the community.

Yakoel noted that all philanthropic activities emerged from the Matanot-Levyonim House on Mizrachi Street, where, from January 1942 onward, every afternoon, even on public holidays and sometimes in the morning, members of the bourgeois elite would gather to exchange ideas and make decisions for the good of the community. This community elite clearly decided to bypass Saby Saltiel whenever possible—even if he was given chairmanship of the committee—and to form an informal council that sought to find solutions to the problems of hunger and illness. Apparently, they consulted among themselves and then took charge of the management of the community's financial and other affairs, since no one had the slightest confidence in Saby Saltiel. The committee thus assumed the role of a **shadow community council**. To understand this development, we must

23 Uziel in Bowman, *The Holocaust in Salonika*, p. 242.
24 Novitch, *Le Passage des Barbares*, p. 21.

not forget the strong presence of wealthy upper-class Jews in the committees of the community during the prewar period, including the community council and the administrative committee, as well as on the boards of numerous welfare foundations taking care of the sick and poor—such as the Baron Hirsch Hospital, Bikur Cholim, the Matanot-Levyonim, and the Talmud Torah (which had all become community institutions). Their obvious presence was closely intertwined with their social weight. Despite its extra-institutional nature, the committee included people with economic potential and social influence. Building on the tradition of the community administration, efforts were made to exercise real power in the management of community affairs.

In the meantime, another person who was to play an important role entered the stage: Jacques Albala, a "happy-go-lucky opportunist," as many thought, who was born in Kastoria and, after spending some time in Austria, arrived in Salonika and started working as a community employee. Like many other Ashkenazi refugees, he was met with some suspicion. The forty-year-old tall, blonde Albala accompanied Saby Saltiel to meetings with the Gestapo, where he acted as interpreter. Gradually, this intruder gained power and importance. When Koretz—who had meanwhile returned from Vienna, where he had been imprisoned—later came into conflict with him, Albala was arrested on charges of corruption by the German military police.

The first serious case of the "abnormal normality" occurred in July 1942, when all men between the ages of eighteen and forty-five were ordered to gather on Platia Eleftherias (Liberty Square) to register for forced labor under the supervision of Greek and German engineers. This event was dealt with in detail in the first part of the book. It should be added that the effects of this forced labor on the community were quickly felt: the Jewish "workers" were brought to their knees by the grueling labor, as well as by hunger and diseases such as malaria, while the poorest families were now deprived of the meager wages that their heads of household had brought home. The need to organize medical aid and to provide food, clothing, and other supplies was all too obvious, as was the need to negotiate with the German authorities. Yakoel himself drafted a memorandum for these negotiations that would put the handling of forced labor conscription (exceptions, but also the possibility of redemption) and medical supervision into the hands of the community.

An agreement was reached on August 29, 1942, signed by *Kriegsverwaltungsrat* (military administration counselor) Max Merten. This agreement provided for the return of 3,000 exhausted workers from different workplaces. The news filled the Jews with joy and was considered a committee success. The committee members went about their work with zeal, while—according to Yakoel—Saby Saltiel and Jacques Albala only put obstacles in their way. Even Koretz, who had ceased being a community employee in September, took part in the negotiations. The following steps were described in great detail by Yakoel: meeting after meeting with Merten in Mizrachi Street and extensive negotiations, whose goal now, with so many Jews dying from exhaustion, was collective redemption from forced labor. An agreement for a redemption payment of an incredible 2.5 billion drachmas was reached on October 17, 1942, which also included the loss of the old Jewish cemetery. The very next day, 100 wealthy Jews were invited to the Matanot-Levyonim Foundation to hear about the agreement. At this meeting, they were asked to offer support. Isaac Aruch recalled the "extraordinary spirit of solidarity."

The first funds were handed over in October 1942, the next installments being paid in November, December, and January 1943. Aruch himself brought the money to Merten, accompanied by Yakoel, Naar, and Pelossov, first in the form of a check and subsequently in cash.[25] Jacques Revah later spoke of solidarity in the service of the common good.[26] Yakoel, by contrast, noted the pettiness of certain rich people who did not respond to the committee's appeal. The honesty of the two witnesses is beyond question. In any case, the committee said that it would be safer

25 Evangelos Hekimoglou, "Merten's Lost Checks and Their Fate: Ransom for the Forced Labor of the Jews of Salonika (1942–1943)," *Thessalonikeon Polis* (Greek), 18 (2005), pp. 40–59.

26 Novitch, *Le Passage des Barbares*, pp. 26–31.

if Koretz assumed responsibility for the financial arrangements rather than the corrupt Saby Saltiel. On December 31, Koretz telegraphed a letter to Asher Moisis in Athens: the amount to be raised was enormous and he requested the support of the Athenian Jews in collecting 500 million drachmas, of which 300 were needed immediately. The task of raising this sum created tensions within the committee, especially with Koretz, and hampered efforts to spread the burden. Merten, Isaac Aruch recalled, promised that "everything would be fine."

From November 1942, all consulates in the city were closed and the confiscation of goods from paper merchants and Jewish-owned printers began; even the cinemas in Jewish possession were confiscated and handed over to the Germans. The city council of Salonika decided to rename all streets bearing Jewish names.

The next turning point was in December 1942: the dismissal of Saby Saltiel, and his "adjutant" Jacques Albala, with Koretz replacing Saltiel. Saby Saltiel was not considered trustworthy in any way. Yakoel and several others in the Central Committee suggested that Gabriel Safarana, a former member of the community assembly, be made chairman. The head of the Gestapo, Dr. Kalmes, suggested that Yakoel take over the position himself, but he refused, and Kalmes ended up proposing Koretz for the position instead. The central committee members advised the rabbi not to assume the chairmanship and to leave the position to a reliable employee of the community such as Eliezer Mitrani. On December 11, 1942, however, Koretz accepted the appointment and in turn appointed Saby Pelossov, Jules Naar, Isaac Benveniste, Solomon Uziel, Beniko Saltiel, Albert Tchenio, and Isaac Angel as his advisors. The last two refused. Isaac Siaki, a former parliament member under P. Tsaldaris, became secretary of the Judenrat. Saby Saltiel and Jacques Albala were dismissed and detained. Yakoel considered the reorganization of the community beneficial in dealing with pressing issues, and the committee's activities were reduced under a new, more capable, and honest leadership. A week earlier, the Jewish cemetery— despite all assurances by Merten that only a part of it would be expropriated—was completely destroyed. On Christmas Eve, the

Jews of Salonika began exhuming and removing the bones of their dead.

At this juncture, in December 1942, the final act of the drama, which was characterized by violence and delusion, began. It seems that the Nazis had recognized the importance of the Jewish community of Salonika as early as the 1930s. A photographer from the Frankfurt Institute for the Study of the Jewish Question published a photograph taken in Salonika in September 1941 in an article entitled "The Warsaw of the Mediterranean." Those tasked with collecting material on the "Jewish question" were reminded of Poland when they saw Salonika, thinking of the numerous poor Jews who had settled in Eastern Europe long ago.[27] The fate of the Jews of Salonika was in fact sealed in early 1942, when Hitler instructed Himmler to set Eichmann's machinery in motion for their deportation.[28]

In January 1943, perhaps even earlier, transports to the Nazi camps in Poland were planned. Now the Judenrat found itself in a trap. Isaac Aruch wondered, "How could we be tempted by their devilish tactics?...There were clever people among us."[29] Eichmann's *Sonderkommando*, under the leadership of Alois Brunner and Dieter Wisliceny, arrived in Salonika on February 2 or 3,[30] with instructions to coordinate the deportation of the Jews from the city. The model of deception and deportation they were to follow was exactly the same as the one Eichmann had introduced in Vienna in 1938 and to which he owed his rise in the SS. After the Wannsee conference, Eichmann's men also resorted to these methods elsewhere: in Berlin in 1942, in Salonika in the spring of 1943, and in France from the summer of 1943.[31]

---

27 Dan Michman, *The Emergence of Jewish Ghettos during the Holocaust* (Cambridge: Cambridge University Press, 2011), pp. 139–141.

28 Bowman, *The Agony*, p. 59ff; Bowman, *The Shoah in Salonika*, pp. 12ff.

29 Novitch, *Le Passage des Barbares*, p. 22.

30 Concerning the exact date, see Daniel Carpi, "A New Approach to Some Episodes in the History of the Jews of Salonika during the Holocaust: Memory, Myth, Documentation," in Minna Rozen, ed., *The Last Ottoman Century and Beyond: The Jews in Turkey and the Balkans, 1808–1945*, vol. 2 (Tel Aviv: Tel Aviv University, The Goldstein-Goren Diaspora Research Center, 2002), p. 263.

31 Hans Safrian, *Eichmann's Men* (Cambridge: Cambridge University Press and USHMM, 2009), p. 7.

Following their arrival in Salonika, Wisliceny and Brunner installed themselves in a requisitioned housing complex at 42 Velissariou Street, very close to the offices of the Jewish community on 13 Sarantaporou Street, and started to make the extermination of the Greek Jews a reality, reinstating Albala, who had been released from prison, as their interpreter. According to Yakoel, on Monday, February 8, 1942, Koretz briefed the Central Committee and other prominent members of the community about the veritable barrage of anti-Jewish measures: a ban on the use of transportation of all kinds after 5:00 P.M.; the wearing of the Star of David; restriction to certain residential districts…[32] Indeed, Jews could only reside in three areas: the Exochon district (from Evzonon to March 25 Street), in the city center (between Egnatia Street, Panagia Chalkeon Square, Dioikitiriou Street, and Langada Street), as well as in the poor neighborhoods of Agia Paraskevi, Régie Vardar, and Baron Hirsch near the train station. The decree of February 6 did not use the term "ghetto," but there is mention of "special districts," while on February 26, the German Ambassador Schönberg spoke of "ghettoization."[33] Spanish and Italian citizens were excluded from these measures. The completion date was set for February 25.

The decree ordering Jews to wear the yellow star was delayed, but it was discussed for a long time, as is demonstrated by a letter from Eichmann's department to the Foreign Ministry of the German Reich dated July 11, 1942.[34] According to a letter to a comrade in Vienna, Alois Brunner seemed to enjoy the work entrusted to him, especially his decree regarding the yellow star: "Dear Rudolf…The weather is becoming more and more beautiful, and our work is progressing terrifically. On February 25 the yellow stars started gleaming here…And the Greek population is so delighted with this marking and ghettoization that I tell myself

---

32 Molho and Nehama, *In Memoriam*, pp. 75–80. For photographs of the German documents, see pp. 151–161.
33 Michman, *The Emergence*, pp. 138–141.
34 "The Trial of Adolf Eichmann", *Record of Proceedings in the District Court of Jerusalem*, vol. 2, pp. 846ff.

what a crime that such measures were not taken earlier."[35] Michael Molho remembers things quite differently: "The Orthodox regarded all these measures in silent grief. Some priests preached pity and sympathy for the persecuted from the pulpit, and teachers advised children to refrain from any provocation and irony in the face of the discriminatory sign."[36]

Solomon Uziel mentions that in February 1943 the Judenrat asked the Central Committee for help (as we have seen, he himself was a member of both), subsequently placing tremendous pressure on the fourteen people attempting to deal with the situation. It is easy to imagine that the situation did not facilitate either quiet discussions and a search for consensus, or the overcoming of personal differences. Subcommittees were formed, and community volunteers, often young students, came forward to assist in the registration of the Jewish population, the issuing of ID cards, and the making of the stars...In addition, a militia staffed by young Jews, under the command of Albala, was created to ensure the implementation of the measures.

The communal leaders worked day and night, discussing, exchanging ideas, and striving to understand and cope with the new situation. And again, the Judenrat sought to mitigate the coercive measures through negotiations; Koretz, however, advocated the immediate implementation of the German orders. To the great despair of the Central Committee, the memorandum prepared for the German authorities together with the Judenrat received no support from Koretz and was never filed. Yakoel explained that the memo requested more time to register, declared the militia superfluous, and considered the discriminatory labeling harmful to children who attended school and were thus separated from their classmates. Until February 25, people could be seen moving through the city laden with suitcases, trunks, and bundles or pulling carts to transport their belongings to their new quarters in the designated neighborhoods; families and friends, but also complete strangers, were accommodated together. They found

35 Safrian, *Eichmann's Men*, p. 7.
36 Molho and Nehama, *In Memoriam*, pp. 92ff.

themselves facing a host of problems, and the haste with which the Germans insisted their decrees be carried out, and Koretz's failure to question them ("the community does not need advice, but work," the chief rabbi said, according to Yakoel) made matters all the more chaotic. The dignitaries of the community continued to deliberate yet had no real room for maneuver, and Koretz seems to have brought everything under his direct control.

* * *

From the days of forced labor negotiations, or the period of concentration in the ghettos in February 1943, when the community dignitaries worked intensively without returning home, a fearful note arrived from Beniko:

> My beloved Valika,
> I'm sorry that I cannot come home. I am still very sad, and my heart is heavy, I want so much to see you, if only briefly. Given my tendency to want to change clothes, shoes, etc., I beg you to send me via Avramico a suitcase containing the blue coat, black shoes, socks, shirts with detachable white collars, handkerchiefs, pajamas, and my briefcase. And if you open Moisico's bag, you will find a big notebook, send that to me too. Moise, my brother, has put himself at our disposal, should you want to go to his house, Uncle Isak too. If you cannot go, then I will try to come and meet you and the children at Mother's house tomorrow. About Zizica, send her to Neftel and tell him that I want to…an appointment on Thursday to go to the administrator because I want to take the house.…
> Hugs to the children,
> Your
> Ben[37]

---

37 For the original French, see the appendix.

Three ID cards were obtained for Beniko Saltiel's family: for Valérie (registration number 22), Dario (number 26), and Beniko's mother Eliza (number 27). They were issued in Greek and German by the Jewish Cultural Community of Salonika (Israilitische kultusgemeinde Saloniki). The last ID card is original, it was issued on February 21 and bears Koretz's signature. The other two, marked "copies," are dated May 30 and May 2 and bear the signatures of Albala or Albala and Koretz.

ID cards of Dario, Valérie, and Eliza Saltiel, issued by the Jewish community in 1943

February 25, 1943, a sunny day, brought a new reality for the Jews. They could only move within their ghettos and had to wear the yellow star on their chest; there were signs in their shop windows declaring them Jewish businesses. Would the behavior of Christians change? Would they henceforth be more susceptible to the Nazi arbitrariness? What would the new situation entail? They were forced to adapt to a new "abnormal normality." This very "abnormal normalcy" is apparent in photographs of a group of young friends, the yellow star on their lapels, smiling at the camera. How strange is the effect of such photographs...On the one hand, they confirm the story that they convey and on the other they undermine it.

Zizy Saltiel with friends, the yellow star attached to their clothes

The practical effects of banning Jews from the public, social, and business spheres were accompanied by the deceptions and mockery of the German authorities. Indeed, the Germans reassuringly promised that a self-governing, autonomous community with its own institutions, chamber of commerce, and police would be created, first in Salonika and later in another resettlement area in distant, icy Cracow. These plans went hand in hand with the next stage—the registration of assets in the first week of March. Kavala, who has studied this material thoroughly, believes that the asset declarations are quite accurate.[38] The more optimistic they were, the more readily they were deceived. Only a few months previously the Jews had bought themselves out of forced labor; maybe they would now be able to buy their lives…The requisition of assets would perhaps serve as a ransom payment. Beniko Saltiel hastened to complete the declaration for his family, detailing his considerable immovable and movable assets.[39] The family now lived in one of the ghettos, at 56 Edmondou Rostan Street, with Beniko's recently widowed mother, who made a separate declaration.

* * *

In the five weeks between February 6 and March 15, the day of the first deportation to Auschwitz, the community collapsed under the stranglehold of the Germans. The Baron Hirsch district, which is adjacent to the railway station and was inhabited by poor Jews, was fenced off with barbed wire. At the same time, certain traitors and collaborators, the most prominent among them Vital Hasson, began their activities: extortion, violence, and humiliation threatened those who dared to oppose his predatory intentions.[40] On March 7, Brunner summoned the Judenrat and hundreds of dignitaries, using Koretz as an interpreter. Brunner announced that from that day on they would all be deported as "hostages." Koretz handed over a list of the names of 104 highly respected

---

38 M. Kavala, *Salonika during the German Occupation*, pp. 267ff.
39 Beniko Saltiel's declaration of assets, HAJCTh, folder 00021: 00507–00510.
40 See "Trial of the Traitors," July 1946, Vital Hasson, Jacques Albala, and others, HAJCTh, folder 00190.1: 00002–00340.

Jews, selected for this purpose in collaboration with the Judenrat, who were to be executed should they attempt to escape from the ghettos in which all the Jews of Salonika were concentrated.[41]

* * *

All the escape routes were now closed, and nobody—the Red Cross, the Church, the Greek authorities—seems to have been able to provide assistance. By order of the Germans, 300 railway carriages arrived at the station. Solomon Uziel writes that new proposals by the Judenrat to ransom the deportees were directed to Merten, adding that the plan to ransom the deportees— according to Merten, of course—was met with opposition from the Nazi organizations in Greece. Yet the unknown destination and the miserable situation in which the overwhelming majority of the Jewish population found itself led to general despair. The two committees consulted repeatedly and tried to drum up food and shoes for the poor. They exchanged opinions and arguments, analyzed the international political situation, and imagined the community as a bone of contention between the Allies and the Germans, as a "hostage" until the end of the war.

The race was an unequal fight. On March 15, the first transport left for Auschwitz. Following hard work and thanks to the mediation of the general governor of Macedonia and the metropolitan bishop, Koretz managed to arrange a meeting with Prime Minister Rallis, who was visiting the city. The encounter indeed took place, but it yielded no positive results. This initiative even cost Koretz his office. He was punished and taken to the Baron Hirsch ghetto with his family. Koretz's absolute reign had lasted for about three crucial and fatal months. With his dismissal, Albala returned to the stage as chairman of the Judenrat. The dance of the cursed trains began…

Some managed to get to Athens and thus save their lives or avoid arrest for the time being, for example Yakoel. The escape was dangerous and required funds that not everyone possessed.

41 Carpi, "A New Approach to Some Episodes."

Beniko's brother, Moise Saltiel, decided to flee to Athens with his wife, Olga, and their young child. However, during an inspection the Germans arrested Olga, and Moise had to force the child to pretend that he did not know his mother. Father and son arrived safely in Athens. Valérie's sister Nella fled to Athens in June with her husband, journalist Sam Modiano, and their two children. Sam had lost his Italian citizenship in 1933, and so his family had been forced to move into one of the ghettos. On the advice of his colleagues, he asked the consul if he could renew his Italian citizenship, and with the new papers the family traveled safely by train to Athens. As the noose began to tighten around the Jews' necks, they hid themselves with the help of Christian friends.

The committee and the Judenrat sought to alleviate the suffering of the Jews of Salonika a little, providing warm clothing, food, and water for the ten-day journey. In March, five transports brought more than 13,000 Jews to Auschwitz-Birkenau. In April, sixteen more transports followed, each with around 3,000 people.

Solomon Uziel later recalled that "it was foreseen" that he and his family would be on the transport that left on May 9, 1943. At the last moment, he was informed that he should stay in Salonika as a member of the community's finance committee, together with Beniko Saltiel, to prepare food parcels and clothing for around 2,000 workers arriving from Thebes. These were men who had been arrested at the end of March, when the deportations had already begun, for use as forced laborers; they were to be transported from Salonika to Auschwitz on the nineteenth and last transport. Solomon Uziel requested that his brother-in-law Ezra Barzilay remain to help him, and his proposal was accepted. So, they set to work, he writes, and, together with Jacques Revah, Eli Modiano, and Solomon Ezrati, they raised funds and bought shirts, pants, and jackets for the 2,000 workers. Isaac Aruch remembered the workers returning exhausted and ragged to Salonika; together with Beniko Saltiel and Solomon Uziel, he had collected clothing for the unfortunate group: "How were we to know that we were procuring their death shirts?" These workers arrived in Auschwitz on August 18, 1943, on the nineteenth transport.[42]

---

42 Czech, *Auschwitz Chronicle*, p. 465. Around 1,800 men, women, and children

In the meantime, an alleged "special transport" was planned for June 1, destined for Theresienstadt in the northwest of Czechoslovakia.[43] This was a camp ghetto, which served as a kind of "showcase" for the representatives of the Red Cross. Mostly it was simply a transit camp on the way to Auschwitz. "Prominent people," used as hostages, were brought there. The leaders of the community of Salonika, dignitaries, and intellectuals were supposed to be sent to Theresienstadt. It seems that they were given preferential treatment, were promised it, or were simply hoping for it. In truth, this train too arrived in Auschwitz-Birkenau on June 8, 1943.[44] Solomon Uziel writes that he certainly wished to be included on this transport, as did Beniko Saltiel, and a document received by Beniko confirms this version: a "receipt" that "the Jew Saltiel Benico," holder of ID card no. 21, made a payment of 501 Reichsmarks for six people. The confirmation bears the community stamp, is signed by Albala, and is dated May 29, 1943, meaning that it was issued three days before the supposed transport was due to leave for Theresienstadt. However, they were not allowed to leave, Uziel writes, because they had to take care of the 2,000 workers, the last Jews of Salonika, who were sent to Poland on August 10/11.

* * *

As of July 28, Spanish citizens were also taken to the Baron Hirsch ghetto, where there were about 100 other people besides them. The families—the Germans deported whole families, not individuals—formed a heterogeneous group:[45] Zvi Koretz with

were on the last transport. Of these, 271 men went to the camps, the remainder were sent directly to the gas chambers.

43 See George E. Berkley, *Hitler's Gift: The Story of Theresienstadt* (Boston: Branden Books, 1993).

44 Czech, *Auschwitz Chronicle*, p. 415: 880 men, women, and children from Salonika. Of these, 220 men and eighty-eight women passed the selection, the rest went directly to the gas chambers.

45 Of this group see the testimonies of Aryeh Koretz (USHMM, RG-50.120.0080); Josette Counio (VHA, 45194); Edgar Counio (VHA, 42145); Lori B. (HVT, 905); Bella (Uziel) Barzilai (VHA, 41749); Zizy (Saltiel) Benveniste (VHA, 21296); Rina (Barzilai) Revah (VHA, 40031); Dario Saltiel (VHA, 45153); Rosy (Levi) Saltiel (VHA, 44581); and Ino Hasson (VHA, 8771).

Acknowledgment of payment issued to Beniko Saltiel for train tickets to Auschwitz, May 29, 1943

his wife and two children; Solomon Uziel and Ezra Barzilay's families of six; the family of Valérie and Beniko Saltiel; community workers such as Alphonse Levi with his wife and small daughter, Rosi; the doctor Jean Allalouf; the families of Moise Castro, Joseph Errera, David Menache; and others—including the families of Albala, Edgar Counio, and Leon Sion, who had collaborated with the Germans throughout and served as unprecedentedly brutal tools of oppression.[46] Following liberation the latter three were sentenced by the Greek judiciary (see below). On August 2, 1943, the train carrying 367 "Spanish" Jews and seventy-four community members departed from Salonika for Germany and Bergen-Belsen. Vital Hasson, the notorious traitor and brutal commander of the ghetto militia, had already escaped from the Baron Hirsch ghetto, while two or three of his protégés boarded the train.

Of Valérie's sisters, as mentioned, Nella Modiano had already fled to Athens with her husband and children. Of Beniko's siblings, Elda and her family had gone to Belgrade, while Moise had escaped

---

46 In the Central Zionist Archives in Jerusalem there is a document dated October 31, 1944, listing the names of eighteen Jews who allegedly collaborated with the Germans during the occupation. From Salonika: Jacques Albala, Jacques Aboav, Vital Hasson, Zvi Koretz, and Marcel Neftel; the German refugees Blumefeld, Kapel, and Levi are also mentioned (folder S25-7841).

to Athens with his young son. There, as was also mentioned, his wife had been arrested and executed. Emily Saul, married to Beniko's younger brother Albert, was, like the other siblings, on the supposed Theresienstadt transport of June 2. She later recalled, "My husband Alberto Saltiel worked for the community. He did not dare to go away. One of his brothers left, Moise. He went with his wife and child. They caught her in Larissa and shot her. When they were caught, Moise hid with the child, they were not discovered, and that's how they survived. But his wife, mother-in-law, and brother-in-law were shot dead. What happened terrified us, it was something that happened in **our** family and had an impact on us."[47]

As was noted above, the Judenräte consisted of people who had already led the community in the prewar period. As elsewhere,[48] in Salonika members of the elite formed the Judenrat and the Central Committee: wealthy individuals and significant figures who had traditionally been involved not only in leading the community but also in the economic and social life of the city. Sam Arditi, Albert Arditi, Albert Tchenio, and Beniko Saltiel had been leading members of the city's Chamber of Commerce and Industry. Thus, they were asked to organize the community, to take protective measures, to negotiate, and to compromise. They did so, most likely with a sense of responsibility and self-confidence. Still, the dilemmas they now faced were entirely different to those they had known before the war. Therefore, their stance became the object of not only rational understanding but also of polemic and legend.[49]

Some of them fled, possessing the necessary resources and connections. Yakov Yakoel tried to, but he was betrayed and arrested in Athens. Those who decided, or were forced, to stay— each for their own reasons and needs, and with their own self-deceptions—were completely isolated. They lost their homes and

---

47 VHA, 37995, see also Emilia Saul's testimony in Kounio-Amarilio and Nar, eds., *Oral Testimonies*, pp. 194–195. Emphasis in the original.

48 Lucjan Dobroszycki, "Jewish Elites under German Rule," in Henry Friedlander and Sybil Milton, eds., *The Holocaust: Ideology, Bureaucracy and Genocide* (New York: Kraus International Publications, 1980), pp. 221–230.

49 Ibid., p. 222.

businesses, their rights and recognition, and the connections and contacts that their involvement in associations and organizations had brought them. Their communication with the outside world, formerly guaranteed via radio, newspapers, and correspondence, stopped, and they learned that the Germans were now using them as hostages. Despite all this, they clung to their illusions, their belief in the agreements and cultural rules. Over time, and as the machinery of deportations began to move, these illusions lost their meaning. They considered the phase of "relative calm" a time of stabilization; the situation had deteriorated, but it was stable. The storm would blow over, the war would end. During this time, the isolation of the Jews from their Christian fellow citizens and their complete powerlessness were sealed. The plans of the Nazis, built on deception, were successfully implemented.

All the Judenräte were caught in a net that instrumentalized their "self-administration." As Zygmunt Baumann wrote,[50] the members of such councils played a mediating role in weakening the Jews, but they had no choice. They were forced into a game of "save what you can," a game of rational action and good intentions that inevitably led to the deaths of many and the—provisional—survival of a few. It was a situation of **choiceless choices**, in Lawrence Langer's paradoxical and pertinent formulation.[51] The involvement of the victims in the perpetrators' actions was part of the Nazi project of mass destruction. According to Dan Diner, **self-destruction through**

---

50 Zygmunt Bauman, *Modernity and the Holocaust* (Ithaca: Cornell University Press, 1989), pp. 117–150, esp. p. 149.

51 Lawrence Langer, *Versions of Survival: The Holocaust and Human Spirit* (Albany: State University Press of New York, 1982), p. 72. Primo Levi's *zona grizia* is a metaphor for the ethically dubious stances that arose in the extreme circumstances of the extermination process. Not only does Levi himself warn against any confusion between victims and perpetrators, but he also insists that those in that "gray area" should not be condemned in retrospect. See also Primo Levi, *La zone grise*. This dimension of Primo Levi's work, including his reluctance to judge, is taken up by Adam Brown. However, in Brown's interesting book, *Judging the "Privileged" Jews: Holocaust Ethics, Representation and the "Grey Zone"* (New York: Berghahn, 2013), different categories of "privileged" Jews (members of the Judenräte, special committees, etc.) are mixed in a way that does not always meet analytical requirements.

self-preservation was the terrible moment of a universally applicable borderline experience.[52]

Aside from the Greek case, we see that in Vienna the lists of candidates for emigration—that is, salvation—were converted into death lists that led to the camps. In Poland, job opportunities with the German authorities were often the only way to survive in the face of terrible marginalization. Unlike those who were saved because they were able to flee, the members of the Judenräte (at least some of them) demonstrated a sense of responsibility to the community. In any case, that was roughly the picture they drew of themselves—then as well as later. Solomon Uziel is emphatic about this point too: "We were captains in the storm...we could not leave the ship." With the offer of work (in Poland) or of money (in the case of Salonika and elsewhere) the Judenräte fought against time, trying to exploit the disparity between the Nazis' desire to destroy and their quest for profit. They also wanted to exploit the tension between the local administration (in the case of Salonika, Max Merten) and the SS officers (in Salonika, Brunner and Wisliceny), who received their orders from Berlin. In many cases, the fate of the Jews depended on the course of the war. The community of Lodz would have been saved if the Red Army had not had to halt their advance and had only marched in a little earlier, as Yehuda Bauer repeatedly emphasized. The existential question of responsibility, which arises in hindsight, remains. However, I am by no means sure that history can give us an answer.

Certainly, the responses of the Judenräte to some extent always depended on local circumstances, as well as on the personalities, capabilities, and moral strength of the people heading them. Yet this issue is difficult to investigate. The Judenräte maneuvered between Scylla and Charybdis: if they carried out the orders, they facilitated the process of annihilation; if they refused, they gave up the idea of slowing down the extermination process—and any delay could prove lifesaving when the war seemed to be coming to an end. Or, worse, the responsibility was handed over to others, with unknown consequences. There was no way out of this dilemma when very

---

52 Dan Diner, *Beyond the Conceivable*, p. 117.

few could grasp the "cultural caesura" that Nazism introduced, denying the most basic forms of thought and overruling all moral presuppositions. Salonika's Judenrat functioned by continuing a long tradition according to which the elite oversaw the community's self-government. The merchants had based their success on rational action, foresight, and belief in the binding nature of agreements. They were familiar with this code, and they behaved according to it: this, in the final analysis, was a mistake. The Germans, in opposition, trusted in their strategies of deception: they encouraged mutual aid and engaged in deceptive activities. As Joseph Ben noted, the Nazis suggested that negotiations might be helpful and that the Judenräte might be able to exert a little influence.[53] Yet Nazism and the occupation had shaken the rational and moral foundations of the world and that is precisely what must not be overlooked in *a posteriori* interpretations.

In May 1943, the last Greek Jews were transported to the Baron Hirsch ghetto. Rosy Saltiel, the six-year-old daughter of community employee Alphonse Levi, recalled that time. "There were," she explained many years later, "**pessimists**, and there were **optimists**: the former tried not to go to the Baron Hirsch camp; the most credulous were the optimists." She also remembered that some managed to escape from the ghetto by hiding in garbage cans and that Christian friends had said to her parents, "Give us Rosy so we can hide her." But how could she be separated from her family?...Rosy also remembered the terror that prevailed in the ghetto, the fear of the next train, and the journey into the unknown. During the day, the ghetto was noisy and militia officers came and went. In the evening they were locked in, and only the militiamen were still on the street. Misery increased the tensions and anger, and any solidarity was lost.

The train, which left Salonika on August 2, arrived at its destination on August 13—the Bergen-Belsen camp located in northwest Germany, near the Celle station—after an eleven-day journey interrupted by many stops.

---

53 Ben, "Jewish Leadership," pp. 341ff. My emphasis.

Chapter 12

Bergen-Belsen: August 1943–April 1945

The Camp

Bergen-Belsen is often described as a strange camp. Indeed, many different policies of the Third Reich converged there.[1] The camp's establishment, purpose, internal history, and its symbolic value were all unique. Although over time it was perfectly integrated into the Nazi system of oppression, it was initially set up to house groups of Jews who were to be exchanged as part of a diplomatic plan. The name of the camp first appears in an official document dated April 1943. One month earlier, Ernst Kaltenbrunner, Reinhard Heydrich's successor as head of the Reich Security Headquarters, had ordered that the lives of certain Jews be spared.[2] Subsequently, the first Jewish candidates for exchange from Poland arrived at the camp in July 1943. Most of them ended up in Auschwitz, and only very few Jews, as we shall see, were actually exchanged.

1   David Cesarani, Tony Kushner, Joanne Reilly, and Colin Richmond, eds., *Belsen in History and Memory* (London: Routledge, 1997).
2   David Cesarani, "A Brief History of Bergen-Belsen," in Suzanne Bardgett and David Cesarani, eds., *Belsen 1945: New Historical Perspectives* (London: Vallentine Mitchell, 2006), pp. 13–21. The most comprehensive history of the camp is Eberhard Kolb, *Bergen-Belsen: Geschichte des "Aufenthaltslagers" 1943–1945* (Hannover: Verlag für Literatur und Zeitgeschehen, 1962). I used the condensed English edition *Bergen-Belsen: From 1939 to 1945* (Göttingen: Vandenhoeck, 1985).

When the British liberated the camp on April 15, 1945, they were confronted with a terrible sight. Photographs, published almost immediately, show victims' corpses piled high, reduced to skeletons, with no name and no personal history. In the first weeks after the liberation, in addition to the 37,000 already murdered at Bergen-Belsen, who were almost exclusively Jews, 13,000 to 14,000 died of exhaustion, typhus, tuberculosis, or dysentery. Initially, war correspondents did not attribute any importance to the fact that the victims were Jews. For the British, the event was more important as a chapter in the military history of liberation from the Nazi yoke than anything else.[3]

Before the war, there were facilities for training German soldiers in the area around the camp, and in 1943 some buildings for the SS were added. In fact, Bergen-Belsen was a complex of camps built at different times and separated by wire fences. Each camp was organized differently in terms of forced labor and oppression. At the end of the central pathway through the camp was a crematorium for the incineration of the dead. The camp consisted of three main sections: the prisoner of war camp, the prisoners' camp (*Häftlingslager*), and the residence camp (*Aufenthaltslager*).

As of 1940, 600 French and Belgian prisoners of war were interned in the prisoner of war camp. After the German invasion of the Soviet Union, about 20,000 to 30,000 Soviet prisoners of war were taken to the camp. The living conditions led to the death of about 100 prisoners per day. This prisoner of war camp consisted of the original prisoners' camp (*Häftlingslager*), to which were added the so-called recuperation camp (*Erholungslager*), the so-called tent camp (*Zeltlager*), the small women's camp (*Kleines Frauenlager*), and the large women's camp (*Grosses Frauenlager*). The *Häftlingslager* housed the approximately 500 prisoners who arrived from other camps in the spring of 1943 to build the residence camp.

---

3 Joanne Reilly and Donald Bloxham, "The Belsen Camp in Historical Context," in Ben Flanagan, Donald Bloxham, and Joanne Reilly, eds., *Remembering Belsen: Eyewitnesses Record the Liberation* (London: Vallentine Mitchell, 2005), pp. 126–139.

The residence camp consisted of four subcamps: the special camp (*Sonderlager*), the neutral camp (*Neutralenlager*), the star camp (*Sternlager*), and the Hungarian camp (*Ungarnlager*). The residence camp was founded in April 1943, when a previously vacant camp area was selected to house Jewish candidates for exchange, who were often referred to as "privileged." Sometimes the residence camp is also called the exchange camp. At first, life there may have been "bearable," but it was never "privileged." Soon the camp came under the authority of the SS Economic and Administrative Main Office, meaning that it was not under the control of the Red Cross inspectors. Thus, prisoners could be evacuated to an extermination camp at any time.

Nazi policy did not preclude the possibility of ransoming Jews that the Allies considered "significant" in exchange for Germans interned in the Allied states or for diplomatic purposes. In addition, the German Foreign Ministry supported the view that Jews holding passports of neutral states should be exempt from deportations in order to avoid diplomatic incidents. It seems that Himmler never gave up on the idea of "setting aside" a small number of Jews as an exchange reserve, and he clung to the decision even after the Final Solution was decreed. With Hitler's verbal approval, Himmler chose to exchange certain Jews if this would entail significant benefits for the Third Reich, especially when Germany began to lose power. In 1943, when millions of Jews had already been deported, the German Foreign Ministry and the SS leadership agreed to keep some Jews to be exchanged for Germans detained by the British and Americans. The negotiations continued even when the systematic annihilation had been set in motion in Slovakia and Hungary. In fact, few such exchanges took place.[4] The overwhelming majority of exchange Jews remained in

4 In 1944, 222 Dutch Jews with Palestinian papers were exchanged for Germans living in Mandatory Palestine; they reached their destination in July 1944, see Abraham N. Oppenheim, *The Chosen People: The story of the '222 Transport' from Bergen-Belsen to Palestine* (London: Vallentine Mitchell, 1996). In January 1945, 136 Jews with papers from South American countries were sent to Switzerland. In July 1944, 1,684 Hungarian Jews from Bergen-Belsen were brought to Switzerland, after Rudolf Kasztner persuaded Eichmann, as a sign

Bergen-Belsen under conditions that steadily worsened, slowly but surely leading to their deaths.

Separated by nationality and by barbed wire, the different groups of prisoners interned in Bergen-Belsen had different experiences. The residence camp, where the deportees from Salonika were also housed, became increasingly full. The first transport with Jews arrived on April 29, 1943, and another followed in mid-June. The June transport included 2,400 Polish Jews who possessed consular documents (*promesas*) certifying that they were to receive passports from Central and South American countries. The tragic story of the betrayal of this promise and its hopes ended with the deportation of most of them to Auschwitz in late 1943 and early 1944.

The Jews from Salonika belonged to the next wave of arrivals. The "Spaniards" were immediately separated and sent to the neutral camp, where they remained until February 1944. After lengthy diplomatic negotiations, they were first taken to the Spanish border and thence to Mandatory Palestine, under relatively tolerable conditions and with an exemption from forced labor. The remaining Jews were housed in the star camp. The star camp owes its name to the fact that the internees kept their civilian clothes but wore the yellow star on their chests. Men and women were housed in separate barracks. The next transport after the arrival of the Greek Jews in the star camp in 1944 consisted of 3,670 candidates for exchange from Holland. In the same subcamp, together with the Greek and Dutch Jews, there were also Jews from North Africa, Belgium, France, Yugoslavia, and Albania.

The transports to Bergen-Belsen in 1944 also included 1,000 sick people from the Mittelbau-Dora camp who were sent there to "recover." Subsequently, in June 1944, 1,683 Hungarian Jews arrived and were accommodated in the Hungarian camp. Bergen-Belsen began absorbing numbers that exceeded its capacity. This affected the hygiene conditions and the food portions, bringing

of goodwill toward the Allies, to release them, see Yehuda Bauer, *Jews for Sale: Nazi-Jewish Negotiations 1933–1945* (New Haven: Yale University Press, 1996).

the situation to crisis point. From August 1944, thousands of Polish and Hungarian Jews from Buchenwald, Flossenbürg, and Auschwitz-Birkenau arrived in Bergen-Belsen. They brought with them terrible news of Jews being murdered in gas chambers. In December 1944, Bergen-Belsen housed 15,000 prisoners. Josef Kramer, the former commander of Auschwitz, took over the leadership of the camp, bringing with him new personnel: Kapos, who had themselves been prisoners in Auschwitz, now took charge of the barracks and forced labor.

As the Red Army advanced, Bergen-Belsen eventually became a reception center for prisoners who had been evacuated from other labor or extermination camps. Thousands arrived, exhausted by the death marches, among them prisoners from Auschwitz and Ravensbrück. In March, the number of inmates reached 42,000, and in April it was 60,000. Without sanitation, without water, without food, and with a typhus epidemic raging, the inmates died en masse. In February 1945, 7,000 people died of hunger, disease, and exhaustion, with 18,000 dying in March, and an additional 9,000 in April.

Once the reasons for exemption from the Final Solution were no longer valid, the Jewish candidates for exchange returned to their original status as victims destined for annihilation.[5] When the gas chambers were no longer in use, the destruction of the Jews was left to starvation, exhaustion, epidemics, and, in second place, executions. In other words, the mass transfer of prisoners from other camps and the concomitant worsening of living conditions meant that Bergen-Belsen was integrated into the comprehensive universe of the Nazi camp system. The overcrowding brought with it the final catastrophe for the prisoners in the form of typhus, dysentery, and starvation. According to Eberhard Kolb, the transformation of a typical concentration camp into a "camp of terror" did not happen by chance. Rather, this was the result of an internal logic of the camp system and the mentality of its

---

5 Christine Lattek, "Bergen-Belsen: From 'Privileged' Camp to Death Camp," in Cesarani, Kushner, Reilly, and Richmond, *Belsen in History and Memory*, pp. 37–71.

"employees." In this sense, Kolb stresses, Bergen-Belsen symbolizes the entire barbarity of crimes committed by the Nazi regime.[6]

The Star Camp

As we have seen, the Jews of Salonika arrived in Bergen-Belsen on August 13, after a journey in cattle cars that was interrupted by many stops. They were housed in the star camp, where the women and young children were separated from the men. Instead of the characteristic striped camp uniforms they wore their own clothes, with the yellow star on their lapels. They did not have a number tattooed onto their forearms. Families could meet during the day. In the dormitories there were bunk beds, initially only with two levels. The regular calls for prisoners to attend a head count could be repeated many times over the course of a day and lasted for lengthy periods, no matter the weather. A large group of inmates worked in the *Schuhkommando* (shoe commando): they spent up to fourteen hours a day extracting valuable leather from the deportees' shoes, which were piled high in front of them. Another task force had to chop down huge tree trunks outside the camp, a heavy and exhausting job. The outdoor work—road construction, moving earth, soil, and so on—was the hardest.

Work in the kitchen was exhausting but preferable because it offered a way to get food. As early as the summer of 1944, food was the prisoners' main concern. Daily life was dominated by exhaustion and hunger, the constant fear of punishment if orders were not carried out to the letter, despair, and the sense of abandonment. When the Dutch Jews arrived, they were also housed in the star camp, as were Jews from Albania, Yugoslavia, and Tripoli, as well as French women who came via the Drancy transit camp.

The "privileges" in the star camp also included a degree of self-government. The ten-member Council of Elders was made up of Greeks and Dutchmen. Jacques Albala became the head of the

6   Kolb, *Bergen-Belsen: From 1939 to 1945*, p. 50.

Jews in the camp, the Jewish Elder, and was responsible for the implementation of the Germans' orders.[7] Along with his wife and child, he lived in a space sectioned off from the rest of the dormitory. Edgar Counio also held an important office: he decided on the distribution of prisoners to the camp workforces. The Council of Elders regulated affairs between the prisoners. In December 1944, Albala was replaced by Walter Hanke, a Dutchman.[8] The last Jewish Elder was the German Jew Josef Weiss, who came from Holland and was a respectable person, in contrast to Albala, who was considered corrupt.[9]

What do we know about the experiences of the prisoners in the star camp? In addition to written[10] and oral testimonies, we possess some diaries that conditions in the star camp allowed inmates to keep. Worth mentioning are the diaries of Abel Herzberg, born in Amsterdam in 1893, Hanna Levy-Hass, born in Sarajevo in 1913, and the son of Chief Rabbi Koretz, Aryeh Koretz, thirteen at the time.[11] Although only Koretz belonged to

---

7   Hetty Verolme recalled that they were received in the camp by Albala. When her father complained to Albala about the unfair treatment of his children, he was punished by being put into solitary confinement. Nevertheless, Albala prevented his removal to another camp, which would have been tantamount to a death sentence. See Hetty Verolme, *Children's House of Belsen* (Perth: Freemantle Press, 2000), pp. 53ff.

8   He came from Dora Camp in March 1944. Before becoming camp elder of all Bergen-Belsen, he had been the elder in Dora. In April 1945 he died of typhus.

9   See Hans-Dieter Arntz, *Der letzte Judenälteste von Bergen-Belsen: Josef Weiss. Würdig in einer unwürdigen Umgebung* (Aachen: Helios, 2012).

10 Albert Bigielman, *J'ai eu douze ans à Bergen-Belsen* (Paris: Editions Le Manuscrit, Fondation pour la Mémoire de la Shoah, 2005); Jacques Saurel, *De Drancy à Bergen-Belsen, 1944–1945: Souvenirs rassemblés d'un enfant déporté* (Paris: Editions Le Manuscrit, Fondation pour la Mémoire de la Shoah, 2006); Tomi Reichental, *I Was a Boy in Belsen* (Dublin: The O'Brien Press, 2011).

11 Abel Jacob Herzberg, *Between Two Streams: A Diary from Bergen-Belsen* (London and New York: I. B. Tauris Publishers, 1997). Hanna Levy-Hass, *Diary of Bergen-Belsen: 1944–1945* (Chicago: Haymarket Books, 2009). The work was first published in Serbian in 1946. Aryeh Koretz, *Yoman Bergen-Belzen, 11.7.1944–30.3.1945* (Hebrew) (Tel Aviv: n.p., 1992). See also Renata Lacqueur, *Bergen-Belsen Tagebuch, 1944–1945* (Hannover: Fackelträger, 1983). The diary was first published in Dutch in 1965. Lacqueur, who later also wrote a thesis regarding diaries from the concentration camps, writes that her book reflects the efforts of an eyewitness to escape reality by writing, leaving it to the

the group of Greek Jews, I will focus on these three diaries, which introduce us to the world of the star camp and reveal to us how it was perceived and experienced by certain prisoners. The diaries enable us to understand what their authors did and did not know, how they interpreted and judged what was happening around them, according to their gender, age, education, profession, and social background; in other words, how very different people perceived the experience of deportation and internment in concentration camps and how they drew strength, seeking refuge in writing. The diaries, written in different languages, cover more or less the same period.[12]

Aryeh Koretz describes what happened to him in his daily life. His testimony is that of a boy forced to grow up quickly. His entries concern his own experiences, his efforts to find a better work placement, to secure food, to survive fever and pain, and to cure himself of the edema caused by the lack of hygiene in the camp. Abel Herzberg, an intellectual and a lawyer, observed the world around him and meditated on the human behaviors resulting from Nazi barbarity. Hanna Levy-Hass, an intellectual and a Communist, also observed the world around her but without losing sight of the vision of another world after liberation. All the diaries, each one in its own way, show us life in the camp day by day and event by event. They depict the bitter experience of expulsion, overcrowding, the exhausting work—even with a fever of 38.5 degrees Celsius people were still considered able to work—and the constant roll calls under a regime of terror. They portray humiliation and punishment,

---

reader's imagination to develop an idea of that reality. For her oral testimony see USHMM, RG-50.030.0370.

12 Herzberg's diary describes the period from August 11, 1944, to April 26, 1945, that of Levy-Hass from August 16, 1944 to April 1945, and Koretz's diary begins in June 14, 1944, concluding on March 30, 1945. Hanna Levy-Hass, a native of Sarajevo, kept her diary in Serbo-Croat but could not publish it in postwar Yugoslavia; she then translated it into French herself. I consulted both the French and later English versions. Aryeh Koretz preferred to keep his diary in Greek and then translated it into Hebrew many years later. Abel Herzberg wrote and published his diary in Dutch and the English translation of the diary is the work of a younger inmate who identified with it.

the increasing hunger and worries about finding, at best, half a piece of bread, as well as the continuing arrival of new masses of wretched human beings, now coming in droves from the other camps, the absence of basic hygiene, lice and typhus, illness and fever, exhaustion and death.

Under such extreme conditions, self-sacrifice and the manifestation of solidarity, as well as selfishness and harshness, reached a climax, as Hanna Levy-Hass and Abel Herzberg both testify. The latter emphasizes the dark side of human behavior: "Who is scum?" asks Herzberg, before answering: "Scum is someone who manages to obtain a crumb more than another. What is honesty? The conviction that in the long run it is **more advantageous** to distribute everything equally...The weak are honest."[13] He was struck by the struggles between people who are no longer young, people who had been highly respected in their hometowns and now argue about every little thing, and he says to himself: "People complain bitterly about each other. But how could it be any different?...Loneliness cries out from us. Four thousand lonely people, that is our community. Judge them but forgive them nothing."[14]

Elderly people who used to have a secure life and whose children were now far away in Poland found themselves hungry and in a far worse position, complaining that they were disadvantaged in the distribution of food. And yet families clung to the idea of abstaining for the sake of kith and kin: a piece of bread for one's partner because one's own hunger could be endured, if at least the other was satiated...[15] By contrast, the lack of understanding between people who had previously experienced marital problems now heightened. A report by Herzberg on community life in the camp is of interest, because it mentions the Greeks in "hut twelve": "On Sunday evenings, when the French, Albanian, and Serbian Jews are the guests of the Greeks, there is singing. Then there is excitement and life in the group. A freedom song, and the rhythm

---

13 Herzberg, *Between two Streams*, pp. 10–11. Emphasis in the original.
14 Ibid., p. 33.
15 Ibid.

is accompanied by handclapping and stamping of feet. The SS finally leave us in peace." He continues:

> Yet the song wells up and the full vitality, the stubborn power of the Jewish nation breaks through. French and Greek, Serbian and Russian songs are sung, most incomprehensible but everyone knows their meaning: "Il faut se tenir"...Then, at the end, the Greek national anthem and after that...Hebrew, *Ha-Tikvah*.[16]

First-class singers, violin virtuosos, Greeks and others, girls performing folk songs; one sees how Jews the world over are similar to one another.[17] In the midst of absolute misery, scenes of solidarity take place: one helps another, a doctor puts a bandage on someone, a woman cooks for a sick person, a warm coat is shared, a mother courageously takes responsibility for an orphaned child...[18] Yet the constant persecution creates an atmosphere of corruption. Herzberg gives a psychogram of all those who have no scruples and act without thought, who became the slaves of the new masters.

Hanna Levy-Hass relentlessly condemns the pettiness and selfishness. "In general," she writes, "everyone continues to display mean and petty habits, selfishness and narrow-mindedness. Out of this comes endless conflicts of interest, friction, and cases of bigotry on top of it all."[19] She continues, describing the distrust that reigns in the camp and the barracks; the lack of interest in anyone else's fate, lack of solidarity and cordiality. Those who act ruthlessly get everything thanks to this opportunistic attitude; they do not care about what happens in the parasite-infested barracks; they do not care about hunger, fever, death, decay, not to mention morality.[20] Gradually, the consciousness of a unifying common destiny is lost, and with it all solidarity. Theft, exploitation, and corruption ensue, a shameless marketplace.

16 Ibid., p. 14.
17 Ibid., p. 129.
18 Ibid., p. 26.
19 Levy-Hass, *Diary of Bergen-Belsen*, pp. 39ff.
20 Ibid., p. 67.

The women somehow survived: They scolded and yelled, but because they had to look after their children, they were forced to be practical, to show a sense of community, and sometimes even sacrifice themselves.[21] "Our mothers in the camps were wonderful,"[22] a French survivor who had come to a camp as a child recalls with gratitude. In the camp, men proved to be weaker than women, both physically and morally, as Levy-Hass emphasized: hunger manifested itself in their faces and in their movements very differently to its manifestation in women. Few preserved their dignity, without cowardice, in the face of the enemy.

In Bergen-Belsen, the prisoners were—at least initially— sorted by nationality. This may have made solidarity within these groups easier, but it also encouraged potential rivalry with other groups. When the Dutch arrived, the Greeks were already among the veterans in the camp, and Albala had been appointed Jewish elder. According to the diary of the young Koretz, there was often friction between his father, the rabbi, and Albala. Bigielman recalled that the "internal leadership" of the prisoners were Greeks and that they were "seriously detested by the others."[23] In his diary, Herzberg, in addition to documenting the daily routine of hunger and death and his thoughts on the fate of the Jewish people, details the function of the "internal leadership" as the successor of the Amsterdam Judenrat (De Joodse Raad voor Amsterdam). In August 1944, he wrote with extraordinary clarity about the role of the Amsterdam Judenrat and its members, who lived with the illusion that they would be able to save lives by clever tactics and avert the worst, as they claimed, or at least delay the implementation of measures.

The Judenräte were nothing more than burial societies that the Third Reich considered essential in burying the Jewish communities that were doomed to die or had already been murdered. They were, therefore, executive organs of planned or completed policies. As such, the Judenräte fulfilled their tasks

21 Ibid., pp. 72–73.
22 Saurel, *De Drancy à Bergen-Belsen*, p. 110.
23 Bigielman, *J'ai eu douze ans à Bergen-Belsen*, p. 99.

to perfection. They made only one mistake: they imagined the undertaker could reach a compromise with death. Nothing lies further from the truth. Death is relentless, merciless...Burial is a necessity, and an undertaker a useful creature. He must just know his place, and above all he must not assume the role of "leader" of mankind.[24]

In Bergen-Belsen, Herzberg continues, there was also a Judenrat called the Council of Elders:

It, too, is primarily the executor of decisions made by the Germans. Members of the *Rat* must dance to the tune of the Third Reich more than others. At the head of the *Ältestenrat* is the *Judenälteste*. He is appointed and dismissed by the commandant. Consistent with the principles of leadership, the other members of the *Rat* are likewise not elected by the internees but appointed by the commandant on the recommendation of the *Judenälteste*. The *Judenälteste* is a Greek [Jacques Albala], a strongly-built fair-haired man who—unlike the other internees—has not lost an ounce of his former weight despite a really incredibly hard working day trotting almost non-stop behind every SS man...The *Judenälteste* receives three times as much to eat as anyone else and is proud of it...This has earned him a reputation of being "corrupt"...For our *Judenälteste* is not so much corrupt, as a kind of robber chief. In reality he is a gangster. Politics is a very popular hunting ground for the robber chief, which largely explains the surprisingly rapid diffusion of Fascist and National Socialist ideas..."[25]

Ironically and with disgust, Herzberg speaks of preferential treatment and the behavior of the Albala family, noting that the Jewish elder lived together with his wife and two-year-old child in a separate area bordered by cupboards and shelves. Nevertheless, he

24 Herzberg, *Between Two Streams*, p. 21.
25 Ibid., pp. 21–22.

describes with respect the advisory body to which the Jewish elder, who also acted as judge, was attached.[26] This body was comprised of experienced lawyers like himself.

On the occasion of the arrival of Jews from Theresienstadt, Herzberg commented on the "self-government" there and in Bergen-Belsen.[27] The disadvantage, he emphasizes, is corruption; on the other hand, the Jews' control over the work assignments, the guarantee of unity, etc., offered an advantage. By dividing the people into work groups, the Council of Elders managed to save hundreds from death by exhaustion.[28] The diary of the young Koretz likewise emphasizes how a particular work assignment could lead to complete exhaustion and the death of the weak.

The legal committee decided, Herzberg continues, that somehow law had to prevail in the camp. According to Herzberg, theft of food was a constant threat, yet everyone was reduced to the same degree of poverty and needed the same calories. The committee met in a separate section of the dormitory. This section was known as the Palace of Justice, the *Palais de Justice*, a name coined by French women who had not quite lost their sense of humor. The elders tried to prevent thefts, which could have fatal consequences for the victims, and intervened in other matters: they acted as mediators and made Albala pardon a woman from Zagreb for showing disrespect.[29] As judges, the chief rabbi of Salonika, Koretz, and a lawyer from Montenegro had to determine the case of a woman who had stolen salt, and another who had stolen a headscarf.[30]

Herzberg also clarifies the limits of the Council of Elders's charitable work with the following example: The Germans demanded 190 women for the *Schuhkommando*; the leadership had to drum them up. If some refused, others would have to pay for it, and all were threatened with collective punishment. Thus, it was vital to ensure discipline. Yet it was unthinkable that Jews

26 Ibid., p. 26.
27 Ibid., p. 122.
28 Ibid., p. 17.
29 Ibid., pp. 138–139.
30 Ibid., p. 61.

would punish other Jews for refusing to work for the Germans. Once a system of cooperation (a more agreeable word for voluntary slavery) has been adopted, gradually a judicial commission also emerged, pronouncing judgements against people who did not want to subject themselves to the German orders.[31]

As we have already seen, the situation in the camp deteriorated sharply: more and more people arrived, and the inmates suffered from overcrowding, hunger, epidemics, death. Kramer, who learned his trade at Auschwitz, took over the leadership, and on December 22 Albala and the Council of Elders were deposed.[32] The Greeks, writes Herzberg, lost the privilege of distributing the packages from the Red Cross.[33] Above all, the Kapo system was now introduced, with non-Jewish prisoners taking the lead. Unlike the Jews, who had never used blows,[34] they provided discipline using punches, clubs, and sticks.[35]

Levy-Hass also notes the changes in the system of "self-government": "Kramer dismissed the Jewish camp commander. The Jews will no longer have a say in the blocks." She herself was more distant from the circle of the council and the judges, condemning them more harshly: "All the administration members are disgraced. To be frank, they were all corrupt, insensitive to the group's misery, completely indifferent."[36] The non-Jewish Kapos used by Kramer—Germans, French, Poles—she continues, were ordinary criminals; they wore striped clothing and beat people for nothing. Their victims were in such pain that often they could not move afterwards. For every supposed crime, even a matter of stashing away a few onions, there was a risk of being put in solitary confinement or being taken to another camp. It was impossible to escape from the camp. "Besides, who would wish to escape? Where to?"[37] Herzberg asked resignedly.

31 Ibid., p. 156.
32 Ibid., p. 185.
33 Ibid., p. 188.
34 Ibid., p. 39.
35 Ibid., p. 191.
36 Levy-Hass, *Diary of Bergen-Belsen*, p. 97.
37 Herzberg, *Between Two Streams*, p. 12.

Nevertheless, there were different forms of resistance in the camp. We have already mentioned efforts at self-organization: protecting universal equality and preventing food theft. We also mentioned the different forms of solidarity and care, and the singing...The Jews' reaction to the Nazis' desire to destroy them was also a form of resistance. Indeed, the prisoners tried in every possible way to preserve their strength: they did not walk fast if they could walk slowly, and if they could stay in bed for five minutes here and there, they did so.[38] Aryeh Koretz also describes his desperate efforts to keep up his strength.

Levy-Hass took care of the children with infinite patience: 110 children between the ages of three and fifteen lived in her barracks. Despite the prohibitions, secretly, without books, with just a few pieces of paper, she organized classes for them. And despite the fact that "bad habits catch on quickly among children in calamitous times and in an overall atmosphere of distrust and fear...Nevertheless, we do what we can, and the children's fundamentally good nature often wins out."[39] A French gentleman took over history lessons,[40] and the French women, in a daring act carried out on the feast of the July 14, sewed rags in the colors of the French flag onto their clothes.[41] Jews from North Africa celebrated *Simchat Torah*; they were, as Herzberg notes, deeply devout and not assimilated like the Dutch Jews and those from the Balkans.[42] *Yom Kippur* was also celebrated, even though this was prohibited. A letter from Josef Weiss to his relatives dated July 1945 reveals that during the Passover festival the Seder night was celebrated in the children's barrack in spring 1945.[43]

Cut off from the outside world, the prisoners felt a great need for news that would provide a solid foundation for the unconfirmed

---

38 Ibid.
39 Levy-Hass, *Diary of Bergen-Belsen*, p. 45.
40 Bigielman, *J'ai eu douze ans à Bergen-Belsen*, p. 94.
41 Saurel, *De Drancy à Bergen-Belsen*, p. 115; see also Bigielman, *J'ai eu douze ans à Bergen-Belsen*, p. 101.
42 Herzberg, *Between Two Streams*, p. 143.
43 See Arntz, *Der letzte Judenälteste*.

information circulating in the camp, largely distributed by the humorously termed "Greek Press Agency" and "Polish Press Agency" (the GRIPA and the PIPA).[44] However, even without outside news, camp inmates knew that the huts being built to house a transport from another camp meant the end of the Third Reich was approaching. As rumors circulated that the war had taken a fortunate turn, the greatest optimists predicted concrete dates and counted the days; when rumors in October 1944 announced that the first cities in the distant homeland had already been freed, Levy-Hass too felt an "eternalized anguish."[45] A few weeks later, the news of the liberation of the Balkans was accompanied by the news that "a federation of Balkan republics has been created with Salonika as its capital."[46]

Herzberg penned a shocking entry on November 8—the day on which 3,000 women from Auschwitz arrived in Belsen with horrifying stories to tell. The children and all those who were not eligible for work were said to have been gassed. "It is impossible to believe such an atrocity."[47] Levy-Hass learned of the gruesome secret in January.[48] She had spoken to Greek women, Poles, and Hungarians who had arrived from Auschwitz and told of the mass murders by gas. A Greek woman told her that only 300 women had survived and she herself saw her whole family go up in smoke. They did not starve to death there, she said, but death was constantly lurking—it was a factory of death.

The newcomers were crowded together in the barracks with the other inmates; in Levy-Hass's barrack, three-tier bunk beds were set up from September. In December, Albala tried to renegotiate the demand that 1,356 people be accommodated in the eight overcrowded barracks. The SS captain told him that the relocation had to be completed.[49] The overcrowding led to chaos, as Levy-Hass's shocking description indicates:

44 Herzberg, *Between Two Streams*, p. 25.
45 Levy-Hass, *Diary of Bergen-Belsen*, p. 86.
46 Ibid., p. 90.
47 Herzberg, *Between Two Streams*, p. 160.
48 Levy-Hass, *Diary of Bergen-Belsen*, pp. 98ff.
49 Herzberg, *Between Two Streams*, p. 176.

Comings and goings, cries of despair, children's sobs, dust, straw everywhere, the stench, the filth, excrement. Quarrels are inevitable, especially between women, either when the beds are being made or when the laundry is being done. We are slaves...unable to take a breath, treated like cattle...humiliated, tormented... beasts.[50]

At first, the inmates responded to the gradual reduction in food rations by using tricks. They enriched their food with endless conversations about food, even exchanging recipes...[51] Yet when hunger invaded the camp, kitchen culture fell by the wayside: "There is hunger on one side of your body, namely the inside and fodder on the outside. Now the problem is: how to make the fodder reach the stomach. That is all."[52] In October 1944, people desperately fought for a few crumbs of bread, and the fear that they would be stolen by a thief or by the Germans increased daily. This was the immediate concern of every individual and of the prisoners in general. As the thin soup became thinner and thinner, the prisoners carefully cut their three-and-a-half-inch slice of bread into two.[53] Worries over a ladle-full of hot water with turnips reached a new climax.

Loden Vogel, the twenty-five-year-old son of a psychiatrist from Amsterdam and a nurse in the camp hospital, describes the hunger, the lice, typhus, and dysentery, the emaciated bodies and death, in a staggering manner, depicting every detail. He heard that a book by French author André Malraux (later French minister of culture) contains reports of camaraderie in the concentration camps, and he would like to read it...On February 15, 1945, he noted: "The huts are full of candidates for the crematorium, skeletons who only get out of bed to collect their food...Excreta lie everywhere on the camp street."[54]

50 Levy-Hass, *Diary of Bergen-Belsen*, p. 54.
51 Ibid., p. 85; see also Herzberg, *Between Two Streams*, p. 25.
52 Herzberg, *Between Two Streams*, p. 9.
53 Levy-Hass, *Diary of Bergen-Belsen*, p. 80.
54 Loden Vogel, who obtained documents from a South American country,

The starved inmates froze over the long winter of 1944–1945; in November it snowed, there were no more coals to warm themselves, their shoes disintegrated, and more and more became sick: dysentery, tuberculosis, skin diseases, edema, fever...This winter, the crematorium operated continuously, and the stench of the burned bodies spread throughout the camp. In October 1944, Levy-Hass mentions the death of a fragile elderly woman in the bed next to hers. The family cried briefly and then removed the corpse. "An ended life, quickly forgotten."[55] At the same time, Herzberg notes: "The harvest of today: F. is dead—exhaustion. Mrs. R. is dead—camp fever, pulmonary infection. F. is dead—exhaustion, dysentery." In December he remarks, "Dying is a transition from death to death."[56] Hanna Levy-Hass also speaks of a death without dying, what she calls a prolonged living death, always and ever present. Men in striped uniforms pushed carts full of skeletons across the path that led to the crematorium.[57]

Time was suspended in the camp.[58] The testimony of Rosy Levi-Saltiel, who came to the camp as a child, is shocking: she speaks of the hours of idleness and constant anxiety. She stayed in the barrack with other young children and waited for her parents to return from work. There were "red beets in a watery soup, and if there was a potato, it was like a feast," she recalled. A few people from Salonika, who were responsible for the distribution of the bread, kept most of it for themselves. Ten-year-old Dario Saltiel had discovered a place where the Germans planted beets: he went there and dug some out. One day, he recalls, a Russian prisoner of war saw him and came with him to dig some up for himself, and the Russian was shot dead by a German guard. All day long, Dario froze and starved, waiting for his sisters to bring him something...

arrived in Bergen-Belsen in April 1944 as an "exchange Jew." For a year, until liberation, he kept a diary, Loden Vogel, *Tagebuch aus einem Lager* (Göttingen: Vandenhoeck and Ruprecht, 2002); the entry from February 1945 was published by Kolb, *Bergen-Belsen*, pp. 86–88.

55 Levy-Hass, *Diary of Bergen-Belsen*, p. 71.
56 Herzberg, *Between Two Streams*, p. 183.
57 Bigielman, *J'ai eu douze ans à Bergen-Belsen*, pp. 98 and 100.
58 Herzberg, *Between Two Streams*, p. 163.

Likewise, Tomi Reichental, another child in Bergen-Belsen, remembers that most of the time he did absolutely nothing. One day was like another: "We were afraid and constantly hungry."[59] There was no place for feelings: "And because love has abandoned us, we also hardly ever cry anymore. Only the children cry: the adults have their stereotypical postures of sorrow."[60] There were no pleasures for the children:

> Fear, nothing but fear...For hours, these poor little mortified creatures standing for hours on end, their bodies filled with terror, their gaze fixed, awaiting whatever might happen. They bury their heads in an old rag, press up against the adults, seeking shelter from the cold and the fear. Only their eyes remain open, alarmed, like those of a hunted animal...[61]

The children from Salonika, Rosy, Dario, and little Rina, remember the corpses, mountains of corpses and the carts in which the corpses were transported...

Some cried. Indeed, "tears of rage and shame"[62] also overcame Levy-Hass. Man's capacity to adapt is unbelievable: the humiliation, the hunger, the lack of room to breathe, the dirt and the communal washing, everyone naked...[63] The prisoners often lost the ability to feel shame when forced to confront the naked bodies of their fellow prisoners, but not always.[64] Bitterness strangled the inmates: "To justify their inhumanity they reproach us with bestiality."[65]

59 Reichental, *I Was a Boy in Belsen*, p. 138.
60 Herzberg, *Between Two Streams*, p. 79.
61 Levy-Hass, *Diary of Bergen-Belsen*, p. 51.
62 Ibid., p. 63.
63 Ibid., p. 88.
64 Concerning shame see Werner Weinberg's words: "It is quite wrong to assume that we inmates of Bergen-Belsen had become like rotting vegetables ourselves. We still had feelings and even more values...I remember that we were indignant over the cases of cannibalism in the camp." See in particular the section entitled "The Shame of Bergen-Belsen," in Werner Weinberg, *Self-Portrait of a Holocaust Survivor* (Jefferson: MacFarland, 1985), pp. 70–72.
65 Herzberg, *Between Two Streams*, p. 110.

Herzberg expresses this bitterness: "Sometimes one wonders if the poets, who wrote and sang of the bitterness of life, had also experienced something like a camp for Jews in Germany, and if not, with what right they had spoken."[66]

If only for reasons of self-preservation, the prisoners were able to laugh at themselves; they were not completely mad yet. They knew that their lives hung by a silk thread, which one calls coincidence.[67] When asked, "What is this camp?" the prisoners' answer comes without hesitation, as Levy-Hass wrote in April 1945:

> This camp is not made to hold civilian deportees or prisoners of war for a specific period of time, to temporarily deprive them of freedom for whatever political, diplomatic, or strategic reasons...No: this camp is consciously and knowingly organized and arranged in such a way as to methodically exterminate thousands of human beings according to a plan. If this continues for only one more month, it is highly doubtful that one single person among us will come through.[68]

Primo Levi remembered the nightmare that plagued him in Auschwitz: He would speak to anyone who came across his path, but nobody believed what he was telling them. Werner Weinberg remembers a "vision" he had one day when he saw some Dutch diamond traders headed straight for the crematorium; there was no point in killing them first and then having to carry them; they knew exactly what to expect, but they had no strength to fight back. Then, writes Weinberg, he had the vision: In thirty years, one will say that all this happened a very long time ago...that if you cannot forgive, you must at least forget...that life continues...[69]

* * *

66 Ibid., p. 140.
67 Ibid.
68 Levy-Hass, *Diary of Bergen-Belsen*, p. 121.
69 Weinberg, *Self-Portrait*, pp. 67–69.

We have very few details about what happened to Valérie, Beniko, and their children during their internment in Bergen-Belsen. Little Dario stayed with his mother and sisters. Germaine Cohen, one of the Greek women who were deported to Auschwitz and taken from there to Bergen-Belsen, one of those who brought with them "the terrible secret" of the gas chambers, many years later recalled: "And one day we went and shouted that they should come, so we could tell them what had been done to us, because they said that the Germans would not harm us. There was only one woman who, seeing our miserable condition, threw us a dress for Claire and a cardigan for me."[70] Germaine Cohen's daughter told me once that her mother always remembered how, when she arrived from Auschwitz in terrible shape, Valérie had given her a woolen jacket...Zizy told me that thanks to her privileged position in the kitchen, she was able to secure a few potato peelings and give them to her sister, Nina.

Beniko Saltiel's family eventually received two telegrams from Mandatory Palestine through the Red Cross. The first is dated August 30, the second September 12, 1944. The telegrams, from Sima Adanya, were addressed to Beniko's mother, Eliza Saltiel, and Beniko Saltiel himself, respectively, at the address "Camp Bergen-Belsen near Celle, near Hannover, Germany." Such telegrams could not contain more than twenty-five words and had to be messages from the family, of a completely personal character. The first read:

> We are always thinking of you, we are with you. We hope, wish, endeavor to see you as soon as possible. Nephew Semtoviko / father with aunt Athina, all well. Kisses. Sima.

And the second:

> We hope you received our news. Full of impatience we anticipate our great joy in embracing you. We are all very well, we hug you all tight. Sima, Elda.

---

70 Germaine Cohen testimony, SFI-VHA, 48674. I am grateful to Pothiti Hantzaroula for directing me to this resource.

Beniko's sister Elda lived in Belgrade with her husband, Sima, and their three daughters, Mary, Regina, and Alice, who were born there. Sima originated from Belgrade. Elda held Greek nationality, Sima and the children Yugoslavian.

Like other Jews,[71] they had remained in the Italian-occupied territories, and their path henceforth is documented in the archives.[72] They were arrested by the Italians and brought to the Kotor-Kavajë camp in Montenegro, on the Adriatic coast. About 200 Jews were interned in this camp in quite good conditions: they were allowed to leave the camp and visit the village, and the Italian soldiers were not particularly hostile to them. On October 22, they were first loaded onto trucks and then taken by ship to Italy. After five days they reached the Ferramonti camp in Calabria, where about 3,800 mostly foreign Jews were imprisoned. The living conditions there were bearable, and the Italian soldiers behaved decently. Six weeks after the overthrow of Mussolini, the prisoners were released. It is likely that emissaries were sent from Mandatory Palestine to facilitate the immigration of those who desired it. Elda, Sima, and the children were among that group.

In Mandatory Palestine they learned that Beniko's family was in Bergen-Belsen. In August and September 1944, they wrote to them, assuring them of their love and trying to offer them some encouragement. The first telegram indicates that they were trying to get them out of the camp, although it is not clear how. In addition, it contains encrypted good news: Their brother, Moise, with his son Semtoviko, was safely hiding with "Aunt Athina" (that is, in Athens).

71 See the similar testimony of Haim "Mile" Pinkas in Aleksandar Gaon ed., *We Survived...: Yugoslav Jews on the Holocaust*, vol. 1 (Belgrade: The Jewish Historical Museum of the Federation of Jewish Communities in Yugoslavia, 2005), pp. 188–207.

72 For information on the Ferramonti camp (in Italian) see Ebrei stranieri internati in Italia durante il periodo bellico: http://www.annapizzuti.it (accessed June 20, 2014).

Telegrams from Sima Adanya to Beniko Saltiel in Bergen-Belsen, August 30 and September 12, 1944

CHAPTER 13

The Lost Train and Liberation:
Tröbitz, April–August 1945

By the end of March 1945, the conclusion of the war seemed to be approaching. Every day the bombs of Allied aircraft were heard. Rumors circulated in the camp: Would the Germans surrender and release the prisoners, or would they kill them? On March 25, all the prisoners of the star camp were taken to the showers for disinfection and delousing. They understood that the camp was being evacuated. As strange as it may sound, the idea of leaving the camp and of the unknown unsettled the prisoners.

On April 6, 7, and 9, 1945, three trains departed from Bergen-Belsen, just a week before the British arrived on April 15. The first train left on April 6 carrying 2,500 inmates, including 400 from the star camp. It departed from the nearby train station, which was about 5 to 6 kilometers away. On April 13, these prisoners were liberated by the American army in the small town of Farsleben, near Magdeburg. The second train left on April 7, taking Hungarian prisoners in the direction of Theresienstadt. On April 9, the third train left with the remaining 2,500 prisoners from the star camp on board. Among them were most of the Greeks. Families were allowed to be in the same wagon.

On its way east, this train meandered for about two weeks, looking for tracks undamaged by the Allied bombardments. Constantly monitored by the SS, the passengers, weakened by typhus and fever, collapsed one by one, and the starving slowly died of exhaustion. The story of the Lost Train was first made public in 1985 by one of its former passengers, the survivor W. Weinberg;[1] Aryeh Koretz, in his 1993 oral testimony, offered an accurate and extremely interesting account.

On the first day the train did not move at all. The passengers could have fled. Yet to where could they turn in Nazi Germany? In addition, they were simply too exhausted. Moreover, they were likely to be disappointed yet again if the war was not really over. The sentries gave the impression of being more relaxed, and so whoever had the strength foraged for food in the area. On the evening of the second day, the first cases of typhus became manifest on the train: high fever, severe headaches, hallucinations. From their time in the camp, the inmates knew that typhus reaches its peak on the fourteenth day. Whoever survives, survives. Doctors among the inmates did everything in their power to help.

The Jews organized themselves and recognized the leadership of Josef Weiss from Holland. They took care of the distribution of food that was found on the way. They buried their dead, the now-daily victims of typhus and exhaustion. On the third day, they reached the small town of Soltau, where they crossed paths with the train transporting the Hungarians. Slowly, with constant stops, they continued in the direction of the Elbe, and arrived at Lüneburg. On April 12, the news of Roosevelt's death reached them, causing concern: what if the Germans were to regain their courage? For the second time they crossed paths with the Hungarians, and, under constant bombardment, the train continued its journey. South of Hamburg it crossed the Elbe and reached Berlin.

Outside of the Berlin train station, the Hungarians crossed their path for the third and last time. For two days the train traveled around Berlin, from the western to the eastern districts. All around them they saw ruins. The Third Reich was collapsing. On the outskirts of the city, they saw hordes of German citizens

1 Weinberg, *Self-Portrait*, pp. 85–115. The account was first published in *Yad Vashem Studies*, 15 (1983), pp. 283–326; see also Joseph A. Pollak, "The Lost Transport," *Commentary* (September 1995), pp. 24–27.

making their way by night, pushing carts with their belongings in front of them. The train turned south: Luckenwalde, Lübben, Lübbenau. They arrived in Brandenburg.

On the morning of April 23, they woke up to find that the sentries had disappeared. (Did it occur to Zizy that on this day she was given the gift of freedom for her twentieth birthday?) Anyone who had the strength to do so got out of the train. Scouts brought food from a nearby village and the news that the Soviet soldiers who had taken up positions there suggested they find accommodation in Tröbitz, which had been abandoned by its residents.[2] The survivors, those who still had the strength to do so, walked to the village. Shortly afterwards, they returned to take the incapacitated and to bury the dead. They entered the empty houses, finding food supplies, water, and clothing. Some could no longer restrain themselves and rushed to satisfy their hunger—soon becoming sick.

It took some time for the Russians to organize medical care for the Jews. Although finally free, many continued to die from typhus. The Soviets imposed a two-month quarantine on them. In the forest an abandoned labor camp for Ukrainians was considered suitable for the isolation of the sick. It was converted into a hospital where the Jews were cared for by Soviet doctors and nurses. Medications and remedies, including the shaving of heads and repeated washing, were limited, but in most cases, they worked...However, they failed in the case of Zvi Koretz. The only rabbi among the survivors died of exhaustion on the morning of June 2, 1945. About 350 prisoners from Bergen-Belsen died after their liberation, not a family was spared...

Valérie, Beniko, and their three children also contracted typhus in May 1945. Beniko died on May 7. He was buried in

2   The area later became part of the GDR. In the version of events told by local residents, the population received the refugees with their doors wide open. Tröbitz became a memorial place for the Shoah in East Germany. At the initiative of the Jews, the cemetery, in which many former prisoners from Bergen-Belsen were buried, was preserved.

Tröbitz.[3] For the remaining four, Dr. Allalouf, also from Salonika, wrote out the following certificates. For Valérie:

Saltiel Valérie, born October 22, 1906, had exanthematous typhus during the month of May 1945.
Tröbitz, June 7, 1945
The attending physician
Dr Jean Allalouf
9 Agia Triada Street, Salonika

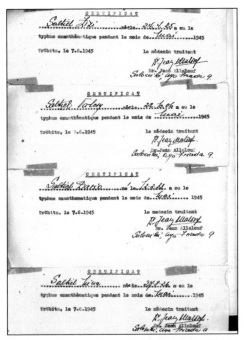

Medical certificates issued in Tröbitz certifying that Valérie, Zizy, Dario, and Nina Saltiel suffered from typhus in May 1945

3   In Tröbitz—along with many others—Beniko's mother Eliza Gatenio-Saltiel died, as did Jacques Albala's three-year-old child. See "Benico Saltiel," Häftlinge des Konzentrationslagers Bergen-Belsen (memorial book of prisoners of the concentration camp Bergen-Belsen), April 1995, https://www.holocaust-denkmal-berlin.de/raum-der-namen/biographien/biographie/10184 (accessed September 12, 2012).

In May, the Dutch returned to their homeland. When Valérie, now a forty-year-old widow, was in the hospital with her youngest son, Dario, she received a letter written in pencil from her eldest daughter. Zizy, who was hospitalized in another wing, possibly in quarantine, wrote:

> My dear Mamica. Your letter with your news makes me happy, but I was sad hearing about Nina—when she will be here, I'll show her—she got it from me. Don't worry. You have three children who adore you and you are most precious to them. Here there has been a lot of activity…Fanny is gone. She was very nice during these days, and she made us laugh a lot. She left very happy, also the…Dutch and your dear Aby. Here…mother the food has changed a bit, we have potatoes and also…but I eat everything. You, mother, how are you doing? Why do you want to leave the hospital? Maybe I'll have to go there on Monday, so I'll be alone there again. Try to stay as long as you can for food, and, after all, you will not get tired and there will be houses because 700 people are gone. The next convoy will be next Friday, so it is a long time for us. Nina must try to regain her strength. She had told Alice that she would come in the morning, but I waited for her all day and in the end, she came in the evening. She promised to send me everything, but I still have nothing, not even a letter. I think she has changed with the disease. If you want, write to her. What is Dario doing? Does he like the hospital? I noticed that he had grown a lot. Fanny has always said how good and kind he was when we were sick, and I am very grateful to him; if I can, I will give him beautiful gifts in Salonika. Mamica, I want to be near you. If there is a transport you must first ask the doctor if you can register me because Monique did something stupid and stayed.
>
> Mamica, be well, and don't worry,
> Zizy[4]

4   For the original French, see the appendix.

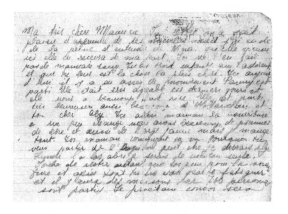

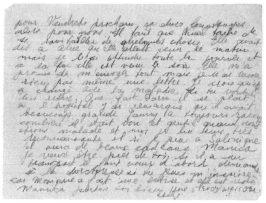

Letter from Zizy to Valérie while hospitalized in Tröbitz, May 1945

This affectionate letter sounds as though it was written by a little girl still seeking the protection of her mother, not by a young woman who had experienced the hardships of the camp. She returns to being an older sister—she quarrels with her sister, who is one year younger than her, and promises gifts to her younger brother, now twelve years old (who matured so quickly in the eighteen months in the camp)—but remains the little daughter who can be happy when someone makes her laugh, who does not want to be alone while the Soviets slowly organize their return. Valérie is now the head of the family.

When the end of the war was announced on the radio on May 8, the community of former inmates was not much impressed, as noted by Weinberg, who writes in detail about that event.[5] On May 12, the 2,200 former prisoners of Bergen-Belsen wrote to Stalin to express their gratitude to the Red Army as well as their hopes of returning to their home countries with the help of the USSR.[6] The letter was written by representatives of all nationalities and was signed on behalf of the Greeks by Chief Rabbi Koretz. They knew that the return could not be achieved overnight. Under the shadow of the still constant threat of typhus, the former prisoners lived in a provisional state. The main concern was to stay alive and obtain enough food.

Under the leadership of Josef Weiss, the council took over the procurement of supplies, the distribution of food, and registering the "members" of this unusual community. Certificates were issued confirming that their holders were passengers on the train from Bergen-Belsen and were liberated in Tröbitz. These certificates, in Dutch or in English, bear the signature of the Dutch lawyer Weiss and the stamp of the mayor's office of Tröbitz, which was sequestered, together with a typewriter. When the Germans returned to the village, they cohabited in an odd fashion with the Jewish survivors, who resided in houses that the Soviets had confiscated. Many of them, including the young Aryeh Koretz, traveled around on bicycles and "traded," exchanging tobacco or whatever they found in the warehouses for milk and eggs.

According to the family stories told, Valérie and her children lived in a house together with the German owner. Presumably, they had already learned about the fate of their relatives in Auschwitz. There was a danger that Valérie, whose husband had also died in the meantime, would now lose her oldest daughter to typhus. She later said that a good-looking Russian doctor saved her life. Her daughter also recalled how she found Christmas baubles in that German house and gave them to Rina, a little girl from Salonika, to play with.

5   Weinberg, *Self-Portrait*, pp. 85–115.
6   Arntz, *Der letzte Judenälteste*, ch. 22.

When the period of quarantine came to an end and a plan for departure became possible, the Soviets organized the return home. The Dutch drove off in Red Cross cars, followed by the French. About 100 people remained in Tröbitz: Serbs, Czechs, Romanians, Hungarians, as well as the Greeks.

CHAPTER 14

The Return: August–September 1945

One day in August, the Soviets announced the departure of a train bound for Romania, Yugoslavia, and Greece. The survivors collected their belongings, some clothes and shoes, and loaded them onto horse-driven carts. They went to the station as free people, the certificates issued by Josef Weiss in their pockets. They got into the carriages to embark on a journey that would last more than a month. There was space enough, but the train moved slowly, with constant stops, each lasting a day or two. It progressed eastward, to Poland, and finally drew close to Katowice. A rumor circulated that they would be taken to Odessa, and from there by ship to Bulgaria and Greece. Finally, the train returned to Germany. It moved so slowly that when you jumped out at one station, you could get back on at the next. The stations at which the train stopped had special kitchens for refugees. Now they too were among the "Displaced Persons." In some cities, representatives of the Jewish community and the JDC awaited them; they received food and a little money. Czechoslovakia, Hungary, Romania, Bulgaria…

Valérie wanted to record in writing the stations of this reverse path from Golgotha, the stages of return to Salonika after two years of hardship. In a curious diary she kept in the year 1973, in which she noted down proverbs and sayings, as well as the birthdays of family members and even recipes, Valérie recorded the route on March 24, twenty-eight years after her return from Bergen-Belsen:

Itinerary of the journey Germany-Greece, in 1945 after the liberation

Germany-Tröbitz,
Luckenwalde Kirstenwald,
Frankurt. Oder
Poland-Posen Ostrave-
Gleinitz Mittenwalde
Czechoslovakia. Luckoz.
Bratislava Galanta
Hungary Budapest Rumania
Bucharest
Bulgaria-Sofia-
Koula
Greece Siderokastro Thessalonika

Despite the sometimes inaccurate orthography, the "route" Valérie recorded here is the same one that Aryeh Koretz also remembered. The train went initially in the direction of Poland. The city of Gliwice in the south of Poland (Upper Silesia) is near Katowice. Close by, the train changed direction and returned to Germany (Mittenwalde station). The list of cities is a commemoration of this "Exodus." What did she think about during this journey, her return home? How impatient was she? What did she imagine for the future, what did she fear? How haunted was she by images from the camp? How did she navigate the difficult and unpredictable everyday life? According to another family story, in Bratislava, Zizy and Nina stood in front of a pastry shop with a dreamy look on their faces. A gentleman went in, bought all sorts of sweets, and offered them to the young women.

An identity card confirms arrival at the border between Greece and Bulgaria, at Sidirokastro/Koula, on September 7. The Greek UNRRA department for DPs confirms in English that Zizy Saltiel, aged twenty, a student, Greek, in parenthesis Jewish, was held prisoner in Germany and was now on her way to Salonika. She was admitted on September 8, and on September 9 she was "disinfected." This identity card also carries a Greek stamp of the

"Return Service of the Ministry of Social Welfare" and the stamp "Hostage." Dario recalled that Moise, his father's brother, who had been hiding in Athens, came to the border to pick them up. He took a taxi and brought them to Salonika. The first thing Dario looked for was olives.

Arrival in Sidirokastro, September 1945

Meanwhile, the council of the Jewish Community of Salonika, chaired by Chaim Saltiel, who had survived in the resistance, met for an extraordinary meeting on September 11. The occasion was the imminent arrival of fifty-three survivors from Bergen-Belsen, where they had been deported "thanks to their preferential treatment by the Germans in 1943." Some of them were accused of having collaborated with the Rosenberg Commando, which was responsible for the persecution and deportation of the Jews, while others were expected to explain their behavior as members of the Judenrat or community committees during the period of the deportations. They were all called to account for the "preferential treatment" that the Germans accorded them, having "sent them to privileged concentration camps, not to the concentration camps and crematoria in Poland." Finally, the council decided that sixteen of them (including the now deceased Koretz) should appear in person before the court. The community also requested that anyone with information should report, instructing the community's lawyers to take the appropriate steps in the chief prosecutor's office.

We will return below to the "privileges" and "guilt" of the survivors. In the first place, it should be remembered that this group, originally so heterogeneous, was now made up of survivors such as Albala, members of the ghetto militia such as Leon Sion, community employees such as Alphonse Levi, the sole survivor of the Judenrat, Solomon Uziel, and of course their families, women and children who had survived. Aryeh Koretz said that in Sidirokastro he found himself confronted for the first time with mistrust and in the Pavlos Melas camp in Salonika he heard the first accusations against his father. Never before, he claimed, had there been such allegations. He also remembered spending the first evening alone with his little sister outside the White Tower, a famous monument on the waterfront in the city center, because his mother was held for a day or two while she was interrogated, before being released.

On July 2, 1946, a trial of thirteen defendants began before the Special Court for Collaborators. The charges included activities in the services of the occupying authorities, assisting with persecution, acts of violence, and denunciations.[1] Although Chief Rabbi Koretz had already died, a summons was issued on June 11 ordering Zvi Koretz, resident of Salonika, address unknown, to appear as a defendant in court. In the subsequent trial, six Jewish defendants were found guilty. Vital Hasson was sentenced to death, while Leon Sion was sentenced to life imprisonment; Jacques Albala received fifteen years in prison, Edgar Counio eight. The Jewish community acted as a plaintiff. Nine days before the trial, on June 24, the council issued an appeal in Ladino: *Queridos Ermanos, Ya sono la hora de la djusticia!* ("Dear Brothers. It is the day of justice!…Our community must take legal action against the rogues and demand justice in the name of the 2,000 survivors and retribution for the 50,000 martyrs,") it read. Whoever had evidence of any crime was asked to bring it before the court, and everyone should attend.

In fact, hundreds of Jews followed the trial, finding it difficult to hold back their anger and grief. The local and Athenian newspapers reported on the event according to their respective political positions, with no shortage of antisemitic comments. One cannot help thinking that only the Jewish collaborators were convicted while many others escaped punishment…

In addition to the certain crimes of which some defendants were accused, fundamental questions, relevant to our subject matter here, were raised during the hearing: What did members of the community know about the Germans' intentions? What kind of camp was Bergen-Belsen?

Regarding the first question, Chaim Saltiel, the leader of the community, was the first to be asked the following question: "Did the accused, the chief rabbi, the community members, and the militia know that the Jews were being sent to extermination?" Chaim Saltiel answered with a categorical "No." "What were they told?" "They were in a hurry to send people to Poland as soon as possible. Nobody knew what would happen, but of course it was certain that nothing good awaited them." One of the defense lawyers asked the witness Sam Nahmias, who was also a community

1   Trial of the Traitors, July 1946, HAJCTh, folder 00190.1: 00002–00340.

lawyer, whether rich Jews could escape that fate, as he himself had done. "Yes," was the answer. "Why did they not escape?" the lawyer was asked. "They did not think they would die." "Why was that not explained to them?" "When? In April?" by which time it was already too late, came the answer, full of bitter sarcasm.

Salvator Counio, an Auschwitz survivor, was summoned[2] by the civilian plaintiffs as a witness and asked to explain "the Bergen-Belsen camp." His answer mixes precise information with imprecise elements, but it is indicative of the general and prevalent perception that this was a camp "for the privileged":

> The Germans had many camps. Birkenau, Auschwitz for annihilation, Buchenwald for political prisoners, and Bergen-Belsen, which consisted of sixteen camps. In two of them prisoners lived under the best conditions. These were the "valuable Jews," i.e., those who had been in the service of the Germans or possessed large fortunes that the Germans had not yet legally appropriated. Industrialists were well cared for until a German got them to sign over their assets, and then the man would be sent to hell. There were others who were sent to Switzerland in exchange for $5,000 that was handed over in the name of the Reich. Belsen had the best camps. The inmates did not get their hair shorn, and they did not have to do hard labor...

In his defense speech, Jacques Albala emphasized that he had only led the militia to protect the Jews and denied using any form of violence. He insisted that he offered his help and did nothing bad to anyone; he was not a traitor. His lawyer placed all responsibility on the Judenrat.

In addition to the official channels of justice, the Jewish community and the Association of Hostages, as they called

2   On the witness testimonies in the case against the collaborators see Eleni Haidia, "The Punishment of Collaborators in Northern Greece," in M. Mazower, ed., *After the War Was Over: Reconstructing the Family, Nation and State in Greece, 1943–1960* (Princeton: Princeton University Press, 2000), pp. 42–61.

the association that the survivors of the camps had set up, also initiated internal procedures. This fact may indicate a lack of confidence in the regular judiciary, or the desire for the matter to be settled within the community and without any outside influence. Perhaps it also reveals a conviction that the case concerned the community first and foremost and only secondly the Greek judiciary. Similar procedures took place elsewhere, for example in Amsterdam.

A few days after his return to Salonika, Solomon Uziel was summoned by the investigator into cases of collaboration with the occupying forces and then immediately released. Afterwards, as he explains in his book, he insisted on being interrogated by the community committee, which then questioned and acquitted him. Later, he gave testimony to the committee of the Association of Hostages and, again on his own initiative, also joined this association.[3] The minutes of these proceedings are to be found in the community archives. The first interrogation concerning "the activities of the Jews returning from the Bergen-Belsen camp for privileged people" took place on March 8, 1946, in the presence of eight members of the community in the offices of the Association of Hostages.[4]

Joseph Nehama,[5] who had been interned for some time in the neutral camp in Bergen-Belsen, together with other Spanish nationals, responded to Uziel regarding the accusations against him: "It speaks against you that there were clever people in the council, of whom you were the smartest. Beniko Saltiel was a fool, as was Koretz. The worst part is that you sought to save yourself, and of course you were aware that people were being deported so they could be eliminated."

3   Uziel, in Bowman, *The Holocaust in Salonika*, pp. 254–256.
4   Interrogation protocols of the committee, HAJCTh, folder 00190.2, two machine-typed pages and twelve handwritten pages in Judeo-Spanish.
5   The well-known historian, a banker by profession. He himself was deported to Bergen-Belsen with his wife and daughter, all in possession of Spanish passports, on August 2. The Spaniards were interned, until their liberation on February 7, 1944, as already noted, in a separate subcamp and under special conditions. They were then taken to Spain and from there to North Africa. Nehama's brother-in-law, the architect Saporta, had escaped from the synagogue in Athens and gone to the mountains.

Uziel defended himself by citing his prewar services to the community council, adding:

> People say that I was the secretary of Koretz and his friend, but I quarreled with him constantly. When the Germans invaded, I was jailed for seventy days and came out only after I signed that I would not be active in the community, otherwise they would shoot me. And still I turned to Saby Saltiel to organize help for the poor...I had no direct relations with the Germans, I was desperate to make the lives of the Jews easier.

Asked by other members of the committee, Uziel made it clear:

> Until the day of registration, there were no deportations. Merten assured us that there would be no deportations, that the workers would be transported to a ghetto, and that they would set up a chamber of commerce, a civic authority, and a police force...We tried to buy ourselves free from the deportation, as well as from forced labor. We all agreed that this was how to proceed and insisted that the rabbi take this step. For this purpose, we committed ourselves to cooperating, to clarify and bring the matter to an end...Mrs. Koretz must have the document.

Subsequently, Uziel explained that one week before the departure of the first transport, when the first 300 cars had already arrived at the station, Koretz had gone to Merten and burst into tears, offering to sign over 50 percent of the community's movable and immovable property in the form of a mortgage from the Bank of Greece. Following this conversation, a telegram was sent to Berlin, but the very next day they ordered him back and told him that the Greeks had protested. And so, the deportations began. Uziel also reported on Koretz's attempt to get help from Rallis and on Koretz's replacement by Albala. A third member of the committee of inquiry, Salvator Counio, reiterated that despite Koretz's "dictatorial attitude," the Judenrat had not rebelled against him. Uziel replied that they had put pressure on Koretz when they were trying to buy their release from deportation, but that when their attempts failed, it made no sense to inform anyone because the facts quickly spread from mouth to mouth.

Nehama insisted that if they knew the Jews in Poland would be sent to their deaths, they were traitors, and Uziel countered him, saying, "We believed that we were being held hostage for our exchange value when peace would come. That was the view of the fourteen."

The members of the Inquiry Committee returned to the matter, noting that Koretz believed some of the favored Jews would remain in Salonika, that Albala knew they would end up in preferential camps, and that, when there were still about 1,000 Jews in the city—"the strongest"—a rumor circulated that they would be going to Theresienstadt.

Uziel provided information regarding his personal history. The members of his family had been aboard the transport of May 9,[6] and he himself had wanted to journey with them. However, he was ordered to stay, and at the last moment he was pulled out of the carriage. Together with Beniko Saltiel, he was ordered to receive the 2,000 Jews who had been sent to forced labor. On June 1, they wanted to leave with the next transport,[7] "to get it over with, once and for all." Yet they were arrested by the militia, which threatened to charge them with sabotage. So, they stayed in Salonika to get clothes for the workers, prepared food for the Spaniards, and when they had finished the lists of holders of Spanish passports, they noticed that seventy-four were missing. There were several arrests "because there were empty carriages," and he himself was arrested. On August 2, they set out with the Spanish nationals.

The trial resumed three years later, on April 25, 1949, at the community offices, continuing for over three months before

---

6   This was the seventeenth transport, which included Jews from Salonika as well as Jews from Thrace and Veria. The train reached Auschwitz on May 16, and 3,823 of those on board were taken directly to the gas chambers.

7   This eighteenth transport, which included twelve members of the Judenrat, was supposed to go to Theresienstadt. However, on June 8, it too reached Auschwitz.

a new twelve-member committee. Yitzhak Tiano stated at the beginning of the session that the committee's work had not been completed in 1946 due to negligence and the departure of some of its members for Athens. It is obvious that this meeting was also initiated by Solomon Uziel himself who, in his letter of January 25, 1948, requested that the situation be clarified. Time had not dampened passions. Members of the committee agreed to investigate allegations and to determine whether the events were the result of malicious intent. Baruch Schiby raised the question of "Jewish conscience," which under certain circumstances "counts for more than the law of the state." Witnesses testified in favor of Uziel. While Saul Molho noted that Uziel was not a good leader, he admitted something that was apparently confirmed by everyone: he did not know that the Jews had been deported for extermination.

These were difficult years in Salonika. The deep pain and anger only too easily led to accusations, some right and some wrong. Some came to light before the Investigations Committee of the Association of Hostages,[8] while many others remained in the dark and floated around in the memories of the survivors.[9]

---

8 A tailor who had been assigned to Bergen-Belsen on January 13, 1945, was asked to respond to the allegations against him. In his defense, he classified certain prisoners according to their guilt: "To assist you in your work, I classify everyone's responsibility as follows: innocent, guilty, doubtful, unknown to me," HAJCTh, folder 12012.

9 After the war, there was a tendency in Israel and other countries to investigate the attitude of the Jews in Manichaean terms, implying that someone who survived could owe this only to some kind of non-radical behavior. In this climate, the case of Rezsö (Rudolf) Kasztner vs. Malchiel Gruenvald took place in Israel in 1954. The latter accused Kasztner of having conducted negotiations with the Germans in Budapest, who had then allowed 1,685 Hungarian Jews, including Kasztner's family, to travel to Switzerland on a special train. Was this a heroic attempt to save at least a few Jews from certain destruction, or a treacherous act motivated by selfish intentions? The court sentenced Kasztner, but in 1958 the Israeli Supreme Court (even though Kasztner had fallen victim to a political assassination in 1957) overturned the decision, stressing that the moral issue of cooperating with the Nazis should not be confused with legal matters. The Supreme Court also stated that this was a commendable cooperation in so far as it was not accompanied by lower motives, and it should not be condemned or regarded as moral misconduct. See also Lawrence Douglas, *The Memory of*

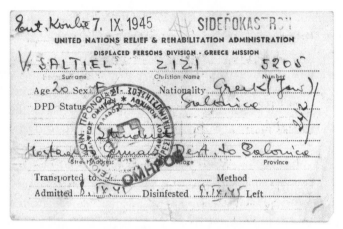

Certificate issued to Zizy Saltiel by the United Nations Relief and Rehabilitation Administration upon arrival in Greece, September 1945

Most likely, if Beniko Saltiel had survived, he would have found himself in the same situation as Solomon Uziel. He too would have been forced to justify himself to clear his name.

Valérie and the children found themselves in the Pavlos Melas camp—the "Displaced Persons Assembly Center Pavlos Melas Barracks"—which received all the survivors returning to Salonika. The certificate they were issued is dated September 16 and confirms the registration of the three children with ID numbers 241, 242, and 243. After registering, they were able to travel onward to Salonika. The certificate bears the stamps of the UNRRA and of the relevant Greek ministry and the remark "Hostage."

＊ ＊ ＊

Valérie and the children had no family waiting for them in Salonika and no home. So, they continued on to Athens, where they received another document. On September 26, 1945, the office of the Greek Red Cross responsible for former prisoners from the concentration camps certified that "Zizy Saltiel, [daughter]

Judgment: Making Law and History in the Trials of the Holocaust (New Haven: Yale University Press, 2001), pp. 154–157.

of Beniko, as evidenced by the documents available, had been a political prisoner of the German occupying authorities in Germany and returned in freedom to Athens on September 19, 1945." The certificate bears the stamps of the Red Cross and the Ministry, each with the remark "Hostage."

According to the bureaucratic terminology of that time, the Jews who had survived the concentration camps were "Displaced Persons," "prisoners," or "political prisoners," depending on which authority was responsible for the document issued. However, they were widows, orphans, dispossessed, holding together the little that they still had and starting a new, "normal" life, especially those who were still young…

Valérie and her daughters, Nina and Zizy, a few months after liberation

CHAPTER 15

A New Life Begins

Building a New Life

T
he Jews returned! The last camp survivor arrived in Salonika in November 1945. In the second part, we saw that some preferred not to return, remaining in the DP camps, where they waited for the coveted visas for the United States or a chance to immigrate to Mandatory Palestine, which was no easy feat. For many, the return to Greece proved to be a stopover before emigration: they came to realize that the land they had been forced to leave was no longer theirs, that they had lost their homes, their money, and all their relatives. Hundreds of orphans prepared for *aliya*, immigration to the land of Israel, with the help of the Jewish Agency in Palestine. Of the ten couples who married at one of the first group weddings in 1946, four went to Israel and three to the US; only three stayed in Salonika.[1] These group weddings were an opportunity for the entire community to celebrate their survival and their sense of solidarity. Yet in Greece, the joy of liberation was soon overshadowed by a cruel civil war, which for many left-leaning Jews meant the continuation of their persecution. All Jews, however, saw how many of the Germans' collaborators, thanks to their excessive nationalism, were able to buy impunity.

1   Lewkowicz, *The Jewish Community of Salonika*, p. 199.

Valérie and the children found their properties in the hands of strangers. They ended up living with a family of non-Jewish friends and soon went to Athens, where Valérie's sister was also residing. Her brother-in-law, Moise, who had been hiding with "Aunt Athina" (as he wrote in his telegram to Bergen-Belsen) had hitherto returned to Salonika and made efforts from there to help his brother's widow and her children return and settle there. The following letter was addressed to them. It includes depressing details from an ordinary everyday life compared to everything they themselves had gone through. Valérie always used to say after the war: "Worries that can be fixed by money (*bela que se se scapa con paras*) are not worries." However, material matters were also part of the postwar landscape.

MOISE S. SALTIEL
Avenue Reine Olga, 123
Salonika November 7, 1945

My dearest Valica,
I have just received almost at the same time your two letters sent via the post office as well as the one that Frosso brought me. I am happy to know you are all in the best of health.

I think it may be best that you agree to live for a while with Frosso until we can find a long-term apartment for you. You will have received my approval by the dispatch sent yesterday. As I tell you in that telegram, I suggest you go by boat, because I think it's the cheapest way, but if it is difficult to get tickets for the boat, then at worst you will have to take a taxi. Also, I think you might have Sofia's company because she too must return to Salonika. Frosso advised me to tell you that when you are about to depart you should message me via Pavlo.

Contrary to what I told you in my last letter about Eleonore's apartment, we could only throw out three of the four tenants who lived there, giving them a gift of 40,000 drachmas each, but the fourth was intransigent and demanded 200,000 drachmas. Salvator Counio is trying to sort things out with this one...

According to the law on housing, I inform you that those who request to take back their apartment have the right to claim the apartment they abandoned when they left here, so in your case you should ask for the apartment where you lived, Edmond Rostand Street No. 56. I have already made the request at the abandoned housing office for this last apartment.

Now I will tell you the story of your possessions that were kept by the famous Miss Péppi: Last Sunday, at 5 o'clock in the afternoon, I went to her brother, who lives on Allatini Street...Péppi was also meant to be at our rendezvous, as per our arrangement. When I got there with Emilie and my friend Kalfoglou, the good Péppi was not there; her brother told us that Péppi had come earlier to ask him to tell us that she could not come to the appointment because she was looking after her baby, but if she had time she would come along later, as soon as she had time. After waiting for three-quarters of an hour, the brother asked me to follow him to his room and told me that Péppi had given him some packages for me. Taking possession of these, I saw that he had given me your overcoat, a nightgown, a jewelry box from Péppi, and on his part he gave me a packet containing papers belonging to dear Beniko, telling me that he had destroyed several other documents fearing a search by the Germans. While checking the contents of the jewelry box in front of Péppi's brother, we were surprised to see that many compartments were entirely empty, while others contained a heap of old stuff like: a pearl necklace, a baroque coral necklace, a broken coral horn, two small nickel-plated wristwatches in very bad condition, and a chain in gold bearing the masonic insignia, two or three small, extra fine bracelets that may have belonged to Zizy or Nina, a white metal bag containing worthless coins, and a small white metal purse as well. After questioning

Peppi's brother and asking him for the rest, the real jewels, he replied that you did not give your good jewelry to Péppi for safekeeping. I tried to get a signature from him for what he gave me, but he refused, saying that he was not the guardian of the jewelry box and that he only knew the state of its contents at the point when Péppi had given it to him to return to me. Now it's up to you to come here and decide what to do…

I await your dispatch announcing your departure and beg you to convey my greetings to the Aloneftis family, to embrace the children and Toto on my behalf. I kiss you affectionately,

Moise

P.S. I am sending you this letter to the Aloneftis family based on your last letter [which said] that you will be staying with them again.[2]

Moise tried to help his brother's widow return to Salonika and deal with practical issues, especially housing, apparently with care and interest. Stories like those of the lost jewels were common in those days, but very often such things were kept safely and returned. After the war, Valérie prepared food for the whole family on the Jewish New Year festival. The meal was served in the old dining room using prewar furniture and cutlery, which was returned to her untouched by those who had hidden it for her.

In December 1945, Valérie, Zizy, Nina, and Dario were back in Salonika. We know this from an application Zizy made at the City Hall to obtain a certificate of registration, which was required in order to obtain a police ID card. Another "identity card" made of thick, pink paper dates from that period and confirms membership in the Salonika branch of the "Association of Jewish Hostages of Poland": serial number 1072; Camp number (meaning the number tattooed onto the forearm of prisoners in Auschwitz): "Bergen-Belsen." On the inside of the two-part card, it was noted

---

2   For the original French, see the appendix.

that Zizy received two blankets and 32,000 drachmas from the JDC in January. Her photo bears the round stamp of the Union with the Star of David in the middle; it shows Zizy smiling and with long hair.

For most Greeks, whether Jewish or not, the years after the war were a time of poverty and homelessness. UNRRA and the

ID issued to Zizy Saltiel by the Association of Hostages

JDC took care of their food and clothing. Many of the Jews could not return to their homes, either because some other unfortunate refugees had found refuge there or because the houses had been occupied by collaborators. Several families lived under the same roof, in the same yard. Although the withdrawal of the laws enacted during the war should have meant an immediate restoration of their houses, they were in fact often faced with drawn-out proceedings hampered by the reluctance of the authorities and the courts. And worse, in line with the usual perverse antisemitic logic, their legal claim for the restitution of their expropriated assets was now used to give the impression that the Jews, known for their greed, were all rich and had hidden treasures. Indeed, in November 1945, *Israilitikon Vima* printed an article highlighting the prevailing situation: "Certain circles in our city, in the service of the interests of those who enriched themselves at the expense of the Jews, are beginning to speak out about the gigantic fortunes allegedly concentrated in the hands of the Jews and are demanding that the return of Jewish assets be stopped."[3]

* * *

In 1947, the care of children was the highest priority for the communities in need of rehabilitation, and a children's center was established in Salonika. A report published in *Evraiki Estia* about the December 1947 *Hanukkah* celebrations there, in which we once again meet Dario and Zizy, reflects the prevailing mood at the time:

> The children had fun together, ate sweets, and had a good time. A theatrical performance was planned for the following day, in the presence of the parents, organized by Dr. Schreiber and the members of the community council...The third scene takes us back to the temple of Solomon, where the Jews went to thank God, who had freed them. One of the children in the center, Dario Saltiel, lit the *Hanukkah* candles... Mr. Salv. Counio spoke on behalf of the community

3 *Israilitikon Vima*, November 23, 1945, cited in Fragiski Abatzopoulou, *The Holocaust in the Testimonies of Greek Jews* (Greek) (Thessaloniki: Paratiritis, 1990), pp. 230–231.

council, saying how touched he was by the excellent results of the work of the children's center...He also extended his thanks and praise for the women and girls who worked for the Center, noting especially Miss Zizy Saltiel...[4]

In the summer camp and children's center

4   *Evraiki Estia*, January 16, 1948.

Zizy Saltiel and others in the summer camp and children's center 1947

Feelings of Guilt

The façade of a "normal life" consisting of work, family, and all sorts of pleasures hid a deep mourning among the Jews. The Jews felt an unsettling strangeness, as described by Jean Améry.[5] No one around them seemed to be interested in their fate, leaving them

5   Jean Améry, *Par-delà le crime et le châtiment: Essai pour surmonter l'insurmontable* (Arles: Actes Sud, 2005). The work was first published in 1966.

estranged and completely alone, banished from all that was once familiar to them and in which they believed, banished even from the story of their own lives. Their nightmare from the camp had come true: no one out there would understand the hunger, the cold, the pain, the fear, the exhaustion, the despair, and the ubiquitous death they had encountered. If they ventured to talk about those things, they soon realized that no one who had not experienced it themselves wanted to listen. Even worse, they were met with a perverse mistrust. Those who did not know the camps were only too willing to believe that only criminals, or at least people who had become criminals, survived there. Or that the camps could not have been all that dreadful; the very fact that these former prisoners had returned to tell the story was proof that things could not have been so awful...[6]

Sometimes even close relatives felt distrust, and the desire for a "normal life" was poisoned by a kind of hierarchy of torment and pain. Yet what did a "normal life" mean? Anger, pain, loneliness, guilt, hope—these feelings collided endlessly. "I'm not among the living, I died in Auschwitz, and no one cared...starting life again is just another expression...If there is one thing that does not start again, it is your life," wrote Charlotte Delbo.[7]

The prisoners already knew from the camp that their experiences would be difficult to put into words and that their return to "normal life" would present a minefield. Renata Lacqueur, who had been interned in Bergen-Belsen, says:

> Will we ever be able to convey what these camp years have meant for us when we talk with someone who has not actually lived through a similar experience himself. What it is like to see from behind barbed wire, tall, green fir trees and new vegetable crops growing along the camp road, what the constant pressure and coercion by SS guards and their perennial checkups really mean.

6   Klüger, *Still Alive*, p. 218.
7   Delbo, *Auschwitz et après*.

How you try all the time to convince yourself that it does not touch you. All this shouting, cursing and kicking that you notice that you're growing older and that you're used to slipping through your fingers in these long years of waiting for the end of oppression. What the months mean when you count them in hours, days and weeks. And in which the only bright spots are sleep, warm soup, and sometimes a ray of sun on the way back to the barracks after another endless roll call in the damp chill of the big center Appell fields. Good moments also, the thoughts and dreams about before. Homesick and more homesick and whether it's the Frenchwomen who sing about "*Paree, Paree,*" or the Italians in their brightly patched Mediterranean get ups or the Greek, Spanish Jews from Salonika. They all think of and yearn for only one single thing: home, going home after the war. And what is home? Will we be able to find our way back from the concentration camp universe into a world in which most of us have no longer any other possessions than the memories of before the war and in which we will live among people to whom our years of imprisonment will only mean—"Oh, there's another one of those who only complain about lost things and tell horror stories."[8]

Hanna Levy-Hass also worried in the camp:

I will definitely remember everything I have seen and experienced and learned, everything that human nature has revealed to me. From this moment on it is encrusted in the depths of my soul...And in normal life. (But what is in essence "normal?" All this, this eternalized anguish or rather what is beyond, before and after?) I will never again be able to forget, I believe all findings and verdicts arrived at here: I will measure each man against the criteria of today's reality, from the perspective of what

8   Renata Lacqueur testimony, USHMM, RG-50.030.0370.

he was or could have been in these conditions of ours. To form an opinion of someone, to have a high opinion of him or not, everything will depend first and foremost on knowing what his behavior, his physical, moral and psychological reaction was or might have been during these dark years characterized by great trial, the force of his character, his emotional endurance.[9]

However, the difficulties that the diaries predicted in the postwar period included yet another factor: guilt. The subliminal reproach of which Ruth Klüger speaks, the often-unbearable guilt of all those who survived,[10] took on enormous dimensions in the case of the Bergen-Belsen survivors. The excerpt from an interview with Renata Lacqueur quoted below clearly illustrates this:

A: If you're being shoved into the gas, it's much, much worse I think than being starved and diseased. I don't know. I think because this is the final victimization because even if you are dying of hunger, even though you're dying of disease, you still have a certain control. If you're being pushed into a shower and it turns out to poison you…This is my fear of the anesthesia also. Anything which is done to me where I can't be in control.

Q: You don't feel like a victim, do you?

A: No, that's why I also feel so guilty and that maybe also the reason why I feel almost frivolous. The fact that I talk about and wear lipstick, the fact that I am "not looking my age" is not an effort. It's just I'm a survivor. By the way, why do you look so good at age 57. That is a matter of skin and haircut and also personality. I love your haircut. I hope it doesn't cost 300 dollars, because mine cost 15.

Q: What do you think that is about that you—I

---

9   Levy-Hass, *Diary of Bergen-Belsen*, p. 86.
10 Lawrence Langer, *Holocaust Testimonies: The Ruins of Memory* (New Haven: Yale University Press, 1991).

understand that Bergen-Belsen is not Auschwitz Birkenau, but in reading your diary it's clear how difficult it was and one did not know whether it was going to end?

A: Unbelievably difficult but not final.

Q: But you didn't know that.

A: That's right, but the people in Auschwitz knew. The smoke, the pipe, the fear of going through the pipe. You know. The smoke of the crematoria. We had no gas in Germany.

Q: But you had a lot of death in Bergen-Belsen?

A: Death?

Q: Death.

A: By the loaves. An unbelievable amount of dying percentage wise because people were dying of disease and starvation, but that's a different death than by being pushed into—I don't know. To me it's much more horrible. Because it's so phony, it's so typical German. You tell them they're going to have a shower. You tell them, "You're going to be disinfected." You're being killed. In Bergen-Belsen they didn't tell you that we're not going to kill you. They said we don't give a shit whether you die. Wir lassen Euch stehen bis Euch die Scheisse runterläuft, "We let you stand here on the appell until the shit comes out of you."[11]

Stanislas Tomkievicz explained that apart from his recurring nightmares, he had only a rather hazy picture of Bergen-Belsen.[12] The reason for this is partly the week-long coma into which he fell as a result of typhus, which wiped out his last memories of the camp and left him with no desire for a new, future-oriented life. After a long time, he managed to uncover what it was from the camp that he had kept hidden in the dark recesses of his memories, memories of a very specific physical suffering: hunger, swollen feet, sores, typhus, pain…

11 USHMM, RG-50.030.0370.
12 Stanislas Tomkievicz, *L'adolescence volée* (Paris: Calmann-Lévy, 1999).

The memories were lost behind a twofold repressed guilt. For one thing, he had left his parents behind when he jumped off the train that led them to certain death, and then he survived as a "privileged" inmate of a camp in which death was not inhaled in the gas chambers but only a daily visitor in the form of hunger, beatings, typhus, exhaustion from forced labor, freezing. So, this "lucky devil" had landed in a camp where he weighed a wholesome 39 kilograms—and not 26—and in which he could even procure a bite of bread for his little nephew...

Every survivor thought that what he had endured was the worst. However, very often he realized that what he had experienced was nothing compared to what a friend had gone through, who in turn acknowledged that his torment could not compete with that of others.[13]

The "surrealistic" aspect of the experience of every single day is expressed in literary depictions. In Amir Gutfreund's novel, *Our Holocaust*, Grandfather Lolek (the "adopted" grandfather who became the replacement for lost family and later the "king of tea," the proverbial miser, but at the same time drove an expensive old car) was a soldier when he fled Poland for Russia, from where he hoped to go to *Eretz Israel*. He had fought in the Jewish Brigade and had participated in major battles with countless casualties. He lost his entire family in the gas chambers, and now he bullied the survivors:

> Grandpa Lolek would rebuke the survivors. "You had terrible *Selektion*? One out of three, they took from you? Ten hours, naked in snow in *Appellplatz*? Well, what coddling! With us, against the Germans at Monte Cassino, if only it was being one out of three! Two nights and two days, person that rests a little, they die. Come on, let's move, no rest. Well, such trouble for you..."[14]

13 Aharon Appelfeld, "Individualization of the Holocaust," in Robert M. Shapiro, ed., *Holocaust Chronicles: Individualizing the Holocaust through Diaries and other Contemporaneous Personal Accounts* (New York: Ktav, 1999), pp. 1–2.
14 Guttfreund, *Our Holocaust*, p. 6.

Nostalgia

A tightly-written four-page letter reached Valérie. It was probably she who, on the margin of the letter that she carefully preserved, noted the date of its arrival (May 6, 1946). The letter had been mailed a month and a half previously, from China!

Shanghai–China
March 15, 1946

My dear Valika,

I do not know where to start and where to stop. This letter, written by our graceful and beautiful girl, Sophie, and which I received just yesterday, has given me three sensations: great joy, deep mourning, and sweet, unforgettable memories.

You can sincerely believe me that as soon as I heard that the filthy Germans had invaded Salonika—and we had already heard about the Germans' atrocities against the Jews—I was with you in spirit, with your husband, children, and beloved siblings. If only I could fly, I would have come to protect you. It was not humanly possible. For so long you have suffered terribly, while I moved about on cargo ships between the submarines and the German airplanes, transporting vital supplies to England to win the war and free you, our enslaved brothers and sisters.

Fate has hit you hard, my Valika. You have lost your beloved husband who did so much for you, solely to make you the happiest wife in the world, and he did.

I feel for you, and I am heartily sorry; may you be consoled by dedicating yourself to his beloved children. May his memory be eternal, and may God forgive him.

I'm surprised, Valikaki, my sweet, that nobody wrote to me to tell me what happened to your brothers and sisters. Albert, the gentleman, the cheerful Peppo, and the amiable Moise and my favorite, little Oscar, are in my thoughts. I hope that everyone and their families are well.

With great joy and emotion and tears of happiness, I have learned that our dear little Valika has returned safe and sound with her charming children. I was so afraid for all of you, after all that I had heard, and was eager to know what was new with you, and now I know. The letter from our sweet Sophika made it clear to me that you were very moved when you learned that I am alive.

My Valika, you are a good, noble soul, you are an angel, a priceless treasure for both your children and all of us who know you, and we will all be with you to comfort you—as best we can—and make you forget all the bitterness this war has forced you to drink. Keep your composure, for the sake of your children...

Your little Zizy (and I think she'll remember me from the last time I took a tram with her), I imagine, will probably be older now than you were when I met you, and she must have become a beautiful and charming woman, an enticing young lady. I hardly remember Nina, she was still small, but she, too, with beautiful parents, can only be beautiful, a perfect doll.

I imagine Didiko as a lovely little Palikari, an exact replica of his mother. *N'est-ce pas?* How I would like to embrace him and kiss him as if he were my own child.

Please, Valika, send me a photograph, if only a small one, of you with the three children and one of you alone. Grant me this favor that I ask of you. I would like to have you in my study and gaze upon you every day.

And then, Sofika's letter reminded me of the sweetest memories of my life, beginning the day I first saw you. You were with Moise at our house, and when you left, I stayed behind, and two dark eyes bore into my heart. I remember that you were wearing a black velvet hat that went right down to your eyes, as was the fashion then. You were just fifteen years old, and from that moment on, I could not think of anything but these two dark, cute little eyes that looked intensely into the world. The next event that made an impression on me and that I remember was when we sat at home with Riketta and you wore that white woolen dress and were the little angel of the evening. While we were dancing, you backed away from me—do you think that I have forgotten these little things? Next comes the memory of the scrapbook that I kept under the pseudonym "Missouri," and you wrote "Magnolia." Right? I would give anything to see this scrapbook again. Then the evening of the Ball d'Enfants in the White Tower. I was up in the gallery and was literally beside myself when you arrived and encouraged me by talking to me and pulling me down by the hand so we could dance.

Then comes the Panthessalian dance at Pentziki's, with the military band playing the "Missouri Waltz" all the time, and you wore this adorable pale rose dress with ruffles at the waist and at the hem, and at the end of the dance, you placed some hyacinths in my hand, something I would never have dared to do (I'm afraid I will not find the dried flowers that I left behind in Athens). That evening you were the most beautiful girl at the ball and in my eyes the most beautiful girl in the world. Really, you were. I could not calm down, I was overflowing with joy that my beautiful Valika preferred me to all other men of my age. I considered myself the happiest person in the world. But, dear Valika, I beg you, if you think fit, to explain to little Zizy that all this was a perfectly harmless romance and that I never even dared kiss your hand. Zizy should know that her mother was the most innocent creature in the world.

Then I remember the slap you gave me in front of the late Afro, which felt like a caress to me. How I would like to be with you now, so that you could give me one more...

Then comes the book (in my memory) that you and Frossika gave me, in which I underlined in ink the phrases that seemed interesting to me, and I wish I had shown them to you, but I did not dare and just ploughed on with the book, afraid to arouse your anger.

And finally, the day of your wedding comes to mind, as we danced, all in white, and I wished you all the happiness of the world. This is one of my sweetest memories. Of course, I also remember the "Would you like a mint?" And also on that Clean Monday[15] at the Karabournaki. I was worried because you were late, and even if many things do not occur to me now, I will always remember them.

During my stay in America, I heard the "Missouri Waltz" played countless times on the radio and remembered you, and all those old memories came to my mind, like a movie. In Portland, Oregon, I met an American naval officer who happened to be from Missouri. We were invited to the house of a friend of mine in which there was a big piano, a grand piano. To thank this officer, I announced to all those invited that I would play the "Missouri Waltz" in honor of the officer. This time I put all the strength of my soul into my playing and gave an excellent performance. Everyone applauded and believed it was for the officer. Nobody knew that this performance was for a certain pair of eyes that moved me so much that I burst into tears. Just believe me when I tell you that they asked me, "What's the matter?"—"What's going on?" I did not answer, and the others explained that I was extremely sensitive, and that the melody made me cry.

Truly, my Valika, I wish you would hear me play this waltz. I'll take care to record a gramophone recording of it and send it to you. Do not forgo the opportunity, my Valika, I'm old enough, and, let's not forget, I've crossed the threshold of forty.

I'll send you a little photograph, the only one I have

---

15 The first day of Lent in the Eastern Church.

here in Shanghai, and when I come back, I'll send you a better one. Write me, that goes without saying, if you want it. I look younger in this photo; five years have passed since then, and half of my hair has turned white.

I await your news and remain—not without asking you to pass my greetings to Miss Zizy and Miss Nina and countless kisses to your charming Didiko—

In sincere love,

Charis

Would you like a mint?

A few months after her return from Bergen-Belsen, Valérie received a tender letter from an old friend, who apparently had fallen in love with her around the year 1920. He is unaware that his spoiled "Valikaki" has lost siblings in addition to her husband, and that the Tchenio and Saltiel families have been almost wiped out. In spite of all that has become known about the horrors of the deportations, he has not yet realized the extent of the catastrophe that has befallen the Jews of Salonika. So, he loses himself in his nostalgia, in the memories of her pretty clothes in the prewar period, of flowers and dances. Did Valérie answer him? We do not know. In any case, there was an abyss that separated those prewar memories from the present, postliberation days.

* * *

On April 4, 1948, Zizy, now betrothed to Dick Benveniste, who had been called to serve in the army, wrote a short letter to her mother from Athens. This typed letter testifies to the momentum of the younger generation and their yearning for a "new life." Zizy had regained her sense of humor. She refers to her "*Mama*" by name— "*très chère Valika*"—and signs off with "Your elder daughter, Zizy." She writes about relatives she has visited, who received her warmly, and those whom she intends to visit. Above all, she asks that she be telegraphed immediately, that she would return if Dick came to Salonika on leave. She talks about how expensive life in Athens is and how much chocolate costs, not to mention a spring coat....In a lively and funny way she describes another relative's visit (for this reason half of the letter is in the Judeo-Spanish): uncle had wanted everyone to go for a walk together, someone else preferred to pay some visits, and Zizy decided to run away to avoid an argument (*Moi, voyant que se les ia fase la notchada de ouerko à cause de moi, je me suis mise dans la caye promettant d'aller Jeudi*). She sends her siblings and "Aunt Truman" greetings and concludes with the words: "I hope you are well, and you have no major worries. Your elder daughter, Zizy" (*J'espere que tu te portes bien et que tu n'as pas beau-coup d'ennuis, ta grande fille Zizi*). And in her own hand she added the following greetings "to sister-in-law, brother-in-law, and niece. Tell Ninette I'm going to write to her, but before that, tell me if I do not make too many mistakes" (*Salutations à ma couniada couniado et nièce. Dis à Ninette que je vais lui écrire, mais dis moi d'abord si je ne fais pas beaucoup de fautes*). Indeed, she made quite a few!

* * *

Shortly before Zizy's wedding, Valérie received a letter from Maurice Faragi, a cousin, from Athens:

Athens, June 18, 1949

My dear Valika,
You would be right to think the worst of me, but you are right in thinking that nothing can alter our common affection. Do you see, my darling, just like you, I hate writing to complain, and for over a year I could have written for no other reason. As you say so well, there are so many things that we could say in person that we cannot entrust to paper...
...Valika, Sofi and I wish your children all the happiness they deserve, you know that your children are for me more than cousins because their mother is more than a sister to me. If the ceremony goes on without us, in our hearts we will always be close to you, and who

knows, things may work out one day and then we will meet again, young and happy as in the past and we will laugh at our present misfortunes…

…My darling, I kiss you all, and wish for nothing else than an end to our troubles,

Maurice

I will send an electric cooker to Zizy and Dick soon. If for some reason this gift does not suit them, please write to me confidentially and I will send something else.[16]

Five years had passed since the end of the war, and the civil war was now coming to an end. Other problems cropped up; life was not easy for anyone. Yet Valérie seems to have been loved by all, by her children, her relatives, her friends. And while mourning those loved ones who were lost in the war years was still a fact of daily life, and nostalgic memories of the prewar period were ever present, nonetheless a few things allowed glimpses into the future: the weddings of children, the grandchildren who would come soon…And all those little things that demand our attention: whether an electric cooker was a suitable wedding present for a young bride and groom in 1949…?

---

16 For the original French, see the appendix.

Moving Forward

For the younger ones, marriage and a wedding ceremony were saviors, a means of plunging into life and bringing order to the chaos of postwar survival. Nina met Phaedon Kondopoulos on an excursion with some girls from her neighborhood. When the war broke out, he had been a student at the polytechnic; he had fled and fought in the Middle East.[17] They fell in love, and in 1947 they were married. Zizy, who had accepted jobs at the JDC and at the children's center, fell in love with Dick Benveniste: they married in 1949. Dario returned to school. He later married, had two children, and named them after Valérie and Beniko.

Valérie Saltiel in the postwar years (1950s)

---

17 Phaedon Kondopoulos was notified by a neighbor who had relations with the Gestapo that the Germans knew about his "illegal" food-buying activities, leading him to flee to the Middle East. He took part in military operations on the Aegean islands, and in a special operation he secretly returned to Salonika to collect information for the English. His report from September 15, 1943, contained insightful false as well as accurate information about the fate of the Jews; it includes many rumors that circulated in the city at the time. The fact that the report was published without commenting on this fact is one of the many disadvantages of the volume it was published in. See Thanos Veremis and Fotini Konstantopoulou, eds., *Documents on the History of Greek Jews: Records from the Historical Archives of the Ministry of Foreign Affairs* (Athens: Kastaniotis, 1998), p. 260.

Epilogue

*Introduire l'autobiographie dans le texte juif, réhabiliter le
Je—le par-ticulier d'où émerge l'universel—, affirmer le
visage, puis procéder au lent effacement de cette affirmation*

Edmond Jabes[1]

This book discusses several hundred of the few Jews from Salonika who survived the Shoah. This is not a success story. Indeed, over the stories of those who survived lies the heavy veil of the extermination of their families and the Jews of their city; their own lives too were marked by untold torments. We should not forget that their stories remain exceptions to a rule: death. Surviving encompassed many aspects, aspects that are encountered here in the form of individuals embodying a wealth of different characteristics: courage, fear, disobedience, subservience, pettiness, ill-will, pride, goodness. And all this was heightened by the war. Yet there were also aspects determined by a society that was caught in the vortex of the war, occupation, and deportation. Chance, too, played a part in this dialectic of the personal and the social to no small extent.

My concern about adequately grasping the complexity of the survival of the Jews of Salonika as a historian was accompanied by —or even born out of—the desire to learn about and understand the history of my own family members. I wanted to understand the uniqueness of their individual life stories in the context of the war, the occupation, and the machinery of annihilation. So, I tried to steer clear of the "biographical illusion" that lends life *a*

---

1   Edmond Jabes, *Le livre du Partage* (Paris: Gallimard, 1987) p.14.

posteriori logic, showing the tension between the freedom of the subject and those necessities that emerged as a result of historical structures. Dick Benveniste "handed me" the plot outline: he was one of the partisan protagonists in the first part of this book. He was the employee in charge of the correspondence of the Jewish community of Salonika, signing the documents from which I learned the story of the deportees in the second part of the book. And, ultimately, he married a young woman who returned from Bergen-Belsen, whose family history can be found in the third part of the book.

The structure of the narrative also responds to a methodological challenge: I wanted to approach the history of the Jews of Salonika in the years of the Shoah by following the paths of groups of people who shared certain experiences, that is, the experience of the camps to which they were deported, the mountains in which they fought, and later, in the first years of the postwar period, their intersecting or diverging lives. By focusing on **groups**, the opportunities and limits of their options for action, their intentions and hopelessness, their resistance and their retreat, became clear. Certainly, the Holocaust cannot be grasped solely by the question of survival. Yet the pervasiveness of the diversity of these lives is extremely important to understanding history.

The further my research progressed, the more I became aware of the deeper meaning of a decision that I had initially made for purely "theoretical" reasons, namely the decision to confront archival sources with personal—written or oral—testimonies, but also to immerse myself in a messy "family archive." The sometimes extremely precise references to the traces left by events in the written testimonies or in the words of the survivors directed me to an understanding of "how" they survived: how did they resist and how did they submit? How did they cope with it, and how were they helped or abandoned by others? How did they escape and how did they stay...? I captured details from speeches, from a photograph, an identity card, or a timeline, hoping that they would guide me and confirm or shatter the stories I told, stories that I wove into a coherent sequence of events. Nevertheless, I did not lose sight of the fact that all this—the events of the war and experience of the concentration camps—destroyed any coherence and consistency.

Perhaps my attitude to all these traces of the past has something to do with a special kind of historical consciousness, typical of a generation of historians who gradually took over from those who themselves were survivors. As Jorge Semprun sarcastically remarked, soon there will not be any more embarrassing witnesses to encumber memory...[2]

Many of us believe that the abundance of discourse about the Holocaust entails the danger of the melodramatic, that talk of the "inexplicable" is used almost ritually to tame the "wild" past. And yet, we must accept the fact that the presence of eyewitnesses in our midst keeps a sense of *aporia* (perplexity) alive. I believe that the reason for this is our realization **that they faced death**. The archive of memory insists on reminding us of the importance of the **proximity of death** and the **dilemmas** faced by the persecuted. These dilemmas resulted from the extreme nature of the events and the limited knowledge people had at that time. The gap between their knowledge at that time and their memories results in the disparity between our knowledge and our ability to write their history. This dynamic of knowledge and of the inexplicable lies at the heart of work on the Holocaust. The world of the persecuted— of those "who were drowned" and of those "who were saved"—was flooded with uncertainties and dilemmas. Will we lose that sense of the extreme and of the complexity of their experiences when these witnesses have left us?

Furthermore, as Geoffrey Hartman pointed out,[3] the witness who bears testimony, even after the event, is still under the shadow of the experience of death. This shadow, which one feels in the personal encounter with survivors, weighs on their public presence. It keeps us from losing sight of the horror, loss, fear, and pain that are at the center of their stories. When the living memory is lost, we will be left with the so-called post memories. As shocking as

---

2   Jorge Sempurn, *Le mort qu'il faut* (Paris: Gallimard, 2001).
3   See Geoffrey Hartman's chapter, "Testimony and Authenticity," in his book *Scars of the Spirit: The Struggle against Inauthenticity* (New York: Palgrave Macmillan, 2002), pp. 85–101.

these may be, in my opinion they in no way guarantee a deeper understanding of the past.

In his last book, Siegfried Kracauer[4] wrote that exiles and historians live between the past and the present. They are seeking familiarity and alienation at the same time. Their art is to reduce as far as possible the disadvantages resulting from the distance and at the same time to take advantage of it as far as that is possible. In the **aftermath of the eyewitnesses**, the archived voices and faces of the survivors of the Shoah may become guides who will open the path for us to write history.

Zizy Saltiel and Dick Benveniste's engagement in 1947

4   Siegfried Kracauer, *History: The Last Things before the Last* (Princeton: Marcus Wiener Publisher, 1995) pp. 83–84.

Appendix*

Letter from Greek Jews in Feldafing to the Jewish Community of Salonika, August 27, 1945:

Feldafing 27.8.46

A la
Communauté Juive de
Athènes,
Mitropol. Nr. 2

Nous juifs grecs, déportés de Salonique et demeurant en Allemagne, en l'occasion de la nouvelle année 5707 nous vous souhaitons bon an "que l'année se termine avec sa malédiction et qu'il commence avec beaucoup de bénédiction." Amen.

Ici inclus vous trouverez une liste avec les noms et prénoms de tous les juifs grecs de la Bavarie et nous vous prions de la publier dans les journaux de votre pays, pour faire savoir à nos parents que nous som- mes vivants et que notre adresse est la suivante:

DP Camp FELDAFING-BAVARIA-GERMANY
UNRRA TEAM No. 109   U.S. Zone

Avec beaucoup de salutations et de bénédictions, nous restons en attendant votre réponse.

vos frères
Samuel Moise

---

*   Original correspondence in French. Full English translations appear throughout the book.

Letter from Beniko Saltiel to his wife Valérie, June 1, 1941

Ma Valika chérie,
Je profite du départ de mon ami et collègue Profil Ephiliades pour t'écrire longuement. Avant tout, je t'écris presque chaque jour par poste en dehors des billets que je t'envoie entremise chauffeurs, amis etc.

De toi rien jusqu'à ce moment et suis bien inquiet. Jani m'a envoyé une lettre entremise Mr Avramidis et Leonidas m'ont dit que sa femme et Mme Eftehia ont étés te voir et cela m'a tranquillisé j'espère vous êtes tous en bonne santé.

Ici la famille en complet. Saltiel et Tchenio se portent à merveille, Papa va de mieux en mieux; il s'est levé hier et assis au fauteuil, heureusement que je suis là car il tenait beaucoup à me voir. Pour moi et les anciens collègues de notre communauté nous sommes bien tranquilles et tu n'as rien à t'inquieter. La bora est définitivement passée. Je reste chez tante Rachel je déjeune à midi chez Olga Saltiel avec maman et les Camhi et quelques fois chez Maurice Molho, et le soir chez oncle Isac. La tante est aux petits soins. J'ai la meilleure chambre avec bain etc. et Moise et oncle Isac se font en quatre pour me faire plaisir. Avec Mme Eftyhia, femme du Dr qui restera a Athènes, téléphone 84233 chez sa tante…je t'ai envoyé une valise pleine avec diverses choses, si tu ne l'as pas encore reçue téléphone et envoie la chercher.

Valika chérie, ici on ne manque de rien en dehors café… l'huile savon et habillement. Le reste en abondance. Cela me fait beaucoup de souci que vous ne mangiez là-bas de pain…etc. et je me demande si cela ne serait pas préférable de retourner ici. Tante Rachel se met à notre disposition, mais je suis sûr que cela ne te conviendra pas à rester. Impossible, à la rigueur on pourrait louer une maison mais sans meubles, lits etc. C'est pour ça que nous trouvons tous que c'est préférable de rester là-bas. D'ailleurs les communications sont très difficiles. Papa pense même que nous resterons a Athènes et l'hiver aussi. Moi si Dieu veut je serai dans une dizaine a Athènes. Je t'ai écris d'acheter sans faute immédiatement, sans tarder, robes chaussures…tout le nécessaire été comme hiver pour les enfants et toi, car ici il n'y a rien et suis sûr il n'y aura pas et a Athènes.

La maison reste avec les meubles et services lits etc. toujours les moussafir et ils ne pensent pas partir. Ce que nous avons ànotre disposition je les ai mis dans deux baoulo. Emma a enlevé tout ça la pauvre et elle a laissé et perdues plusieurs choses à elle. Comme habillement d'après ce que j'ai vu vous n'avez rien ici ni les enfants ni toi. L'autre maison a nous aussi est...celle d'Olga Molho et les bureaux, mais il n'y a pas à ce faire du mauvais sang ici c'est général. J'espère que tu as retiré de l'argent de la Banque. Si Mr Ephiliadis trouve quelque chose en chemin il t'achètera et règle lui, en le remerciant. A Mme et Mr Mavrakis mes meilleures amitiés a Niko Ekaterini, que Jani m'ecrive si Mr Antonakis s'est remis de sa maladie et où est-il. A Mr...et...amitiés de...que Mr Haralambos et sa femme, Mr et Mme...

Et toi prends les enfants embrasse les a Zizi, Nina et Diko. J'embrasse fort et tendrement,

Ton

Ben

Extract from the fourth letter from Beniko Saltiel to his wife Valérie:

Valika chérie, aujourd'hui je complète mes quarante ans et je te remercie pour tes souhaits...la prochaine fois...tous ensemble nous fêterons.

Le mois de juin est passé, il reste encore un mois à passer et ensuite con bueno nous serons réunis. Si les choses vont bien tu viendras ici et resterons chez Emma, autrement et probablement j'irai là-bas et resterons a Kifissia jusqu'en Septembre, ensuite nous prendrons une maison meublée à Athènes, car pour plusieurs raisons il se peut que je sois obligé d'aller là-bas. En tout cas écris moi si pour affaire manger tu t'arranges et ton opinion pour ce que je t'ai écris.

Extract from the fifth letter from Beniko Saltiel to his wife Valérie

Ici cela va comme je t'ai déjà écris. Les Karayanides cherchent toujours des maisons et des meubles qu'ils emportent et beaucoup de monde reste sans lit et de ce fait la vie devient bien insupportable et tu comprends bien que la question venir ici est impossible pour le moment. Au contraire je te répète dans une vingtaine de jours je serai là-bas…

Letter from Beniko Saltiel to his wife Valérie, July 9, 1941:

Ma Valika chérie,
Enfin j'ai de tes nouvelles par les lettres du 3 et 4 courant et elles m'ont fait autant de plaisir que de peine. Plaisir de savoir les enfants en bonne santé et de savoir que ma femme chérie pense beaucoup à moi, déplaisir de savoir que vous souffrez beaucoup question estomac. Avec Mr Gavrielides je t'ai envoyé une lettre et malgré ce que je t'ai écrit jusqu' à ce jour et ce qu'il te dira verbalement, après tes lettres j'ai changé d'avis et trouve que c'est préférable que vous veniez ici, car je m'en voudrais beaucoup si vous souffrez inutilement pour question manger.

Ici comme je te l'ai plusieurs fois dit, il y a viande, poisson, cher mais on trouve, légumes et fruits beaucoup, sucre et café presque pas, des riz et macaroni très peu et très cher, du pain on peine et il y aura les deltion comme à Athènes. N'empêche qu'on mange bien et avec des amis et payant cher on a tout.

Pour ce si vous souffrez là-bas c'est préférable de venir ici ou aller d'ailleurs ensemble bien entendu.

J'ai écrit à Maurice Farragi à Volo qu'il écrive si là-bas on mange bien et on pourrait trouver une maison meublée.

En tout cas, à peine tu recevras cette lettre tu me répondras si à la rigueur tu voudrais aller à Volo bien entendu si Maurice m'écrira que là c'est convenable comme vie et habitation, ou si tu préfères venir à Salonique. Moi aussi je veux beaucoup être ensemble, à toi de me dire si la vie là-bas est impossible comme manger.

Note from Beniko Saltiel to his wife Valérie, February 1943

Ma Valika chérie,
Je suis désolé de ne pouvoir aller à la maison. Je suis encore très chagriné et le cœur est très gros pour pouvoir aller au moins vous voir. Pour ce comme tu connais mes habitudes de vouloir changer l'habit, souliers etc., je te prie beaucoup de m'envoyer avec Avramico une valise contenant l'habit bleu, les souliers noirs, des bas, des chemises aux faux cols blancs, des mouchoirs, un pyjama, mon sac. Et ouvre le sac de Moisico, il y a un gros cahier, envoie le moi dans la valise. Moise mon frère se veut à notre entière disposition pour aller chez lui, oncle Isac aussi. Enfin, je tacherai si tu ne le peux pas d'aller vous rencontrer avec les enfants chez maman demain. A Zizica envoi la chez Neftel dis-lui que je veux le voir qu'il…un rendez-vous jeudi pour aller chez le commandant car je tiens à prendre la maison.
…beaucoup embrasse les enfants
Ton
Ben

Letter from Zizy to her mother, written in Tröbitz

Ma chère Mamica. Ta lettre m'a fait plaisir d'attendre de tes nouvelles mais j'ai eu de la peine d'entendre de Nina, qu'elle vienne ici, elle en recevra de ma part. Toi ne t'en fais pas de mauvais sang. Tu as trois enfants qui t'adorent et que tu leur es la chose la plus chère. Ici aujourd'hui il y a eu assez de mouvement. …Fanny est partie. Elle était très agréable ces derniers jours et elle nous a beaucoup fait rire. Elle est parti très heureuse, aussi les…d'Hollandais et ton cher Aby. Ici…maman la nourriture a un peu changé nous avons beaucoup de pommes de terre et aussi de…mais je mange tout. Toi maman comment ça va. Pourquoi tu veux partir de l'hôpital ? Peut-être je devrai aller Lundi là-bas, alors je serai de nouveau seule. Tache de rester autant que tu peux pour la nourriture et après tout tu ne vas pas te fatiguer et il y aura des maisons car 700 personnes sont partis. Le prochain convoi sera pour Vendredi prochain ça dure longtemps alors pour nous. Il faut que Nina tache de se ravitailler de quelques choses. Elle avait dit à Alice qu'elle allait venir le matin mais je l'ai attendue toute la journée et à la fin elle est venue le soir. Elle m'a promis de m'envoyer tout mais je n'ai encore rien, pas même une lettre. Je crois qu'elle a changé avec la maladie. Si tu voulais lui écrire. Que fait Dario? Il se plait à l'hôpital? J'ai remarqué qu'il avait beaucoup grandi. Fanny a toujours raconté combien il était bon et gentil quand nous étions malade et moi je lui suis très reconnaissante et si je peux à Salonique il aura de beaux cadeaux. Mamica je veux être près de toi. Si il y a un transport il faut d'abord venir demander à la doctoresse si tu peux m'inscrire car Monique a fait une bêtise et elle est resté.

Mamica, portes toi bien, μην στεναχωριέσαι

Zizi

Letter from Moise Saltiel to Valérie, November 7, 1945

MOISE S. SALTIEL
Avenue Reine Olga, 123
THESSALONIKI, le 7 Novembre 1945

Ma très chère Valica,

Je viens de recevoir presqu'en même temps tes deux lettres parvenues par la Poste ainsi que celle que Frosso m'a apporté. Je suis heureux de vous savoir tous en parfaite santé.

Je trouve que c'est peut-être la meilleure solution d'avoir accepté à aller habiter pour quelque temps chez Frosso et ceci jusqu'au jour où nous pourrons trouver un appartement définitif pour toi. D'ailleurs tu as dû recevoir mon approbation par dépêche datée d'hier. Comme je te le disais dans cette dernière je te suggérais de rentrer par bateau car j'estime que c'est la voie la meilleur marché, mais à la rigueur si il est difficile d'obtenir des billets pour le bateau alors tu seras obligée ben entendu de prendre place dans un taxi. Également je trouve que tu auras peut-être la compagnie de Sofia qui doit rentrer elle aussi à Salonique. Puis lorsque tu seras sur le point de partir, Frosso m'a conseillé de te dire que tu m'avises par dépêche par l'entremise de Pavlo...

Contrairement à ce que je te disais par ma dernière lettre concernant l'appartement d'Eleonore, on a pu seulement mettre dehors les trois des quatre locataires qui habitaient là-bas, en leur donnant un cadeau de 40,000 drahmes à chacun mais la quatrième se montrant intransigeant demandant 200,000 drs., Salvator Counio tâche de s'arranger avec celui-ci...

Selon la Loi sur la Stégassis, je t'informe que pour ceux qui demandent à reprendre leur appartement ils ont droit de faire la demande pour l'appartement qu'ils ont abandonnés lors de leur départ d'ici, donc en ce qui te concerne il faut demander pour l'appartement où tu habitais, sois rue Edmond Rostand No 56. J'ai déjà fait la demande aux Bureaux de la Stégassis pour ce dernier appartement.

A présent je te raconterai l'histoire de tes effets gardés par la fameuse Mlle Péppi : Dimanche dernier j'ai été à 5H de l'après-midi, chez le frère de celle-ci, qui habite sur la rue Allatini au Diable vert, et ceci sur rendez-vous pris avec elle où elle devait être aussi présente. Enfin, lorsque je me suis rendu là-bas en compagnie d'Emilie et de mon ami Kalfoglou, la bonne Péppi n'était pas là; son frère nous a dit que Péppi était venue plus tôt pour le prier de nous dire qu'elle ne pouvait pas venir au rendez-vous car elle était de service avec son bébé, mais si elle avait le temps elle serait venue. Après avoir attendu durant trois-quarts d'heure, le frère m'a prié de le suivre dans sa chambre pour me dire que Péppi lui a donné quelques paquets pour moi. En prenant possession de ceux-ci je trouve qu'il me donnait, ton paletot, une chemise de nuit, la bonbonnière de la part de Péppi et de sa part il m'a donné un paquet contenant des papiers au cher Benico me déclarant qu'il a fait disparaitre plusieurs autres documents craignant une perquisition de la part des allemands. En contrôlant le contenu de la bonbonnière devant le frère de Péppi, nous sommes restés étonnés de constater que d'abord tous les écrins étaient vides et qu'il y avait un tas de vielles bricoles, comme : un collier en perles de bois, un collier de corail baroques, une corne cassée en corail, deux petites montres bracelet nickelées en très mauvais état, puis une chaine parait-il en or avec le symbole maçonnique, deux ou trois petits bracelets extra fins qui appartenaient peut être à Zizi ou à Nina, un sac en métal blanc contenant des pièces de monnaie sans valeur et un petit porte-monnaie en métal blanc également. Après avoir questionné le frère de Péppi lui demandant le reste, soit les véritables bijoux, il m'a répondu que vous ne lui avez pas donné à Péppi à garder vos bons bijoux. J'ai tâché d'avoir de son frère une signature pour ce qu'il me donnait, mais il s'est refusé alléguant que ce n'était pas lui qui gardait la bonbonnière et qu'il connaissait l'état du contenu au moment où Péppi lui avait remis cette boite pour me la rendre. A présent c'est à toi de venir ici et de décider ce que tu dois faire…

En attendant ta dépêche m'annonçant ton départ je te prie de transmettre mes salutations aux Aloneftis, d'embrasser les enfants et Toto de ma part. Je t'embrasse bien affectueusement.

Moise

P.S. Je t'adresse la présente chez les Aloneftis me basant suivant ta dernière lettre que tu iras de nouveau habiter chez eux.

Letter from Maurice Faragi to Valérie, June 18, 1949:

Athènes, le 8 juin 1949

Ma chère Valica,
Tu aurais raison de penser le plus grand mal de moi, mais tu as parfaitement raison en pensant que rien ne peut altérer notre commune affection. Vois-tu mon chéri, de même que pour toi, je déteste écrire pour me plaindre et depuis plus d'un an je n'aurais pu écrire pour rien d'autre, comme tu dis si bien, il y a tant de choses qu'on pourrait raconter de vive voix et qu'on ne peut confier au papier…

Valica, Sofi et moi souhaitons à tes enfants tout le bonheur qu'ils méritent, tu sais que tes enfants sont pour moi plus que des cousins car leur mère est pour moi plus qu'une sœur. Si la cérémonie se passera sans nous, de cœur nous serons toujours près de vous et qui sait les choses vont peut-être s'arranger un jour et alors nous nous retrouverons, jeunes et heureux comme dans le passé et nous rirons de nos malheurs présents…

Ma chérie, je vous embrasse tous très fort, et je n'ai rien d'autre à souhaiter que la fin de nos maux.

Maurice

Je vais envoyer un de ces jours à Zizi et à Dick une cuisine électrique, si pour une raison ou une autre ce cadeau ne leur va pas, je te prie de m'écrire en confidence afin que j'envoie autre chose.

Bibliography

Archives

Yad Vashem Archives

O.3 – Testimonies Department of the Yad Vashem Archives.
M.1 – Central Historical Commission (CHC) of the Central Committee
of Liberated Jews in the US Zone, Munich.

Other Archives
American Jewish Archives, Cincinnati, Ohio (AVA).
Fortunoff Video Archive for Holocaust Testimonies (HVT).
Historical Archive of the Jewish Community of Thessaloniki
(HAJCTh).
Holocaust Memorial Museum of Washington Archives (USHMM).
JDC Archives (Archives of the American Jewish Joint Distribution
Committee), NY.
The Steven Spielberg Jewish Film Archive of The Hebrew University
of Jerusalem.
The Central Zionist Archives, Jerusalem.
The Wiener Holocaust Library, London.
Visual History Archive of the University of Southern California
Shoah Foundation (VHA).

Newspapers
Israilitikon Vima, Salonika, November 1945–October 1947.
Evraiki Estia, Athens, March 1947–December 1962.
The Times, London.

Palestine Post, Jerusalem, 1932–1950.

Databases and Internet Sources

Archives of the Greek Radio and Television (ERT), https://archive.ert.gr/.

Centropa Jewish Witness to a European Century, http://www.centropa.org.

Database of Greek-Jewish Holocaust Survivors' Testimonies, http://gjst.ha.uth.gr/en/index.php.

Foreign Jews in Italy during the War, http://www.annapizzuti.it_

Jewish Women's Archive, http://jwa.org.

Kavvadas, Christos, "Joseph (Johnny) Mano: A Jewish Volunteer in the War of '40, Then Guerilla ELAS and, finally, a Soldier in the Greek Army during the Civil War" (Greek), *Lefkas Island* (blog), July 14, 2014, http://www2.puresight.com/blcp.html?ps895prm=1633079701.

Michalakis, Kostas, "The Jews and the Sanatorium" (Greek), *Sanatorio Archive* (blog), October 2011, http://sanatorio-archives.blogspot.gr/p/blog- page_28.html.

National Committee for Attending Deportees (DEGOB), http://degob.org.

Raum der Namen, https://www.holocaust-denkmal-berlin.de/raum-der-namen/biographien.

Survivors Voices, Holocaust Center for Humanity, https://www.holocaustcenterseattle.org/21-survivor-resources/survivor-videos.

Voices of the Holocaust, https://voices.library.iit.edu/.

Wisconsin Historical Society: Oral Histories: Wisconsin Survivors of the Holocaust, https://www.wisconsinhistory.org/HolocaustSurvivors/.

Printed sources

Abatzopoulou, Fragiski, *The Holocaust in the Testimonies of Greek Jews* (Greek) (Thessaloniki: Paratiritis, 1990).

Ainsztein, Reuben, *Jewish Resistance in Nazi Dominated Eastern Europe* (New York: Elek,1974).

Aly, Götz, *Into the Tunnel: The Brief Life of Marion Samuel, 1931–1943* (New York: Metropolitan Books, 2007).

Améry, Jean, *Par-delà le crime et le châtiment: Essai pour surmonter l'insurmontable* (Arles: Actes Sud, 2005).

Anastasiadis, Stratis, *From Resistance to Disillusionment: Salonika, Bulkes, Vitsi* (Greek) (Thessaloniki: Epikendro, 2013).

Antelme, Robert, *L'espèce humaine* (Paris: Gallimard, 1957).

Antoniou, Giorgos, and Dirk Moses, eds., *The Holocaust in Greece* (Cambridge: Cambridge University Press, 2019).

Antoniou, Giorgos, Stratos Dordanas, Nikos Zaikos, and Nikos Marantzidis, eds., *The Holocaust in the Balkans* (Greek) (Thessaloniki: Epikendro, 2001).

Apostolou, Andrew, "The Exception of Salonika. Bystanders and Collaborators in Northern Greece," *Holocaust and Genocide Studies,* 14:2 (2000), pp. 165–196.

———, "The Exception of Salonika: Greek Christian Reactions to the Holocaust" (PhD diss., St. Anthony's College, Oxford, 2007).

Appelfeld, Aharon, "Individualization of the Holocaust," in Robert M. Shapiro, ed., *Holocaust Chronicles: Individualizing the Holocaust through Diaries and other Contemporaneous Personal Accounts* (New York: KTAV Publishing House, 1999), pp. 1–18.

———, *Ve Haza'am Od Lo Nadam* (Hebrew) (Or Yehuda: Kineret, Zemorah-Bitan, 2008).

Arad, Yitzhak, Israel Gutman, and Abraham Margaliot, eds., *Documents on the Holocaust, Selected Sources on the Destruction of the Jews of Germany and Austria, Poland, and the Soviet Union* (Jerusalem and Lincoln: Yad Vashem and University of Nebraska, 1981).

Arendt, Hannah, "The Stateless People," *Contemporary Jewish Record,* 8:2 (1945), pp. 137–153.

———, *Eichmann in Jerusalem: A Report on the Banality of Evil* (New York: Viking Press, 1963).

_____, *The Origins of Totalitarianism* (New York: Harcourt Brace Jovanovich, Publishers, 1973).

_____, *The Jewish Writings* (New York: Schocken, 2007).

Arntz, Hans-Dieter, *Der letzte Judenälteste von Bergen-Belsen: Josef Weiss. Würdig in einer unwürdigen Umgebung* (Aachen: Helios, 2012).

Bankier, David, *The Jews are Coming Back: The Return of the Jews to Their Country of Origin after World War II* (Jerusalem: Yad Vashem; and New York: Berghahn, 2005).

Bauer, Yehuda, *Flight and Rescue: Brichah* (New York: Random House, 1970).

_____, "Forms of Jewish Resistance during the Holocaust," in John K. Roth and Michael Berenbaum, eds., *Holocaust: Religious and Philosophical Implications* (New York: Paragon House, 1989), pp. 136–155.

_____, "Jewish Resistance and Passivity in the Face of the Holocaust," in François Furet, ed., *Unanswered Questions: Nazi Germany and the Genocide of the Jews* (New York: Schocken Books, 1989), pp. 235–251.

_____, *The Jewish Emergence from Powerlessness* (Toronto: University of Toronto Press, 1979).

_____, "The Judenräte: Some Conclusions," in Israel Gutman and Cynthia J. Haft, eds., *Patterns of Jewish Leadership in Nazi Europe 1933–1945: Proceedings of the Third Yad Vashem International Conference, April 4–7, 1977* (Jerusalem: Yad Vashem, 1979), pp. 393–405.

_____, *Jews for Sale: Nazi-Jewish Negotiations 1933–1945* (New Haven: Yale University Press, 1996).

_____, *History of the Holocaust* (New York: Franklin Watts, 2001).

_____, *Rethinking the Holocaust* (New Haven: Yale University Press, 2001).

Bauman, Zygmunt, *Modernity and the Holocaust* (Ithaca: Cornell University Press, 1989).

Bédarida, François, "Le temps présent et l'historiographie contemporaine," *Vingtième Siècle: Revue d' histoire*, 69 (2001), pp. 153–160.

Ben, Joseph, "Jewish Leadership in Greece during the Holocaust," in Israel Gutman and Cynthia J. Haft, eds., *Patterns of Jewish Leadership in Nazi Europe 1933–1945: Proceedings of the Third Yad*

Vashem International Conference, April 4–7, 1977 (Jerusalem: Yad Vashem, 1979), pp. 118–123.

Benveniste, Rika, "The Leadership of the Jewish Community of Salonika during the Nazi Occupation," *Ianos* (Greek), 2 (1982), pp. 118–123.

———, ed., *The Jews of Greece during the Occupation* (Greek) (Thessaloniki: Vanias, 1998).

———, "The Historiography of the Holocaust in Greece: A Survey," *Sychrona Themata* (Greek), 76/77 (2001), pp. 104–109.

———, "On the Historiography of the Shoah: The International Scene and the Greek Perspectives," in K. Gardika, A. M. Droumbouki, V. Karamanolakis, and K. Raptis, eds., *The Long Shadow of the 1940s. Heritages and Memories: War, Occupation, Resistance, Civil War* (Greek) (Athens: Alexandria, 2015).

———, *Luna: An Essay in Historical Biography* (Greek) (Athens: Polis, 2017).

Benveniste, Rika, and Hantzaroula Pothiti, "After the Tempest: The Post-Holocaust Years in the Netherlands and Greece," *Historein*, 18:1–2 (2019), https://ejournals.epublishing.ekt.gr/pfiles/journals/14/editor-uploads/issues/776/main776.html?1=776&2=18605.

Benz, Wolfgang, "Germans, Jews and Antisemitism in Germany after 1945," *Australian Journal of Politics and History*, 41:1 (1995), pp.118–129.

Berkley, George E., *Hitler's Gift: The Story of Theresienstadt* (Boston: Branden Books, 1993).

Berkowitz, Michael, and Suzanne Brown-Fleming, "Perceptions of Jewish Displaced Persons as Criminals in Early Postwar Germany: Lingering Stereotypes and Self-fulfilling Prophecies," in Avinoam J. Patt and Michael Berkowitz, eds., *We Are Here: New Approaches to Jewish Displaced Persons in Postwar Germany* (Detroit: Wayne State University Press, 2010), pp. 167–193.

Beze, Eleni, "Greek Jews: Memories and Identities after World War II" (Greek) (PhD diss, University of Thessaly, Volos, 2021).

———, "Being Leftist and Jewish in Greece during the Civil War and Its Aftermath: Constraints and Choices," *Historein*, 18:2 (2019), https://doi.org/10.12681/historein.14601.

Bigielman, Albert, *J'ai eu douze ans à Bergen-Belsen* (Paris: Editions Le Manuscrit, Fondation pour la Mémoire de la Shoah, 2005).

Blatman Daniel, *The Death Marches: The Final Phase of Nazi Genocide* (Cambridge: The Belknap Press of Harvard University Press, 2011).

Boder, David P., *Topical Autobiographies of Displaced Persons: Recorded Verbatim in DP Camps with a Psychological and Anthropological Analysis* (Los Angeles: National Institute of Mental Health, 1957).

Borowski, Tadaeusz, *This Way for the Gas Ladies and Gentlemen* (London: Penguin Books, 1976).

———, *Postal Indiscretion: The Correspondence of T. Borowski* (Evanston: Northwestern University Press, 2007).

Bourlas, Moisis: *Greek, Jew, and Leftist* (Greek) (Skopelos: Nisides, 2009).

Bouroutis, Andreas K., *The Holocaust in Salonika: The Italian Stance and the Jewish Pupils of Umberto Primo* (Greek) (Athens: Alexandria, 2020).

———, ed., *After the War: Salonika and the Fate of the Jewish Assets* (Greek) (Athens: Alexandria, 2021).

Bowman, Steven B., ed., *The Holocaust in Salonika, Eyewitness Accounts* (New York: Bloch Publishing Company, 2002).

———, *Jewish Resistance in Wartime Greece* (London: Vallentine Mitchell, 2006).

———, *The Agony of Greek Jews, 1940–1945* (Stanford: Stanford University Press, 2009).

———, "The Shoah in Salonika," in Randolph L. Braham. ed., *The Holocaust: Essays and Documents* (New York: East European Monographs, 2009), pp. 11–30.

Braham, Randolph L., The Jewish Councils: An Overview," in François Furet, ed., *Unanswered Questions: Nazi Germany and the Genocide of the Jews* (New York: Schocken Books, 1989), pp. 252–274.

Breitman, Richard, *Official Secrets. What the Nazis Planned, What the British and the Americans Knew* (London: Hill and Wang, 1999).

Brenner, Michael, "Displaced Persons and the Desire for a Jewish National Homeland," in Dan Stone, ed., *Post-War Europe: Refugees, Exile and Resettlement (1945–1950)* (Gale Digital Collection, 2007).

Brown, Adam, *Judging the "Privileged" Jews: Holocaust Ethics, Representation and the "Grey Zone"* (New York: Berghahn, 2013).

Browning, Christopher R., *Collected Memories: Holocaust History and Post-War Testimony* (Madison: University of Wisconsin Press, 2003).

Bruttmann, Tal, Annette Wieviorka, and Joly Laurent, eds., *Qu'est-ce qu'un déporté? Histoire et mémoires des déportations de la Seconde Guerre Mondiale* (Paris: CNRS, 2009).

Carpi, Daniel, "A New Approach to Some Episodes in the History of the Jews of Salonika during the Holocaust: Memory, Myth, Documentation," in Minna Rozen, ed., *The Last Ottoman Century and Beyond: The Jews in Turkey and the Balkans, 1808–1945*, vol. 2 (Tel Aviv: Tel Aviv University, The Goldstein-Goren Diaspora Research Center, 2002), pp. 259–290.

Cesarani, David, "A Brief History of Bergen-Belsen," in Suzanne Bardgett and David Cesarani, eds., *Belsen 1945: New Historical Perspectives* (London: Vallentine Mitchell, 2006), pp. 13–21.

Cesarani, David, Tony Kushner, Joanne Reilly, and Colin Richmond, eds., *Belsen in History and Memory* (London: Routledge, 1997).

Cohen, Beth B., *Case Closed: Holocaust Survivors in Postwar America* (New Jersey: Rutgers University Press, 2007).

———, "From Case File to Testimony: Reconstructing Survivors' First Years in America," in Bruce Zuckerman, ed., *The Impact of the Holocaust in America: The Jewish Role in American Life* (West Lafayette: Purdue University Press, 2008), pp. 1–30.

Cohen, Boaz, *Israeli Holocaust Research: Birth and Evolution* (London: Routledge, 2013).

Cohen, Boaz, and Rita Horvath, "Young Witnesses in the DP Camps: Children's Holocaust Testimony in Context," *Journal of Modern Jewish Studies*, 11:1 (2012), pp. 103–125.

Cohen, Gérard Daniel, "Naissance d'une nation: Les personnes déplacées de l'après- guerre européen," *Genèses*, 38 (March 2001), pp. 56–78.

———, "Between Relief and Politics: Refugee Humanitarianism in Occupied Germany 1945–1946," *Journal of Contemporary History*, 43:3 (2008), pp. 437–449.

———, *In War's Wake: European Refugees in the Postwar Order* (Oxford: Oxford University Press, 2011).

Cole, Tim, *Traces of the Holocaust: Journeying in and out of the Ghettos* (London and New York: Continuum, 2011).

Confino, Alon, "Fantasies about the Jews, Cultural Reflections on the Holocaust," *History and Memory*, 17:1/2 (2005), pp. 296–322.

———, *Foundational Pasts: The Holocaust and Historical Understanding* (Cambridge: Cambridge University Press, 2012).

Czech, Danuta, *Auschwitz Chronicle: 1939–1945* (New York: Henry Holt and Company, 1990).

Dekel, Ephraim, *Brichah: Flight to the Homeland* (New York: Herzl Press, 1973).

Delbo, Charlotte, *Auschwitz et après II: Une connaissance inutile* (Paris: Editions de Minuit, 1970).

Dellopoulou, Hari, "1945: The First Trials against Jewish Collaborators in the Special Court in Athens: A Peculiar Source of Information," *Ta Istorika* (Greek), 62 (2015), pp.189–200.

Dimitriou, Dimitrios N., "The Participation of the Jews in the National Resistance," *Chronika* (Greek), 104 (1989), pp. 3–6.

Dimitriou, Panos, *From the Depths of My Heart: Chronicle of a Life, of an Era* (Greek) (Athens: Themelio, 1997).

Diner, Dan, *Beyond the Conceivable: Studies on Germany, Nazism, and the Holocaust* (Berkeley: University of California Press, 2000).

Dinnerstein, Leonard, *America and the Survivors of the Holocaust* (New York: Columbia University Press, 1982).

Dobroszycki, Lucjan, "Jewish Elites under German Rule," in Henry Friedlander and Sybil Milton, eds., *The Holocaust: Ideology, Bureaucracy and Genocide* (New York: Kraus International Publications, 1980), pp. 221–230.

Dodos, Dimosthenis, *The Jews of Salonika in the Elections of the Greek State, 1915–1936* (Greek) (Athens: Papazisis, 2005).

Dordanas, Stratos, "German Occupation Authorities and Greek Administration," in V. Gounaris and P. Papapolyviou, eds., *The "Blood Tax" in Occupied Thessaloniki: Foreign Domination, Resistance and Survival* (Greek) (Thessaloniki: Paratiritis, 2001), pp. 91–121.

———, *Greeks against Greeks: The World of the Security Battalions in Occupied Salonika, 1941–44* (Greek) (Thessaloniki: Epikentro, 2006).

———, "Extermination and Plunder: Agency for the Custody of Jewish Properties," in Giorgos Antoniou, Stratos Dordanas, Nikos Zaikos, and Nikos Marantzidis, eds., *The Holocaust in the Balkans* (Greek) (Salonika: Epikentro, 2011), pp. 331–352.

_____, *The German Uniform in Mothballs: The Survival of Collaborationism in Macedonia, 1945–1974* (Greek) (Athens: Estia, 2011).

Douglas, Lawrence, *The Memory of Judgment: Making Law and History in the Trials of the Holocaust* (New Haven: Yale University Press, 2001).

Drosaki, Eleftheria, *In Salonika: From War to Occupation and Resistance* (Greek) (Thessaloniki: Odyseas, 2000).

Droumbouki, Anna-Maria, *An Endless Negotiation: The Reconstruction of the Jewish Communities and German Reparations, 1945–1961* (Greek) (Athens: Potamos, 2019).

Elefantis, Angelos, *They Took Athens from Us…Rereading History, 1941–1950* (Greek) (Athens: Vivliorama, 2002).

Etmektsoglou, Gabriella, "The Holocaust of Greek Jews," in Christos Chatziiosif and Prokopis Papastratis, eds., *History of Greece in the Twentieth Century: World War II, 1940–1945. Occupation-Resistance* (Greek) (Athens: Vivliorama, 2010), pp. 175–196.

Feldman, Yael, and Steven Bowman, "Love and War on Mount Olympus: Jewish Participation in the Greek Resistance," *Thetis*, 4 (1997), pp. 253–257.

Fellow Fighters: Greek Jews in the National Resistance (Greek) (Athens: Jewish Museum of Greece, 2014).

Fink, Ida, *A Scrap of Time and Other Stories* (New York: Random House, 1987).

Fleischer, Hagen, *Im Kreuzschatten der Mächte: Griechenland 1941–44: Okkupation, Resistance, Kollaboration* (Frankfurt am Main: Peter Lang, 1986).

Fleming, Katherine E., *Greece: A Jewish History* (Princeton: Princeton University Press, 2008).

Friedländer, Saul, *Nazi Germany and the Jews: The Years of Persecution, 1933–1939* (New York: Harper Collins, 1997).

_____, *The Years of Extermination: Nazi Germany and the Jews, 1939–1945* (New York: Harper Collins, 2007).

Friedman, Philip, "Pseudo Saviors in the Polish Ghettos: Mordecai Haim Rumkowski of Lodz," in Philip Friedman and Ada June Friedman, eds., *Roads to Extinction: Essays on the Holocaust*, 2nd ed. (New York and Philadelphia: The Jewish Publication Society of America, 1980), pp. 333–378.

Gaon, Aleksander, ed., *We Survived…: Yugoslav Jews on the Holocaust.* Vol. 1 (Belgrade: The Jewish Historical Museum of Federation of Jewish Communities in Yugoslavia, 2005).

Gay, Ruth, *Safe among the Germans: Liberated Jews after World War II* (New Haven: Yale University Press, 2002).

Geller, Jay Howard, *Jews in Post-Holocaust Germany, 1945–1953* (Cambridge: Cambridge University Press, 2005).

Genizi, Haim, *America's Fair Share: The Admission and Resettlement of Displaced Persons, 1945–1952* (Detroit: Wayne State University Press, 1993).

Georgiadou, Vasiliki, and Alkis Rigos, eds., *Auschwitz: The Event and Its Memory: Historical, Social, Psychoanalytical, and Political Aspects of the Genocide* (Greek) (Athens: Kastaniotis, 2007).

Giere, Jacqueline, "We're on Our Way, but We're Not in the Wilderness," in Michael Berenbaum and Abraham J. Peck, eds., *The Holocaust and History: The Known, the Unknown, The Disputed, and the Reexamined* (Indiana: Indiana University Press, 1998), pp. 699–715.

Gilbert, Shirli, "'We long for Home': Songs and Survival amongst Jewish DPs," in Avinoam J. Patt and Michael Berkowitz, eds., *We Are Here: New Approaches to Jewish Displaced Persons in Postwar Germany* (Detroit: Wayne State University Press, 2010), pp. 289–307.

Glass, James M., *Jewish Resistance during the Holocaust: Moral Uses of Violence and Will* (New York: Palgrave Macmillan, 2004).

Gourgoulianis, K. I., and A. Kordatzi-Prasa, *The First Mountain Sanatorium: One Struggle, Many Lives* (Greek) (Volos: General State Archives, University of Thessaly, 2013).

Grammes, Philip, "Sports in the DP Camps, 1945–1948," in Michael Brenner and Gideon Reuveni, eds., *Emancipation through Muscles: Jews and Sports* (Lincoln: University of Nebraska Press, 2006), pp. 187–212.

Gross, Jan T., "Themes for a Social History of War Experience and Collaboration in the Politics of Retribution in Europe," in I. Deák, J. T. Gross, and T. Just, eds., *The Politics of Retribution in Europe* (Princeton: Princeton University Press, 2000), pp. 15–36.

_____, *Neighbors: The Destruction of the Jewish Community in Jedwabne, Poland* (Princeton: Princeton University Press, 2001).

_____, *Fear: Antisemitism in Poland after Auschwitz: An Essay in Historical Interpretation* (Princeton: Princeton University Press, 2006).

Grossmann, Atina, "Victims, Villains, and Survivors: Gendered Perceptions and Self-Perceptions of Jewish Displaced Persons in Occupied Postwar Germany," *Journal of the History of Sexuality,* 11:1–2 (2002), pp. 291–318.

_____, *Jews, Germans, and Allies: Close Encounters in Occupied Germany, 1945–1949* (Princeton: Princeton University Press, 2007).

_____, "Entangled Histories and Lost Memories: Jewish Survivors in Occupied Germany, 1945–1949", in Avinoam J. Patt and Michael Berkowitz, eds., *We Are Here: New Approaches to Jewish Displaced Persons in Postwar Germany* (Detroit: Wayne State University Press, 2010), pp. 14–30.

_____, "Grams, Calories, and Food: Languages of Victimization, Entitlement, and Human Rights in Occupied Germany, 1945–1949," *Central European History,* 44:1 (2011), pp. 118–148.

Grossmann, Kurt R., *Refugees, DPs, and Migrants* (New York: Institute of Jewish Affairs and World Jewish Congress, 1962).

Gutfreund, Amir, *Our Holocaust* (New Milford and London: The Toby Press, 2000).

Gutman, Israel, "Jewish Resistance: Questions and Assessments," in Israel Gutman and Gideon Greif, eds., *The Historiography of the Holocaust Period* (Jerusalem: Yad Vashem, 1988), pp. 641–677.

_____, *The Jews of Warsaw, 1939–1943: Ghetto, Underground, Revolt* (Bloomington: Indiana University Press, 1989).

_____, *Resistance: The Warsaw Ghetto Uprising* (New York: Houghton Mifflin, 1994).

Gutman, Israel, and Avital Saf, eds., *She'erit Hapletah, 1944–1948: Rehabilitation and Political Struggle: Proceedings of the Sixth Yad Vashem International Historical Conference, October 1985* (Jerusalem: Yad Vashem, 1990).

Ha-Elion, Moshe, *Las Angustias del Enferno: Las passadias de un Djidio de Saloniki en los campos de eksterminasion almanes Aushwitz,*

Mauthausen, Melk i Ebensee (Ladino) (Beersheva: Centre Moshe David Gaon, Ben-Gurion University, 2007).

Haidia, Eleni, "The Punishment of Collaborators in Northern Greece," in M. Mazower, ed., *After the War Was Over: Reconstructing the Family, Nation and State in Greece, 1943–1960* (Princeton: Princeton University Press, 2000), pp. 42–61.

Handrinos, Iasonas, G., *Fellow Fighters: EAM and the Jews of Greece* (Greek) (Athens: Psifides, 2020).

Hantzaroula, Pothiti, "The Social Dimension of Memory in Holocaust Survivors' Testimonies," in R. B. Bouschoten et al., eds., *Bridging Generations: Interdisciplinarity and Life-Histories in the Twenty-First Century* (Greek) (Volos: Oral History Association, 2013), pp. 217–234.

———, *Child Survivors of the Holocaust in Greece: Memory, Testimony and Subjectivity* (London: Routledge, 2020).

Harrison, Earl G., *The Plight of the Jews in Europe: A Report to President Truman* (New York: Reprinted by the United Jewish Appeal, 1945).

Hartman, Geoffrey, *Scars of the Spirit: The Struggle against Inauthenticity* (New York: Palgrave Macmillan, 2002).

Hekimoglou, Evanghelos, "Merten's Lost Checks and Their Fate: Ransom for the Forced Labor of the Jews of Salonika (1942–1943)," *Thessalonikeon Polis* (Greek), 18 (2005), pp. 40–59.

Hekimoglou, Evanghelos, and Anna Maria Droumpouki, eds., *The Day After the Holocaust* (Greek) (Thessaloniki: Jewish Museum of Thessaloniki, 2017).

Herzberg, Abel Jacob, *Between Two Streams: A Diary from Bergen-Belsen* (London and New York: I. B. Tauris Publishers, 1997).

Heymont, Irving, *Among the Survivors of the Holocaust, 1945: The Landsberg DP Camp Letters of Major Irving Heymont* (Cincinnati: American Jewish Archives, 1982).

Hilberg, Raul, *Perpetrators, Victims, Bystanders: The Jewish Catastrophe, 1933–1945* (New York: Harper Perennial, 1992).

———, *The Destruction of the European Jews*, 2nd ed. (New Haven: Yale University Press, 2003).

Hilliard, Robert H., *Surviving the Americans: The Continued Struggle of Jews after Liberation* (New York: Seven Stories Press, 1997).

Hilton, Laura, "The Black Market in History and Memory: German

Perceptions of Victimhood from 1945 to 1948," *German History*, 28:4 (2010), pp. 479–497.

Hionidou, Violetta, *Famine and Death in Occupied Greece, 1941–1944* (Cambridge: Cambridge University Press, 2006).

Holian, Anna, *Between National Socialism and Soviet Communism: Displaced Persons in Postwar Germany* (Ann Arbor: University of Michigan Press, 2011).

———, "The Ambivalent Exception: American Occupation Policy in Post War Germany and the Formation of Jewish Refugee Spaces," *Journal of Refugee Studies*, 25:3 (2012), pp. 452–473.

Hondros, Ioannis L. "The Greek Resistance, 1941–1944: A Reconsideration," in G. Iatridis, ed., *Greece in the Decade 1940–1950: A Nation in Crisis* (Greek) (Athens: Themelio, 1984), pp. 69–90.

Jabès, Edmond, *Le livre du Partage* (Paris: Gallimard, 1987).

Jockush, Laura, "A Folk Monument for Our Destruction and Heroism: Jewish Historical Commissions in Displaced Persons Camps in Germany, Austria, Italy," in Avinoam J. Patt and Michael Berkowitz, eds., *We Are Here: New Approaches to Jewish Displaced Persons in Postwar Germany* (Detroit: Wayne State University Press, 2010), pp. 31–73.

———, "Memorialization through Documentation: Holocaust Commemoration among Jewish Displaced Persons in Allied Occupied Germany," in Bill Niven and Chloe Paver, eds., *Memorialization in Germany since 1945* (London: Palgrave Macmillan, 2010), pp. 181–191.

———, *Collect and Record! Jewish Holocaust Documentation in Early Postwar Europe* (Oxford: Oxford University Press, 2012).

Kaftantzis, Giorgos, *The University of Salonika during the Occupation* (Greek) (Salonika: Paratiritis, 1983).

Kaposi, David, "Judge or Not to Judge: The Clash of Perspectives in the Scholem Exchange," *Holocaust Studies: A Journal of Culture and History*, 14:1 (2008), pp. 93–116.

Kavala, Maria, "Hunger and Survival in Occupied Greece," in Vasilis Panagiotopoulos, ed., *History of Modern Hellenism, 1770–2000, Greece at War, 1940–1949* (Greek) vol. 8 (Athens: Ellinika Grammata, 2004), pp. 49–62.

———, "Salonika during the German Occupation (1941–1944): Society,

Economy, Persecution of Jews" (Greek) (PhD diss., University of Crete, Rethymnon, 2009).

———, *The Destruction of the Jews of Greece 1941–1944: A Multifaceted History* (Greek) (Athens: Hellenic Academic EBooks, 2015).

———, ed., *Modern Greek Jewry: Dynamic Presence, Painful Absence* (Greek) (Thessaloniki: University Studio Press, 2020).

Kedros, Andreas, *The Greek Resistance, 1940–1944* (Greek) (Athens: Themelio, 1976).

Kenan, Orna, *Between Memory and History: The Evolution of Israeli Historiography of the Holocaust, 1945–1961* (New York: Peter Lang, 2003).

Kerem, Yitzhak, "New Findings on Greek Jewish Heroism in the Holocaust," *Sephardic Horizons*, https://www.sephardichorizons. org/Volume2/Issue2/kerem.html.

Kershaw, Ian, *Hitler, the Germans and the Final Solution* (New Haven and London: Yale University Press, 2008).

Klüger Ruth, *Still Alive: A Holocaust Girlhood Remembered* (New York: The Feminist Press, 2001).

Kochavi, Arieh J., *Post-Holocaust Politics: Britain, the United States, and the Jewish Refugees, 1945–1948* (Chapel Hill: The University of North Carolina Press, 2001).

Kogon, Eugen, Hermann Langbein, and Adalbert Ruckerl, *Les chambres à gaz secret d'État* (Paris: Editions de Minuit, 1984).

Kokkonen, Susanna, "Jewish Displaced Persons in Postwar Italy 1945–1951," *Jewish Political Studies Review*, 20:1/2 (2008), pp. 91–106.

Kolb, Eberhard, *Bergen-Belsen: From 1939 to 1945* (Göttingen: Vandenhoeck, 1985).

Kolinski, Eva, *After the Holocaust: Jewish Survivors in Germany* (London: Pimlico, 2004).

Königseder, Angelika, and Juliane Wetzel, *Waiting for Hope: Jewish Displaced Persons in Post-World War Germany* (Evanston: Northwestern University Press, 2001).

Koretz, Aryeh, *Yoman Bergen-Belzen, 11.7.1944–30.3.1945* (Hebrew) (Tel Aviv: no publisher, 1992).

Kossoy, Edward, "The Gęsiówka Story: A Little-Known Page of Jewish Fighting History," *Yad Vashem Studies*, 32 (2004), pp. 323–350.

Kounio-Amarilio, Erika and Albertos Nar, eds., *Oral Testimonies of*

Jews of Salonika on the Holocaust (Greek) (Thessaloniki: Paratiritis, 1998).

Kousouris, Dimitris, *Trials of the Collaborators, 1944–1949: Justice, State Continuity, and National Memory* (Greek) (Athens: Polis, 2014).

Kracauer, Siegfried, *History: The Last Things before the Last* (Princeton: Markus Wiener Publishers, 2013).

Kyriazopoulos, Dimitris (Fotinos), *Western Macedonia: Free Greece during the Occupation. Memoirs from the National Resistance, 1940–1944* (Greek) (Thessaloniki: Kodikas, 2004).

La Capra, Dominick, *Writing History, Writing Trauma* (Baltimore: John Hopkins University Press, 2001).

Lacqueur, Renata, *Bergen-Belsen Tagebuch, 1944–1945* (Hannover: Fackelträger, 1983).

Lagrou, Pieter, *The Legacy of Nazi Occupation: Patriotic Memory and National Recovery in Western Europe, 1945–1965* (Cambridge: Cambridge University Press, 2000).

Lampsa, Karina, and Yakov Schiby, *Life from the Start: The Migration of Greek Jews to Palestine (1945–1948)* (Greek) (Athens: Alexandria, 2010).

———, *Rescue: World's Silence, Resistance in the Ghettos and the Camps. Greek Jews during the German Occupation* (Greek) (Athens: Capon, 2012).

Langer, Lawrence, "The Dilemma of Choice in the Death Camps," *Centerpoint*, 4 (1980), pp. 222–231.

———, *Versions of Survival: The Holocaust and Human Spirit* (Albany: State University Press of New York, 1982).

———, *Holocaust Testimonies: The Ruins of Memory* (New Haven: Yale University Press, 1991).

Lattek, Christine, "Bergen-Belsen: From 'Privileged' Camp to Death Camp," in David Cesarani, Tony Kushner, Joanne Reilly, and Colin Richmond, eds., *Belsen in History and Memory* (London: Routledge, 1997), pp. 37–71.

Lavsky, Hagit, *New Beginnings: Holocaust Survivors in Bergen-Belsen and the British Zone in Germany, 1945–1950* (Detroit: Wayne State University Press, 2002).

Levi, Primo, *If This Is a Man* (London: Penguin Books, 1988).

———, *The Truce* (London: Abacus, 1998).

_____, *La zone grise: Entretien avec Anna Bravo and Federico Cereja* (Paris: Éditions Payot & Rivages, 2014).

Levin, Dov, *Fighting Back: Lithuanian Jewry's Armed Resistance to the Nazis, 1941–1945* (New York: Holmes and Meier Publishers, 1985).

Levine Melamed, Renee, "The Memoirs of a Partisan from Salonika," *Nashim*, 7 (2004), pp. 151–173.

Levy-Hass, Hanna, *Diary of Bergen-Belsen: 1944–1945* (Chicago: Haymarket Books, 2009).

Lewkowicz, Bea, *The Jewish Community of Salonika: History, Memory, Identity* (London: Vallentine Mitchel, 2006).

Malignac, Georges, "Personnes Déplacées," *Population*, 3:4 (1948), pp. 737–741.

Malkki, Lisa, *Purity and Exile: Violence, Memory, and National Cosmology among Hutu Refugees in Tanzania* (Chicago: University of Chicago Press,1995).

Mankowitz, Zeev W., *Life between Memory and Hope: The Survivors of the Holocaust in Occupied Germany* (New York: Cambridge University Press, 2002).

Marantzidis, Nikos, *Yaassin Millet/Long Live the Nation: Refugees, Occupation, and Civil War, Ethnic Identity and Political Behavior among the Turkish-Speaking Orthodox Greek of Western Pontos* (Greek) (Heraklion: University of Crete Press, 2001).

Margaritis, Giorgos, *From Defeat to Revolt. Greece: Spring 1941–Fall 1942* (Greek) (Athens: Politis, 1993).

Mariot, Nicolas, and Claire Zalc, *Face à la persécution: 991 juifs dans la guerre* (Paris: Seuil, 2010).

Marrus, Michael R., *The Unwanted: European Refugees from the First World War through the Cold War* (New York and Oxford: Oxford University Press, 1985).

_____, *Jewish Resistance to the Holocaust* (London: Mecklermedia, 1989).

_____, "Jewish Resistance to the Holocaust," *Journal of Contemporary History*, 30:1 (1995), pp. 83–110.

Matsas, Joseph, "The Participation of the Greek Jews in the National

Resistance, 1940–1944," *Journal of the Hellenic Diaspora*, 17 (1991), pp. 55–68.

Matsas, Michael, *The Illusion of Safety: The Story of the Greek Jews during the Second World War* (New York: Pella, 1997).

Mazower, Mark, *Inside Hitler's Greece: The Experience of Occupation, 1941–1944* (New Haven: Yale University Press, 1993).

———, ed., *After the War Was Over: Reconstructing the Family, Nation and State in Greece, 1943–1960* (Princeton: Princeton University Press, 2000).

———, "The Cold War and the Appropriation of Memory. Greece after Liberation," in István Déak, Jan T. Gross, and Tony Just, eds., *The Politics of Retribution in Europe: World War II and Its Aftermath* (Princeton: Princeton University Press, 2000), pp. 212–232.

Michel, Henri, "Jewish Resistance and the European Resistance Movement," *Yad Vashem Studies*, 7 (1968), pp. 7–16.

Michman, Dan, "Judenrat," in Judith Tydor Baumel and Walter Lacqueur eds., *The Holocaust Encyclopedia* (New Haven: Yale University Press, 2001), pp. 370–377.

———, *Pour une historiographie de la Shoah* (Paris: Press Editions, 2001).

———, "Jewish Leadership in Extremis," in Dan Stone, ed., *The Historiography of the Holocaust* (Basingstoke and New York: Palgrave Macmillan, 2004), pp. 319–340.

———, *The Emergence of Jewish Ghettos during the Holocaust* (Cambridge: Cambridge University Press, 2011).

Moisis, Asher, *Legacy*, Introduction and commentary by Rafail Moisis (Athens: Asher Moisis, 2011).

Molho, Michael, and Joseph Nehama, *In Memoriam: Homage aux victimes juives des Nazis en Grèce* (Thessaloniki: Jewish Community of Thessaloniki, 1948).

Molho, Rena, "Myths and Reality on the Extermination of the Jews of Salonika," *Athens Review of Books* (Greek), 27 (2013), pp. 38–42.

———, "La reconstruction de la communauté juive de Salonique après la Shoah," in Esther Benbassa, ed., *Salonique: Ville juive, ville ottomane, ville grecque* (Paris: CNRS, 2014), pp. 117–138.

_____, *The Holocaust of Greek Jews: Studies on History and Memory* (Greek) (Athens: Patakis, 2014).

Myers Feinstein, Margarete, "Jewish Women Survivors in the Displaced Persons Camps of Postwar Germany," *Shofar: An Interdisciplinary Journal of Jewish Studies*, 24:4 (2006), pp. 67–89.

_____, *Holocaust Survivors in Postwar Germany, 1945–1957* (Cambridge: Cambridge University Press, 2010).

Myers, Margarete L., "Jewish Displaced Persons: Reconstructing Individual and Community in the US Zone of Occupied Germany," *Leo Baeck Year Book*, 42 (1997), pp. 303–324.

Naar, Devin E., "From the 'Jerusalem of Balkans' to the Golden Medina: Jewish Immigration from Salonika to the United States," *American Jewish History*, 93:4 (2007), pp. 435–473.

Nar, Albertos, *Seated by the Sea...Studies and Articles on the Jewish Community of Salonika* (Greek) (Thessaloniki: University Studio Press, 1997).

Nar, Leon A., *Jewish Members of the Parliament, 1915–1936* (Greek) (Athens: Foundation of the Greek Parliament, 2011).

_____, *In Salonika Again: The Hesitant Return of Greek Jews to the Native Place (1945–1946)* (Greek) (Athens: Polis, 2018).

Nazis and the National Resistance in Greece: Seven Secret Reports of the General Military Staff, with an introduction by Michalis Lyberatos (Greek) (Athens: Dromon, 2012).

Novitch, Miriam, *Le Passage des Barbares: Contribution à l'histoire de la déportation et de la résistance des Juifs Grecs* (Paris: Presses du Temps Présent, 1967).

Oppenheim, Abraham N., *The Chosen People. The Story of the '222 Transport' from Bergen-Belsen to Palestine* (London: Vallentine Mitchell, 1996).

Ouzan, Francoise, *Ces Juifs dont l'Amérique ne voulait pas: 1945–1950* (Paris: Complexe, 1999).

Ouzan, Françoise, and Gerstenfeld Manfred eds, *Postwar Jewish Displacement and Rebirth: 1945–1967* (Leiden: Brill, 2014).

"Pages of the National Resistance: A Flyer by EAM to save the Jews," *Chronika* (Greek), 108, November–December 1989, p. 12ff.

Papapolyviou, Petros, "Resistance intra muros," in V. Gounaris and P. Papapolyviou, eds., *The "Blood Tax" in Occupied Thessaloniki:*

Foreign Domination, Resistance and Survival (Greek) (Thessaloniki: Paratiritis, 2001), pp. 41–90.

Patt, Avinoam J., *Finding Home and Homeland: Jewish Youth and Zionism in the Aftermath of the Holocaust* (Detroit: Wayne State University Press, 2009).

———, "Living in Landsberg, Dreaming of Deganiah: Jewish Displaced Youths and Zionism after the Holocaust," in Avinoam J. Patt and Michael Berkowitz, eds., *We Are Here: New Approaches to Jewish Displaced Persons in Postwar Germany* (Detroit: Wayne State University Press, 2010), pp. 98–135.

———, "Stateless Citizens of Israel: Jewish Displaced Persons and Zionism in Post War Germany," in Jessica Reinisch and Elizabeth White, eds., *The Disentanglement of Populations: Migration, Expulsion and Displacement in Postwar Europe, 1944–49* (Basingstoke: Palgrave Macmillan, 2011), pp. 162–182.

Patt, Avinoam J., and Michael Berkowitz, eds., *We Are Here: New Approaches to Jewish Displaced Persons in Postwar Germany* (Detroit: Wayne State University Press, 2010).

Paulsson, Gunnar S., *Secret City: The Hidden Jews of Warsaw, 1940–1945* (New Haven: Yale University Press, 2002).

Pinson, Koppel S., "Jewish Life in Liberated Germany: A Study of the Jewish DPs," *Jewish Social Studies*, 9:2 (1947), pp. 101–126.

Plaut, Joshua Eli, *Greek Jewry in the Twentieth Century, 1913–1983: Patterns of Jewish Survival in the Greek Provinces before and after the Holocaust* (Madison: Fairleigh Dickinson University Press, 2000).

Pollak, Joseph A., "The Lost Transport," *Commentary* (September 1995), pp. 24–27.

Poznanski, Renée, "Reflections on Jewish Resistance and Jewish Resistance in France," *Jewish Social Studies*, 2:1 (1995), pp. 124–158.

Poznanski, Renée, "Résistance juive, résistants juifs: Retour à l'histoire," in Jean-Marie Guillon and Pierre Laborie, eds., *Mémoire et Histoire: La Résistance* (Toulouse: Privat, 1995), pp. 227–245.

———, *Propagandes et Persécutions: La Resistance et le problème juif 1940–1944* (Paris: Fayard, 2008).

Protopapas-Kikitsas, Sarandis, *The Tenth Division of ELAS: National Resistance in Macedonia, 1941–1944* (Greek) (Athens, 1978).

Proudfoot, Malcom, *European Refugees, 1939–1952: A Study in Forced*

Population Movement (Evanston: Northwestern University Press, 1956).

Rabinovici, Doron, *Eichmann's Jews: The Jewish Administration of Holocaust Vienna, 1938–1945* (London: Polity, 2011).

Rayski Adam, "The Jewish Underground Press in France and the Struggle to Expose the Nazi Secret of the Final Solution," in Michael J. Berenbaum and Abraham J. Peck, eds., *The Holocaust and History: The Known, the Unknown, the Disputed, and the Reexamined* (Bloomington: Indiana University Press, 1998).

Refael, Shmuel, ed., *Benetivei She'ol. Yehudei Yavan Bashoah: Prakei Edut* (Hebrew) (Jerusalem: Institute for the Study of the Jews of Salonika and Organization for Greek Survivors of the Concentration Camps, 1988).

Reichental, Tomi, *I Was a Boy in Belsen* (Dublin: The O'Brien Press, 2011).

Reilly, Joanne, and Donald Bloxham, "The Belsen Camp in Historical Context," in Ben Flanagan, Donald Bloxham, and Joanne Reilly, eds., *Remembering Belsen: Eyewitnesses Record the Liberation* (London: Vallentine Mitchell, 2005), pp. 126–139.

Reinisch, Jessica, "Preparing for a New World Order: UNRRA and the International Management of Refugees," in Dan Stone, ed., *Post-War Europe: Refugees, Exile and Resettlement, 1945–1950* (Reading: Gale Cengage Learning, 2007).

Ritzaleos, Vasilis, "The Greek Orthodox Church in Salonika and the Holocaust," in Giorgos Antoniou, Stratos Dordanas, Nikos Zaikos, and Nikos Marantzidis, eds., *The Holocaust in the Balkans* (Greek) (Thessaloniki: Epikentro, 2011), pp. 295–330.

Ritzaleos, Vasilis, "The Jewish Community of Kavala under Bulgarian Occupation: Organization, Exploitation, Dissolution (1942–1944)," in V. Dalkavoukis, E. Pashaloudi, I. Skoulidas, and K. Tskekou, eds., *Narratives on the 1940s: From the Occupied State's Discourse to Postmodern Historiography* (Greek) (Thessaloniki: Epikendro, 2012), pp. 69–90.

Rosenberg, Göran, *A Brief Stop on the Road from Auschwitz* (London: Granta, 2014).

Rozen, Minna, "Jews and Greeks Remember their Past: The Political

Career of Rabbi Tzvi Koretz (1933–1943)," *Jewish Social Studies*, 12:1 (2005), pp. 111–166.

Rozett, Robert, "Jewish Resistance," in Dan Stone, ed., *The Historiography of the Holocaust* (New York: Palgrave Macmillan, 2004), pp. 344–63.

Safrian, Hans, *Eichmann's Men* (Cambridge: Cambridge University Press and USHMM, 2009).

Salem, Stella, "The Old Jewish Cemetery of Salonika," *Chronika* (Greek), 181 (2005), pp. 6–17.

———, "Jews' Assets during the German Occupation and afterwards (1940–1949)," in M. Kavala, ed., *Modern Greek Jewry: Dynamic Presence, Painful Absence, the Present* (Greek) (Salonika: University Studio Press, 2020), pp. 183–224.

Saltiel, Leon, "Dehumanizing the Dead: The Destruction of Thessaloniki's Jewish Cemetery in the Light of New Sources," *Yad Vashem Studies*, 42:1 (2014), pp. 11–46.

———, *The Holocaust in Thessaloniki: Reactions to the Anti-Jewish Persecution, 1942–1943* (London: Routledge 2020).

Salvatici, Silvia, "Help the People to Save Themselves: UNRRA Relief Workers and European Displaced Persons," *Journal of Refugee Studies*, 25 (2012), pp. 1–24.

Saurel, Jacques, *De Drancy à Bergen-Belsen, 1944–1945: Souvenirs rassemblés d'un enfant déporté* (Paris: Editions Le Manuscrit, Fondation pour la Mémoire de la Shoah, 2006).

Savosnick, Robert, *I Did Not Want to Die: From Norway to Auschwitz* (Jerusalem: Yad Vashem, 2021).

Schwarz, Ghita, *Displaced Persons: A Novel* (New York: William Morrow, 2010).

Segalman, Ralph, "The Psychology of Jewish Displaced Persons," *Jewish Social Service Quarterly*, 23 (1947), pp. 361–369.

Segev, Tom, *The Seventh Million: The Israelis and the Holocaust* (New York: Picador, 1993).

Sempurn, Jorge, *Le mort qu'il faut* (Paris: Gallimard, 2001).

Shapiro, Leon, *The History of ORT: A Jewish Movement for Social Change* (New York: Schocken Books, 1980).

Shepard, Ben, *The Long Road Home: The Aftermath of the Second World War* (New York: Anchor, 2011).

Slatt, Vincent E., "Nowhere to Go: Displaced Persons in Post-V-E Day Germany," *Historian*, 64:2 (2002), pp. 275–294.

Sloan, Jacob, ed., *Notes from the Warsaw Ghetto: The Journal of Emmanuel Ringelblum* (New York: McGraw-Hill, 1958).

Spengler-Axiopoulou, Barbara, "Methodological Thoughts for a Historical Approach to the Holocaust: The Case of Salonika," *Sychrona Themata* (Greek) 52–53 (July/December 1994), pp. 85–88.

———, "Solidarity and Offering Help to the Greek Jews during the German Occupation, 1941–1945," in Rika Benveniste, *The Jews of Greece during the Occupation* (Greek) (Thessaloniki: Vanias, 1998), pp. 13–28.

Spiliotis, Susannne-Sofia, "An Affair of Politics Not Justice: The Merten Trial (1957–1959) and Greek-German Relations," in Mark Mazower, ed., *After the War Was Over: Reconstructing the Family, Nation and State in Greece, 1943–1960* (Princeton: Princeton University Press, 2000), pp. 293–302.

Stone, Dan, "Holocaust Historiography and Cultural History," *Dapim: Studies on the Holocaust*, 23 (2009), pp. 52–55.

Tec, Nechama, *Jewish Resistance: Facts, Omissions, and Distortions* (Washington, D.C.: United States Holocaust Memorial Museum, Miles Lerman Center for the Study of Jewish Resistance, 1997).

The Trial of Adolf Eichmann: Record of Proceedings in the District Court of Jerusalem, vol. 2 (Jerusalem: Ministry of Justice, 1992).

Tomkievicz, Stanislas, *L'adolescence volée* (Paris: Calmann-Lévy, 1999).

Traverso, Enzo, *Fire and Blood: The European Civil War, 1914–1945* (New York: Verso, 2016).

Trunk, Isaiah, *Jüdenrat: The Jewish Councils in Eastern Europe under Nazi Occupation* (New York: MacMillan, 1972).

Tsatsou, Ioanna, *Diary during Occupation* (Greek) (Athens: Estia, 2000).

Tydor, Baumel Judith, "DPs, Mothers and Pioneers: Women in the She'erit Hapletah," *Jewish History*, 11:2 (1997), pp. 99–110.

Tzafleris, Nikos, "Survival and Resistance in Volos under the Occupation (1941–1944)" (Greek) (PhD diss., University of Thessaly, Volos, 2007).

———, "Persecution and Rescue of the Jews of Volos during the Holocaust in Greece (1943–1944)," in Dan Michman, ed., *Hiding,*

Sheltering, and Borrowing Identities: Avenues of Rescue during the Holocaust (Jerusalem: Yad Vashem, 2017), pp. 125–144.

_____, "Rebuilding the Jewish Communities after the Holocaust: The Relief Programme of the American Joint Distribution Committee in Post-War Greece," *Historein*, 18:2 (2019), https://doi.org/10.12681/ historein.14583.

Uziel, Baruch, and David Benveniste, eds., *Saloniki: Ir Va'em Be'Israel* (Hebrew) (Jerusalem and Tel Aviv: Institute for the Research of Salonikan Jewry, 1967).

Uziel, Daniel, *Arming the Luftwaffe: The German Aviation Industry in World War II* (Jefferson: MacFarland, 2012).

Uziel, Solomon Meir, *Savuni gam sevavuni beshem Adonai ki amilam* (Ladino) (Salonika, 1953).

Vafiadis, Markos, *Memoirs (1940–1944)* (Greek) (Athens: Papazisis, 1985).

Vafopoulos, Giorgos Th., *Pages of an Autobiography* (Greek) (Thessaloniki: Paratiritis, 1971), pp. 180–182.

Varon-Vassard, Odette, *The Emergence of a Difficult Memory* (Greek) (Athens: Estia, 2013).

Vasilikou, Maria, "Politics of the Jewish Community of Salonika in the Inter-War Years: Party Ideologies and Party Competition" (PhD diss., University College London, London, 1999).

Venia Hadari, Ze'ev, *Second Exodus: The Full Story of Jewish Illegal Immigration to Palestine, 1945–1948* (London: Vallentine Mitchell, 1991).

Veremis, Thanos, and Fotini Konstantopoulou, eds., *Documents on the History of Greek Jews: Records from the Historical Archives of the Ministry of Foreign Affairs* (Athens: Kastaniotis, 1998).

Verolme, Hetty H., *Children's House of Belsen* (Perth: Freemantle Press, 2000).

Vers la paix et l'équité: Récommendation du American Jewish Committee (New York: The American Jewish Committee, 1946).

Vogel, Loden, *Tagebuch aus einem Lager* (Göttingen: Vandenhoeck and Ruprecht, 2002).

Voglis, Polymeris, *Greek Society during the Occupation, 1941–1944* (Greek) (Athens: Alexandria, 2004).

_____, "Surviving Hunger: Life in the Cities and the Countryside during the Occupation," in Robert Gildea, Olivier Wieviorka, and Anette Warring, eds., *Surviving Hitler and Mussolini: Daily Life in Occupied Europe* (Oxford and New York: Berg Publishers, 2006), pp. 16–41.

Weinberg, David, *Recovering a Voice: West European Jewry after the Holocaust* (Liverpool: Littman Library of Jewish Civilization, 2015).

Weinberg, Werner, *Self-Portrait of a Holocaust Survivor* (Jefferson: MacFarland, 1985).

Weiss, Aharon, "Jewish Leadership in Occupied Poland: Postures and Attitudes," *Yad Vashem Studies*, 12 (1977), pp. 335–365.

Weiss, Aharon, "The Historiographical Controversy Concerning the Character and Functions of the Judenrats," in Israel Gutman, ed., *The Historiography of the Holocaust Period: Proceedings of the Fifth Yad Vashem International Conference, March 1983* (Jerusalem: Yad Vashem, 1988), pp. 679–696.

Wetzel, Juliane, "Les camps pour personnes déplacées juives en Allemagne de 1945 à 1957," *Vingtième siècle: Revue d'Histoire*, 54 (1997), pp. 79–88.

Wiesel, Elie, *Night* (New York: Hill and Wang, 2006).

Wieviorka, Annette, *Auschwitz: 60 ans après* (Paris: Robert Laffont, 2005).

_____, *Ils étaient juifs, résistants, communistes* (Paris: Denoël 2020).

Wyman, Mark, *DPs: Europe's Displaced Persons, 1945–1951* (Ithaca: Cornell University Press, 1998).

Yakoel, Yomtov, *Memoirs 1941–1943* (Greek), ed. and introduced by Fragiski Abatzopoulou (Thessaloniki: Paratiritis, 1993).

Zalc, Claire, Tal Bruttmann, and Ivan Ermakoff, eds., *Pour une Microhistoire de la Shoah* (Paris: Seuil, 2012).

Zanna, Virginia, *Diary of War, 1940–1941* (Greek) (Athens: Ermis, 1979).

Zertal, Idith, *From Catastrophe to Power: Holocaust Survivors and the Emergence of Israel* (Berkeley: University of California Press, 1998).

Bibliography of Works in Greek

Αμπατζοπούλου, Φραγκίσκη, *Το Ολοκαύτωμα στις μαρτυρίες των Ελλήνων Εβραίων* (Θεσσαλονίκη: Παρατηρητής, 1990).

Αναστασιάδης, Στρατής, *Από την αντίσταση στη διάψευση. Θεσσαλονίκη, Μπούλκες, Βίτσι* (Θεσσαλονίκη: Επίκεντρο, 2013).

Αντωνίου, Γιώργος, Στράτος Δορδανάς, Νίκος Ζάικος, και Νίκος Μαραντζίδης, επιμ., *Το Ολοκαύτωμα στα Βαλκάνια* (Θεσσαλονίκη: Επίκεντρο, 2001).

Βαφειάδης, Μάρκος, *Απομνημονεύματα (1940–1944)* (Αθήνα: Παπαζήσης, 1985).

Βαφόπουλος, Γιώργος Θ., *Σελίδες Αυτοβιογραφίας* (Θεσσαλονίκη: Παρατηρητής, 1971).

Βαρών-Βασσάρ, Οντέτ, *Ανάδυση μιας δύσκολης μνήμης: Κείμενα για τη γενοκτονία των Εβραίων* (Αθήνα: Εστία, 2013).

Βερέμης, Θάνος, και Φωτεινή Κωνσταντακοπούλου, επιμ., *Οι Έλληνες Εβραίοι. Στοιχεία μέσα από διπλωματικά και ιστορικά έγγραφα του Υπουργείου Εξωτερικών* (Αθήνα: Καστανιώτης, 2000).

Βόγλης, Πολυμέρης, *Η ελληνική κοινωνία στην Κατοχή, 1941–1944* (Αθήνα: Αλεξάνδρεια, 2004).

Γεωργιάδου, Βασιλική, και Άλκης Ρήγος, επιμ., *Άουσβιτς. Το γεγονός και η μνήμη του: Ιστορικές, κοινωνικές, ψυχαναλυτικές και πολιτικές όψεις της γενοκτονίας* (Αθήνα: Καστανιώτης, 2007).

Γιακοέλ, Γιομτώβ, *Απομνημονεύματα, 1941–1943*, επιμ., Φραγκίσκη Αμπατζοπούλου (Θεσσαλονίκη: Παρατηρητής, 1993).

Γουργουλιάνης, Κωνσταντίνος Ι., και Αννίτα Κορδατζή-Πρασσά, *Το πρώτο ορεινό σανατόριο. Ένας αγώνας, πολλές ζωές* (Βόλος: Γενικά Αρχεία του Κράτους και Πανεπιστήμιο Θεσσαλίας, 2013).

Δελλοπούλου, Χάρη, «1945: Οι πρώτες δίκες δοσιλόγων-καταδοτών

Εβραίων στο Ειδικό Δικαστήριο Αθηνών: μια ιδιότυπη πηγή πληροφοριών», *Τα Ιστορικά,* 62 (2015), σ. 189-200.

Δημητρίου, Δημήτριος Ν., «Η συμμετοχή των Εβραίων στην Εθνική Αντίσταση», *Χρονικά,* 104 (1989), σ. 3-6.

Δημητρίου, Πάνος, *Εκ Βαθέων: Χρονικό μιας ζωής και μιας εποχής* (Αθήνα: Θεμέλιο, 1997).

Δορδανάς, Στράτος, «Γερμανικές αρχές Κατοχής και ελληνική Διοίκηση», Βασίλης Γούναρης και Πέτρος Παπαπολυβίου, επιμ., *Ο φόρος του αίματος στην κατοχική Θεσσαλονίκη. Ξένη Κυριαρχία, Αντίσταση και Επιβίωση* (Θεσσαλονίκη: Παρατηρητής, 2001), σ. 91-121.

Δορδανάς, Στράτος, *Έλληνες εναντίον Ελλήνων: Ο κόσμος των Ταγμάτων Ασφαλείας στην κατοχική Θεσσαλονίκη 1941-44* (Θεσσαλονίκη: Επίκεντρο, 2006).

Δορδανάς, Στράτος, «Εξόντωση και λεηλασία: Η Υπηρεσία Διαχειρίσεως Ισραηλιτικών Περιουσιών (ΥΔΙΠ)», Γιώργος Αντωνίου, Στράτος Δορδανάς, Νίκος Ζάικος, και Νίκος Μαραντζίδης, επιμ., *Το Ολοκαύτωμα στα Βαλκάνια* (Θεσσαλονίκη: Επίκεντρο, 2011), σ. 331-352.

Δορδανάς, Στράτος, *Η γερμανική στολή στην ναφθαλίνη: Επιβιώσεις του δοσιλογισμού στη Μακεδονία, 1945-1974* (Αθήνα: Εστία, 2011).

Δροσάκη, Ελευθερία, *Εν Θεσσαλονίκη: Από τον πόλεμο, την κατοχή και την αντίσταση* (Θεσσαλονίκη: Οδυσσέας, 2000).

Δρουμπούκη, Άννα-Μαρία, *Μια ατελείωτη διαπραγμάτευση: Η ανασυγκρότηση των ελληνικών εβραϊκών κοινοτήτων και οι γερμανικές αποζημιώσεις, 1945-1961* (Αθήνα: Ποταμός, 2019).

Δώδος, Δημοσθένης, *Οι Εβραίοι της Θεσσαλονίκης στις εκλογές του Ελληνικού κράτους, 1915-1936* (Αθήνα: Παπαζήσης, 2005).

Ελεφάντης, Άγγελος, *Μας πήραν την Αθήνα…Ξαναδιαβάζοντας την Ιστορία 1941-1950* (Αθήνα: Βιβλιόραμα, 2002).

Ετμεκτσόγλου, Γαβριέλλα, «Το Ολοκαύτωμα των Ελλήνων Εβραίων», Χρήστος Χατζηιωσήφ και Προκόπης Παπαστράτης, επιμ., *Ιστορία της Ελλάδας του 20ου αιώνα. Β' Παγκόσμιος Πόλεμος 1940-194:. Κατοχή-Αντίσταση,* τ.3 (Αθήνα: Βιβλιόραμα, 2010), σ. 175-196.

Ζάννα, Βιργινία, *Ημερολόγιο Πολέμου, 1940-1941* (Αθήνα: Ερμής, 1979)

Καβάλα, Μαρία, «Πείνα και επιβίωση: Αντιμετώπιση των στερήσεων στην κατεχόμενη Ελλάδα», Βασίλης Παναγιωτόπουλος, επιμ.,

Ιστορία του Νέου Ελληνισμού, 1770–2000, τ. 8: *Η Ελλάδα στον Πόλεμο, 1940–1949* (Αθήνα: Ελληνικά Γράμματα, 2004), σ. 49–62.

Καβάλα, Μαρία, *Η Θεσσαλονίκη στη γερμανική Κατοχή (1941–1944): Κοινωνία, οικονομία, διωγμός Εβραίων* (Ρέθυμνο: Πανεπιστήμιο Κρήτης, 2009).

Καβάλα, Μαρία, *Η καταστροφή των Εβραίων της Ελλάδας 1941–1944: Μια ιστορία με πολλές πτυχές* (Αθήνα: Ελληνικά Ακαδημαϊκά Ηλεκτρονικά Συγγράμματα, 2015).

Καβάλα, Μαρία, επιμ., *Νεότερος Ελληνικός Εβραϊσμός: Η δυναμική παρουσία, η οδυνηρή απουσία, το σήμερα* (Θεσσαλονίκη: University Studio Press, 2020).

Καφταντζής, Γιώργος, *Το Πανεπιστήμιο της Θεσσαλονίκης τον καιρό της Κατοχής* (Θεσσαλονίκη: Παρατηρητής, 1983).

Κέδρος, Ανδρέας, *Η Ελληνική Αντίσταση, 1940–1944* (Αθήνα: Θεμέλιο, 1976).

Κούνιο-Αμαρίλιο, Έρικα, και Αλμπέρτος Ναρ, επιμ., *Προφορικές μαρτυρίες των Εβραίων της Θεσσαλονίκης για το Ολοκαύτωμα*, Εισαγωγή Φ. Αμπατζοπούλου (Θεσσαλονίκη: Παρατηρητής, 1998).

Κουσουρής, Δημήτρης, *Δίκες Δοσιλόγων, 1944–1949: Δικαιοσύνη, συνέχειες του κράτους και εθνική μνήμη* (Αθήνα: Πόλις, 2014).

Κυρατζόπουλος-Φωτεινός, Δημήτριος, *Δυτική Μακεδονία. Η ελεύθερη Ελλάδα της Κατοχής. Απομνημονεύματα Εθνικής Αντίστασης* (Θεσσαλονίκη: Κώδικας, 2004).

Λάμψα, Καρίνα, και Ιακώβ Σιμπή, *Η ζωή από την αρχή: Η μετανάστευση των Ελλήνων Εβραίων στην Παλαιστίνη (1945–1948)* (Αθήνα: Αλεξάνδρεια, 2010).

Λάμψα, Καρίνα, και Ιακώβ Σιμπή, *Η Διάσωση: Η σιωπή του κόσμου, η αντίσταση στα γκέτο και τα στρατόπεδα. Οι Έλληνες Εβραίοι στα χρόνια της Κατοχής* (Αθήνα: Καπόν, 2012).

Μαραντζίδης, Νίκος, *Γιασασίν Μιλλέτ/Ζήτω το Έθνος: Προσφυγιά, Κατοχή και Εμφύλιος, εθνοτική ταυτότητα και πολιτική συμπεριφορά στους Τουρκόφωνους ελληνορθόδοξους του Δυτικού Πόντου* (Ηράκλειο: Πανεπιστημιακές Εκδόσεις Κρήτης, 2001).

Μαργαρίτης, Γιώργος, *Από την ήττα στην εξέγερση. Ελλάδα: Άνοιξη 1941–Φθινόπωρο 1942* (Αθήνα: Πολίτης, 1993).

Μόλχο, Μιχαήλ, και Ιωσήφ Νεχαμά, *In Memoriam: Αφιέρωμα εις την μνήμην των Ισραηλιτών θυμάτων του Ναζισμού εν Ελλάδι* (Θεσσαλονίκη: Ισραηλιτική Κοινότητα Θεσσαλονίκης, 1973).

Μόλχο, Ρένα, *Το Ολοκαύτωμα των Ελλήνων Εβραίων: Μελέτες Ιστορίας και Μνήμης* (Αθήνα: Πατάκης, 2014).

Μόλχο, Ρένα, «Μύθοι και πραγματικότητα για την εξόντωση των Εβραίων της Θεσσαλονίκης», *Athens Review of Books*, 27 (2013), σ. 38–42.

Μωυσής, Ασέρ, Ρ., *Κληροδότημα*, Εισαγωγή και Επιμέλεια Ραφαήλ Μωυσής (Αθήνα: Καπον, 2011).

Μπεζέ, Ελένη, *Έλληνες Εβραίοι: Μνήμες και ταυτότητες μετά τον Β' Παγκόσμιο Πόλεμο* (Βόλος: Πανεπιστήμιο Θεσσαλίας, 2021).

Μπενβενίστε, Ρίκα, «Η ηγεσία της Ισραηλιτικής κοινότητας της Θεσσαλονίκης στη διάρκεια της ναζιστικής Κατοχής», *Ιανός*, 2 (1982), σ. 118–123.

Μπενβενίστε, Ρίκα, επιμ., *Οι Εβραίοι της Ελλάδας στην Κατοχή* (Θεσσαλονίκη: Βάνιας, 1998).

Μπενβενίστε, Ρίκα, «Η ιστοριογραφία για το Ολοκαύτωμα στην Ελλάδα», *Σύγχρονα Θέματα*, 76/77 (2001), σ. 104–109.

Μπενβενίστε, Ρίκα, «Για την ιστοριογραφία της Shoah: Το διεθνές πλαίσιο και οι προοπτικές στην ελληνική ιστοριογραφία», Κ. Γαρδίκα, Α. Μ. Δρουμπούκη, Β. Καραμανωλάκης, και Κ. Ράπτης, επιμ., *Η μακρά σκιά της δεκαετίας του '40. Πόλεμος-Κατοχή-Αντίσταση-Εμφύλιος*, τόμος αφιερωμένος στον Χάγκεν Φλάισερ (Αθήνα: Αλεξάνδρεια, 2015), σ. 153–170.

Μπενβενίστε, Ρίκα, *Λούνα: Δοκίμιο ιστορικής βιογραφίας* (Αθήνα: Πόλις, 2017).

Μπουρλάς, Μωυσής, *Έλληνας Εβραίος και Αριστερός* (Σκόπελος: Νησίδες, 2009).

Μπουρούτης, Ανδρέας, Κ., επιμ., *Μετά τον πόλεμο: Η Θεσσαλονίκη και η τύχη των εβραϊκών περιουσιών* (Αθήνα: Αλεξάνδρεια, 2021).

Μπουρούτης, Ανδρέας Κ., *Το Ολοκαύτωμα στη Θεσσαλονίκη: Η ιταλική στάση και οι Εβραίοι μαθητές του Ουμπέρτο Πρίμο* (Αθήνα: Αλεξάνδρεια, 2020).

Ναρ, Αλμπέρτος, *Κειμένη επί ακτής Θαλάσσης...Μελέτες και άρθρα για την Εβραϊκή Κοινότητα της Θεσσαλονίκης* (Θεσσαλονίκη: University Studio Press, 1997).

Ναρ, Λεών Α., *Οι Ισραηλίτες βουλευτές στο ελληνικό Κοινοβούλιο (1915-1936)* (Αθήνα: Ίδρυμα της Ελληνικής Βουλής, 2011).

Ναρ, Λεών Α., *Ξανά στη Σαλονίκη: Η μετέωρη επιστροφή των Ελλήνων Εβραίων στον γενέθλιο τόπο* (Αθήνα: Πόλις, 2018).

Οι Ναζί για την εθνική αντίσταση στην Ελλάδα: Επτά απόρρητες εκθέσεις του Γενικού Επιτελείου του Χίτλερ, εισαγωγή Μιχάλης Λυμπεράτος (Αθήνα: Δρόμων, 2012).

Παπαπολυβίου, Πέτρος, «Η αντίσταση εντός των τειχών», Β. Γούναρης και Π. Παπαπολυβίου, επιμ., *Ο φόρος του αίματος στην κατοχική Θεσσαλονίκη* (Θεσσαλονίκη: Επίκεντρο, 2019), σ. 41-90.

Πρωτόπαπας-Κικίτσας, Σαράντης, *Χη Μεραρχία του ΕΛΑΣ: Εθνική Αντίσταση στη Μακεδονία 1941-1944*, επιμ. Ν. Μάργαρης (Αθήνα, 1978).

Ριτζαλέος, Βασίλης, «Η ελληνική ορθόδοξη Εκκλησία της Θεσσαλονίκης και το Ολοκαύτωμα», Αντωνίου Γιώργος, Στράτος Δορδανάς, Νίκος Ζάικος, και Νίκος Μαραντζίδης, επιμ., *Το Ολοκαύτωμα στα Βαλκάνια* (Θεσσαλονίκη: Επίκεντρο, 2001), σ. 295-330.

Ριτζαλέος, Βασίλης, «Η εβραϊκή κοινότητα Καβάλας στον έλεγχο των Βουλγαρικών Αρχών Κατοχής: οργάνωση, εκμετάλλευση, διάλυση (1942-1944)», Β. Δαλκαβούκης, Ε. Πασχαλούδη, Ι. Σκουλίδας, και Κ. Τσέκου, επιμ., *Αφηγήσεις για τη δεκαετία του 1940: Από το λόγο του κατοχικού κράτους στη μετανεωτερική ιστοριογραφία* (Θεσσαλονίκη: Επίκεντρο, 2012), σ. 69-90.

Σαλέμ, Στέλλα, «Το παλιό νεκροταφείο της Θεσσαλονίκης», *Χρονικά*, 181 (2005), σ. 6-17.

Σαλέμ, Στέλλα, «Η ακίνητη περιουσία των Εβραίων της Θεσσαλονίκης κατά τη διάρκεια της γερμανικής Κατοχής μέχρι το τέλος της δεκαετίας (1940-1949)», Μαρία Καβάλα, επιμ., *Νεότερος Ελληνικός Εβραϊσμός: Η δυναμική παρουσία, η οδυνηρή απουσία, το σήμερα* (Θεσσαλονίκη: University Studio Press, 2020), σ. 183-224.

«Σελίδες Εθνικής Αντιστάσεως: Προκήρυξη του ΕΑΜ για τη σωτηρία των Εβραίων», Χρονικά 108 (November-December 1989), σ. 12 κ.ε.

Σπένγκλερ-Αξιοπούλου, Μπάρμπαρα, «Αλληλεγγύη και βοήθεια προς τους Εβραίους της Ελλάδας κατά τη διάρκεια της γερμανικής Κατοχής 1941-1945», Ρ. Μπενβενίστε, επιμ., *Οι Εβραίοι της Ελλάδας στην Κατοχή* (Θεσσαλονίκη: Βάνιας, 1998), σ. 13-28.

Σπένγκλερ-Αξιοπούλου, Μπάρμπαρα, «Μεθοδολογικές σκέψεις για μια ιστορική προσέγγιση του Ολοκαυτώματος: η περίπτωση της Θεσσαλονίκης», *Σύγχρονα Θέματα*, 52-53 (Ιούλιος-Δεκέμβριος, 1994), σ. 85-88.

Συναγωνιστής: *Έλληνες Εβραίοι στην Εθνική Αντίσταση* (Αθήνα: Εβραϊκό Μουσείο Ελλάδος, 2014).

Τσάτσου, Ιωάννα, *Φύλλα Κατοχής* (Αθήνα: Εστία, 2000).

Τζαφλέρης, Νίκος, *Επιβίωση και Αντίσταση στον Βόλο στην Κατοχή (1941-1944)* (Βόλος: Πανεπιστήμιο Θεσσαλίας, 2007).

Φλάισερ, Χάγκεν, *Στέμμα και Σβάστικα: Η Ελλάδα της Κατοχής και της Αντίστασης, 1941-1944*, 2 τ. (Αθήνα: Παπαζήσης 1995).

Χανδρινός, Ιάσονας Γ., *Συναγωνιστές: Το ΕΑΜ και οι Εβραίοι της Ελλάδας* (Αθήνα: Ψηφίδες, 2020).

Χεκίμογλου, Ευάγγελος, «'Οι χαμένες επιταγές' του Μέρτεν: Τα λύτρα για την εξαγορά της υποχρεωτικής εργασίας των Εβραίων της Θεσσαλονίκης (1942-1943)», *Θεσσαλονικέων Πόλις*, 18 (2005), σ. 40-59.

Χεκίμογλου, Ευάγγελος, και Άννα-Μαρία Δρουμπούκη, επιμ., *Την επαύριον του Ολοκαυτώματος* (Θεσσαλονίκη: Εβραϊκό Μουσείο Θεσσαλονίκης, 2017).

Χόνδρος, Ιωάννης Λ., «Η ελληνική αντίσταση 1941-1944: Επανεκτίμηση», Γ. Ι. Ιατρίδης, επιμ., *Η Ελλάδα στη δεκαετία του 1940-1950: Ένα έθνος σε κρίση* (Αθήνα: Θεμέλιο, 1984), σ. 69-90.

Index